Marketing Countries, Places, and Place-associated Brands

Marketing Countries, Places, and Place-associated Brands

Identity and Image

Edited by

Nicolas Papadopoulos

Distinguished Research Professor of Marketing and International Business, Sprott School of Business, Carleton University, Ottawa, Canada

Mark Cleveland

Dancap Private Equity Chair in Consumer Behavior, DAN Department of Management and Organizational Studies, University of Western Ontario, London, Canada

Edward Elgar
PUBLISHING

Cheltenham, UK • Northampton, MA, USA

Published by
Edward Elgar Publishing Limited
The Lypiatts
15 Lansdown Road
Cheltenham
Glos GL50 2JA
UK

Edward Elgar Publishing, Inc.
William Pratt House
9 Dewey Court
Northampton
Massachusetts 01060
USA

Paperback edition 2022

A catalogue record for this book
is available from the British Library

Library of Congress Control Number: 2021943586

This book is available electronically in the **Elgar**online
Business subject collection
http://dx.doi.org/10.4337/9781839107375

ISBN 978 1 83910 736 8 (cased)
ISBN 978 1 83910 737 5 (eBook)
ISBN 978 1 0353 0680 0 (paperback)

Printed and bound in Great Britain by TJ Books Limited, Padstow, Cornwall

To my wife, Irinela, who has been with me in everything I do including this book. Without her nothing in life or work would ever have been possible.
Nicolas Papadopoulos

To 'my better half', Jane, my wife and best friend, and to my son Ryan and my daughter Madison. Thank you for bearing with me!
Mark Cleveland

And to the hundreds of scholars and practitioners from whom we have learned and who have lent us their wisdom so that we may stand on the shoulders of giants.
Nicolas Papadopoulos and Mark Cleveland

Contents

Figures

Tables

About the editors

Nicolas Papadopoulos is Distinguished Research Professor of Marketing and International Business at the Sprott School of Business of Carleton University in Ottawa, Canada, where he has served as Director, Associate Dean (Research), IB Teaching Area Coordinator, Director of the IB Study Group, and Chancellor's Professor.

He worked with Exxon, 3M, and P&G before turning to his academic career, and has maintained close ties with the business community through consulting, executive training, and other engagements. In research, Nicolas is known worldwide as a leading scholar in country and place images, country and place branding, and international market selection. He has over 340 publications, including 15 books and more than 90 journal articles and book chapters, and has given invited keynote addresses at such events as the Multicultural Marketing Conference (Mexico), 9th Congress of the Società Italiana di Marketing (Italy), Export Summit IV (Greece), and Consumer Research Summit on Place & Identity (UK), as well as well over 100 other presentations and seminars.

His research has been covered extensively in interviews and feature stories internationally, ranging from *The Strategist* in India to *La Reforma* (Mexico) and *The Economist* (UK), and has been recognized through numerous honours and distinctions. He has received the Capital Educators Award from the Ottawa Centre for Research and Innovation; Carleton University's Davidson Dunton Lectureship Award, Graduate Mentorship Award, and two Research Achievement Awards; the Outstanding Service or Best Reviewer awards from various journals; and 10 best paper awards, including most recently the 2019 Best Paper Award in International Business of the Administrative Sciences Association of Canada. He is an Honorary International Member of the Società Italiana di Marketing, and is currently serving on the Senior Advisory Board of *International Marketing Review* and the *Journal of Product and Brand Management* (UK), on the Editorial Review Boards of the *Journal of International Business Studies*, *Journal of International Marketing* (US), and five other journals, and as Associate Editor (IB) of the *Canadian Journal of Administrative Sciences*.

Mark Cleveland is a Western Faculty Scholar and the Dancap Private Equity Chair in Consumer Behavior at the DAN Department of Management and

Organizational Studies of the University of Western Ontario in London, Canada. He is a former Director of Western's Collaborative Graduate Program in Migration and Ethnic Relations. As the coordinator of the Consumer Behavior area, he teaches numerous courses at graduate and undergraduate levels. Since 2013, Dr Cleveland has been an Associate Editor for the journal *International Marketing Review.* He is on the editorial board of several other journals, and he has served as a Guest Co-editor for several journals as well as Track Chair for numerous conferences.

His research interests are interdisciplinary, spanning marketing, consumer behavior, social psychology, and international business, with a special focus on globalization, identity and culture; cross-cultural consumer behavior; cosmopolitanism, xenocentrism, materialism, and consumer ethnocentrism; international market segmentation, promotion, and branding; sustainability and green marketing; and psychometrics. To date, he has conducted research on consumers living in 22 countries. He has authored, co-authored, or edited more than 100 publications, including 43 journal articles, 3 book chapters, a book on global consumer culture, and 51 conference papers. He has presented his research at conferences spanning five continents.

His scholarly work has more than 5000 citations on *Google Scholar*, and his research has been featured in prominent media outlets including *The New York Times, The Globe and Mail, Psychology Today*, and *CBC's Marketplace.* Mark has been a consultant for numerous organizations, including *McKinsey & Company, McCann Worldgroup*, and *Industry Canada.* He has received many awards for his scholarly activities, including three best paper awards, Western's Faculty Scholar Award, and the Hans B. Thorelli Award, from the American Marketing Association, for an article that has made the most significant and long-term contribution to international marketing theory or practice.

About the contributors

Mikael Andéhn is an Associate Professor at the School of Business and Management of Royal Holloway, University of London, UK. His research interests include issues pertaining to brands, critical marketing and management studies, international marketing, tourism, and the commercial relevance of place. His work has been featured in journals such as *Journal of Travel Research, Marketing Theory, Tourism Management, Organisation,* and *International Marketing Review.*

Boris Bartikowski is Professor of Marketing at Kedge Business School in Marseille, France. His research emphasis is in the areas of cross-cultural consumer behavior, online marketing, and brand management. He serves as an Associate Editor of the *Canadian Journal of Administrative Sciences.* His work has been published in journals such as *Journal of Business Research, British Journal of Management, Journal of Business Ethics, Psychology & Marketing,* and *European Journal of Marketing.*

Fabian Bartsch is an Associate Professor in Marketing at IESEG School of Management, France. His research interests include cross-cultural consumer behavior, the country of origin effect, and global consumer culture(s). To date, his work has been published in the *Journal of International Business Studies, Journal of International Marketing, International Marketing Review,* and *Journal of Business Research.*

Mark Cleveland is Dancap Private Equity Chair in Consumer Behavior at the University of Western Ontario (London, Canada). He is an Associate Editor for the *International Marketing Review.* Mark's research interests are interdisciplinary and centre on globalization, cross-cultural consumer behavior, and green marketing. With more than 50 published articles and chapters, his work has more than 5000 Google Scholar citations and has appeared in prominent media, such as *The New York Times.* His numerous commendations include Western's Faculty Scholar Award and the AMA's Hans B. Thorelli Award.

Alia El Banna is Profesor Ayudante Doctor at Universidad Francisco de Vitoria in Spain, before which she worked as a Senior Lecturer in Marketing and Head, Centre for International Business and Marketing Research, at the University of Bedfordshire Business School in the UK. Her research focuses on the multidimensional construct of 'place' and how the images of countries and other places affect domestic and foreign consumers, influence the attraction of tourists, investors, and skilled workers, and interact with culture, identity, belonging, and heritage.

Magdalena Florek is Associate Professor at the University of Economics and Business in Poznań, Poland. Co-founder and board member of the International Place Branding Association. Co-founder and member of the board of "Best Place – The European Place Marketing Institute". Senior Fellow at the Institute of Place Management. Consultant and co-author of numerous branding and promotion strategies for towns, cities, and regions in Poland. Member of the Editorial Boards of, for example, *Place Branding and Public Diplomacy* and *Journal of Destination Marketing and Management.*

Robert Govers is the author of the award-winning book *Imaginative Communities: Admired Cities, Regions and Countries* (2018). He is an independent government advisor, founding chairman of the International Place Branding Association, co-editor of the quarterly journal *Place Branding and Public Diplomacy*, and a contributor to *Apolitical*, the *World Economic Forum Agenda* and the *Economist Intelligence Unit Perspectives.*

Jonathan Grix is a Professor of Sports Policy in the Business and Law Faculty at Manchester Metropolitan University, UK and leads the Faculty's Sport Policy Unit. He is a global academic leader in the area of sport politics. His latest books include *Sport Politics* (2016) and *Entering the Global Arena: Emerging States, Soft Power Strategies and Sports Mega-Events* (with Paul Brannagan and Donna Lee, 2019). Jonathan is the Editor-in-Chief of the leading *International Journal of Sport Policy and Politics.*

Henrik Halkier is Professor of Tourism and Regional Development at Aalborg University, Denmark, and Dean of the Faculty of Humanities. He has published on the politics of regional development policy, knowledge dynamics in regional innovation and tourism development, and on policies and governance of tourism destination development. His publications include contributions on Denmark, Britain, and Europe, and his current research interests are place branding, sustainable destination development, and synergies between food and tourism in local and regional development.

Anna M. Hersperger, Prof. h.c. Dr, heads the Land-Use Systems Group at the Swiss Federal Research Institute WSL where she is also a member of the WSL Directorate. Her work focuses on landscapes as changing human-environmental systems and, specifically, on understanding the role of spatial planning and land-use policies in changing metropolitan regions by evaluating planning and policy instruments and processes. She holds Master's degrees from the ETH Zurich and Arizona State University and a PhD from Harvard University.

Andrea Insch's research expertise is inter-disciplinary, connecting marketing, urban studies, and tourism. Designed to contribute to the debate on the role and impacts of place branding for cities, nations, and their stakeholders, her main research activity is focused on several sub-themes – the interplay of cities branding and urban development, resident engagement with city branding, and value derived from country-of-origin images. Andrea is on the Editorial Advisory Board of the *Journal of Management History* and is the Book Review Editor for the journal *Place Branding & Public Diplomacy*.

Laura James is Associate Professor of Tourism and Regional Change at Aalborg University, Denmark. Her research interests include destination development and regional change, tourism policy, and sustainability in tourism. She has previously written about 'green' place branding and policy tourism in Sweden and the use of the SDGs in place branding. Laura is currently working on a collaborative project that explores the social, economic, and environmental impacts of cruise tourism on communities in Greenland, Iceland, Norway, and Russia.

Mihalis Kavaratzis is Associate Professor of Marketing at the University of Leicester School of Business, UK and holds a PhD on City Marketing. Mihalis is co-founder of the International Place Branding Association and a Senior Fellow of the Institute of Place Management. He has published some of the most-cited work in the field and has co-edited (amongst others) *Inclusive Place Branding* (with M. Giovanardi and M. Lichrou, 2017) and *Rethinking Place Branding* (with G. Warnaby and G.J. Ashworth, 2015).

Nina Kramareva holds a PhD in Sport Politics from the University of Birmingham, UK. She studies sports mega-events in so-called non-liberal states and in Russia in particular. She is also interested in the role of sport in ideology and national identity formation processes.

Jean-Noël Patrick L'Espoir Decosta is an Associate Professor at the Australian National University Research School of Management. His research interests include interdisciplinary approaches to the study of tourism, an evidence-based approach to management, tourism education and research, and destination branding. His work has been featured in journals such as *Annals of Tourism Research, Journal of Travel Research, Tourism Management, International Marketing Review*, and *Journal of Consumer Culture*.

Peter Magnusson (PhD, Saint Louis University) is Professor and Chair of the Department of Marketing at The University of Texas Rio Grande Valley, USA. His recent research topics include consumer animosity, country of origin marketing, and export marketing strategy. Peter has published in, for example, *Journal of International Business Studies*, *Journal of the Academy of Marketing Science*, and *Journal of International Marketing*.

Michela Matarazzo is Professor of International Business at G. Marconi University of Rome, Italy. She has been an elected board member at the Società Italiana Management (2013–2018). Her research interests include international business with a special focus on consumer behaviour, country image, international corporate reputation, and SMEs' internationalization and market entry modes, also in relation to the digital context. She has authored and co-authored 100 publications, including journal articles, conference papers, book chapters, and three books on firms' internationalization and cross-border M&As.

Dominic Medway is a Professor of Marketing in the Institute of Place Management at Manchester Metropolitan University, UK. Dominic's work is primarily concerned with the complex interactions between places, spaces, and those who manage and consume them, reflecting his academic training as a geographer. He is extensively published in a variety of leading academic journals, including: *Environment and Planning A*, *European Journal of Marketing*, *Journal of Environmental Psychology*, *Marketing Theory*, *Mobilities*, *Space and Culture*, *Tourism Management*, and *Urban Geography*.

Eduardo Oliveira studies place branding and spatial planning processes, and the embedding of both in governance. His current research focuses on analysing the effectiveness of place branding as a strategic spatial planning instrument in supporting the social and economic development of metropolitan regions, whilst assessing its effect on environmental sustainability. His works have been published in several academic journals and books. Eduardo is a postdoctoral research associate at the University of Kiel, Germany and guest researcher at the WSL in Switzerland.

Nicolas Papadopoulos is Distinguished Research Professor of Marketing and International Business at the Sprott School of Business of Carleton University in Ottawa, Canada. His research focuses on international strategy and buyer responses to it and includes international expansion, place images and branding, and global market systems. He has over 340 publications including 15 books and over 90 journal articles and book chapters, he serves on nine editorial review or senior advisory journal boards, and his work has been recognized through numerous distinctions.

Ioana S. Stoica is a PhD candidate and Lecturer at the University of Bedfordshire Business School in the UK. Her research addresses the concepts of co-creation, identity, and residents' participation in the context of branding places with a negative reputation. Her teaching expertise involves international business and marketing, digital marketing, and marketing analytics.

Anette Therkelsen is Associate Professor of Tourism and Market Communication at Aalborg University, Denmark, and Vice-Dean of Research at the Faculty of Humanities. Her research interests focus on place branding at different geographical scales and various aspects of place-related consumer practices. Anette has published internationally on these topics and has acted as PI on several research projects on tourism-related place development. She is currently working on a research project on sustainable tourism development.

Gary Warnaby is Professor of Retailing and Marketing, based in the Institute of Place Management at Manchester Metropolitan University, UK. His research interests focus on the marketing of places (particularly in an urban context), and retailing. Results of this research have been published in various academic journals in both the management and geography disciplines. He is co-editor of *Rethinking Place Branding: Comprehensive Brand Development for Cities and Regions* (Springer, 2015) and *Designing with Smell: Practices, Techniques and Challenges* (Routledge, 2017).

Stanford A. Westjohn (PhD, Saint Louis University) is Associate Professor of Marketing in the Culverhouse College of Business at the University of Alabama, USA. His research interests include international marketing strategy and consumer behavior particularly as it relates to global branding and positioning. Stan's research has been published in *Journal of International Business Studies*, *Journal of International Marketing*, and *Journal of the Academy of Marketing Science*.

Candace L. White is a Professor in the School of Advertising and Public Relations at the University of Tennessee, USA, where she teaches international public relations. Her research interests include the role of global corporations as non-state actors in public diplomacy, and how corporate social responsibility and CSR communication affect the image and national reputation of the country with which the corporation is associated. She is a Faculty Fellow of the Howard H. Baker, Jr. Center for Public Policy in the area of global security.

Rick T. Wilson, PhD, is an Associate Professor of Marketing at Texas State University, USA. His research interests include place branding, investment promotion, out-of-home advertising, and creativity in advertising. Dr Wilson's research has been published in journals such as the *Journal of Advertising*, *Journal of Advertising Research*, *International Journal of Advertising*, and *Journal of Place Management and Development*. Before becoming a professor, he worked in the fields of marketing and international business for

12 years as a senior product manager for AT&T, Vodafone Group, and TelePacific Communications.

Sebastian Zenker, PhD, is Professor (with special responsibilities) at the Copenhagen Business School (CBS), Department of Marketing, Denmark. He is widely considered one of the pioneering scholars in the field of place marketing and branding. His current research interests are in place brand management with the special target groups of residents and tourists, as well as conflicts and crises in places. His work has been presented at various international conferences, book chapters, and prestigious peer-reviewed journals, including *Environment and Planning A*, *Tourism Management*, *International Journal of Research in Marketing*, and *Psychological Science*.

Katharina Petra Zeugner-Roth is an Associate Professor in Marketing at IESEG School of Management, France. Her research interests are centered in cross-cultural consumer behavior topics such as consumer dispositional variables, the country of origin effect, and ethical considerations. To date, her work has been published in journals such as *Marketing Letters*, *Journal of International Marketing*, *Journal of Retailing*, *Management International Review*, and *Journal of Business Research*.

Introduction: the 'country' vs. 'place' and 'marketing' vs. 'branding' conundrum

Nicolas Papadopoulos and Mark Cleveland

TO BEGIN ... WHY 'PLACE'?

We have made elsewhere the claim that 'place' is an omnipresent, central, and critical part of human life, and one of many sources on the Internet (www .rhymezone.com, 2020) conveniently provides a *partial* list of no fewer than *486* common phrases that include 'place' and help to show how true that claim is. Here are some extracts from the list:

- Some phrases use 'place' figuratively or in a sense mostly different from its meaning in this book, but it can still be instructive to consider how broadly the word is used – as in, for example, a *first-place finish, in the first place, placing a premium on, staying in place, being put in one's place* or *being commonplace, having one's heart in the right place*, and being psychologically in *a good place* or *a bad place*.
- At the other end are numerous phrases that, whether directly or indirectly, clearly refer to physical or mindset places, such as *place name, place of birth*, being *in the right place at the right time, between a rock and a hard place, out of place* or *all over the place*, and having *pride of place* or *a hiding place*.
- In between these are references to *place settings* or *place cards* at a formal dinner and *having a place at the table*, as well as *place mats*, numerous uses of 'place' in popular culture such as the TV series *Melrose Place, Archie Bunker's Place*, and *Peyton Place*, and *no place to go* and *no place to hide* unless we find *a place to be*.
- Then there are geographically-specified *watering places*, like those zebras use in Africa, *holy places* like Mecca, Medina, or Jerusalem, *places of worship* including Hindu or Shinto temples, Christian churches, and Muslim mosques, *polling places* and *census-designated places, resting places, nesting places, principal places* (a.k.a. headquarters) or just *places of business, meeting* and *gathering places*, events *taking place at X*, organ-

1

izations from firms to espionage agencies that have *an agent in place*, and *dwelling places*.

- And of course there is *no place like home* – but still, for the eventuality that one does not have a 'home' place as such, there are many types of *mythical, imaginary, or dreamed-of* places, from the Garden of Eden, Camelot, El Dorado, Valhalla, Nirvana, and Shangri-La to *a place to call home, a place of our own, a place to grow*, and *our place in the sun*.

The list from which we selected the sample of 48 phrases above does also include several more that are directly related to marketing and the theme of this book, which obviously deserve special treatment here. These include not just the all-important *marketplace* but also *place of origin, sense of place, place attachment, place theory, place branding, place identity*, and *place management*.

Just add a few key missing terms (e.g., place *marketing*, place *belongingness*), ensure that it is well understood that a 'country' is just as much a 'place' as a 'city' or 'town' (e.g., *country* origin, *national* identity, *nation* branding), and, given the enormous importance of place in life, there is a natural expectation that there would also be an enormous amount of research on it, that those dealing with place marketing would have all the necessary know-how to do their job effectively, and everything would, well, *fall into place*.

Unfortunately, this is not the case. Instead, in a near-literal sense, we are *all over the place*.

PLACES AND COUNTRIES, MARKETING AND BRANDING, AND SILOS OF KNOWLEDGE

Things haven't *fallen into place* because, while indeed research in the area is vast and practice in it is burgeoning worldwide, both are split into two sets of silos which turn what might have indeed been a truly enormous amount of knowledge into a fragmented landscape of scholars and practitioners. In a nutshell, some study or practice 'place' and some 'country', some speak of 'marketing' while others speak of 'branding', and there is little or no interchange of ideas between the silos within each set.

Actually there are several silos in this field when considering the areas that study or practice it. To name just a few: (a) *Place branding* (PB) deals mostly with places at the *sub-national* level (e.g., cities, towns, tourism regions) and either focuses on *branding* as such, which is just a sub-part of one (Product) of the four elements of the marketing mix, or includes other parts of the mix, thereby fuelling the misconception that 'marketing = branding'; (b) Instead, *country-of-origin* and *country image* (COO/CI) research is positioned at the nation-state level, focuses more broadly on *marketing*, and deals almost exclusively with how a country and its *products* are viewed by consumers; (c) The parallel stream of *Nation branding* (NB) focuses on the *country* level but from the narrower lens of *branding*, as indicated by its title; (d) Research and practice in tourism destination image (TDI) cover both national and sub-national entities and both marketing and branding but are limited to a single sector; (e) Environmental *psychology* is interested in such issues as place belongingness and identity, while identity theory adopts a broader *socio-cultural* perspective and *ethnicity* studies a narrower context that focuses on a single demographic characteristic.

All of the above areas draw from a variety of disciplines in the social sciences, such as sociology, anthropology, psychology, human or urban geography, political science, and economics, which is a very positive characteristic of knowledge development in this area, and one from which practitioners using this research also benefit and to which they add their own knowledge from their own backgrounds. However, with just a few exceptions that do little but confirm the rule, the main areas of interest here (PB, COO/CI, NB, TDI) do not 'talk' amongst themselves. At base, since 'place' is not just a physical entity comprising landscape elements but a mental construction of how people view it, a common starting place for all these disciplines is the phenomenon of place *image*. Yet as chapters of this book show, 'image' itself means different things in different disciplines, as do 'identity', 'product', 'consumer', and even 'place' itself. As a result, instead of learning from each other, each of the relevant areas has its own perspectives, approaches, and methods, inevitably resulting in different conclusions as to what matters and why.

OBJECTIVES, CONTRIBUTORS, STRUCTURE, AND CONTENT OF THIS BOOK

A most obvious result of silos in knowledge is that advances in one area are not often (if at all) used by scholars and practitioners working in another. The dearth of idea exchange across fields (e.g., COO rarely draws on TDI or PB, and PB rarely uses methodologies developed in COO) means that studies in one area reinvent wheels that others consider 'old hat', while wheels in need of more research fall in-between silo cracks.

Given the above, our purpose in launching this project and therefore the objective of this book is:

> To integrate and synthesize the latest in research on the images, marketing, and branding of all levels of 'place' and of the people, peoples, products, and brands associated with them, taking into account the perspectives of both research and practice and of both sellers and buyers.

We are very happy and proud to say that, with excellent contributions from a stellar cast of authors, we and they believe that this objective has been achieved.

Rather than issuing a broad 'Call for Chapters', an easier approach that is typical in similar projects but can result in near-random collections of contributions, we first did our homework, by adding in-depth research on the leading scholars in the field to what we already knew about many of them, to identify and invite a select group whose members would meet three key criteria: they would be at the cutting edge of know-how in their respective areas, prepared to address important topics from an indicative list we supplied, and hailing from various countries so as to provide an internationally-applicable perspective on the issues.

We were gratified by the response, as virtually all of those we invited became excited over the book's objectives and agreed to participate. In all, the star ensemble of authors in this volume consists of *28 leaders of thought from 22 universities in 13 countries* (Belgium, Denmark, Italy, France, Poland, Spain, Switzerland, Ukraine, and the UK in Europe, Australia and New Zealand, and Canada and the United States) – a broad scope that assures state-of-the-art and international-minded coverage of the topics. The contents reflect a major departure from the status quo and make fresh and original contributions that can be classified in two main types: state-of-the-art syntheses of research within individual sub-disciplines, and integrative cross-disciplinary works that bring disparate approaches under one roof.

We ourselves have read more and learned more during the development of this project than we could possibly describe, and, together with our contributors, we invite readers to join us in learning from this volume's content, which is briefly described below.

Following this Introduction to the book by the co-editors, the place phrase in the title of Part I speaks to what we described above: we are 'all over the place' even though we all also are 'birds of a feather', since we all deal with the *images* of things: of places (and yes, including countries, since they too are 'places'), their people, and their products which local people and many others elsewhere consume. Chapter 1, written by Warnaby and Medway, two seasoned and globally recognized place experts who often work together, uses the setting of an iconic church in Manchester to drive home the reality that all places, from neighbourhoods to nations (and beyond) are indeed worthy of our attention. Chapter 2, by Kavaratzis and Florek, two equally known place experts who also work together, discuss place branding using the standard '5 Ws and 1 H' of journalism (why, who, what, when, where, how). In Chapter 3, Papadopoulos and Cleveland, who dabble in both the 'place' and 'country' sides of the silo fence, examine how concepts used by only one side can also be fruitfully applied to the other. And in Chapter 4, Sebastian Zenker, a pioneer in place marketing and branding, poses six propositions that expose and challenge current assumptions in place research.

Each of the next two parts deals with one of the two parts of the silos – Part II with 'place' and Part III with 'country'. Part II begins with Magdalena Florek's Chapter 5, which looks into brand models by integrating thoughts from state-of-the-art knowledge in both place and commercial product branding. Chapter 6, by the multicultural team of Alia El Banna and Ioana Stoica, focuses on an aspect that is central to much, if not most, of contemporary thought in place branding: the role of residents, who can both co-create as well as, if their views are not properly addressed, co-destruct a place brand. In Chapter 7, Andrea Insch uses her expertise in urban studies to expand on the nature and role of residents through the broader concepts of peoplescapes, placemaking, and identity in the context of a culturally diverse world. And in Chapter 8, Cleveland and Papadopoulos expand specifically on the 'identity' construct even more, by introducing such space metaphors as the 'gravitational pulls' of identity and 'consumption constellations' (and yes, 'space' is also a 'place') to examine the 'fabric' of interrelationships between persons, places, and time.

Part III focuses on 'the other side', that of countries, whose images indeed produce a very rich smorgasbord of thoughts and effects that have been documented abundantly in country of origin research. The place phrase that opens this part is a play on the common saying that "a picture is worth a thousand words" by replacing 'picture' with 'place' – whose worth is indeed that much and, more likely, much more. Chapter 9, by Andéhn and L'Espoir Decosta, both well-known scholars on country images and their effects, throws the gauntlet to COO researchers by heavily critiquing the current state of thinking and asking for new perspectives in that area. In Chapter 10, the team of Magnusson and Westjohn, two of the most prolific and cited COO researchers, zero-in on one of the most important antecedents of the images of countries and places, and present new research to buttress its importance in place marketing and branding: stereotyping. Chapter 11, by Cleveland, Papadopoulos, and Bartikowski, further elaborates on the various levels of place-related social and product identity, using the literature on consumer dispositions to examine in depth how products and places are inextricably connected. Chapter 12, written by the team of Bartsch and Zeugner-Roth that has already left an indelible mark on current COO thought, uses the elaboration likelihood model to examine the known central and peripheral routes in human information processing and consider how advertising cues are internalized and affect consumers' marketplace responses. And in Chapter 13 Michela Matarazzo takes us to a different 'place' where she is a notable thought leader – the effects on buyers' perceptions of products when their producer's 'home' country changes through cross-border acquisitions and offshoring.

Last but not least, Part IV presents yet another smorgasbord, this time of topics critical for a full understanding of country/place marketing/branding, through six chapters that discuss research advances and setbacks with a focus on how various concepts are applied and the interrelationships (the 'Associations' in the part's title) between them.

Chapter 14 is written by Rick T. Wilson, an expert in all three of the main subjects he deals with – advertising, place branding, and investment promotion agencies working to attract foreign investors – who presents a strategic place branding and advertising model that is of great interest to both researchers and managers.

The next three chapters cover three issues that are essential in understanding what place marketing and branding are all about and how far managers' practices reach in shaping the communities and countries we live in. For Chapter 15 Eduardo Oliveira, an innovative and prolific researcher, is joined by Anna Hersperger, head of the Land-Use Systems Group at the Swiss Federal Research Institute WSL, to consider the nature and importance of strategic spatial planning in relation to place branding. In Chapter 16, Candace White uses her deep knowledge in media and communications to explore the influence of popular culture on the image of countries and their products, with a focus on perhaps the biggest cultural exporter of them all: the United States. And for Chapter 17 Nina Kramareva, who works on sports mega-events and their role in national identity formation, joins Jonathan Grix, a globally leading scholar on the business and politics of sport, to focus on how hosting events such as the Olympic Games interacts with and affects a country's image and overall welfare.

Next, in Chapter 18 Anette Therkelsen and her colleagues Laura James and Henrik Halkier, all located in Denmark, speak to one of the hottest topics of the day and one that will be with us for a long time to come – place sustainability, using the case study of Aalborg, a Danish city in a country that is among the forerunners in working toward sustainability and therefore most appropriate for discussing it.

The above assemblage, or even parade, of topics of major contemporary interest written by authors of know-how and wisdom, could not conclude without calling upon one of the most recognizable voices in the 'place' profession: Robert Govers. In Chapter 19, the prolific author, independent consultant, Founding Chairman of the International Place Branding Association, and Co-editor of the journal *Place Branding and Public Diplomacy*, among many other accomplishments, offers his views on the place branding area's past, considers its future, ties both into the COVID-19 pandemic that has affected the entire world in ways previously hard to imagine, and challenges all of us, authors and readers alike, to think, think, think, about how to enhance and establish the *relevance* of place marketing among those who matter: the people who live in places and those who manage them on the people's behalf.

The book's Epilogue by the co-editors takes us back to where we began, using a well-known place phrase in its title, "Between a Rock and a Hard PLACE", and followed by eight sections whose subtitles, quite naturally, are also prefaced by well-known place phrases relevant to the corresponding themes. The aim here is to reorganize the contributions into a selected set of challenges, arising from the chapters described above, in order to provide readers with our reflections about future place-associated research expeditions.

The epilogue uses the Ship of State metaphor of a ship sailing in the ocean to stress how, just as the affairs of a state and the course of a ship commonly face rough seas, so does the country/place marketing/branding Ship we are trying to run, whether as editors, authors, and research or practitioner readers. As the old saying goes, the fun is in the journey, and ultimately reaching a 'perfect' destination is untenable in any case – so we can only hope you will join us in navigating through the high seas that confront us to ensure that, at the very least, we keep moving in the right direction.

PART I

'Birds of a feather, all over the place': my neighbourhood, my town, my country

1. Conceptions of place: from streets and neighbourhoods to towns, cities, nations, and beyond

Gary Warnaby and Dominic Medway

INTRODUCTION

In this chapter, our aim is to provide an overview of different conceptualis-ations of place, which we argue is an essential precondition for developing any understanding of place marketing and branding, whether this be at the localised street-level, or – at the opposite end of the spatial scale – nationally or supra-nationally. By way of initial definition, we begin by outlining Agnew's (1987) tripartite conceptualisation of place in terms of *location, locale*, and a *sense of place*. We then discuss some particular characteristics of place – which, we posit, can be regarded as conceptual antecedents of place market-ing/branding – and arguably make the marketer's task in this spatial context more complex than those stereotypical instances (for example, fast-moving consumer goods) for which much marketing and branding theory has been developed. Thus, interrelated geographical notions of *scale* and *territory* are explored. To demonstrate the practical manifestations of our theoretical argu-ments, we use examples – in particular, St Ann's Square in Manchester, UK, at the street level; and at the opposite end of the spatial scale, the Oresund region, encompassing parts of Denmark and Sweden. We conclude by discussing the implications for place marketing/branding activity.

DEFINING PLACE

Agnew's (1987) tripartite definition considers place in terms of *location, locale*, and a *sense of place. Location* is the point on the Earth's surface where a place is found (and indeed, locational advantage in relation to other, 'competing' places is a common trope of place marketing messages). *Locale* is described by Cresswell (2004) in terms of "the material setting for social relations – the actual shape of place within which people conduct their lives"

(p. 7). In other words, it refers to the settings in which both informal and institutional social relations are constituted. *Sense of place* refers to the emotional attachment that people have to place, which "reinforces the social-spatial definition of place from the **inside**" (Agnew, 1987, p. 27; emphasis in the original), thereby potentially creating an identification between individuals and a place. We will illustrate these different aspects of place using the particular example of St Ann's Square in Manchester.

St Ann's Square was established in 1720, on the site of an annual fair dating from the thirteenth century. It was a "select residential area" with formal rows of trees, and represented the first major development away from the medieval centre of the city around the cathedral, half a kilometre to the north (Hartwell, 2001). The only surviving building from this period is St Ann's Church, at the southern end of the square (see Figure 1.1). The Act of Parliament that granted the church's construction (1709–1712) stipulated that a space 30 yards wide should be reserved for the fair which had previously been held at this location (and which continued there until it moved to another part of the city in 1823). This space became St Ann's Square, and the other buildings currently surrounding the open space of the square were constructed in various styles over

Source: Author's own photo archive.

Figure 1.1   *St Ann's Church*

a long period (see Hartwell, 2001, pp. 199–202, for more detail of the current architecture of the square). In 1970, St Ann's Square was the first conservation area designated by Manchester City Council, and the area was fully pedestrianised in 1993 (Manchester City Council, 2009).

If Agnew's (1987) notion of location refers to the point on the Earth's surface where a place exists, then standing at latitude 53.4817° N and longitude 2.2458° W places us right outside St Ann's Church. Looking north, one sees St Ann's Square, which on a January day can appear a somewhat bleak urban vista. However, at certain times during the year, the space is animated by periodic specialist markets (Warnaby, 2013) or occasionally, music performances (for example, open-air concerts as part of the Manchester Jazz festival – see Oakes and Warnaby, 2011), as shown in Figures 1.2 and 1.3. When such events take place, they could be regarded as manifestations of Agnew's second aspect of *locale*, referring to settings in which formal and institutional social relations are constituted, and they change the dynamic of the space in question. Moreover, looking across the square in late May 2017, one would have seen a carpet of floral and other tributes as St Ann's Square became an epicentre of remembrance for the victims of the Manchester Arena bombing (Burnip,

Source: Author's own photo archive.

Figure 1.2   *Christmas Market, St Ann's Square*

Source: Author's own photo archive.

*Figure 1.3   The Steve Oakes Quartet performing in St Ann's Square as
part of the Manchester Jazz Festival*

2017). This demonstrates Agnew's notion of *sense of place*, potentially creating an identification with – and feelings of attachment to – place.

The inherent convolution of these issues is intimated by Cresswell and Hoskins (2008), who suggest that place "simultaneously evokes a certain materiality (it has a tangible material form to it) and a less concrete realm of meaning" (p. 394). These material and phenomenological aspects thus come together in a particular location. Highlighting the importance of the *experience* of place, the authors continue by also emphasising that place also involves different levels of practice and performance, a recognition that place is a 'lived' concept. To capture such complexities Cresswell (2004) describes the notion of place as "slippery", stating:

> Place is not a specialized piece of academic terminology. It is a word we use daily in the English-speaking world ... As we already know what it means it is hard to get beyond that common-sense level in order to understand it in a more developed way. Place, then, is both simple (and that is part of its appeal) and complicated. (p. 1)

We now move to discuss some other ways in which the characteristics of 'place' may be conceptualised, as this may have particular implications for how spatial entities may be marketed and branded. Our discussion begins by examining ideas about *scale*.

SCALE

Marston et al. (2009) highlight that in the discipline of geography the concept of scale has been the subject of much theorising and has multiple definitions. For our purposes, we take what they term a *social production* or *social construction* standpoint with regard to scale, which has, they argue, proved very influential. Resonating with the title of the current chapter (which mentions spatial scales in a hierarchy from street to nation), these authors suggest that spatial scales "do not ... rest as fixed platforms for social activity and processes that connect up or down to other hierarchical levels, but are instead *outcomes* of those activities and processes, to which they in turn contribute through a spatially uneven and temporally unfolding dynamic" (p. 665, emphasis in the original).

Again, we can take the example of St Ann's Square in Manchester, at the basic spatial level of the street, to illustrate "the idea that social processes – and hence scales – mutually intersect, constitute and rebound upon one another in an inseparable chain of determinations" (Marston et al., 2009, p. 665). From a sociological standpoint, Hubbard and Lyon (2018) define the street *inter alia* in terms of a conduit for various types of flows, which connects people in various ways thereby enabling community and place-making practices. Moreover, as these authors note, streets are "also woven into the social fabric of the city in multiple ways, adjoining any number of buildings, public facilities, open spaces and commercial venues, and providing some form of interaction and relationality between them" (p. 940). This relationality may occur at a variety of spatial scales, with streets potentially connected to things both near and far.

Thus, in St Ann's Square this spatial relationality is evident, with the retailers occupying the buildings that bound the open space of the square, seen for example in their choice to locate there, and in their day-to-day operations. With regard to location, Bennison et al. (1995) note that, particularly for multiple retailers (who may have hundreds of stores in their network), locational decisions are made at various interlinked scales. These scales range from more strategically-oriented *macro*-level decisions (for example, the proposed geographical coverage of a store network), through the *meso*-level (for example, decisions relating to issues such as the delineation of store catchment areas), and *micro*-level. Brown (1992) states that micro-level location decisions relate to individual stores, especially in terms of the appropriateness – or otherwise

– of their precise position within a locale. Furthermore, the globalising trends within many retail supply chains and the internationalisation of retail formats (see Dawson et al., 2008) mean that the individual retail outlet is just the end point of a complex and potentially global network of scalar interdependencies.

These notions resonate with Massey's (1991) contention of a "progressive sense of place", where "what gives a place its specificity is not some long internalized history but the fact that it is constructed out of a particular constellation of social relations, meeting and weaving together at a particular locus" (p. 27). In a specific retail context, this leads Crewe and Lowe (1995) to discuss the emergence of new spatial configurations: "On the one hand the globalisation of retailing continues to weave complex interdependencies between geographically distant locations and tends towards global interconnection and dedifferentiation. On the other hand new patterns of regional specialisation are emphasising the importance of place and reinforcing local uniqueness." (p. 1879).

Indeed, in a situation where the homogenising tendencies of retailing have been highlighted (in terms of creating 'clone towns' for example – see New Economics Foundation, 2004), creating some form of a 'sense of place' by differentiating retail provision in order to reinforce local uniqueness is a key objective of many place management/marketing agencies (Warnaby et al., 2005).

Such attempts at spatial differentiation can have an explicit temporal aspect. In St Ann's Square, this is manifest in the numerous specialist themed markets that have happened there. Some of these market themes are explicitly national in orientation (for example, a French Market and a Moroccan Berber Market), with traders from those countries setting up stalls for the duration of the event, and in so doing incorporating St Ann's Square (albeit temporarily) into different, broader configurations of spatial capital flows. At the same time, since 'France' and 'Morocco' refer to nation-states, 'Berber' to ethnicity, and 'St Ann's Square' to the English/Christian tradition, this mix yields a hybridised place experience that might appeal particularly to cosmopolitan consumers. Similarly, the appropriation of urban space for the purposes of music production and consumption is evident in the use of St Ann's Square as one of the venues for the annual Manchester Jazz Festival. This allows the Square to become a node in a wider circuit of artistic production and has wider implications for place marketing activities (Oakes and Warnaby, 2011).

Indeed, even the materiality of the locale, in the form of the fabric of buildings around St Ann's Square, is linked to broader patterns of spatial connectivity. Drawing on Ingold's (2004) contention that a building "is a condensation of skilled activity that undergoes continual formation even as it is inhabited, that it incorporates materials that have life histories of their own and may have served time in previous structures" (p. 240), Edensor (2012) considers how the sandstone of St Ann's Church is imported from Runcorn, Darley Dale in Derbyshire, and Hollington in Staffordshire. This resonates with Massey's (1991) contention that an understanding of the 'character' of a place is constructed by linking that place to other places.

This notion of scale has potential implications for the marketing and branding activities of places. In conceptual terms, Boisen et al. (2011, p. 136) distinguish between place marketing and branding, suggesting that marketing is "concerned with the whole issue of a demand-driven approach to places, and thus can be seen as a broad term". In contrast, place branding is "a more specific marketing instrument" applied to a particular place, the goal of which "would be to add value to the place in the broad sense". However, a practical consideration here relates to how 'place' is delineated. In this respect, there may be scalar discrepancies between the functional goals of place marketing/ branding organisations (which, in line with the spatial "hierarchy from street to nation" that we mentioned at the start of this section, may correspond to more traditional urban, regional, and national levels of institutions of governance), and the resulting place brand images held by different target groups. These perceived images may not necessarily align with the usual scales of governance, which could, in turn, result in "incongruence in the intentionally orchestrated and communicated brand images" of the places in question (Boisen et al., 2011, p. 146). Such issues bring us to a second key characteristic that may inform our thinking about place in this context, namely *territory*.

TERRITORY

The notion of 'territory' has been usually thought of in terms of a distinct, boundaried space affected by a certain control or a regular set of behaviours (see Kärrholm, 2007, 2012, for a review). In the context of place marketing/ branding, the spatial extent of the place in question is often determined by the jurisdictional areas of the agencies responsible for this activity and/or political administrative areas, which (as mentioned above) may exist at a variety of spatial scales.

Adopting a perspective that in many ways resonates with the communication imperatives of place marketing/branding, Kärrholm (2007, 2008) argues that territories potentially arise through processes of producing, maintaining, and assigning spaces with meaning. This echoes Brighenti's (2010) view that territory is "not an absolute concept. Rather, it is always relative to a sphere of application or a structural domain of practice" (p. 61), and consequently, territory is "better conceived as an act or practice rather than an object or physical space" (p. 53). For our purposes, this domain of practice relates to place marketing/branding activities, and in this context, the role of boundaries is perhaps more nuanced than more traditional conceptualisations of territory allow.

Brighenti highlights the importance of *boundaries*, which he argues, "are a constitutive prerequisite of territory" (2010, p. 60), and therefore the making of a territory is "inherently related to the drawing of certain boundaries" (2014, p. 2). This has implications, not only for delineating the nature of the spatial entity that is the subject of branding initiatives, but also for determining the locus of responsibility for those activities. Thus, some spatial entities that are marketed/branded might have very clear boundaries. For example, nation-states have very clear administrative jurisdictions – evident in the fact that one needs a passport in order to enter or leave their territory.

At the opposite end of the spatial scale, there are other smaller spatial entities which also have very clear boundaries. Within many towns and cities, for example, there exist business improvement districts (BIDs). There is no single consensus definition of what constitutes a BID (Hoyt, 2004; Ward, 2007). However, in general terms BIDs are developed in locations where property owners (or occupying businesses) within a clearly delineated spatial area elect to make a collective contribution (in the form of a levy, for a specific time period) to secure private capital to fund activities (often incorporating marketing and promotion) to improve the attractiveness and spatial competitiveness of their area (Ward, 2007). For our discussion, the crucial element of this definition of a BID is the fact that there is a 'hard' boundary – a business clearly has to be within the BID area and to be paying the levy in order to enjoy the benefits that accrue from the BID's activities.

In contrast to above examples of nation-states and BIDs, other spatial entities could be considered as 'fuzzy' places (Warnaby et al., 2010), where administrative and jurisdictional boundaries are much more amorphous. Echoing the work of, for example, Paasi (2002, 2010) and Hospers (2006), Warnaby et al. (2010) highlight the *regional* as a spatial scale that may, in particular, be shaped as much by symbols, social practice, and consciousness as by 'hard' territorial boundaries. In such 'created' – or 'imagined' – places, boundaries can "become the object of an on-going work of enactment, reinforcement, negation, interpretation and negotiation" (Brighenti, 2010, p. 62), leading to an understanding that the creation of a place (which can then be the subject of marketing/branding activities) is an active and dynamic endeavour.

Paasi (2002) notes that regions emerge, develop, and exist through a process of 'institutionalisation', which is the outcome of the simultaneous and interconnected working of four different forces (or what he terms, 'shapes'). These include:

- *The territorial shape*: the degree to which an area is distinct from other areas in spatial terms. A key question here is whether the territorial borders of the region in question are clearly defined, recognisable, or even agreed upon.

- *The symbolic shape*: the development of regional symbols. Such symbols may include the name of the region, the occurrence of the area on maps, flags, and typical landmarks. These elements are visible aspects of a region that may evoke a shared feeling.
- *The institutional shape*: the area's institutions that are necessary to maintain the territorial and symbolic shape of a region. Examples include the formation of administrative bodies, educational centres, and development agencies.
- *The shape connected with the identity of an area*: the extent to which the region is 'rooted' in the consciousness and social practices of people, being both individuals and groups. This shape can refer to the regional identity of the inhabitants, that is, the identification of individuals with the region. It could also include the constructed identity of the region per se (i.e., its desired reputation or brand), pointing to those elements of nature, culture, and regional life that are chosen by regional groups, such as political bodies, to distinguish their area from other regions.

Hospers argues that these 'shapes' could be the starting points for the development of a distinctive place brand, and considers their role in the context of the Oresund Region (Hospers, 2004, 2006), in terms of trying to 'solidify' this archetypal 'fuzzy' place.

The Oresund Region (also spelled as Øresund in Danish and Öresund in Swedish) is a transnational metropolitan area in northern Europe, centred on the Oresund strait and the two cities that lie on either side of it, namely: Copenhagen, Denmark and Malmö, Sweden. The region is connected by the Oresund Bridge, which spans the strait at its southern end. Such a link between Denmark and Sweden had been proposed from the late nineteenth century (Löfgren, 2004), but it had been a controversial idea (Dekker and Hallin, 2001) and it was not until 2000 that the bridge was finally completed. The building of this iconic structure proved to be hugely symbolic in cementing the idea of the Oresund Region (Löfgren, 2004). Indeed, after the opening of the bridge, an Oresund 'identity' has been extensively promoted (see Hospers, 2004, 2006, for more detail).

IMPLICATIONS FOR PLACE MARKETING AND BRANDING

Warnaby (2009) has suggested that the practice of place marketing/branding is influenced by two key factors: (1) the complexity of the place 'product'; and (2) the complexity of the organisational mechanisms for its marketing. Drawing on the above discussion regarding the characteristics of place, we continue by considering the implications for marketing and branding activities in this explicitly spatial context.

The Place Product

Warnaby et al. (2002) suggest that one of the defining characteristics of marketing places involves the commodification of certain (typically urban) attributes to promote a positive image of the place as a holistic entity. This consequently raises the issue of how these attributes – or what Sleipen (1988) terms 'contributory elements' to the place as a whole – can be classified as a precursor to choosing which ones might be highlighted as part of the representation of a place for the purposes of marketing/branding.

Van den Berg and Braun (1999) introduce an implied scalar perspective into this process by identifying three levels of the (urban) place product, comprising:

*   Level 1 – The individual urban goods and services, which can be marketed as discrete attractions/facilities. They can also be combined to create ...
*   Level 2 – Clusters of related services, which can be marketed to attract particular segments of place users. Clusters can also coalesce to create an overall perception of ...
*   Level 3 – The urban agglomeration as a whole, which is mainly concerned with identity and image building for the urban place as a holistic entity. This activity can be open to various interpretations, because different combinations of individual goods/services and clusters may be promoted to distinct market segments (Ashworth and Voogd, 1990).

Here the focus is primarily on tangible elements, but the place 'product' can also comprise 'soft conditions', including, for example, quality of life, place atmosphere, housing market conditions, levels of tolerance and openness, and the diversity of the population (Musterd and Murie, 2010). These factors relate to the more phenomenological 'experience' and 'feel' of the (urban) place and can have an important role to play in place marketing/branding:

> The vagueness and subjective nature of these terms provides a lack of clarity but also offers flexibility and thus major opportunities for politicians and city managers. They may also favour these terms because the idea that urban amenities are good for the urban economy provides the opportunity to connect (physical) urban development agendas and social agendas with economic agendas. (Musterd and Murie, 2010, p. 25)

The resulting place marketing/branding 'representation work' will involve the conscious communication of selective aspects of specific localities or areas to target audiences (Ward and Gold, 1994). Hubbard and Hall suggest that, for the purposes of marketing, places are "constituted through a plethora of images and representations" (1998, p. 7). Indeed, the use of "visual symbols" (Kotler et al., 1999) has been identified as central to place marketing, evident in the widespread use of a collage approach. This was described by Gold (1994, p. 22) as "perhaps the most distinctive feature of place promotional advertising", comprising "between three and six photographs of the place concerned along with a portion of descriptive text". More recently, the use of such techniques is also evident in relation to place marketing websites (Warnaby, 2015). This resonates with notions of an 'assemblage', defined in terms of the entity formed from the coming together of parts (Anderson, 2012), and "whose properties emerge from the interactions between [those] parts" (Delanda, 2006, p. 5).

In a place context, Anderson (2012, p. 571) highlights that ideas about place as an assemblage are consistent with "a turn towards what have been termed 'relational places'", noting that "[t]he notion of (terrestrial) place has thus changed from one that is sedentary and stable to one that is open to conditionality and emergence". Places can thus be regarded as inevitably 'provisional', because they are "constructed by people doing things, and in this sense are never 'finished' but are constantly being performed" (Cresswell, 2004, p. 37). Similarly, in a marketing/branding context, Warnaby and Medway (2013, p. 351) suggest "the place emerges as a text constantly rewritten by human actions", which brings us to the second distinguishing aspect of place marketing/branding, namely: how those responsible for these activities organise themselves.

Organisational Mechanisms for Place Marketing/Branding

Linking back to notions of territory discussed above, if, as Brighenti (2010) notes, territory can be regarded in relational terms, and conceived of as an act or practice, this begs the question of who is involved in the development of place branding strategies. This issue is a long-established theme in academic inquiry into place branding. For example, Ashworth (1993) suggests three possible producers of the place 'product':

- The assembler of the various elements of the place product – in other words, the individual goods and services and their combination into clusters, as discussed above, as is often the case in the tourism industry;
- Governments and their agencies (which may operate at varying spatial scales), who "concern themselves with coordinating, stimulating, subsidising and occasionally even operating various facilities as well as engaging in much generalized place promotion" (p. 645);

- The place consumer, who creates their own unique place product from the variety of facilities and attributes available.

The relationality inherent in such perspectives is manifest in, for example, van den Berg and Braun's (1999) notion of *organising capacity*, defined in terms of "the ability to enlist all actors involved and, with their help, to generate new ideas and to develop and implement a policy designed to respond to fundamental developments and create conditions for sustainable development" (p. 995).

Van den Berg and Braun (1999) identify various factors contributing to organising capacity. These include the *administrative organisation*, namely, the formal institutional governance framework, which, linking back to scale issues discussed above, relates to administrative jurisdictional areas and so on. They also note the existence of more relationally-oriented entities such as *the strategic network*, described in terms of "patterns of interaction between mutually dependent actors that evolve around policy problems or projects" (p. 996) – in this context, place marketing/branding activities. In addition, other 'relational' factors such as *leadership*, *vision and strategy*, and *societal* and *political support*, are identified as contributing to organising capacity, and thereby helping to achieve place competitiveness.

Such issues of relationality are explicitly developed in a place branding context in Hankinson's (2004) conceptualisation of *relational network brands*. Here, Hankinson suggests a place brand is represented by a core brand (incorporating *personality*, *positioning*, and *reality*), and four dynamic categories of brand relationships (that is, between the brand and consumers, media, infrastructure elements, and primary service providers), "which extend the brand reality or brand experience" (p. 114). In discussing these issues, he highlights the importance of building relationships with key place stakeholders. Again, a scalar perspective is evident here – as Van den Berg and Braun state (1999): "functional urban relations do not stop at municipal borders and cities need to form strategic partnerships with other towns to market the metropolitan region or even a wider conurbation." (p. 998).

CONCLUDING COMMENTS

This chapter began by providing an overview of different geographically informed conceptualisations of place, which we argued are an essential precondition for developing any understanding of place marketing and branding. Drawing on this discussion, we continued by examining how the practice of place marketing and branding is influenced by the complexity of both the place 'product' and those organisational mechanisms responsible for delivering it. In essence, this reduces down to two interrelated questions: (1) what exactly is it that is being marketed/branded; and (2) who, or what institutional arrangements, is/are responsible for doing this? The complexity of places, as illustrated throughout the preceding discussion, means that answers to these two questions are complex too.

On the one hand, this news is not new. Scholars in the field of place marketing and branding have argued for some time that places are different from conventional products, and that any place-focused marketing efforts need to be aware of this. Thus, previous work has emphasised the variegated nature of the place product, and the fact that it is assembled and perceived in multifarious ways, across nested and often overlapping jurisdictions. In this respect, a given place will emerge as a polysemic text that means different things to different people/organisations, and is also likely to be the subject of marketing and branding effort from more than one source. As Warnaby and Medway (2013, p. 357) explain:

> The nature of a place is therefore constantly rewritten (for better or worse) by the creative force of human actions (intentional or unintentional, constructive or destructive). Places in this respect are products which we 'do' – and even how a place is perceived is arguably a form of 'doing'. A common observation of place products is that they are multi-sold, but this is because a place can be more than one product simultaneously.

In this chapter, we have attempted to get under the skin of how place, or places, 'work'; in turn, this has helped reveal the demands this puts on those entrusted with the deceptively straightforward task of marketing and branding them. We can see, for example, how particular challenges might emerge over the interdependency and interwoven nature of different place scales (BID, district, city, region, nation-state, and so on), or what might be called the 'place marketing palimpsest'. This is then coupled with potential overlap, confusion, and even disagreement over the place boundaries of these scalar entities and their associated territories. In marketing and branding terms this is a situation that presents, to say the least, a 'tough gig'.

Analogies can sometimes seem trite in these situations, but bear with us. Imagine you work for a fast-moving consumer goods company, similar to one known for its famed '57 varieties'. Your new position is to head up a marketing team for the company's favourite and best-selling condiment product – for the sake of similitude we can call it 'Happy Place' or 'HP' sauce. You are initially delighted to take this role on; indeed, it seems like a certain promotion from your previous job of working on the production line. A few days in, however, the nature of the task at hand begins to reveal itself as a truly poisoned chalice. Your first idea is to pin down what the key ingredients of the sauce are, as you think you might be able to use this information to get a unique marketing angle or branding refresh on the product itself. However, nobody in the company seems to know or be able to agree on the ingredients, or even the package sizes for that matter; and some online market research suggests that existing consumers also have different views and understandings about what is and what is not (and what should and should not be) in HP sauce. Yet worse is still to come! A couple of weeks into the job and you find out, purely accidentally by reading down an email trail, that there are at least two other teams within the company who are working on separate marketing and branding campaigns for HP sauce. You did not know about them and they did not know about you. And then, perhaps most bizarre of all, one of your team members stumbles across a successful online marketing campaign of a gourmet food retailer that favourably promotes HP sauce as one of the quality products in its specialist Christmas hampers.

This analogy could continue, but it has probably been stretched far enough in demonstrating the potential challenges that those responsible for marketing and branding places might typically face when compared to those working with fast moving consumer goods products. These challenges might be sum-marised as a lack of agreement amongst interested stakeholders about: what the place product actually is, or what its constituent elements are or should be; where this product's boundaries lie or what its size and areal coverage are; and the individuals, institutions, or organisations that are responsible for marketing the place product. We suggest that the most effective way of addressing these challenges is to understand the importance of collaborative behaviour and communication, and mutually supportive attitudes, amongst all relevant place stakeholders.

Some existing work within the field has already highlighted the critical role of such stakeholder interaction in urban place-related contexts (see, for example, Le Feuvre et al., 2016). It would seem that this stakeholder-focused and inclusive approach is key to ensuring that place marketing and branding campaigns are coherent, consistent, and, ultimately, effective, at bringing together multiple voices and viewpoints in a smart pluralistic manner. Such a process should better allow the scalar and territorial differences and interde-pendencies within and between places, along with any associated complexities in the place product and the organisational mechanisms responsible for its marketing, to be successfully accommodated to serve a common good.

REFERENCES

Agnew, J.A. (1987), *Place and Politics: The Geographical Mediation of State and Society*, Boston: Allen & Unwin.
Anderson, J. (2012), 'Relational places: the surfed wave as assemblage and conver-gence', *Environment and Planning D: Society and Space*, 30, 570–587.
Ashworth, G. (1993), 'Marketing of places: what are we doing?', in G. Ave and F. Corsico (eds), *Urban Marketing in Europe*, Turin: Torino Incontra, pp. 643–649.

Ashworth, G.J. and H. Voogd (1990), 'Can places be sold for tourism?', in G. Ashworth and B. Goodall (eds), *Marketing Tourism Places*, London: Routledge, pp. 1–16.

Bennison, D., I. Clarke and J. Pal (1995), 'Location decision making: an exploratory framework for analysis', *International Review of Retail, Consumer and Distribution Research*, 5 (1), 1–20.

Boisen, M., K. Terlouw and B. van Gorp (2011), 'The selective nature of place branding and the layering of spatial identities', *Journal of Place Management and Development*, 4 (2), 135–147.

Brighenti, A.M. (2010), 'On territorology: towards a general science of territory', *Theory, Culture & Society*, 27 (1), 52–72.

Brighenti, A.M. (2014), 'Mobilizing territories, territorializing mobilities', *Sociologica*, 8 (1), 1–25.

Brown, S. (1992), *Retail Location: A Micro-Scale Perspective*, Aldershot: Avebury.

Burnip, L. (2017), 'A city's grief: Manchester's St Ann's Square filled with a sea of flowers, balloons and cards as the city mourns victims of Monday's bombing', *The Sun*, 26 May, accessed 1 June 2020 at https://www.thesun.co.uk/news/3657127/manchester-st-anns-square-bombing-attack-tributes-picture/.

Cresswell, T. (2004), *Place: A Short Introduction*, Oxford: Blackwell Publishing.

Cresswell, T. and G. Hoskins (2008), 'Place, persistence, and practice: evaluating historical significance at Angel Island, San Francisco and Maxwell Street, Chicago', *Annals of the Association of American Geographers*, 98 (2), 392–413.

Crewe, L. and M. Lowe (1995), 'Gap on the map? Towards a geography of consumption and identity', *Environment and Planning A*, 27, 1877–1898.

Dawson, J., A. Findlay and L. Sparks (2008), *The Retailing Reader*, London, UK and New York, USA: Routledge.

Dekker, H. and P.O. Hallin (2001), 'The discursive nature of environmental conflicts: the case of the Öresund link', *Area*, 33 (4), 391–403.

Delanda, M. (2006), *A New Philosophy of Society: Assemblage Theory and Social Complexity*, London: Continuum Books.

Edensor, T. (2012), 'Vital urban materiality and its multiple absences: the building stone of central Manchester', *Cultural Geographies*, 20 (4), 447–465.

Gold, J.R. (1994), 'Locating the message: place promotion as image communication', in J.R. Gold and S.V. Ward (eds), *Place Promotion: The Use of Publicity and Marketing to Sell Towns and Regions*, Chichester: John Wiley & Sons, pp. 19–37.

Hankinson, G. (2004), 'Relational network brands: towards a conceptual model of place brands', *Journal of Vacation Marketing*, 10 (2), 109–121.

Hartwell, C. (2001), *Pevsner Architectural Guides – Manchester*, New Haven, CT, USA and London, UK: Yale University Press.

Hospers, G.-J. (2004), 'Place marketing in Europe – the branding of the Oresund region', *Intereconomics*, September/October, 271–279.

Hospers, G.-J. (2006), 'Borders, bridges and branding: the transformation of the Øresund region into an imagined space', *European Planning Studies*, 14 (10), 15–33.

Hoyt, L. (2004), 'Collecting private funds for safer public spaces: an empirical examination of the business improvement district concept', *Environment and Planning B: Planning and Design*, 31 (3), 367–380.

Hubbard, P. and T. Hall (1998), 'The entrepreneurial city and the "new urban politics"', in T. Hall and P. Hubbard (eds), *The Entrepreneurial City: Geographies of Politics, Regimes and Representations*, Chichester: John Wiley & Sons, pp. 1–23.

Hubbard, P. and D. Lyon (2018), 'Introduction: streetlife – the shifting sociologies of the street', *The Sociological Review*, 66 (5), 937–951.

Ingold, T. (2004), 'Buildings', in S. Harrison, S. Pile and N. Thrift (eds), *Patterned Ground: Entanglements of Nature and Culture*, London: Reaktion Books, pp. 238–240.

Kärrholm, M. (2007), 'The materiality of territorial production', *Space & Culture*, 10 (4), 437–453.

Kärrholm, M. (2008), 'The territorialisation of a pedestrian precinct in Malmö: materialities in the commercialisation of public space', *Urban Studies*, 45 (9), 1903–1924.

Kärrholm, M. (2012), *Retailising Space: Architecture, Retail and the Territorialisation of Public Space*, Farnham: Ashgate Publishing.

Kotler, P., C. Asplund, I. Rein and D. Haider (1999), *Marketing Places Europe: Attracting Investments, Industries, and Visitors to European Cities, Communities, Regions and Nations*, Harlow: Financial Times Prentice Hall.

Le Feuvre, M., D. Medway, G. Warnaby, K. Ward and A. Goatman (2016), 'Understanding stakeholder interactions in urban partnerships', *Cities*, 52, 55–65.

Löfgren, O. (2004), 'Concrete nationalism? Bridge building in the new economy', *Focaal – European Journal of Anthropology*, 43, 59–75.

Manchester City Council (2009), 'St Ann's Square Conservation Area – History', Manchester City Council, accessed 1 June 2020 at http://www.manchester.gov.uk/ info/511/conservation_areas/144/st_anns_square_conservation_area/2.

Marston, S., K. Woodard and J.P. Jones III (2009), 'Scale', in D. Gregory, R. Johnston, G. Pratt, M.J. Watts and S. Whatmore (eds), *The Dictionary of Human Geography* (5th edn), Chichester: Wiley-Blackwell, pp. 664–666.

Massey, D. (1991), 'A global sense of place', *Marxism Today*, June, pp. 24–29.

Musterd, S. and A. Murie (2010), 'The idea of the creative or knowledge-based city', in S. Musterd and A. Murie (eds), *Making Competitive Cities*, Chichester: Wiley-Blackwell, pp. 17–32.

New Economics Foundation (2004), *Clone Town Britain: The Loss of Local Identity on the Nation's High Streets*, London: New Economics Foundation.

Oakes, S. and G. Warnaby (2011), 'Conceptualising the management and consumption of live music in urban space', *Marketing Theory*, 11 (4), 405–418.

Paasi, A. (2002), 'Bounded spaces in the mobile world: deconstructing regional identity', *Tijdschrift voor Economische en Sociale Geografie*, 93 (2), 137–148.

Paasi, A. (2010), 'Regions as social constructs, but who or what "constructs" them? Agency in question', *Environment and Planning A*, 42 (10), 2296–2301.

Sleipen, W. (1988), *Marketing van de Historische Omgeving*, Breda: Netherlands Research Institute for Tourism. Cited in G. Ashworth and H. Voogd (1990), *Selling the City: Marketing Approaches to Public Sector Urban Planning*, London: Belhaven.

Van den Berg, L. and E. Braun (1999), 'Urban competitiveness, marketing and the need for organising capacity', *Urban Studies*, 36 (5–6), 987–999.

Ward, K. (2007), 'Business improvement districts: policy origins, mobile policies and urban liveability', *Geography Compass*, 1 (3), 657–672.

Ward, S.V. and J.R. Gold (1994), 'Introduction', in J.R. Gold and S.V. Ward (eds), *Place Promotion: The Use of Publicity and Marketing to Sell Towns and Regions*, Chichester: John Wiley & Sons, pp 1–17.

Warnaby, G. (2009), 'Towards a service-dominant place marketing logic', *Marketing Theory*, 9 (4), 403–423.

Warnaby, G. (2013), 'Synchronising retail and space: using urban squares for competitive place differentiation', *Consumption Markets and Culture*, 16 (1), 25–44.

Warnaby, G. (2015), 'Rethinking the visual communication of the place brand: a contemporary role for chorography?', in M. Kavaratzis, G. Warnaby and G. Ashworth (eds), *Rethinking Place Branding: Comprehensive Brand Development for Cities and Regions*, Cham: Springer Verlag, pp. 175–190.

Warnaby, G. and D. Medway (2013), 'What about the "place" in place marketing?', *Marketing Theory*, 13 (3), 345–363.

Warnaby, G., D. Bennison and B.J. Davies (2005), 'Retailing and the marketing of urban places: a UK perspective', *International Review of Retail, Distribution and Consumer Research*, 15 (2), 191–215.

Warnaby, G., D. Bennison and D. Medway (2010), 'Notions of materiality and linearity: the challenges of marketing the Hadrian's Wall place product', *Environment and Planning A*, 42 (6), 1365–1382.

Warnaby, G., D. Bennison, B.J. Davies and H. Hughes (2002), 'Marketing UK towns and cities as shopping destinations', *Journal of Marketing Management*, 18 (9/10), 877–904.

2. Place brands: why, who, what, when, where, and how?

Mihalis Kavaratzis and Magdalena Florek

INTRODUCTION

Place branding has been studied rather intensely, at least for the last 20 years. While there is no doubt that significant progress has been achieved in terms of conceptualising the discipline as well as refining the practice, several issues remain unresolved. This chapter attempts to clarify parts of the evident confusion around place brands by taking stock of several approaches that are evident in the literature and can be observed in practice. These various approaches are grouped together as potential answers to core questions that surround place brands.

The aim of this stock-taking is both to consolidate the advancement of the place branding field and to contribute to a clearer 'mapping' of the field so that directions for its future might be deduced. In this sense, the chapter provides complementary thoughts and ideas to a set of publications with similar aims. For instance, we are attempting to complement the review by Lucarelli and Berg (2011), who have outlined the main approaches adopted by place branding studies, and Gertner's (2011) meta-analysis of the literature. More specifically, we aim at extending the attempt by Warnaby et al. (2015) to answer six urgent questions surrounding the field: the 'why', 'who', 'what', 'when', 'where', and 'how' of place branding. Knowing that in all scientific enquiries, when one question is answered it opens the way for a series of new questions to be raised, the chapter highlights potential answers to the basic questions before going ahead to ponder on a tentative future research agenda.

BRIEF OVERVIEW OF DIFFERENT APPROACHES TO PLACE BRANDING

In general, there are significant challenges in place branding associated with the peculiarities, and even the appropriateness or inappropriateness, of treating places as 'marketable assets'. Different approaches have been adopted in the literature to the value and implementation of place branding. While a series of scholars and practitioners welcome the use of place branding (although not always justifying their support), others criticise the discipline and its practice.

Within the studies that adopt a – more or less – positive attitude, several different streams of approaches and aims can be distinguished. A managerial stream focuses on the process through which political decision makers and the consultants they hire can develop the place brand to increase the competitiveness of a given place (e.g., van Ham, 2008; Moilanen and Rainisto, 2009). A series of publications have attempted to explore in more depth the theoretical foundations of place branding (e.g., Kavaratzis, 2004; Govers and Go, 2009; Papadopoulos, 2004, 2011).

A major stream has dealt with the issue of destination branding, that is treating places as brands in order to attract visitors (e.g., Morgan et al., 2002; Cai, 2002). Another stream of publications has sought to explore how place branding might be put into practice (e.g., Anholt, 2007; Braun, 2011) and how to evaluate its impact (e.g., Zenker, 2011; Florek, 2012). A more recent stream is characterised by a cultural approach to place branding and establishes cultural explanations of the process through which place brands are created, identifying roots in the place's culture (e.g., Aitken and Campelo, 2011) and place identity (e.g., Mayes, 2008; Kalandides, 2011; Kavaratzis and Kalandides, 2015).

On the other hand, the 'critical stream' includes publications that see behind branding a suspicious political agenda and identify significant social consequences (e.g., Greenberg, 2008). A common criticism is that place branding is a tool that various elites use in order to pursue their own interests and execute their strategies within neoliberal urban governance (Colomb, 2011). Broudehoux (2001, p. 272), for example, sees city branding as a field where "dominant groups use spatial and visual strategies to impose their views". A particular discussion relates to the effects of place branding on the physical appearance of the city (e.g., Evans, 2015) and on the effects of the evident widespread use of cultural and entertainment branding on the place's social character (e.g., Evans, 2003).

Through both approaches mentioned above, an advanced conceptualisation of the field is arguably closer than ever before. This can be demonstrated, for instance, by a clearer comprehension of the differences between branding, marketing, and promotion (Boisen et al., 2018) or by a refined understanding of the role and value of branding for communities (Govers, 2018). The current emphasis of research and theory is placed on the role of various stakeholders in place branding and an exploration of approaches alternative to the dominant managerial approach. Also, place brands are now increasingly analysed in terms of their cultural value and the place branding process is regarded as a production of cultural meanings (e.g., Aitken and Campelo, 2011; Saraniemi, 2011; Kavaratzis and Hatch, 2013).

The role of various stakeholders – importantly including the residents – has been highlighted under a wider understanding of the 'co-creation' of place brands. This highlights the significance of internal audiences and stresses the fact that place brands are not formed through traditional communications but are co-created by a multitude of people who encounter and appropriate them as they interact. Such understanding is now reflected in part of the literature that emphasises the role of residents (e.g., Braun et al., 2013; Eshuis et al., 2014) and their satisfaction (e.g., Insch and Florek, 2010), the role of stakeholders (e.g., Merrilees et al., 2012; Klijn et al., 2012), the grounding of the place brand in the 'sense of place' (e.g., Campelo et al., 2014; Papadopoulos et al., 2012), and the possibilities of a more participatory approach to place branding (e.g., Kavaratzis and Kalandides, 2015; Zenker and Erfgen, 2014).

THE FUNDAMENTAL QUESTIONS AROUND PLACE BRANDS

Several questions surrounding the theory, practice, and study of place brands form the foundations of the future of the discipline and are raised here. Partial answers have been given to some of the questions in the literature or, at least, there are sound suggestions on how to go about answering them. Since the questions are not fully answered, raising them again helps provide a structure for the ongoing conversation and debate. These fundamental questions are: (1) *why* are brands important for places; (2) *who* are the key agents responsible for place branding; (3) *what* are the ingredients out of which place brands are formed; (4) *when* is the time to brand; (5) *where* do the branding processes occur, with the answers to these core questions combining to provide the approach adopted towards the practice-oriented question; and (6) *how* can the place brand be managed?

Of course, discussion of these questions below is rife with overlap and does not claim to be exhaustive. Furthermore, probably the correct answer to all questions would be: all those at the same time, despite their contradictory natures, oppositional characters, and conflicting (implicit or explicit) interests. The questions are raised below in order to assist in sketching the future of the conversation and debate around place branding, by providing a structure and initial list of topics from which to start clarifying the aspects of place branding that remain unclear.

The 'Why' of Place Brands

The first core question concerns the reasons why place brands are developed and studied. Why do places attempt branding in the first place? Why do scholars keep studying it? Why is the investment in place branding useful or necessary? What does it offer to our understanding of places, place management, place development and, ultimately, what does it mean to society? Possible answers include the following:

- *To fight in the arena of inter-place competition*: this is the most common justification given for the relevance and significance of place brands as well as the most common reason stated for the popularity of place branding as a practice. In this logic, the place brand is a useful tool that places use as they compete with each other for limited, free-moving financial, human, or cultural resources as well as for target groups such as tourists, businesses, and residents. The place brand is assumed to help in securing a desired position within these global flows of people and capital. The usefulness of branding is thought to lie precisely in its ability to assist places in winning 'place wars' or in surviving in the competitive arena. As a consequence, the reason for place branding is *to distinguish from other places and their offer.*
- *To find strategic guidance for place development*: this logic assumes that the usefulness of place brands is their potential to be used as an 'imagined future'; as an ideal scenario for the place's conditions. Place brands are thought to provide a vision for the place's future and an integrated direction for the planning and implementation of various sorts of activities and measures that will help achieve this vision.
- *To find the basis for stakeholder cooperation*: this is a logic that views the place brand as 'common ground' for the various stakeholders to set a collective goal and work together towards achieving it. The place brand is thought to provide the general framework under which actions of different stakeholders can complement and reinforce each other and collectively produce the desired result.
- *To find solutions to practical/functional place-related problems*: this is a more functional and instrumental view of place brands that assumes that a place brand provides the context in which several specific and time-bound issues can be solved. For instance, how to attract investment for a planned project, how to take advantage of a tourist resource in the area, or how to increase usage of a recently redeveloped site.
- *To assist in place identity construction*: this view situates place branding within the wider place identity process (i.e., the process that allows places to acquire and establish a character). It takes into consideration the ways in which individuals and groups of people both affect and are affected by the place brand in their ongoing construction and reconstruction of the place's identity and the way in which they relate to the place. At the same time, the place brand is thought to be a tool in the hands of groups that attempt

to influence the character of the place in specific ways (e.g., to serve their political or economic interests).

- *To maximise positive place experience*: this view assumes that place brands are crucial for the way in which places are experienced by their consumers (residents, visitors, investors, and so on). Place brands are thought to shape the expectations people have of a place and thus the experience they expect to have, which, in turn, is thought to lead to increased satisfaction that people derive out of such experience. This makes place brands useful in the managerial effort to align the expectations people have of a place with the actual place reality.

The 'Who' of Place Brands

A second core question concerns the agents that play key roles in the construction, communication, and management of place brands. Who are the key agents in place brand formation? Who is actually constructing place brands or influencing their construction? How do the interactions between the key agents influence the branding process? Who should take responsibility for the process? And what is the role of leadership? Different answers can be provided depending on the following possible views:

- *Institution/organisation-based* views that mainly refer to dominant groups and the systems they design. Such groups are the local financial, political, or cultural elites and can be authorities, major businesses, closely related industries, as well as consultants.
- *Individual-based* views that accept that the major players in place brand construction are the place's users as they make use of and experience it, for example as they visit a place or as they live their everyday lives.
- *Group-based* views that accept that groups of individuals form different brands as they appropriate the place and its brand in their own, particular ways. This leads to differences between the place brand formation and evaluation as these are undertaken by tourists, residents, investors, by young and older individuals, and so on.
- *Societal* views that attempt to incorporate within individual-based or group-based views the influence of the social/cultural context and how this alters individual meanings towards a more collective perspective.

The 'What' of Place Brands

The third core question concerns the elements that constitute the place brand – the things that place brands are 'made of'. What are the resources and materials out of which place brands are crafted? What are the ingredients that key agents use and combine to form place brands? Answers that could be (and have been) suggested include:

- *Promotional devices and identity claims*: a very common answer assumes that the main resources for place brand construction can be found in official, intentional, and coordinated communication by local stakeholders (most commonly tourism offices or place branding agencies and local authorities). This is a managerial view that approaches place branding as a powerful and persuasive promotional activity.
- *Place-making elements*: this is a more nuanced view that finds the essence of place brands in understanding 'sense of place' and how it changes over time. This view assumes a much stronger link between the place and the brand and conceptualises branding as a wide and complex set of processes rather than isolating its promotional character.
- *Narratives or place stories*: this view finds the main resources used for place brand formation in the general 'story' of the place as this is narrated by various possible story-telling organisations, people, objects, and devices (obviously going well beyond tourism offices and place branding agencies). Emphasis is placed on the historical aspects of the place as well as the understanding of collective meanings through 'narration'.
- *Discursive/interactive formations*: this view extends the above notion of narratives to finding the main resources for place brand formation in conversations and interactions between and among people, landscapes, and other representations. The emphasis is on the collective construction of the meaning of place as this is undertaken in social actuality and through social interactions, including direct and indirect experiences with the place. Such interactions tend to construct particular versions of the place and the place brand which change across time and space.

The 'When' of Place Brands

The next core question concerns the temporal aspect of place brands and the process of their formation. When are place brands formed? When is the time to brand? What are the dynamics of the process? And when does the place brand become more relevant to people? Again, a range of possible answers would include:

- *Place brands as ongoing processes*: this is a proactive view of place brands that assumes they are constantly produced, redefined, and evolving entities. The place brand under this view is intrinsically linked to the processes that construct the place's identity and image.

- *Place brands as time-bound projects*: for politicians, consultants, and other practitioners who are assigned or assume the responsibility to formally organise the branding of a place, the place brand might be thought of as a project or a set of projects. Under this view, the place brand project is to be undertaken within a limited period of time with specifically assigned resources and concrete expected outcomes.
- *Place brands as decision making mechanisms*: this is a customer-centred view of place brands that assumes that place brands become relevant and assume their significance when people need to make place-related decisions such as relocation, choice of holiday, choice of place to study, and so on.
- *Place brands as results of gathering momentum*: in this view, the place brand becomes a force that is able to capitalise on the momentum gathered due to certain circumstances of local significance whether internally or externally initiated. Examples of such circumstances include the 'common goal' found in the period before the organisation of a significant event (e.g., the Olympic Games or another major sport/cultural event) or the collective feeling of success after such an event. The momentum might be gathered after such prompts as a discovery of local significance, after the development of a seemingly fashionable idea, or when a local leader inspires such a momentum.
- *Place brands as results of major changes*: this is a rather reactive view of place brands that calls place branding (normally understood as place re-imaging) to help with reasserting the major characteristic of the place's economic or social base.

The 'Where' of Place Brands

The next core question concerns the locus of the place brand, examining where place brand formation and evaluation occur. Where is the place brand formed? Is it formed in the place itself or somewhere else? Possible answers here vary significantly and are arguably crucial for answering all other questions:

- *In people's minds*: this answer conceptualises the place brand as a property of individual place users rather than a feature of the place itself. This individual mental formation of the place brand is based on associations that individuals hold with the place and its brand and the ways in which these associations are culturally dependent and dynamic. This leads to the widely established assertion that different individuals have a different place brand in their minds.
- *In the place itself*: this is an objectivist view that approaches the place brand as a given, objective property of the actual place that is assumed

to be almost independent of individuals. The assumption is that the (officially) constructed place brand can invoke very similar – or even exactly the same – connotations and feelings for different individuals because it is based on objective, 'real' features of the place.

- *In social interactions in and around the place*: this view is in line with the social-interactionist answers to all previous questions and sees the place brand as a practice situated within processes of place formation. This is initiated, formed, and constantly redefined through the interactions between people over place brand elements (place and brand as networks).
- *In discourses and narratives*: this is a similar view that approaches the place brand as a cultural formation, which is generated and acquires meaning through the narratives of different people and organisations in the past and present. Collectively these narratives might be presenting a coherent place story, which then becomes the place brand.

The 'How' of Place Brands

The above questions concern the nature of place brands as phenomena. The combined answers to these questions determine how people understand the nature of the place branding endeavour and, therefore, what people see as the purpose, power, and limitations of place brand management. How can place brands be directed by key agents towards desired directions? How should place brand management be understood and undertaken? Different answers to this 'how' question would include:

- *Place branding as promotion*: an extension of the view of place brands as promotional devices and identity claims as seen above, this view assumes that place branding includes a set of promotional activities intended to appeal to specified appropriate target groups.
- *Place branding as image/reputation management*: a slightly wider view that sees place branding as aiming to create a favourable place image and a general, positive place reputation to underpin all development efforts. Most commonly, place branding is thought of as a process of place re-imaging (given that place images already exist) in order to 'correct' a negative image or to increase awareness of the place.
- *Place branding as an identity construction exercise*: in line with the view of place brands as part of the place identity construction process mentioned above, this approach assumes that place branding aims at stimulating and facilitating the constant reconstruction of place identity, reinforcing people's identification with the place, and increasing place-attachment.
- *Place branding as a power exercise*: this is a critical view that situates place branding within wider struggles of political, administrative, finan-

cial, and social power. It is most commonly assumed that place branding works to conceal such power struggles and to impose elite-led interests and directions while suppressing opposing voices. This is possible through a 'spectacularisation' of these interests under the 'glitter' of the place brand.

- *Place branding as a community-building exercise*: in this view, the main aim of place branding is to identify common ideas and directions for the future of the community and to produce collectively generated place stories and visions. This is in line with the view of the place brand as the basis of stakeholder cooperation examined under the 'why' question.

THE FUTURE?

Some of the questions outlined in the previous sections are arguably more significant and more pressing, while other questions have been dealt with more extensively and more effectively. The main aim of the above is to offer a map for further advancement of the field. It is certain that each commentator and scholar and each practitioner has his or her preferences concerning all the above, based on personal backgrounds, ontological predispositions, and ideological approaches. Furthermore, the varying capacities in which different people engage with place branding also affect the answers and relative significance of the questions.

The questions above are better thought of as the themes that outline the field and map the intellectual territory occupied by place branding. Like all maps, they don't dictate or even indicate the route one should follow but, rather, they depict the possible routes that one might decide to follow. The questions are offered as possible areas of exploration and as opportunities for creative cross-fertilisation rather than the 'correct' ways in which to undertake research. Combined, the questions indicate further areas to be explored; some of them are highlighted below.

In the near future, the place branding scholarly community will need to address a series of challenges and questions that remain unsolved and unanswered, with implications for both theory and practice. Some have been the subject of discussion for many years, and some appear due to the development of the place branding domain itself and perhaps more so because of the new circumstances or trends.

One of the persistent unresolved issues around place branding is whether there is a need to discuss different types of the construct depending on whether the place being branded is a city, a region or a country. There is one intrinsic attribute of places that is directly relevant to this, namely that places exist within a hierarchy of nesting spatial scales (Boisen et al., 2011). This characteristic of places is often reflected in administrative or political entities that are responsible for designing and implementing the branding effort. Place branding, therefore, can be practised at different spatial scales from the neigh-bourhood, through the city to the region, national state, or even continental scales. This, however, becomes a challenge because such scales may nest comfortably within each other – even with mutually reinforcing brands – or may interact less comfortably and even contradict each other's brand, giving rise to significant tensions and frictions.

Such scale shadowing may be welcomed or avoided by particular scale brands seeking to associate with perceived benefits or disassociate from per-ceived costs of other scales. For example, at the micro scale, every real estate broker attempts to manage a geography of inclusion or exclusion of specific locations. Their attempt is to capitalise actively on whatever images and per-ceptions of the specific street, neighbourhood, suburb, and so on are deemed positive, while also actively disconnecting from all negative associations that other higher place scales might be inflicting. While there are general principles and even persuasion techniques that seem to be applicable in all place scales, it is rather obvious that place branding is not one and the same for all places but that different treatment might be warranted. The neighbourhood and the country are too dissimilar to be covered by one and the same model of place brand management. It might be more useful for the discipline to recognise the differences and explicitly deal with the different place scales separately.

Following a similar logic, another persistent issue that would need attention in a practical sense relates to the tensions between branding a place as a place of residence, a place to visit, and a place in which to invest. Because these place functions present different challenges and very often serve radically different (and conflicting) interests, they tend to be treated as separate with dis-tinct branding organisations responsible for each. However, as the most recent studies (e.g., Rabbiosi, 2016; Zenker et al., 2017) show, their disconnection is not only ineffective but also invalid.

Another problem lies in understanding the real effects of place branding on places. Hankinson (2015) sees the difficulties in the measurement of per-formance of place brands in the complex value creation process but considers the measurement as essential. From diverse perspectives such as tourism (Pike, 2007), investment (Jacobsen, 2012), and urban policy (Kavaratzis and Ashworth, 2008), authors call for better understanding of place brand perfor-mance and suggest including different indicators and metrics (Florek et al., 2019). Measurement of the effectiveness and efficiency of city branding is, however, challenging and requires clear and unambiguous understanding of what is being measured and how it should be done. Although there is a consid-erable number of place brand performance approaches and indicators, the main problem remains that they do not embrace the multifaceted and interdiscipli-nary nature of place brand.

At the same time, there is a need to reflect on fundamental theoretical questions including a better understanding of how brands and space mutually shape each other. Recent work points to the direction of place branding studies that recognise the importance of multidimensional and inclusive approaches as well as the need to sustain the distinctive qualities of place (e.g., Saraniemi, 2011; Campelo et al., 2014; Kavaratzis and Kalandides, 2015). The future research agenda needs to include critical place branding research which will seek new, participative models of place branding, investigate its spatial dimensions, and explore the social (co-) construction of city meanings among locals, visitors, marketers, and other place stakeholders. The research agenda should also consider different perspectives and views on places, people, brands, and their relations as we know from geography, psychology, sociology, marketing, public management, and other related disciplines. However, a question arises concerning how to make use of these disciplinary perspectives and how to integrate their achievements in order to gain a better understanding of place branding and/or of the progress in its development (integration through *agglomeration, loose-assemblage, clustering, distillation* or *fusion*, per Satija, 2001).

Eshuis and Edwards (2013) highlight the common criticism that branding "is a form of spin that prevents the public from gaining a proper understanding of their government's policies" but they also find evidence that branding can "potentially be a participatory process in which the feelings and emotions of citizens are included" (p. 1066). The widespread acceptance of such understanding would be very welcome indeed, allowing place branding to have a greater and more positive influence on people's quality of life.

REFERENCES

Aitken, R. and Campelo, A. (2011), 'The four Rs of place branding', *Journal of Marketing Management*, 27(9/10), 913–933.

Anholt, S. (2007), *Competitive Identity: The New Brand Management for Nations, Cities and Regions*, Basingstoke: Palgrave Macmillan.

Boisen, M., Terlouw, T. and Van Gorp, B. (2011), 'The selective nature of place branding and the layering of spatial identities', *Journal of Place Management and Development*, 4(2), 135–147.

Boisen, M., Teerlow, K., Groote, P. and Couwenberg, O. (2018), 'Reframing place promotion, place marketing and place branding – moving beyond conceptual confusion', *Cities*, 80, 4–11.

Braun, E. (2011), 'Putting city branding into practice', *Journal of Brand Management*, 19(3), 257–267.

Braun, E., Kavaratzis, M. and Zenker, S. (2013), 'My city – my brand: the role of residents in place branding', *Journal of Place Management and Development*, 6(2), 18–28.

Broudehoux, A.M. (2001), 'Image making, city marketing and the aesthetization of social inequality in Rio de Janeiro', in N. Alsayyad (ed.), *Consuming Tradition, Manufacturing Heritage*, London: Routledge, pp. 273–297.

Cai, L. (2002), 'Cooperative branding for rural destinations', *Annals of Tourism Research*, 29(3), 720–742.

Campelo, A., Aitken, R., Thyne, M. and Gnoth, J. (2014), 'Sense of place: the importance for destination branding', *Journal of Travel Research*, 53(2), 154–166.

Colomb, C. (2011), *Staging the New Berlin: Place Marketing and the Politics of Reinvention Post-1989*, London: Routledge.

Eshuis, J. and Edwards, A. (2013), 'Branding the city: the democratic legitimacy of a new mode of governance', *Urban Studies*, 50(5), 1066–1082.

Eshuis, J., Klijn, E.H. and Braun, E. (2014), 'Place marketing and citizen participation: branding as strategy to address the emotional dimensions of policy making?', *International Review of Administrative Sciences*, 80(1), 151–171.

Evans, G. (2003), 'Hard branding the cultural city: from Prado to Prada', *International Journal of Urban and Regional Research*, 27(2), 417–440.

Evans, G. (2015), 'Rethinking place branding and place making through creative and cultural quarters', in M. Kavaratzis, G.J. Ashworth and G. Warnaby (eds), *Rethinking Place Branding: Comprehensive Brand Development for Cities and Regions*, Cham: Springer.

Florek, M. (2012), 'Measurement of city brand equity', *Actual Problems of Economics*, 2(7), 130–139.

Florek, M., Herezniak, M. and Augustyn, A. (2019), 'You can't govern if you don't measure: experts' insights into place branding effectiveness assessment', *Journal of Place Management and Development*, 12(4), 545–565.

Gertner, D.A. (2011), 'A (tentative) meta-analysis of the "place marketing" and "place branding" literature', *Journal of Brand Management*, 19, 112–131.

Govers, R. (2018), *Imaginative Communities: Admired Cities, Regions and Countries*, Antwerp: Reputo Press.

Govers, R. and Go, F. (2009), *Place Branding: Virtual and Physical Identities, Glocal, Imagined and Experienced*, Basingstoke: Palgrave Macmillan.

Greenberg, M. (2008), *Branding New York: How a City in Crisis was Sold to the World*, London: Routledge.

Hankinson, G. (2015), 'Rethinking the place branding construct', in M. Kavaratzis, G. Warnaby and G.J. Ashworth (eds), *Rethinking Place Branding: Comprehensive Brand Development for Cities and Regions*, Cham: Springer International Publishing, pp. 13–31.

Insch, A. and Florek, M. (2010), 'Place satisfaction of city residents: findings and implications for city branding', in G.J. Ashworth and M. Kavaratzis (eds), *Towards Effective Place Brand Management: Branding European Cities and Regions*, Cheltenham, UK and Northampton, MA, USA: Edward Elgar Publishing, pp. 191–204.

Jacobsen, B.P. (2012), 'Place brand equity: a model for establishing the effectiveness of place brands', *Journal of Place Management and Development*, 5(3), 253–271.

Kalandides, A. (2011), 'The problem with spatial identity: revisiting the "sense of place"', *Journal of Place Management and Development*, 4(1), 28–39.

Kavaratzis, M. (2004), 'From city marketing to city branding', *Place Branding and Public Diplomacy*, 1(1), 58–73.

Kavaratzis, M. and Ashworth, G. (2008), 'Place marketing: how did we get here and where are we going?', *Journal of Place Management and Development*, 1(2), 150–165.

Kavaratzis, M. and Hatch, M.J. (2013), 'The dynamics of place brands: an identity-based approach to place branding theory', *Marketing Theory*, 13(1), 69–86.

Kavaratzis, M. and Kalandides, A. (2015), 'Rethinking the place brand: the inter-actional formation of place brands and the role of participatory place branding', *Environment and Planning A*, 47, 1368–1382.

Klijn, E.H., Eshuis, J. and Braun, E. (2012), 'The influence of stakeholder involvement on the effectiveness of place branding', *Public Management Review*, 14(4), 499–519.

Lucarelli, A. and Berg, P.O. (2011), 'City branding: a state-of-the-art review of the research domain', Journal of Place Management and Development, 4(1), 9–27.

Mayes, R. (2008), 'A place in the sun: the politics of place, identity and branding', *Place Branding and Public Diplomacy*, 4(2), 124–135.

Merrilees, B., Miller, D. and Herington, C. (2012), 'Multiple stakeholders and multiple city meanings', *European Journal of Marketing*, 46(7–8), 1032–1047.

Moilanen, T. and Rainisto, S. (2009), *How to Brand Nations, Cities and Destinations: A Planning Book for Place Branding*, Basingstoke: Palgrave Macmillan.

Morgan, N., Pritchard, A. and Pride, R. (eds) (2002), *Destination Branding: Creating the Unique Destination Proposition*, London: Butterworth-Heinemann.

Papadopoulos, N. (2004), 'Place branding: evolution, meaning, and implications', *Place Branding and Public Diplomacy*, 1(1), 36–49.

Papadopoulos, N. (2011), 'Of places and brands', in Andy Pike (ed.), *Brands and Branding Geographies*, Cheltenham, UK and Northampton, MA, USA: Edward Elgar Publishing, pp. 25–43.

Papadopoulos, N., El Banna, A., Murphy, S.A. and Rojas-Méndez, J.I. (2012), 'Place brands and brand-place associations: the role of "place" in international marketing', in S. Jain and D.A. Griffith (eds), *Handbook of Research in International Marketing*, 2nd edn, Cheltenham, UK and Northampton, MA, USA: Edward Elgar Publishing, pp. 88–113.

Pike, S. (2007), 'Consumer-based brand equity for destinations', *Journal of Travel & Tourism Marketing*, 22(1), 51–61.

Rabbiosi, C. (2016), 'Place branding performances in tourism local food shops', *Annals of Tourism Research*, 60, 154–168.

Saraniemi, S. (2011), 'From destination image building to identity-based branding', *International Journal of Culture, Hospitality and Tourism Research*, 5(3), 247–254.

Satija, M.P. (2001), 'Relationships in Ranganathan's colon classification', in B.A. Carol and R. Green (eds), *Relationships in the Organization of Knowledge*, Dordrecht: Springer, pp. 199–210.

Van Ham, P. (2008), 'Place branding: the state of the art', *The Annals of the American Academy of Political and Social Science*, 616(1), 126–149.

Warnaby, G., Ashworth, G.J. and Kavaratzis, M. (2015), 'Sketching future for place branding', in M. Kavaratzis, G. Warnaby and G.J. Ashworth (eds), *Rethinking Place Branding: Comprehensive Brand Development for Cities and Regions*, Cham: Springer International Publishing, pp. 241–248.

Zenker, S. (2011), 'How to catch a city? The concept and measurement of place brands', *Journal of Place Management and Development*, 4(1), 40–51.

Zenker, S. and Erfgen, C. (2014), 'Let them do the work: a participatory place branding approach', *Journal of Place Management and Development*, 7(3), 225–234.

Zenker, S., Braun, E. and Petersen, S. (2017), 'Branding the destination versus the place: the effects of brand complexity and identification for residents and visitors', *Tourism Management*, 58, 15–27.

3.   Will the twain ever meet? 'Place' vs. 'country' in research and practice

Nicolas Papadopoulos and Mark Cleveland

"You've got pretty good taste", she said. "I like Italian suits, actually" he replied.
"I've had a couple of British suits, and they were okay,
but they felt ... constructed. Like I was wearing a building.
But the Italians – they know how to make a suit."
(John Sandford, *Secret Prey*, 1999)

In this quote from one of his novels, Sandford praises one *country* while teasing another in unflattering terms – while a character in another novel berates a famous *city* and its people, in fact drawing on one of the iconic elements that have contributed to its positive reputation: "Vienna was not a big city and never has been: it is a little provincial town where narrow-minded peasants go to the opera, instead of the pig market, to exchange spiteful gossip" (Len Deighton, *Spy Line*, 1989).

Countries, cities, and other places are also often portrayed in music and other art works. One popular song, for example (Steve Tyrell, *New York is Where I Live*, 2009), ties various types of places to recognizable characteristics that make them desirable: *Cities* like Los Angeles for seeing 'the stars', New Orleans to enjoy blues music, Las Vegas for gambling, or San Francisco to which "my heart I give" (in a tip of the hat to another famous song from 1962, Tony Bennett's "I Left My Heart in San Francisco"), as well as *states*, including Texas for baby back ribs and Alaska for ice skating, and *countries*, in this case Germany for cars and Italy for shoes – but each stanza concludes with a verse that stresses the value of home, with "But New York is where I live".

Such references to various kinds of places in popular works reflect the relevance of 'place' in human life. As Relph (1976) stressed in his pioneering work, which helped to launch humanistic geography and its interest in 'place', "To be attached to places and have profound ties with them is an important human need ... [yet this] is the least recognized need of the human soul" (p. 38). Today, growing interest in the importance of place is found in several disciplines and in both scholarly and applied work – but what exactly is 'place'?

'PLACE MATTERS' – BUT *WHICH KIND* OF 'PLACE'?

Juxtaposing Relph's (1976) view with the quotes from fictional works just above points to the central theme of this chapter: the latter are quite clear as to the 'kind' of place they refer to – but which 'places' was Relph referring to? One's home? Neighbourhood? City? Country? A trade bloc? Our planet, perhaps? Does 'attachment' refer only to one's home or might it extend to where one goes to skate on ice or the origin of the car one buys? And what are the scholarly and managerial implications depending on how one answers? Addressing such questions is the overall goal in the sections that follow.

As practicing managers or scholarly researchers, we are hampered when putting together our reports or articles by the need to be 'serious' and 'evidence-based'. We *are* 'serious', indeed, but both fiction and non-fiction works for broader audiences are much free-er to express their creators' thoughts. They do not worry much about stereotyping their objects or over-generalizing and prefer to avoid qualifiers (the academic's and manager's stock-in-trade!), thus sacrificing accuracy to make their key message more effective. In doing so they may be less scientifically correct but have at least two key strengths over our work: (a) they *drive points home to many more people more effectively*, thus tending to sustain commonly held beliefs in societies at large; and at the same time, (b) they *reflect* those commonly held beliefs, thus creating a feedback loop whose participants play back their views to each other, each buttressing and strengthening the other's.

We do not ignore the obvious chicken-and-egg question in this loop, let alone the ugly consequences of malicious stereotyping whose effects harm its targets. As Gloria Steinem, the noted women's rights activist, stressed in a widely quoted 1971 speech, differences in gender and race are visible and therefore easy to spot, having thus served as the main criteria for classifying people into groups and for stereotyping, and discriminating against, those that are considered inferior to others. Notwithstanding their great importance, addressing such issues is well beyond the scope of this chapter – but our focus on *place* speaks to yet another characteristic that can act as a calling card: it may not be as visible or as responsible for discrimination as gender and race, but it acts as a powerful differentiator of the places themselves as well as of the people and products associated with them. It makes a difference to both locals and/or others, for example ...

- ... whether one states London's posh Belgravia as one's place of birth and lifelong residence instead of the city's poorer boroughs, notwithstanding that the respective residents' sense of attachment to their places may be similarly strong in all cases.

- ... that Denmark and other Scandinavian countries rank at the top of the 153-country World Happiness Report, while Poland is 43rd (UN/WHR, 2020), as also reflected in a novel: "The Poles have a style of melancholy that is ... a world-embracing philosophy impervious to cheer" (Len Deighton, *Hope*, 1995).
- ... that a country may be perceived as friendlier and more world-minded in global terms than another: "He asked, 'American?' I replied, 'Canadian,' which I'd been taught is good cover for Americans in certain parts of the world ... Thank God for Canada." (Nelson DeMille, *Up Country*, 2002).
- ... whether a product's origin matches that origin's image, as Jaffe and Nebenzahl (2006) teach us when they ask whether Switzerland can be a reasonable made-in place for a luxury car in buyers' minds (their answer is a 'no').
- ... whether a city government does not take into account the multicultural makeup of its residents when designing a resident-based place branding campaign and hopes that they all will see it positively.
- ... that consumers have different expectations from a movie made in Hollywood, Bollywood, or Nigeria's Nollywood instead of the UK, Italy, or France, just as much as whether the chocolates come from Switzerland, the avocados from Mexico, or the software from Silicon Valley versus other origins.

Place images in both fiction and non-fiction most often are close to, or at least not too far from, 'reality', whether actual or perceived. Few might choose Alaska-made suits, opt for Italy as a place to skate on ice, be unaware of New York's moniker as "the city that never sleeps", or buy into the idea of a Swiss-made luxury car. More importantly, images highlight some of the core competencies of the named places, such as Italian design, German engineering, Belgravia's pedigree, and Vienna's opera (which the novel acknowledges, even if twisted into a venomous negative to suit a character's views).

In fact, in another novel John Sandford (*Silken Prey*, 2013) highlights competencies of two places he previously left without praise, when the same character chastises a friend who complimented him on his 'French' shoes: "English. English shoes. French shirts, Italian suits. Try to remember that." We readily acknowledge that, as academic writers, we cannot possibly compete with the 'bite' of works addressed to broader audiences – and so this chapter is sprinkled with more quotes from such works where we feel they express a point better than we ever could.

Place, they all say explicitly or implicitly, *matters*. Which leaves us with the question: What 'place'?

Levels and Kinds of 'Place'

As signalled above, we adopt the view that from a place setting at the dinner table to the universe at large, all are 'places'. While there are obvious differences depending on what level of place one studies or manages, much of the task of marketing places, their people, and their products always revolves around the place's *image*. Stated differently, from a marketing perspective, *all* places and place brands are *joined at the hip by how people perceive them, and therefore by the construct of 'place image'*.

Yet as the opening quotes show, the notion of place is treated rather loosely and very often confusingly. Clearly, when one says 'Italian suits' one has Milan in mind, not Palermo in Sicily, just like Japanese Kubota farm tractor exports to 'France' is more likely to refer to its agricultural regions than to Paris. Conversely, why is it common to say 'Italian' instead of 'Milan' for suits – but 'Kobe' instead of 'Japanese' beef? Why does Tyrell elect to speak of a *city* for the blues (New Orleans), a *state* for skating (Alaska), and a *country* for cars (Germany), instead of alternatives which would have been just as relevant in his song's context (ignoring, for a moment, the question of rhyming), respectively a *state* (Mississippi), a *country* (Sweden), and a *city* (Detroit)? And what does "Visit Canada" mean to foreign tourists for a country that is as diverse as its over 5,500 km length suggests, and where various regions experience temperature extremes of over +40C in summer and below −40C in winter?

The key notions related to places of all kinds manifest themselves in societal belief structures and expressions that often are loose and confusing, and are tapped in disciplines from a variety of conceptual origins that have evolved independently from each other. We posit that this has had the unintended and unfortunate consequence of leading to a 'Great Divide' among scholars and managers who are, after all, embedded in the same societies, and hail from the same variety of disciplines, as everyone else. Specifically,

- On one side are those who deal with *subnational* places, which in the vast majority of cases is taken to mean *cities and towns*, tends to be *inward*-oriented toward the interests of *residents* and in '*bringing things to*' a place (e.g., tourism and inward investment), and is positioned mostly within the *domestic* marketing context.
- On the other side are those who deal with *countries*, which in the vast majority of cases means the *nation-state*, tends to be more *outward*-oriented toward domestic and foreign *consumers* and in '*bringing things into* or *taking them out of*' the place (e.g., domestic vs. foreign products); and is positioned in the *international* marketing context.

This divide has resulted in a dearth of holistic thinking on 'place' and, therefore, in reducing the effectiveness of advances in scholarship and applied know-how in this domain.

Objectives, Approach, and Limitations

This chapter has three main goals: to highlight similarities and differences between the 'subnational place' vs. 'country' sides of the divide, to discuss their complexities as fields of study and decision making, and to highlight ways in which each side can benefit from the other.

The fact that the 'place' discipline deals almost exclusively with places at the subnational level, while the same term also applies by definition to all levels, can be a source of confusion in this discussion which deals with both. For clarity, therefore, we use *place* and *country* to refer respectively to the *subnational* and *national* sides of the disciplinary divide, and use 'geographically defined area' (GDA) or other suitably clear terms (e.g., 'all levels of place') to encompass both sides.

For other concepts we use the generic terms, letting the context define the meaning except when it is necessary to specify it; this includes, for instance, product/brand (any offering), consumer (any stakeholder public), city or region (any subnational urban or other area), and marketing (any part of the marketing mix, including branding within 'product'). Finally, to prevent clutter and avoid redundancy, we do not cite past relevant research for concepts that are well understood and widely shared, limiting citations only to specific points or for concepts that may not be familiar to all readers, and provide only basic citations (name, title, year) for non-academic works (a full list of references is available on request).

The three main sections that follow highlight key differences between place and country research, discuss implications arising from these differences, and present concluding thoughts for the road ahead.

THE WORLDS OF 'PLACE' AND 'COUNTRY': DIFFERENT IDEAS, CONSTRUCTS, METHODS, AND FOCI

At the core of any discipline lies its fundamental paradigm, which draws on a variety of theories and in turn points to the key ideas and construct(s) used to research, understand, and practice in the area. Unfortunately, the term 'paradigm' itself has been used rather loosely in GDA research and so no single paradigm can be identified as the guiding light in either place or country thinking. For instance, using just a small sample of past studies, research on place has been based on the paradigms of 'co-creation', 'rural development', and 'democratic governance', and country studies on the paradigms of 'equity theory', 'cue', and 'belief disconfirmation', as well as on the 'traditional research paradigm' in country-of-origin research (whichever this may be, since it is not defined in the study that referred to it, the wording can have any number of meanings, and an 'origin paradigm' remaining elusive at best).

Rather than trying to unravel the intricacies of what paradigms are, or attempting to trace their underlying theories which simply are too many and diverse to discuss here, we focus on the main constructs, research methods, and foci used by each side of the divide since these can be identified and compared more readily.

'Place' and 'Country' *Think* Differently: Commonly Used Constructs

In line with the different orientations in place- versus country-based thinking, the constructs used in each area differ and the difference is also reflected in popular culture. On the place side, for instance, and consistent with Relph's (1976) emphasis on place attachment, a character in a novel "had felt it in all his love and hate for this city ... 'I want to believe in one place,' he said. 'I want it in my blood.'" (Olen Steinhauer, *The Bridge of Sighs*, 2003). A comparable view in the country domain focuses on others: "He thought of Americans as a decadent people whose idea of refinement is fluffy toilet paper" (Trevanian, *Shibumi*, 1981). This section compares and contrasts the different concepts that permeate scholarly thinking in each of the two domains.

Constructs in place research

Our review of the place literature in social and environmental psychology, humanistic and urban geography, behavioural economics, political science, cultural anthropology, sociology, and other cogent disciplines shows that all tend to gravitate toward the 10 constructs listed below. Their meaning is known to those on the *place* side or can generally be deduced from the relevant terms, and while some seem very similar (e.g., attachment and bonding) each has a differently-nuanced, but materially so, definition.

Place attachment	Place identity
Place bonding	Social identity
Place belongingness	Place attraction
Place rootedness	Place involvement
Place dependence	Sense of place

Constructs in country research

The variety of disciplines that study place underscores its importance and ubiquitousness in human life, and social psychology provides much of the theoretical input for studies in international marketing. Our review identified 18 psychological dispositions of consumers toward their own and/or other countries. As with place, their meaning is known to those on the *country* side or can be deduced from the respective terms, and in this case two recent detailed reviews can be accessed by readers interested in exploring them in more depth (Bartsch et al., 2016; Papadopoulos et al., 2018).

It is also important to note that the constructs are arranged in two columns mostly for facility: those on the right have distinct definitions and are not necessarily the obverse of the ones on the left. For example, 'nationalism' denigrates other countries and considers one's own to be superior to them, 'patriotism' reflects one's love for one's country no matter how superior or inferior one perceives it to be, and neither of these two constructs is a direct opposite of 'internationalism' on the left.

Cosmopolitanism	Ethnocentrism
Internationalism	Nationalism
Globalism	Patriotism
Worldmindedness	Parochialism
Universalism	Provincialism
Xenocentrism	Localism
Xenophilia	Xenophobia
Topophilia	Topophobia
Affinity	Animosity

Constructs of place and country: the missing links

The preceding two lists underscore the 'great divide' in GDA research: the place constructs are rarely looked at by country scholars and practitioners, and vice versa. It is not possible to examine here all or even most of the possibilities where concepts used only by one side could also be used fruitfully by the other, but a small handful of sample cases should suffice to make the point.

- *Attachment* is used in place works to refer to one's relationship with a location of residence. This begs the question: is this kind of relationship not similar to that engendered by *patriotism*? Whether a resident of Prague is attached to the city, to Czechia, or both, why is *place* attachment rarely (if ever) studied in *country*, and patriotism in *country* but not *place*, research?

That patriotism derives from 'patria' and is thus related to the country seems irrelevant: whatever 'Xism' one may call it, the construct reflects place love and belongingness, making it hard to imagine why each of the two domains uses different theories and paradigms to study the same kinds of people's feelings, instead of exchanging ideas and insights with each other.

- *Nationalism* may reflect a preference for 'things local' (which relates it to *localism*) but is also used to refer to ignorance and narrow-mindedness, making it akin to *parochialism* – yet neither of these two constructs is encountered in place research or used in place branding practice.
- *Ethnocentrism* (from 'ethnos', an ethnicity *regardless of where in the world its members live*) is studied in international marketing extensively but at the 'nation'-state level (which may include ethnicities *within its borders*). Ethnos and nation are very often and wrongly used interchange-ably in many disciplines (Papastephanou, 2012) even though they are diametrically different, but either way both make ethnocentrism a 'con-struct *non grata*' in subnational place works. Yet using insights from the rich country literature at the place level is a pressing necessity today. For example, ethnic populations in multicultural cities may be ethnocentric in relation to their place of residence, place of origin/heritage, or both (e.g., El Banna et al., 2018), and some ethnic groups may oppose a place branding campaign that other residents support, leading to problems that could have been avoided if resident ethnocentrism had been taken into account.
- Scholars and practitioners working on place draw on self- and social-identity theory and probably know more about *place* identity than any other mar-keter, while those working on country also draw on the same core concepts but know more about *national* and *ethnic* identity – yet each side insists on reinventing its own wheel, neither referring to research in, or availing itself of insights from, the other.
- There is no reason to believe that such concepts as animosity, affinity, or nationalism, which are studied in country but not subnational research, are not relevant to the latter as well. Cities and regions also vie to attract tour-ists, investors, or residents, and while cooperative cross-place approaches are often encouraged, competition (even if termed 'friendly rivalry') is closer to the norm. Examples that readily come to mind include Los Angeles vs. New York, Hyderabad vs. Bangalore, Scotland vs. England, intense inter-city animosities over their respective sports teams, and of course major regional disputes leading to armed conflict (e.g., Crimea, Nagorno-Karabakh, Kashmir).
- Similarly, Cleveland and Balakrishnan (2019) have examined interactions between such constructs as cosmopolitanism, xenocentrism, and admira-tion at the national level that could well be key explanators of behaviour

subnationally as well: we do not know whether *intra*-national affinities and rivalries may be due to one city or another being strongly 'cosmopolitan' or strongly 'parochial', since such constructs generally are not part of the place research lexicon.

- Cultural heritage is often used in place branding and has a long history in place research, and recently has started making inroads in country research. However, the latter seems to have opted for developing its own research approaches drawing solely or mostly from what it knows best ('country'!) instead of accessing insights from existing know-how ('place'!). Yet the multifaceted nature of heritage means that many 'country' studies deal mostly with subnational entities (articles dealing with 'Italian' heritage focus, for example, on Chianti wines, Pompeii antiquities, and Florence fashion). As well, given their respective foci, there is a dearth of either place or country research on supra-national regional heritage – although it may be directly related with how places within such regions are viewed and understood (e.g., *European* fashion, *African* crafts, *Latin American* music, *South Asian* textiles).

The constructs behind the constructs: what we don't know could hurt us
Within the overarching GDA research field, place branding looks at such constructs as attachment and belongingness, country research at patriotism and nationalism, and, in tourism, destination branding at attractiveness and sense of place. But what lies *behind* such concepts? Our review of the literature in the disciplines shown earlier also revealed a number of additional constructs that are relevant here:

Self-(also 'Idio'-)centrism	Alter-(also 'Allo-')centrism
Traditionalism	Nostalgia
Neophobia	Affect
Dogmatism	Homophily
Hostility	Admiration
Antipathy	Materialism
Disaffect	Religiosity
Racism	Political ideology

These constructs are elaborated upon in the studies cited above and, as before, the left–right arrangement does not reflect correspondence between the terms. Three summary observations are called for. First, these constructs are broader and also applied to study other aspects of the human condition and are not, like those in the two previous sections, directly related to place, although they can be used in studying it. Second, some reside in the individual and are better understood in that context (e.g., dogmatism, self-centrism a.k.a. egotism), while others can also be readily applied to the societal level (e.g., nostalgia in Japan, materialism in individualistic and Calvinist societies, religiosity more so in some countries than elsewhere). Third and most relevant here, *any of them may be the primary antecedent behind constructs on either side of GDA research.*

Take, for instance, resident resistance to a city-proposed place branding initiative. Is opposition due to residents 'not liking' the initiative, perhaps feeling it does not express what their city is all about? Or might it be because the city is characterized by higher levels of resistance to change, perhaps driven by *traditionalism* ('we're just fine as we are, why change'), *neophobia* ('we don't like new-fangled things, what's this story with "branding" a city anyway'), or *disaffect* ('yeah, now they remembered we're part of the city too')? Similarly, *racism* may result in nearby residents not shopping at a particular neighbourhood because of its racial composition, regardless of how nicely it may have branded itself; or, *political ideology* may lead to rejecting nation branding campaigns that are perceived as conflicting with current political beliefs (e.g., deep inter-regional divisions in the 2020 US election). And needless to say, *affect*, which is emotion-based and has recently emerged in psychology as a more important antecedent of behaviour than cognition, may well be the major driver in forming positive dispositions toward places at any level.

Country studies have studied some of these constructs in depth (e.g., affect, religiosity) and others less so (e.g., racism, admiration), but most of them are not part of the subnational research repertoire except for occasional references to them in passing.

'Place' and 'Country' Do *Research* Differently: Different Methods, Different Measures

It is a well known axiom in research that one cannot study a phenomenon without affecting it, and fiction, as in so many other instances, expresses this rather succinctly: "My trouble is, everywhere I go, I come too and spoil it" (John le Carré, *The Tailor of Panama*, 1996). The way that a researcher may affect the object of observation depends highly on his or her point of view, and so differences in the paradigms and constructs used by each side of the GDA field also affect how each goes about researching, understanding, and practicing their respective areas. The summary in Table 3.1 highlights the general tendencies characterizing each.

A more detailed list of research approaches would be unwieldy, but this summary readily illustrates that the two sides of GDA research differ substantively on all counts. Perhaps a tongue-in-cheek comment can further buttress

Table 3.1   *Paradigms and constructs used by GDA silos: 'place' vs.*
                     'country'

Research...	... on *'place'*, is *often or mostly*	... on *'country'*, is *often or mostly*
Object	Locals' and others' views of place	Views anywhere of country, people, products
Design	Conceptual Qualitative	Empirical Quantitative
Approach	Interpretive (phenomenological, hermeneutical) Historical research Single places or place clusters	Cross-sectional surveys (exploratory, descriptive, correlational, causal) Experiments Comparative cross-cultural/-national
Fieldwork	Focus groups/depth interviews Ethno-/video-/ netnography Narrative, storytelling Case studies Content analysis	Self-administered surveys Interviewer-led/assisted surveys Lab, field, or panel experiments Multi-stage/-phase (e.g., interviews > focus group > survey 1 > survey 2)
Subjects	Smaller samples, mostly locally Key informants, elite interviews Subject experts Residents Tourists Business/Government	Larger samples, mostly foreign & domestic Consumers Students Organizational buyers, investors Tourists Secondary corporate data ('big data')
Measures	Logical argumentation Open-ended questions	Independent and dependent variables Closed bipolar adjective or Likert scales
Analysis	Recording, coding, interpretation of responses, observations	Regression, analysis of variance (ANOVA) Factor analysis (exploratory, confirmatory) Structural Equation Modelling (SEM)

the fundamental differences between the two areas: often it feels as if one cannot possibly publish a study on *place* if 'residents' and 'co-creation' are not mentioned at least once, and as if one cannot possibly publish a study on *country* if it does not include an elaborate SEM with its attendant statistical details.

An additional four observations on the different research approaches in typical place and country studies within the GDA umbrella are necessary here. First, good research leading to good and useful findings arises from *replication* and *triangulation*. Our review suggests that place research is generally better at replication, enabling conclusions that certain concepts apply across a variety of locales (e.g., a consensus that city brand co-creation is hard to achieve but works). On the other hand, triangulation is generally absent from the subnational domain and found more often in country research.

Second, longitudinal research is scarce and studies typically are 'one-shot, one-time' in both domains, which means that challenging traditional wisdom to enhance the credibility and usefulness of findings by incorporating the temporal element is relatively absent in both cases.

Third, both country and place studies have embraced the notion of 'brand personality', but, we feel, not carefully enough. The original work on human personality identified no fewer than 17,953 traits (Allport and Odbert, 1936), which were later distilled into the Big-5 theory of personality in the 1980s, applied to brands in the 1990s, and carried over to place brands after that. However, while the human version of the construct appears to have universal applicability, its use in the GDA field has resulted in many different conceptualizations, reflecting a lack of stability across various contexts. In fact, virtually all personality-based GDA studies begin by developing their own 'Big-X', with 'X' standing for seven to almost 20 constructs. This variability is not surprising, considering that many of the nearly 18,000 traits may be relevant to a particular situation – but be that as it may, it is also not surprising that this nascent research stream has yet to produce consistent findings.

Fourth, those working in place vs. country research do not 'talk' to one another much, because, we feel, they do not 'understand' each other well enough. For instance, place models quite commonly treat image as the *dependent* variable (resulting from efforts to improve a place), whereas country research views it as an *independent* attribute (its effects on consumer views of its products). Furthermore, place research and practice also seem "Obsessed with identity" (subhead of a CNN story on place attachment; Wong, 2020), and, while country studies also take interest in this construct, they may be said to be more 'obsessed with end results'. As a sample practical implication of this distinction, country research examines a much broader range of factors than do place studies, including potential target markets (e.g., producers, domestic and foreign end-consumers, industrial buyers, investors, tourists, students, skilled workers, immigrants, expatriate managers), sources that affect their views (e.g., schooling, news media, popular culture, ads by and/or ownership of domestic and foreign products, family and friends, cross-cultural interactions from living, working, or travelling abroad), and dependent varia-bles (e.g., evaluation, preference, and/or ownership, and intent or willingness to try, buy, recommend, reward, avoid, punish, or boycott, countries/people and their products).

In summary, each side of the divide treats its favourite themes in detail but neither interacts with nor borrows insights from the other so as to build a dia-logue that would be to the benefit of both.

'Place' and 'Country' *Focus* Differently: Is It Place Marketing, Place Branding, or Both?

Place images and 'brands' are formed from myriad inputs, including what fictional works say about them. Concerning Russia, for example, a novel notes that the country "is little more than a petrol station with a flag on top. They export oil and natural gas, but manufacture nothing worth mentioning" (David Lagercrantz, *The Girl in the Spider's Web*, 2015). While such inputs affect the images of places, they may do so differently from the marketing and branding perspectives – and while these differences may appear quite obvious at first sight, the way the terms are used in GDA research suggests that the matter is more complicated than it seems.

The formal definitions of the American Marketing Association see market-ing as the all-inclusive term and refer, among others, to the 4Ps (Product, Price, Place (distribution), Promotion), with Product including the 'brand', defined as any feature that distinguishes an offering (products and services, places, people, ideas) from others. Accordingly, branding is the 'marketing practice' that helps to shape and define a brand in the minds of target audiences. Given these definitions, the 'marketing and branding' expression that is often used in place research is akin to saying 'cars and Toyota' or 'furniture and table', or even 'place and country' in the context of this chapter, and therefore is *prima facie* wrong: the second term in each case is part of the first and cannot be cast as a separate item, as the additive 'and' suggests.

This does not mean, of course, that 'place branding' cannot stand by and be practiced in itself. In fact, Kavaratzis (2004) was among the first who saw city *branding* as a new phase in the evolution of city *marketing*, a trend confirmed in a recent comprehensive review of 1,172 journal articles on place research which noted a shift from place marketing to place branding (Vuignier, 2016). However, even a cursory look at the literature shows that such discussion focuses almost exclusively on *communication* – namely, and regardless of whether one speaks of marketing, branding, or both, on the *Promotion* part of the 4Ps. Place characteristics (e.g., natural or urban environment, technologi-cal strengths) are considered as givens or discussed as 'product design' areas needing improvement, but *Price* (with the exception of tourism studies), *Place* (channels, supply chains, logistics, market coverage), and other elements within *Product* (e.g., packaging, labelling, warranties, associated services) are rarely studied.

One important consequence of these differences is that place thinking adopts mostly a *seller's* perspective ("How should our brand be communicated to target audiences?"), while country research and much of the associated practice mostly uses a *buyer's* perspective ("What do our domestic and foreign target markets think of our brand, and why?").

IMPLICATIONS, RAMIFICATIONS, AND EDUCATED GUESSES

The way that both non-fiction and fiction works refer to various levels of 'place' reflects both the differences between levels as well as, in many cases, the rather 'loose' approach in distinguishing across levels. For instance, when the Ancient Roman advocate and statesman Cicero (106–43 BCE) wrote, in a letter to his friend Atticus after moving to a new villa, that "I have put out my books and now my house has a soul", he was clearly equating place to a *house*. By contrast, a poem calls London 'a man's' and Paris 'a woman's' town, continues by referring to Venice as a city to dream in and Rome as one to study, but concludes that "when it comes to living, there is no place like home" (Henry Van Dyke, *America for Me*, 1909) – thus mentioning four *cities* first but then defining 'home' at the *country* level.

When one examines the landscape of place versus country scholarship and managerial practice in the GDA divide, one is tempted to ask, or rather, exclaim (hoping again that readers will forgive the colloquialism): "*What is the matter with you people!* Why do you insist on hiding each in your own cocoon instead of opening up to your sibling fields? A place is a place is a place no matter what kind of place it is! Why don't you just *talk* about it with each other!"

GDA Research and Management: Are We There Yet?

We phrased the colloquial exclamation in the paragraph above provocatively with the deliberate intent of countering it: we believe that the criticism it implies would be misplaced, unfair, facile, and wrong.

- *Misplaced*: Divides such as what we experience in GDA are common in scholarship and management as well as in human thought at large (witness such typical slurs as 'ivory tower', 'bureaucrats', 'ruthless profiteers', 'conslutants' [*sic*], 'talking heads', or 'tree huggers', levelled at various valuable sectors of human activity by those in other sectors). For better or worse, we are not alone.

- *Unfair*: From a time perspective both place and country research are infants. Philosophy, physics, and geography have a history of over 2,000 years, and behavioural sciences such as psychology and sociology came of age in the 1800s. In contrast, the centrality of 'image' in human behaviour was *first* put forth by Boulding (1956), and in products and tourism by Dichter (1962) and Hunt (1975); modern marketing was born in the 1950s and *environmental* psychology, *humanistic* geography, and *international* marketing in the 1970s; and *Place Branding and Public Diplomacy* (PBPD) and the *Journal of Place Management and Development* (JPMD) were not launched until, respectively, 2004 and 2008. It takes time to grow up, and we have not had it yet.
- *Facile*: GDA thinking cannot be divorced from marketing, which itself is presently experiencing a period of upheaval. Belk (2020) has stressed that "marketing lays dying" and needs "a funeral eulogy ... both as a practice and as an academic discipline", partly due to "the shift in control of brands from marketer to consumer" (p. 168), and 'brand' has been elevated to a term for all and sundry (Queen Elizabeth of the UK has been called one of "the top ten brand images in the world"; Lee, 2013). Such thoughts seem rather relevant in the GDA context: it is no wonder that the 'twain' have not yet met as place and country struggle to account for, respectively, the roles of residents and consumers, not to mention dealing with broader issues with which marketing itself has difficulty, including the rise of branding.
- *Wrong*: Our area has been endowed with many noted thinkers, from Simon Anholt to Gregory Ashworth, Adamantios Diamantopoulos, Saeed Samiee, and the team of Israel Nebenzahl and Eugene Jaffe, to name just a few. They and many others who could be named have made both sides of the divide among the most researched, and most substantively evolved and advanced, disciplines in our time.

Therefore, to cycle back to the exclamation above, '*nothing is wrong with us people*'! Having dealt at length and in depth with our 'partisan' issues, we are now on the cusp of turning to such bigger and broader ones as merging 'place' and 'country', and evolving a better understanding of branding within marketing, in GDA thinking at large. At the same time, while the above comments explain and excuse the lack of integration under our umbrella discipline, they do not provide licence for continuing 'as-is' and we believe we are not anywhere near to where we ought to be.

Advances Versus the Legacy of Disciplinary Origins

The place vs. country differences highlighted in the preceding sections are not, of course, absolute. Like good academics, we deliberately avoided making 'unsubstantiated assertions' by offering additional citations as needed and using such qualifiers as 'often', 'virtually', 'most', and so on. Indeed, some scholars and managers on either side of the divide have used the thinking or research approaches of the other, studies in tourism have examined both national and subnational 'destinations', and place consultants have specialized in one area but also dabbled in the other. Furthermore, some recent studies have begun to focus on integrating the place–country perspectives in both country- and place-oriented journals (respectively, Stöttinger and Penz, 2019, and Suter et al., 2020).

However, these are the exceptions that prove the rule. Understanding why the two sides differ requires a brief diversion to the origins of the respective disciplines.

- Place scholarship emerged primarily from urban planning and geography studies. For instance, the editors and all contributors in Gold and Ward's (1994) pioneering book hailed from those parent disciplines. It is perhaps not surprising that even the book's title was a terminological marketing 'salad', juxtaposing 'selling' (a throwback to marketing thinking of the 1930s) 'towns and regions' ('country' excluded) and adding 'and Marketing' to 'Publicity', reflecting the 'marketing = *promotion*' view of its content. This urban/regional orientation is behind today's subnational focus: The Institute of Place Management defines the field as aiming to "improve *locations*" (emphasis added), and our review of a random sample of volumes showed that over 95 per cent of its journal's content deals with subnational and often sub-city entities (e.g., Lak et al., 2019).
- Country scholarship evolved after Dichter's (1962) reference to "the little phrase 'Made in'", which lies behind this area's focus on 'country-of-origin'. In turn, this has been the subject of intense debate to this day as to whether the 'origin' of products matters in consumer behaviour (in spite of mountains of evidence that it does), which of 'made-in', 'country', or 'brand' origin matters the most (it depends on the context), and whether accuracy in 'origin' perceptions among consumers matters (it does not, as Magnusson et al. (2011) and several others have proven), since at issue in a globalized world is not so much (if at all) where a product is made but the place with which its managers elect to associate it.

In fact, Peter van Ham's much-quoted 2001 article "The Rise of the Brand State" in *Foreign Affairs* brought *nation* branding to the fore more than a century after the assumed beginnings of *place* branding in the 1870s (Gold and Ward, 1994), both serving to buttress the *country/place* divide – while also reflecting a consequential historical anachronism, since systematic marketing has been practiced for millennia. For instance, it was used to attract athletes and spectators to the Olympics in antiquity; to brand Ancient Rome as SPQR (*Senātus Populusque Rōmānus*, The Roman Senate and People) on everything from military standards to coinage; and to present Memphis versus Thebes as 'the' major tourism centre in Ancient Egypt 4,000 years ago (Casson, 1994). All such cases involved Promotion (e.g., stone or metal inscriptions, papyrus pamphlets, word-of-mouth) as well as the full marketing mix (e.g., agents and supply chains, roadside markers, coin distribution, monetary and psychic pricing, place and merchandise design and improvement). The absence of long-term historical research is yet another factor that perpetuates misunder-standings of the place–country divide and impedes the evolution of a holistic view of the GDA field.

Of Missing Links and Pressing Opportunities

There seems little reason to say more about the large number of differences between place and country thinking which were discussed in detail in the preceding sections. There are, however, three issues that we have only touched upon before, which are important enough to require some further elaboration, and one that is so important as to deserve re-stressing.

Whither place-associated brands?
The relationship between a nation's image and its products has been studied intensely in country research; several content analyses of magazine ads in various countries have shown that place connections are used extensively in both B2B and B2C brand advertising (e.g., Papadopoulos et al., 2012; Zeugner-Roth and Bartsch, 2020), and A.C. Nielsen (2016) has reported that 75 per cent of global consumers specifically consider *brand* origin a key driver in purchase decisions.

On the other hand, place scholarship does deal with signature regional *products* (most often in the terroir-influenced agri-food sector), but its inward ori-entation generally limits this interest to examining their benefits for the region and their role in its identity (e.g., Fusté-Forné, 2020). The impact of brands on subnational place images among consumers internationally is rarely consid-ered, in spite of the numerous cases where a brand's origin is widely known (e.g., Starbucks/Seattle) or is included in its name (London Fog, Maybelline New York, L'Oréal Paris are among the best-known examples), and therefore this represents an area that is as yet largely unexplored, calls for attention, and can benefit from insights developed in country studies.

Investment is welcome but investors are not understood
Since most of the research on 'country', 'place', and foreign direct investment (FDI) itself focuses, respectively, on the behaviour of end consumers,
residents, and firms, the potential role of place image in investor behaviour is,
with only a few exceptions (e.g., Wilson and Baack, 2012), among the most
under-researched fields in GDA scholarship.

Interviewees in a study of FDI promotion agencies that we carried out in
four countries stressed that investment location choice is influenced by 'soft'
factors. Connecting Holland to tulips "makes sense", one said; "symbols help
people recognize the country" before examining other attributes in more depth.
Others noted that soft factors could be "equally important for a tourist or an
investor", pointing at the negative effects of "disjointed messaging" across
sectors; that as many as "nine out of ten SMEs" select the UK "because the
CEO's daughter had secured a place at a university or private school" there;
and that inter-*city* rivalry often leaves investors "bewildered", signalling
a preference for country-level coordination in selecting the most appropriate
location for each case, the alternative leading to failure and an investor "telling
their 100 buddies back home" that the *country* is not the right place to go.

Similar findings have been reported in the few studies that have focused on
other types of industrial buyers, suggesting that the role of *image* in both B2B
and FDI represents an area in need of more research and much deeper understanding than we presently have.

The lack of longitudinal research hurts
Articles in a 1997 *European Journal of Marketing* special issue (no. 3/4)
pointed to a postmodern marketing trend toward social fragmentation, coun-
tered by neo-tribalism as individuals regroup around tribes, each with its own
identity, interests, values, and icons. However, we are now almost a quarter
century past the time when this trend was identified. Since people in both
national and subnational places comprise tribes, each with several subtribes,
the matter is relevant to GDA thinking: did the trend materialize? Is it still with
us today? Why or why not? We do not know, and this is just one case in point
where the broader impacts of globalization can be considered over the long
term, both in marketing generally and within GDA scholarship.

Country–place cross-pollination can help – a lot
The need to integrate the two sides of the divide has been central to this entire
chapter, but we feel its importance warrants stressing it again. Differences
in perspective emanate from how countries are viewed from each side of the
divide: essentially, and subject to only a few exceptions, neither subnational
nor national research and practice view 'country' as a 'place', and, as a result,
neither feels that the other's perspective is relevant to its purposes.

Yet as we noted previously, the two areas are 'joined at the hip'. For instance, place studies emphasize attachment and belonging, but country research also discusses such similar concepts as patriotism and ethnocentrism: "It is sweet and fitting to die for your country" wrote Horace in 23 BCE ("Dulce et decorum est pro patria mori"; Odes III.2.13); "I love my country because it is mine", echoed the 14th-century Armenian poet Stephan Orbelian (Gelven, 1994); and more recently, in a novel set in Africa: "O Botswana, my country, my place" (Alexander McCall Smith, *The No. 1 Ladies' Detective Agency*, 2002).

It would take both the 'place' and 'country' sides recognizing the obvious, that 'country is a place', to begin the integrative work that waits to be carried out. But once this acknowledgement is made, such work should be easier because, if for no other reason, the relevant concepts are portable. Wong (2020), for example, brings a country construct into a discussion of subnational places when stressing that "taken to the extreme, *place attachment* often brings out *xenophobic* ... behaviors" (emphasis added) – and a novelist asks, "What would people do to preserve a safe harbor? What countries do to protect their borders, what individuals do to protect their homes" (Louise Penny, *Bury Your Dead*, 2010).

CONCLUDING THOUGHTS AND THE WAY AHEAD

We learn about and experience places of all kinds in a near-infinite variety of ways. The image of the cowboy, that "magical blend of macho man and tamed beast ... [is] a metaphor for the nation itself", notes a movie critic (Monk, 2004, p. D1), and Hornby's (1992) learning about locations in Europe came mostly "not from school, but from away games or the sports pages" (p. 70). Place images find their way into our minds every time we watch a movie, read a book, or watch a sports game, not to mention watch the news, see an ad, or buy a country's product. There are *a lot* of such images, and so, how do our minds cope?

One answer, which can be highly useful in GDA scholarship of any kind, can be found in our *mental schemata*. These incorporate *everything* we internalize about *everything*, from objects and events to feelings and stereotypes, all organized hierarchically and connected through nodes into associative networks. In the place context, discovery of a new planet in outer space, a region for vacationing, a restaurant in our city, or a desk for our home office, will trigger associations that affect one or more levels of the hierarchical string *universe–earth–continent–country–region–city–neighbourhood–street–home–room*. Importantly, a *schema* reflects the complete *image* of its object: India's may include the Ganges and the Taj Mahal and Brazil's the Amazon and Rio de Janeiro, along with both countries' populations, languages, religions, iconic sports (e.g., cricket vs. soccer/football), exports (e.g., textiles and software vs. coffee and aircraft), and much more.

Since such images reside in the mind they influence, while also being a part of, people's local, ethnic, and national identities as well as their attitudes and behaviours toward their own and other places – and therefore mental schemata can serve as a or 'the' paradigm that may enable the 'great divide' in GDA to be no longer.

Whether using this or some other paradigm, one is needed in order to enable us to address the challenges in the road ahead. We still do not have answers to several critical questions, including but not limited to:

- Which level of 'place' matters more, and in what contexts? Bordeaux or French wines? In FDI, Ghaziabad to attract investment in electronics or Delhi, of which it is a part?
- What images does a place versus its people evoke? 'Sicily' is viewed positively and 'Sicilians' negatively (Morello, 1999), while both Canada and Canadians have positive images in global polls and our own research. What are the relevant implications? Country studies know much more about this than place research.
- Are the Behavioural Activation vs. Inhibition Systems in personality theory (BAS/BIS; Gray, 1981) relevant to GDA personality-based research? To the best of our knowledge, neither place nor country studies have ever included them.
- What role, if any, do language or music play in place/country image formation and marketing? In a speech to the Académie Française, the Nobel laureate Albert Camus defined his *homeland* as the French *language* ("*Ma patrie, c'est la langue française*"). In fiction, dialects are integral parts of identity: "The women went wild for him. French accent and all" (Olen Steinhauer, *The Confession*, 2004), and "Enderby drawled in that lounging Belgravia cockney which is the final vulgarity of the English upper class" (John le Carré, *Smiley's People*, 1980). And, perhaps most evocatively, in an 1897 theatre play on the life of Cyrano de Bergerac, the famous French swordsman prompts the shepherd Bertrandou to play his fife and take him and his fellow Gascons to "the hill where mist still lingers ... the glade, the heath, the forest way ... the green of spring on the Dordogne ...", urging them to "Listen, Gascons. It is all Gascogne" (Anthony Burgess, *Cyrano de Bergerac*, 1991). It would seem that such elements, perhaps seen as 'peripheral' since they are rarely included in relevant studies, could be studied in research and considered in management practice for great benefit to both.
- Might insights from country and/or place research and practice be able to help in resolving the many issues that each faces within its own side of the

divide? For instance, in country research we still do not have a clear idea of what 'origin' means (e.g., made-in? brand origin? country-of-origin? product–place image? brand–place association?), and in place studies our review of a sample of several articles shows that the relationship between such core constructs as *place attachment* and *place identity* is also unclear (e.g., conclusions include that the two have the same meaning; are similar but distinct; either is a component of the other; either is the overarching place construct; both are parts of sense of place). Clearly, progress in 'cleaning house' is needed for integration of the houses to truly advance.

Place, whatever its incarnation may be, matters to all humans, is researched intensively in several disciplines, and is used heavily by both buyers and sellers. Therefore, it needs to 'find its place' as a critical and dominant construct in both GDA and general marketing and management research and practice, and both sides of the current divide have made substantive advances to that end but are not 'there yet'. Perhaps it is best to leave the last word to Levitt (1984), who, in one of his most famous quotes, stressed that "Data do not yield information except with the intervention of the mind. Information does not yield meaning except with the intervention of imagination" (p. 99).

We have data, we have information, and we most certainly have minds. We also have a lot of imagination, and it seems that with just a bit more of it 'the twain shall meet' and the sky will be the limit for the future of inquiry into, understanding of, and practice on, geographically defined areas.

REFERENCES

A.C. Nielsen (2016). *Nielsen: Nearly 75% of Global Consumers List Brand Origin as Key Purchase Driver*, 26 April. Accessed 2 October 2020 at http://www.nielsen.com/ca/en/press-room/2016/nielsen-75-percent-of-global-consumers-list-brand-origin-as-key-purchase-driver.html.

Allport, G.W. and Odbert, H.S. (1936). Trait-names: a psycho-lexical study. *Psychological Monographs*, 47(1), i–211.

Bartsch, F., Riefler, P. and Diamantopoulos, A. (2016). A taxonomy and review of positive consumer dispositions toward foreign countries and globalization. *Journal of International Marketing*, 24(1), 82–110.

Belk, R. (2020). Resurrecting marketing. *AMS Review*, 10(3–4), 168–171.

Boulding, K.E. (1956). *The Image: Knowledge in Life and Science*. Ann Arbor, MI: University of Michigan Press.

Casson, L. (1994). *Travel in the Ancient World*. Baltimore, MD: Johns Hopkins University Press.

Cleveland, M. and Balakrishnan, A. (2019). Appreciating vs venerating cultural outgroups: the psychology of cosmopolitanism and xenocentrism. *International Marketing Review*, 36(3), 416–444.

Dichter, E. (1962). The world customer. *Harvard Business Review*, 40(4), 113–122.

El Banna, A., Papadopoulos, N., Murphy, S.A., Rod, M. and Rojas-Méndez, J.I. (2018). Ethnic identity, consumer ethnocentrism, and purchase intentions among bi-cultural ethnic consumers: 'divided loyalties' or 'dual allegiance'? *Journal of Business Research*, 82(1), 310–319.

Fusté-Forné, F. (2020). Savouring place: cheese as a food tourism destination landmark. *Journal of Place Management and Development*, 13(2), 177–194.

Gelven, M. (1994). *War and Existence: A Philosophical Inquiry*. University Park, PA: Penn State Press.

Gold, J.R. and Ward, S.V. (1994). *Place Promotion: The Use of Publicity and Marketing to Sell Towns and Regions*. Chichester: Wiley.

Gray, J.A. (1981). A critique of Eysenck's theory of personality. In H.J. Eysenck (ed.), *A Model for Personality*, New York, NY: Springer-Verlag, pp. 246–276.

Hornby, N. (1992). *Fever Pitch: A Fan's Life*. New York, NY: Riverhead Books.

Hunt, J.D. (1975). Image as a factor in tourism development. *Journal of Travel Research*, 13(3), 1–7.

Jaffe, E.D. and Nebenzahl, I.D. (2006). *National Image & Competitive Advantage: The Theory and Practice of Place Branding*. Copenhagen: Copenhagen Business School Press, 2nd edn.

Kavaratzis, M. (2004). From city marketing to city branding: towards a theoretical framework for developing city brands. *Place Branding and Public Diplomacy*, 1(1), 58–73.

Lak, A., Ramezani, M. and Aghamolaei, R. (2019). Reviving the lost spaces under urban highways and bridges: an empirical study. *Journal of Place Management and Development*, 12(4), 469–484.

Lee, C. (2013). Why Prince George will never be King. *The New Republic*, 25 October. Accessed 10 October 2020 at https://newrepublic.com/article/115358/why-prince-george-will-never-be-king.

Levitt, T. (1984). The globalization of markets. *Harvard Business Review*, 61(3), 92–102.

Magnusson, P., Westjohn, S.A. and Zdravkovic, S. (2011). 'What? I thought Samsung was Japanese': accurate or not, perceived country of origin matters. *International Marketing Review*, 28(5), 454–472.

Monk, K. (2004). The good, the bad and the different. *Ottawa Citizen*, 5 March.

Morello, G. (1999). Nouns vs. adjectives in country-of-origin communication. *Marketing and Research Today*, 28(1), 10–14.

Papadopoulos, N., El Banna, A., Murphy, S.A. and Rojas-Méndez, J.I. (2012). Place brands and brand–place associations: the role of 'place' in international marketing. In S. Jain and D.A. Griffith (eds), *Handbook of Research in International Marketing*, Cheltenham, UK and Northampton, MA, USA: Edward Elgar Publishing, pp. 88–113.

Papadopoulos, N., Cleveland, M., Bartikowski, B. and Yaprak, A. (2018). Of countries, places and product/brand place associations: an inventory of dispositions and issues relating to place image and its effects. *Journal of Product & Brand Management*, 27(7), 735–753.

Papastephanou, M. (2012). Deconstructing the ethnos–nation distinction. *Journal of Politics and Law*, 5(4), 147–158.

Relph, E. (1976). *Place and Placelessness*. London: Pion Limited.

Stöttinger, B. and Penz, E. (2019). Balancing territorial identities: how consumers manage their ethnic, regional, and national identities in daily life and consumption situations. *International Marketing Review*, 36(5), 805–827.

Suter, M.B., Borini, F.M., Coelho, D.B., de Oliveira Jr, M.M. and Machado, M.C.C. (2020). Leveraging the country-of-origin image by managing it at different levels. *Place Branding and Public Diplomacy*, 16(3), 224–237.

UN/WHR (2020). *United Nations World Happiness Report*. Paris: UN Sustainable Development Solutions Network.

Vuignier, R. (2016). Place marketing and place branding: a systematic (and tentatively exhaustive) literature review. *IDHEAP Working Paper*, 5/2016.

Wilson, R.T. and Baack, D.W. (2012). Attracting foreign direct investment: applying Dunning's location advantages framework to FDI advertising. *Journal of International Marketing*, 20(2), 96–115.

Wong, K. (2020). Why everyone thinks their city is best – a look at place attachment. *CNN – Cable News network*, 1 December. Accessed 2 December 2020 at https://www.cnn.com/travel/article/place-attachment-theory-city-bias-wellness/index.html.

Zeugner-Roth, K.P. and Bartsch, F. (2020). COO in print advertising: developed versus developing market comparisons. *Journal of Business Research*, 120(11), 364–378.

4. Six propositions for place marketing: a critical discussion of the current state of our field

Sebastian Zenker

INTRODUCTION TO A CRITICAL RE-THINKING

Many articles about marketing places (like a couple of my own) start with the statement that places today are competing intensely with each other for investments, tourists, companies, talents, or attention in general (e.g., Cleave et al., 2016; Jansson and Waxell, 2011; Zenker et al., 2013). The ongoing debate about the impact of globalization – including the easier movement of production, workforce, and capital, as well as the increasing prevalence of tourism worldwide – seems to strengthen this idea (Turner, 2010). However, is place marketing really all about competition?

The question is very relevant because in practice we see a strong tendency to cooperate, not to compete, with places building so-called interregional joined brands (Pasquinelli, 2015). One might argue that competition boosts cooperation – or maybe the market is not as competitive as we think. This is one example of an assumption that is so deeply rooted in our thinking that we do not question it anymore. Being snared in this idea may limit our research and practical suggestions to issues of competition, when we should be asking more questions about cooperative approaches (e.g., Hankinson, 2015).

Fortunately, starting from a rather humble base, the academic discussion on place marketing and branding has improved in recent years and we have begun a process of critical re-thinking of our previous assumptions (e.g., Ashworth et al., 2015; Boisen et al., 2018; Kavaratzis and Kalandides, 2015). To build on (and hopefully enhance this trend), this chapter is presented as an opinion piece – driven primarily by my personal observations and supplemented by major research findings.

A second issue concerns the way that the discipline evolved over time. In the early days of place marketing and branding publications, scholars focused extensively on wordings, definitions, and attention, but knowledge has grown considerably since then. This growth has led place marketing and branding to become a highly interdisciplinary topic. While valuable, this development presents a particular challenge, since researchers and practitioners from, say, marketing are not talking the same language as urban planners, sociologists, or architects. Unsurprisingly, then, even many contemporary articles do not use up-to-date definitions of place marketing, misunderstanding it as a limited approach to place promotion. We in the academic community should defend our discipline to guard against inadequately conceived conceptual development and poorly executed methodologies.

As a third and related issue, and notwithstanding the field's ongoing growth, place marketing and branding has yet to fully mature and may even be criticized for a degree of complacency in terms of advancing its theorizing and empirical rigor. Other disciplines improved their empirical and theoretical skills and raised the bar for publications. For example, while single case studies remain common in place marketing, they would be considered sub-standard by many high-ranked academic journals. Such journals look for empirical results undergirded by a solid theoretical foundation and for more generalizability than can be derived from simple practitioner problems. In place marketing and branding, we are proud of our close link between the practical and academic spheres. However, we often forget about the need to improve general knowledge and further develop place branding as an academic field.

PLACE MARKETING AND BRANDING IN PRACTICE AND THEORY

Even today, place marketing and branding is a growing but not fully matured research field (Vuignier, 2017). It involves different spatial scales and target groups (Ashworth and Voogd, 1990; Kotler et al., 1993). Metaphorically, place marketing is the family tree, with offshoots such as city or regional marketing (focus on spatial scale) and destination or location marketing (focus on specific target groups) serving as the branches (for a deeper discussion see: Berglund and Olsson, 2010; Braun, 2008; Kavaratzis, 2008).

In the last decade, place marketing has adopted place branding as one of its main strategies (Boisen et al., 2018; Kavaratzis and Kalandides, 2015; Medway and Warnaby, 2014). The increasing numbers of meta-analyses (e.g., Acharya and Rahman, 2016; Andersson, 2014; Chan and Marafa, 2013; Lucarelli and Berg, 2011; Lucarelli and Brorström, 2013; Gertner, 2011; Vuignier, 2017) all highlight the exponential growth in contributions, but also criticize the lack of theoretical and conceptual background – as well as the sometimes low empirical standards used.

This lack of scientific rigor is surprising, since place researchers have the opportunity to borrow numerous concepts, theories, and methods from many different disciplines. Unfortunately, there has been limited work on translating current knowledge from other disciplines for use in our field. Consequently, we are often stuck at the same level of discussion, which is burdened further by the fact that we sometimes still rely on false definitions or limit our thinking to common assumptions. To address these problems, I will outline six propositions, the first three to set boundaries, mainly addressing practitioners, and the next three to expand our academic discussion beyond common assumptions.

Place Marketing and Branding Are Not Limited to Promotion

In practice (as well as sometimes in theory), the terms and concepts used in place marketing and branding often lack a proper definition and consistent usage. As a result, place marketing (including the branding of places) is often mistaken as place selling. However, there is a strict differentiation between marketing and selling, where "selling is described as a supply-oriented process seeking to find the right consumers for the existing products, [while] marketing is described as a demand-oriented process seeking to find the right products for targeted consumers" (Berglund and Olsson, 2010, p. 14). While the two may work in conjunction, they cannot be used interchangeably. Thus, a focus solely on the promotional aspects of marketing disregards the central aim and broader range of marketing and branding, namely: to satisfy the consumer's needs and wants.

Since the 1990s, business models have evolved to accommodate this distinction (Homburg et al., 2000; Vargo and Lusch, 2004), with companies detaching marketing from sales and further differentiating between strategic and operational marketing. The strategy department, usually nestled in company management, develops strategies and orchestrates product changes, while the operational department implements said strategies and collects market data. However, in the realm of places, this development is still largely neglected, leaving us with a marketing model rooted in the 1960s.

Following Braun (2008, p. 43), place marketing can be defined as "the coordinated use of marketing tools supported by a shared customer oriented philosophy, for creating, communicating, delivering, and exchanging urban offerings that have value for the city's customers and the city's community at large", with place branding serving as one such marketing tool. Furthermore, the aim of place marketing is "to maximize the efficient social and economic functioning of the area concerned, in accordance with whatever wider goals have been established" (Ashworth and Voogd, 1990, p. 41). These definitions highlight three very important points: first, place marketing is a demand-oriented approach, focused on the place consumer and not the seller. Second, it is a management function where active governance is centrally important. Third, increasing social functions is as pivotal to the aims of place marketing as is economic improvement.

In all fairness, the main reason that this is even today an issue to discuss is, in all probability, the strong influence of practitioners (and especially consultants) in the field. It is especially the places themselves that are asking for this reduced promotional view. From my personal consultancy experience, I would say this is for two reasons: first, people working in the field do not have a holistic place marketing education, but come from very different fields (with sometimes very outdated definitions of marketing). Second, the structure of place governments is all too often perpetuating 'silo thinking', such as separating city-planning or political decision making very much from place marketing units. For us as academics, this calls for educating more and working to help tear down these outmoded silo walls within places.

A Place Brand is Not a Logo and Slogan

Even though academia discussed this for at least a decade (and came to a consensus here, I would say; e.g., Govers, 2013), unfortunately, in practice we still too often have to fight the 'urban myth' that the place brand is the logo and slogan (Medway and Warnaby, 2014). Defining a brand can be difficult since there are multiple viewpoints, but no shared definitions. Most consultants and policymakers focusing on the logo and slogan refer to the very popular definition of a *product* brand supplied by the American Marketing Association (2020, no page): "a brand is a name, term, design, symbol, or any other feature that identifies one seller's good or service as distinct from those of other sellers." From this they

> distil that place branding is about designing logos and slogans for places, while forgetting that the essence of it is to make something identifiable as distinctive. The name or logo is the tool for identification and recognition, but the core of branding is to make sure that consumers attach distinctive associations to this entity. (Govers, 2013, p. 71)

In line with Govers' (2013) arguments, the place branding field has proposed that the essential feature of a brand is "nothing more and nothing less than the good name of something that's on offer to the public" (Anholt and Hildreth, 2005, p. 164). In this sense, brands are markers for offerings, ideally creating easier choices for customers by promising a certain level of quality and reducing risk, thereby building trust between the consumer and the brand (Keller and Lehmann, 2006). Therefore, a place brand *can* be defined as the 'reputation' of a place.

Other researchers have tried to incorporate other related aspects of a brand into their place brand definition. According to Keller (1993), the 'good name' or 'reputation' exists as a network of associations constitutes 'brand knowledge' in consumers' minds. This knowledge about a brand is built through their 'brand awareness' (i.e., the extent to which customers are aware of a brand's complete feature-set) and 'brand image' (i.e., perceptions about a brand as reflected by the brand associations held in memory). Based on their evaluations of those associations, customers then develop an overall 'brand attitude'. Building on these assumptions, Zenker and Braun (2017, p. 275) define a place brand as "a network of associations in the place consumers' mind based on the visual, verbal, and behavioral expression of a place and its stakeholders. These associations differ in their influence within the network and in importance for the place consumers' attitude and behavior." Similarly, Kavaratzis and Kalandides (2015) had earlier criticized this idea of brands as sums of mental associations and highlight in their definition the interaction between these associations and the non-static nature of the place brand association.

However, there are more definitions out there – for instance, some with a stronger focus on the social construction of brand meanings (Lucarelli and Brorström, 2013), or the relationship of brands to the construct of place as such (Boisen et al., 2011). Amidst their differences, they all imply that the branding concept must extend beyond a simple logo and slogan discussion. A logo and slogan can be expressions of a brand concept (as communication tools), but not the brand itself – and failure to realize this can be harmful to a place's image. While place slogans can give some meaning (Medway and Warnaby, 2014), the slogan's tendency to simplify messages can create serious problems (see later discussion about place brand complexity). As such, it is not surprising that place brand managers do not generally find that type of communication to be terribly effective (Braun et al., 2014).

This raises the question: how much energy should places even commit to logos and slogans? Govers (2013, p. 71) argues that because "places already have (more often than not meaningful) names and landmarks, the amount of time and investment generally spent on designing logos and slogans as opposed to actual reputation management for places, seems to be a waste." In other words, a place brand *can* have a logo and a slogan as a graphical and linguistic expression of an underlying brand concept. They *may* be useful elements in a place's secondary communication, but they *should not* comprise the entirety of the brand.

We as academics can only continue to teach practitioners these differences and approaches. Yet even after more than 13 years in the field myself, this is still one of the first lessons I always find it necessary to reiterate to managers – and therefore we should not underestimate the resistance of practitioners to thinking differently.

You Cannot Make a Brand – Only Influence It

The approach taken by many consultancies is to start with the idea that they can 'brand a place' or 'develop a brand for places'. Job titles like 'place brand manager' create the illusion that brands can be created, changed, managed, or owned. However, no matter the brand definition used, it is obvious that we have relatively little influence over the creation or modification of a brand.

Rome's ancient heritage, for instance, provides such dominant associations that a complete image reinvention seems impossible. However, history is not the only factor that influences the place image (Braun, 2008); subordinate place levels also affect people's perceptions. A city in Europe, by mere virtue of country-level associations, might be perceived as relatively safe (even though crime rates could be as high as in South America), while a city in Africa – even if extensively developed – may struggle with associations like poverty or political instability (Sihlongonyane, 2015).

This problem is compounded by the fact that people tend to make assumptions about a place, drawing on stereotypes even in the absence of real associations. Let us take an example: What do you think about Horsens, Denmark? My first associations were 'small', 'dull', 'beach' (everything in Denmark seems close to a beach), 'nature', and 'quiet'. However, I have never been to Horsens; I instead relied on my general associations with Denmark and some added assumptions (if I have never heard of it before, it must be small and unimportant). Now, let us say I learn the following: Horsens State Prison is the oldest (built in 1856) state prison in Denmark, as well as one of the largest. This could immediately change my perception, adding a 'prison image' and associations about 'crime rates'. However, I might next learn that the prison was closed down in 1998, and that from 2010 onward the buildings and surroundings became available for different cultural events. For instance, Metallica performed a famous open-air concert within the old prison walls in 2010 to an audience of 40,000, and the area is now regularly visited by national and international stars (Jørgensen, 2014). This might erase my association of 'quietness', but not necessarily erase the 'crime' association (that could also depend on one's attitudes toward bands like Metallica or toward celebrities in general).

This example shows that we cannot build brands, but we can influence them by nudging or spinning the reputation, image, or meaning in a certain direction. In essence, we can try to perform brand*ing*, with the '*ing*' emphasizing the difference between the object and the process. However, that influence should not be overstated, since brand ownership is limited (Braun et al., 2013; Kavaratzis and Kalandides, 2015). A place belongs to its stakeholders, so if, for instance, residents try to construe Horsens as a quiet place, it would be futile to try and curb them.

Place Branding Is about Dealing with Complexity

Because place brands cannot be owned in a conventional sense and are beholden to multiple stakeholders, place brand managers need a different approach to branding in order to properly capture the complexity of a place. In product branding, companies typically need simple and unique messages in order to attract customers and differentiate their products in the market. In translating this common strategy, which entails defining a core brand and selecting a brand positioning, place officials inevitably narrow the communicated brand to a simple place denominator (in practice, often called the place identity or 'place DNA'). Unfortunately, this tends to exclude different opinions and identities (if a place is branded as 'young and creative', then what do we make of the many people who do not fit that image?). As with the logo and slogan discussion before, such simplification may cause more problems than it solves.

Thus, the classical branding approaches must be questioned, and more complex concepts are needed (Anholt, 2009). A branding strategy that allows for complexity should incorporate different topics into a prioritized selection of brand themes. In doing so, the place brand can accommodate complexity while still focusing on its core values, thereby allowing place managers the flexibility needed to accommodate a larger variety of messages and stakeholders (Kavaratzis and Kalandides, 2015). The issue of complexity is crucial here, since a good place branding strategy is not one of reduction, but possibilities. According to Zenker and Petersen (2014), place complexity could be both quantitative (many different themes, such as a good place to make business, a cultural place, a university city) and with different qualities. These qualities consist of 'ambiguity' (e.g., having poor and wealthy residents at the same district) and the 'degrees of entropy' (i.e., the level of how organized the complexity is). Therefore, a good place branding strategy avoids the 'one-fits-all' approach (Zenker and Braun, 2017), and instead carefully selects from and clearly prioritizes its many available themes, topics, policies, and target groups to address place complexity.

In practice, this approach is still rarely found. The City of Hamburg (Germany), for instance, tried to incorporate 17 different governmental units into one place marketing holding, to ensure that the different stakeholders and customer-groups are represented in their branding strategy. In addition, their brand analysis highlighted twelve brand themes (e.g., city at the waterfront, Hamburg Metropolitan Region, shopping hub, international trading hub; HMG, 2020) to ensure a level of complexity representing a 1.9 million inhabitant city (5 million within the metropolitan region). However, in terms of ambiguity and degrees of entropy, this is still a very top-down organized approach and not a grassroots movement (that a full complexity-driven strategy would also incorporate).

Forget about Uniqueness

According to Kotler et al. (1993, p. 18), place marketing and branding aims to promote "the place's values and image so that potential users are fully aware of the place's distinctive advantages." In addition, Govers (2013) argues that branding aims to influence consumers to attach distinctive associations to the entity of places. As such, we all follow the idea that uniqueness is the key to differentiating and, ultimately, winning the competition between places. We see this in practice when places try to construct flagship buildings, like the Guggenheim museum in Bilbao, in order to seem unique. In classic marketing textbooks, these efforts would fall under the domain of 'unique selling proposition' (USP) and 'added value' for the customer. Zenker (2011) states that one of three dimensions for evaluating place associations is the differentiation between unique and common place association. While it is true that 'unique vs. common' is one of the three dimensions for evaluating place associations, its importance is debatable.

For instance, what truly makes Hamburg different from, say, Rotterdam? Both places offer a similar package: a place to settle down, visit, grow, learn, work, recover, love, hate, have fun, or get bored. In marketing, we call these 'me-too-products', those that offer the same features as the big brands albeit with easier availability and/or a lower price. Those products are not necessarily unique – but they are able to fulfil customers' needs. That is true of most places. It is not the one unique thing, but the arrangement of common things that add value to the consumers of places. One student may search for a very green city with a modest level of urbanity and cultural offerings, while another may want a crowded urban place that still offers easy access to nature – but both are searching for a university city. Thus, we should rather understand marketplaces as a symphony of different instruments, or a meal composed of myriad ingredients. A place's uniqueness is more about the assemblage of common parts than about any particular landmark. Research or academic debates on this aspect are, however, non-existent.

Place Branding Is Not Only about Competition

As written in the introduction, one of our underlying assumptions about places is that they are in strong competition with each other. There are many good arguments for that assumption, as places throughout history have fought and competed for resources, people, or attention. We further assume that globalization has exacerbated this competition by allowing capital, goods, and people to move more easily (Turner, 2010) – but in reality, how much does Hamburg compete with Toronto or Seoul for talents? Zenker et al. (2013) showed that Berlin is the biggest competitor in terms of talents for the city of Hamburg and vice versa. On an international scale, places only compete in very specific categories (e.g., the harbours of Rotterdam and Hamburg as an entrance to the European market). This raises questions about the validity of international city rankings, since comparing cities in Europe with those of North America or Asia is akin to comparing apples with oranges.

On a smaller scale, we do see instances where the idea of competition and differentiation is firmly rooted: municipalities fight for separation from larger places (Frederiksberg, for instance, which is an independent municipality surrounded by the city of Copenhagen); suburbs try not to be seen as the big city. However, as Boisen and colleagues (2011) state, places and their borders are only institutional and artificial boundaries: they only work if people accept them and fill them with meaning. If people do not care, place differentiation does not occur. Case in point: the Copenhagen Business School does not mind being located in the Frederiksberg municipality (thus technically it is not located in Copenhagen) but does not call itself the Frederiksberg Business School.

Amidst entrenched ideas about competition, it is becoming increasingly apparent that place branding can revolve more around cooperation than differentiation. For example, the city of Hamburg – despite competing for talents with Berlin – created a joint cruise ship offer with Berlin, since international tourists are interested in both places. A growing number of metropolitan regions like Hamburg, Stockholm, and Copenhagen are joining forces with their surrounding municipalities, convinced that they can improve their offerings by including them instead of trying competitively to defeat them. The same happens in regional and interregional branding (Pasquinelli, 2015). Therefore, I would argue that our research focus and argumentation could afford to shift more from competitive to cooperative strategies. This so-called *competition–cooperation paradox* is not even new in business research, where competing companies still often join forces (Gnyawali et al., 2016), and it is time to address this perspective much more in our research within the place marketing domain.

CONCLUSION

In this chapter, I presented six propositions, of which the first three are mainly oriented to practitioners: (1) place marketing and branding are not limited to promotion; (2) a place brand is not a logo and slogan; and (3) a place brand cannot be made, only influenced. While to those of us in academia these statements may look obvious, from a practical perspective these are still not accepted as standard wisdom or even common sense and so we still need to keep making the case and defending these boundaries,

The next three propositions are intended to expand our academic thinking: (4) place branding is about dealing with complexity; (5) place branding is not about uniqueness; and (6) place branding is not only about competition. As assumptions become entrenched, it is necessary to step back and critically assess their validity.

All of the above lead to a conclusion that place marketing and branding is still a great field of research with practical utility – as long as we are willing to push beyond our comfort zones. Following Kuhn's structure of scientific revolutions (Kuhn, 2012), we began our investigations of alternative concepts to theorize and understand our world. As the next step now, we have entered a pre-paradigm phase, where we as scholars have to make sense out of this previously little 'anarchic period' of research. Our goal must be to move to a next phase, where new paradigms will be agreed on and a true scientific revolution in thinking will become visible.

Science should always be a domain for discussion and development, but this is only possible if we work hard to maintain an atmosphere of debate. While there are sometimes unavoidable politics involved in academic publishing (such as referencing everybody to please potential reviewers or ignoring poor academic work to not displease anyone), it is important that these not impede the discussion, and to recognize that sometimes conflict is necessary for scientific advancement. Maybe we need to show more courage and be more edgy on this. Many journals offer a publication type called 'viewpoints', 'commentaries', or 'opinion pieces' as one way of shorter and faster publications. One idea or opinion about a published paper could be discussed with this type of publication, and in this context, it is good that this book specifically invited a few such 'opinion pieces', including mine, as a matter of encouraging discussion and debate rather than just of expediency. In publications of this kind, we can criticize problems with scientific rigor, broaden the discussion, add new angles, and create better knowledge – replicating the spirit of the general big debates in academia from the 1960s and 1970s to our field.

Thus, it is in this spirit that I put forth this 'call to arms': I invite your reaction to the thoughts in this chapter and your initiative to discuss articles, definitions, or propositions – tear them apart, change them, or substantiate them with content from your discipline. Only by engaging in critical and constructive debate can we improve our field of research.

REFERENCES

Acharya, A. and Rahman, Z. (2016). Place branding research: a thematic review and future research agenda. *International Review on Public and Nonprofit Marketing, 13*(3), 289–317.

American Marketing Association (2020). *Definitions of Marketing.* Accessed 10 July 2020 at https://www.ama.org/the-definition-of-marketing-what-is-marketing/.

Andersson, I. (2014). Placing place branding: an analysis of an emerging research field in human geography. *Geografisk Tidsskrift-Danish Journal of Geography, 114*(2), 143–155.

Anholt, S. (2009). Should place brands be simple? *Place Branding and Public Diplomacy, 5*(1), 91–96.

Anholt, S. and Hildreth, J. (2005). Let freedom and cash registers ring: America as a brand. *Place Branding and Public Diplomacy, 1*(2), 164–172.

Ashworth, G.J. and Voogd, H. (1990). *Selling the City: Marketing Approaches in Public Sector Urban Planning.* London: Belhaven Press.

Ashworth, G.J., Kavaratzis, M. and Warnaby, G. (2015). The need to rethink place branding. In: M. Kavaratzis, G. Warnaby and G. Ashworth (eds), *Rethinking Place Branding* (pp. 1–11). Heidelberg: Springer.

Berglund, E. and Olsson, K. (2010). Rethinking place marketing – a literature review. In *50th European Regional Science Association Congress,* Jönköping, Sweden, 19–23 August.

Boisen, M., Terlouw, K. and van Gorp, B. (2011). The selective nature of place branding and the layering of spatial identities. *Journal of Place Management and Development, 4*(2), 135–147.

Boisen, M., Terlouw, K., Groote, P. and Couwenberg, O. (2018). Reframing place promotion, place marketing, and place branding – moving beyond conceptual confusion. *Cities, 80*(October), 4–11.

Braun, E. (2008). *City Marketing: Towards an Integrated Approach.* PhD thesis, Erasmus University Rotterdam.

Braun, E., Eshuis, J. and Klijn, E.-H. (2014). The effectiveness of place brand communication. *Cities, 41*(1), 64–70.

Braun, E., Kavaratzis, M. and Zenker, S. (2013). My city – my brand: the different roles of residents in place branding. *Journal of Place Management and Development, 6*(1), 18–28.

Chan, C.-S. and Marafa, L.M. (2013). A review of place branding methodologies in the new millennium. *Place Branding and Public Diplomacy, 9*(4), 236–253.

Cleave, E., Arku, G., Sadler, R. and Gilliland, J. (2016). The role of place branding in local and regional economic development: bridging the gap between policy and practicality. *Regional Studies, Regional Science, 3*(1), 207–228.

Gertner, D. (2011). Unfolding and configuring two decades of research and publications on place marketing and place branding. *Place Branding and Public Diplomacy, 7*(2), 91–106.

Gnyawali, D.R., Madhavan, R., He, J. and Bengtsson, M. (2016). The competition–cooperation paradox in inter-firm relationships: a conceptual framework. *Industrial Marketing Management, 53*(February), 7–18.

Govers, R. (2013). Why place branding is not about logos and slogans. *Place Branding and Public Diplomacy, 9*(2), 71–75.

Hankinson, G. (2015). Rethinking the place branding construct. In: M. Kavaratzis, G. Warnaby and G. Ashworth (eds), *Rethinking Place Branding* (pp. 13–31). Heidelberg: Springer.

HMG (2020). *The Brand Hamburg*. Hamburg Marketing GmbH. Accessed 30 September 2020 at https://marketing.hamburg.de/the-brand-hamburg.html.

Homburg, C., Workman, Jr, J.P. and Jensen, O. (2000). Fundamental changes in marketing organization: the movement toward a customer-focused organizational structure. *Journal of the Academy of Marketing Science*, *28*(4), 459–478.

Jansson, J. and Waxell, A. (2011). Quality and regional competitiveness. *Environment and Planning A*, *43*(9), 2237–2252.

Jørgensen, O.H. (2014). Developing a city brand balance sheet – using the case of Horsens, Denmark. *Place Branding and Public Diplomacy*, *11*(2), 148–160.

Kavaratzis, M. (2008). *From City Marketing to City Branding. An Interdisciplinary Analysis with Reference to Amsterdam, Budapest and Athens*. PhD thesis, University of Groningen.

Kavaratzis, M. and Kalandides, A. (2015). Rethinking the place brand: the interactive formation of place brands and the role of participatory place branding. *Environment and Planning A*, *47*(6), 1368–1382.

Keller, K.L. (1993). Conceptualizing, measuring, and managing customer-based brand equity. *Journal of Marketing*, *57*(1), 1–22.

Keller, K.L. and Lehmann, D.R. (2006). Brands and branding: research findings and future priorities. *Marketing Science*, *25*(6), 740–759.

Kotler, P., Haider, D.H. and Rein, I. (1993). *Marketing Places: Attracting Investment, Industry, and Tourism to Cities, States, and Nations*. New York: The Free Press.

Kuhn, T.S. (2012). *The Structure of Scientific Revolutions* (4th edn). Chicago, IL: University of Chicago Press.

Lucarelli, A. and Berg, P.O. (2011). City-branding: a state-of-the-art review of the research domain. *Journal of Place Management and Development*, *4*(1), 9–27.

Lucarelli, A. and Brorström, S. (2013). Problematizing place branding research: a meta-theoretical analysis of the literature. *The Marketing Review*, *13*(1), 65–81.

Medway, D. and Warnaby, G. (2014). What's in a name? Place branding and toponymic commodification. *Environment and Planning A*, *46*(1), 153–167.

Pasquinelli, C. (2015). Network brand and branding: a co-opetitive approach to local and regional development. In: S. Zenker and B.P. Jacobsen (eds), *Inter-Regional Place Branding: Best Practices, Challenges and Solutions* (pp. 39–49), Heidelberg: Springer.

Sihlongonyane, M.F. (2015). The rhetorical devices for marketing and branding Johannesburg as a city: a critical review. *Environment and Planning A*, *47*(10), 2134–2152.

Turner, B.S. (2010). Theories of globalization: issues and origins. In: B.S. Turner (ed.), *The Routledge International Handbook of Globalization Studies* (pp. 3–22), New York, NY: Routledge.

Vargo, S.L. and Lusch, R.F. (2004). Evolving to a new dominant logic for marketing. *Journal of Marketing*, *68*(January), 1–17.

Vuignier, R. (2017). Place branding & place marketing 1976–2016: a multidisciplinary literature review. *International Review on Public and Nonprofit Marketing*, *14*(4), 447–473.

Zenker, S. (2011). How to catch a city? The concept and measurement of place brands. *Journal of Place Management and Development*, *4*(1), 40–52.

Zenker, S. and Braun, E. (2017). Questioning a 'one size fits all' city brand: developing a branded house strategy for place brand management. *Journal of Place Management and Development, 10*(3), 270–287.

Zenker, S. and Petersen, S. (2014). An integrative theoretical model for improving resident-city identification. *Environment and Planning A, 46*(3), 715–729.

Zenker, S., Eggers, F. and Farsky, M. (2013). Putting a price tag on cities: insights into the competitive environment of places. *Cities, 30*(February), 133–139.

PART II

'A case of mistaken identity?': residents and identity politics in place and space

5. In search of a place brand identity model

Magdalena Florek

INTRODUCTION: BRAND IDENTITY VERSUS PLACE IDENTITY

Brand identity and *place* identity are terms and phenomena broadly covered in literature on the subject in their respective areas. On the other hand, *place brand* identity is relatively rarely presented comprehensively in the literature on place branding. Nevertheless, it has been presented as key and central to the process of branding of places or destinations (Anholt, 2007; Baxter et al., 2013, Morgan et al., 2002; Kavaratzis and Hatch, 2013). Therkelsen (2007, cited in Kvistgaard et al., 2015) emphasizes that the goal of destination branding is to create a coherent, unique, and differentiated identity.

In this context, several perspectives can be indicated with an analysis of the concept of place brand identity which come from the interpretation of place identity and brand identity.

Brand Identity

Place brand identity can and does draw heavily from traditional management-oriented research, which defines brand identity as "a unique set of brand associations that the brand strategist aspires to create and maintain" (Aaker, 1996, p. 68) or as "a long lasting and stable reference" (Kapferer, 2008, p. 37). As such, the branding literature has tended to define brand identity as an internal construct that emanates from the organization to target groups; in other words, brand identity defines what managers want the brand to be and remain over time (Aaker, 1996; Kapferer, 2008), and this does not necessarily match, or even approximate in many cases, the consumer perspective. According to this understanding, brand identity is a creation of managerial decision-making and should define and precisely specify the meaning, intention, and vocation of the brand (Kapferer, 1992; Keller, 1998).

At the same time, brand identity allows managers to define the limits of brand positioning, the concept put forth by Ries and Trout (1981) in an assumption that consumers make choices by comparing competing brands. In these circumstances, the role of brand management is to create the brand's unique position in consumers' minds on the basis of an attractive set of strong associations (Keller, 1998). Figure 5.1 sums up these relationships.

Figure 5.1   Relations between brand identity, positioning, and image

However, creation of this position is not limited to the brand's promotion activity; instead it is perceived as any efforts related to a brand and initiated by it which may be interpreted by the target groups. In this context, brand identity determines the strategy and furthers the selection of the marketing tools for executing this strategy. Brand identity communicated this way results in a subjective brand image (Tybout and Calkins, 2005). This is because a brand's structure is based upon reducing the difference between reality and perception as well as the way perception can be affected.

Therefore, the literature on branding typically depicts brand identity as a unique and key brand idea. This approach unveils two major features of brand identity: its aspirational nature (the desired associations indicate a brand's aspirations related to what the brand wants to be known for) and durability, although research on the latter has often been questioned. Da Silveira et al. (2013) have reviewed approaches to this matter and point out that the practitioner-oriented literature suggests that durability stands for "constant yet flexible" (Interbrand, 2007), that is, trying to agree on which parts of the brand values should remain constant and which should be flexible. According to Collins and Porras (1994, p. XV), durability means "preserving core values and purpose, while changing cultural and operating practices, specific goals and strategies". Interbrand (2007), for example, proposes a 70/30 principle for global branding: 70 percent of the brand must remain absolutely consistent and static and 30 percent can be flexible and dynamic, ensuring that the brand can evolve.

In contrast to this managerially-driven perspective on brand identity, insights from social theories (see the review by Botschen and Mühlbacher,

2019) definitely suggest that brand identity is "dynamic, reciprocal, and iterative in nature" (Scott and Lane, 2000, p. 45). From a social constructivist perspective, identity is "neither a given nor a product" but one which is contextual, pluralistic, results from negotiation, is social, and is discursive (de Fina et al., 2006, p. 2). Thus, identity is a co-created phenomenon that emerges from continuous dialectic processes of interaction in social contexts (Csaba and Bengtsson, 2006; Gioia, 1998). A study by Gioia et al. (2010) of organizational identity formation confirms that identity originates among and is affected by both insiders (i.e., the organization's members, if an organization; the brand managers, if a brand) and outsiders, including all other stakeholders, from local residents to institutions and target groups elsewhere. With reference to all of those who participate in the creation, maintenance, and change of identity, Hatch and Schultz (2004, p. 378) propose a simple definition: "Identity is a relational construct formed in interaction with others". Gioia et al. (2000, p. 64) put forward an argument that "the apparent durability of identity is somewhat illusory" because of the ongoing interrelationships between identity and image, which means that both local and other consumers, as holders of a brand's image, are also co-creators of brand identity.

In the case of organizational brand identities, companies present themselves as driven by organizational values, purpose, core competences, and an envisioned future (Collins and Porras, 1996). With regard to corporations, identity describes 'who we are as an organization', therefore identity holders not only take part in the creation of organizational identity but are also shaped by it (Brown et al., 2006).

As Da Silveira et al. (2013, p. 29) have summarized, "the concern for what brand identity really is, whether the internal vision of the brand managers, the external perceptions of the consumers, or a combination of both perspectives, as expressed in current frameworks, reflects the blurred distinction between brand identity, brand image, and brand positioning".

Today, when marketing communication is no longer a single-way process but rather one co-established by all its links, each component of the process influences itself permanently. We deal here with a triangle of the stimulus (identity) – perceptions (image) – response (experience) (Govers and Go, 2009, p. 30). In the case of place brands, the situation is even more complicated because a place is an open, live entity. For this reason, as Mayes (2008, p. 125) has justly and critically pointed out, "while acknowledging the richness of place identity, place branding [still] rests on the assumption that it is the practice or art of distilling the essence of the place" and that its task is to uncover "what a specific place is and also the identity it wants to project". Therefore, the authenticity and credibility of the whole place branding approach lies in recognizing place identity first.

Place Identity

The term 'place identity' was introduced to environmental psychology in the late 1970s. Proshansky (1978, p. 155) defined it as "those dimensions of self that define the individual's personal identity in relation to the physical environment by means of a complex pattern of conscious and unconscious ideas, feelings, values, goals, preferences, skills, and behavioral tendencies relevant to a specific environment". Thus Proshansky et al. (1983) describe place identity as individuals' incorporation of places into a larger concept of self, but Peng et al. (2020) have criticized that suggestion for its tendency to emphasize the individualistic dimensions of place identity. Subsequent studies have suggested a genuinely social understanding of place identity by showing how places might become significant and contested arenas of collective being and belonging (Peng et al., 2020).

Therefore, in the discussed context, it is worth following Paasi's (2009) proposal to understand place identity in a twofold way, namely as: (1) the place identity of a place, and (2) the people's place-related identity. In this approach, place identity encompasses features of nature, culture, and people that are used in the discourses and classifications of science, politics, cultural activism, regional marketing, tourism, governance, and political or religious regionalization (Peng et al., 2020), which distinguish one place from other places (Paasi, 2009). Groote and Haartsen (2008) have defined place identity as a combination of physical and man-made processes, specific elements and structures in places, and meanings ascribed to places. As Peng et al. (2020) have concluded, "place identity can be anything that makes a place identifiable within the spatial system and there are no fixed components of place identity" (p. 4). At the same time "place identities are residents' interpretation of place elements" (Kerr and Oliver, 2015, p. 67), and so people's place identity refers to individuals' identification with a place.

Notably, alongside place identity there is a number of other constructs developed by environmental psychologists to define and measure individuals' relations with places which are also linked internally, such as place attachment (Giuliani and Feldman, 1993; Lewicka, 2008) or a sense of place (Lalli, 1992; Campelo, 2015). Hernández et al. (2010) have argued, for example, that "place attachment is an affective–emotional bond with residence places, whereas place identity is a cognitive mechanism, a component of self-concept and/or of personal identity in relation to the place one belongs to" (p. 281).

This is of special meaning to place branding, since *people's* place identity and the *place* identity of a place overlap. Both embody subjective or emotional bonds between people and the physical world. As the interaction between people and a place is a mutual, dynamic, and ongoing process, the creating and fostering of place identity is also mutual, dynamic, and circular (Ramos et al., 2016). As Kerr and Oliver (2015) have pointed out, ideally the identities held by residents need to be considered with place branding strategies, and "understanding shared identities and how they represent daily life is crucial to creating an authentic place brand" (p. 68).

With reference to the scientometric review, past research generally analyses *people's* place identity and *place* identity against two perspectives: external looks or internal thoughts (e.g., Peng et al., 2020). Any changes in these components, brought about either by external forces (e.g., natural disasters, spatial planning, globalization) or internal growth (e.g., regional development or promotion) would impact a place's identity and the inhabitants' identities.

Taking the above perspective into account, it is worth referring to Warnaby (2011, based on Agnew's (1987) work) who has outlined a three-part definition of a place: (1) location, which is the geographical area that provides the setting of social interactions; (2) locale, which is the setting of informal and institutional social relations; and (3) a 'sense of place', or the subjective and emotional feeling that people attach to places. Together, these three components represent a place and influence both the content and the form of place marketing activities.

PLACE BRAND IDENTITY

Place branding scholars agree that a strong positive place brand identity can build a reputation that can differentiate one place from another in order to achieve some level of competitive advantage (Anholt, 2005; Skinner, 2008; Govers, 2011). By adapting Kapferer's (2008) proposal concerning commercial brands to place brand identity, the latter can be defined by answering crucial questions such as: What is the vision and meaning of the place? What makes it different? What meaning makes people aware of it? What are its core values? (Hakala et al., 2010).

Skinner (2018) has confirmed that place brand identity comprises elements from the physical and natural environment (i.e., from within its territorial and geographical borders); from its economic, legal, political system and culture; and, finally, from various symbolic and sensory elements that contribute to the way a place presents itself to the world, either authentically or through the staging of sports, music, art, or other cultural mega-events.

With reference to Noordman (2004), Govers and Go (2009) have identified four constructive elements of identity: structural (location, history); semi-static (size, physical appearance, inner mentality); changing signifiers (great events, great heroes, food, architecture, arts, literature, popular culture, language, traditions, rituals, folk); and coloring features (past symbolism, past behavior, communication). Campelo (2015) has added that it is through bonds between people and place, people and landscape, and people and people in a place that meanings are constructed, developed, and ascribed to physical features. Hence, place *brand* identity cannot be analyzed or defined without *place* identity, and raises doubts as to whether identifying place brand identity is at all possible (Kalandides, 2012) given the multidimensional complexity of 'place'.

We can assume tentatively that place brand identity derives from place identity but represents a strategic choice to create the desired image and competitive advantage. In line with this view, Kerr and Oliver (2015) have recommended starting with the innate elements and features of a place, or its revealed place identity set, and linking this with a designed place identity, in order to achieve the objective of reflecting and expressing place identities in communication (Kavaratzis and Hatch, 2013). This is because the way in which brand image is created in the audience's minds is to some extent based on 'hints' on the part of the brand/place owner who sends out signals which, decoded and interpreted, become meaningful. Hence the audience creates an image by means of a network of associations formed over a long time as a result of accumulating numerous stimulators (Luque-Martínez et al., 2007, p. 335).

Drawing on this thinking, Baxter et al. (2013) posit a three-way model that links the innate elements of a place (revealed identity) to its competitive position (competitive identity) and place brand (designed identity). All three constructs are linked with bi-directional arrows, since their relationships and the process of place brand creation are dynamic, and in this connection the authors stress two important points: first, that the revealed identity must be investigated and re-thought on an ongoing basis, since the notion of what a place 'is' changes all the time; and second, that the designed identity components must also be re-visited often to ensure that they are current and relevant (after all, other places change what they 'are' too) as well as in tune with the identities held by the residents.

Hence, the engagement of a local community is widely discussed and supported in place branding research (e.g., Houghton and Stevens, 2010; Insch and Florek, 2010). As Campelo (2015) has concluded, a place brand needs to include the local community, its habits, and sense of place. As a result, unlike product brands, place brands are more likely to succeed from 'the bottom up' – that is, starting their growth from and with the people they represent (Gnoth, 2002). But just like organizations, residents are the identity holders of place and they have views about 'who (or what) we are as a place'. Co-production of place identity refers to the meaning-making process involving residents (Kerr and Oliver, 2015).

Therefore, place brand identity is something not finished, it is "a process, never immobile or fixed" (Kalandides, 2011, p. 37). As Kavaratzis and Hatch (2013) have commented, the identity-definition process is a constant dialogue among stakeholders and its output will be input for the distinct branding process. As a result, the set of values or attributes that differentiate a place from others should not only create a sense of identity for internal stakeholders, but should also appeal to external audiences – as it the case, for example, in tourism destination branding.

In this spirit, Botschen et al. (2017) have discussed future brand identity. In their approach, the process starts with an analysis of the historically grown and established identity of a specific place. The intended place brand identity, consisting of attracting socio-cultural meanings and the driving core competence of the particular place brand, is created, defined, and translated into concrete multisensory touchpoint experiences and the corresponding behavioral rules. Next, necessary alignments for fulfilling the corresponding code of conduct and the enduring achievement of multisensory experiences are designed and implemented. The intended place brand identity materializes and becomes multisensory-perceivable. Typically, these alignments concern the structural and procedural adaptations and roles and the behavioral modifications. Positively resonating touchpoint interactions and experiences continuously charge the intended place brand. The circular process moves to its next stage, further supporting the evolution of the 'new' place brand, which itself remains dynamic.

Kerr and Oliver (2015) have concluded that there are misunderstandings between place identity and place brand identity. The former is pluralistic and fluid while the latter is selected and designed and more formally communicated. Therefore, of key importance to places in this process is the way of developing place brand identity.

BRAND IDENTITY MODELS AND THEIR APPLICATION TO PLACES

In the last decades, leading marketing scholars have developed frameworks and models to conceptualize brand identity, the best-known including Aaker (1996), de Chernatony (1999), Kapferer (1992), and Upshaw (1995). However, Konecnik Ruzzier and de Chernatony (2013) argue that most of these models concern commercial products and services sectors, leaving place branding with no widely accepted models. According to their review, while some of the existing place branding models include a brand identity perspective, they do not go into details.

Indeed, in the literature on the subject we can find many frameworks of place branding that do not focus specifically on the components or the structure of place brand identity. These models also take quite different perspectives on place branding, with Berrada (2018) having identified 17 variations that have been put forth, ranging from 'brand-' and 'place-' to 'local-' 'city brand-', 'national-', and 'nation-brand-' identity.

In order to present the issue and the related challenges, it is worth analyzing the evolution of brand identity models in the business/corporate sector and, as a result, examining the possibilities of applying them to place branding as well as identifying the postulated elements of the models' structure.

Product Brand Identity Models

The best known and commonly used models were created with reference to product brand identity and, not surprisingly, they relate to single products (or families of products) in the traditional sense of the term. These models tend to have an external perspective (the consumer's), are managed from the inside, and focus on creating the brand image in a specific target group. To name but a few of the models proposed by academics and practitioners alike, these include the Prism (Kapferer, 1992), the Brand Wheel (Ted Bates Worldwide, 1980), the Brand Pyramid (de Chernatony, 2006), the Bull's Eye, developed and modified by commercial brands (e.g., Johnson & Johnson; Urde, 2013), Interbrand's brand blueprint (Blackett and Boad, 1999), and the Brand Code (Gad, 2001). Such models are successfully put into practice in business but, for the reasons stated above, including but not limited to the multidimensional complexity of and multiple stakeholders in 'place', they can only be used in a limited way in branding places. As will be discussed later in this chapter, the Brand Wheel and Brand Pyramid are often applied in place branding following some modifications.

At this point it is worth taking a closer look at the Bull's Eye model, which actually shares many elements with other models and defines the six key elements which build up brand identity. They include:

- The values represented by a brand – defining reference areas important to the brand.
- Brand personality – a set of human features associated with a brand, performing symbolic as well as self-expression functions in relation with the brand's audience.
- Brand proposition – a generally defined brand offer for the target group, a synthetic approach to brand benefits.
- Functional and emotional benefits – directly referring to the brand audience's needs. The emphasized benefits should be of importance to the audience and, at the same time, differentiate themselves from the competitors.
- The benefits indicate why a brand is to be chosen by the audience, how it is better, what it can offer that is special and unique and that no other brand has.

- Substantiators – the basis for the benefits' credibility or facts/arguments which will make the audience believe in the promises made by a brand.
- Brand essence/core – a crucial, abridged definition of the brand differentiator which should underlie the positioning. Brand essence stems directly from the proposition and represents a synthetic approach to what is most important in the brand.

The starting point in defining specific elements is insight into the needs, expectations, and viewpoints of the target group. Therefore, the model uses insights through buyer research as inputs and results in formulating consumer 'takeout' or the desired way in which the target group perceives the brand and intends to act toward it, as its output. In her work for cities and regions, the author of this chapter has applied (with some reservations) the Bull's Eye method and confirmed that it can be implemented for clearly-defined target groups and also look for shared values across different groups, which should ultimately lead to specifying 'brand essence' universal to many groups (e.g., see Florek and Janiszewska, 2013).

Another example is the Brand Code model (Gad, 2001), which takes into account the role of a brand in the society as well as a brand vision and therefore presents some potential links with places. Both elements are of special significance in the context of place brand management as decisions made by local authorities largely rely on the social aspect of a brand's functioning and the consequences of activities for future place development.

The Brand Code defines brand identity in six areas: mission, vision, values, product, positioning, and styling. If some of its elements were treated in relation to places (e.g., 'vision' of a place rather than a product), to some extent the model can be useful in some cases, such as small places with a clear-cut offer for a specific target group or when a place intends to create a separate identity(ies) for one or more specific target groups. On the other hand, bundling up many groups and/or offers (i.e., attributes, benefits, values, etc.) within a single identity by means of such a model may be problematic. In such a case, the process would have to focus on areas common to various groups with different needs and to account for the relative importance of each compared to the others. Figure 5.2 shows the main elements of this method with a general adjustment for the place branding context. Notably, this model includes both the 'external' user perspective and the bi-directional arrows between constructs, in line with important elements that differentiate 'place' from 'business' branding.

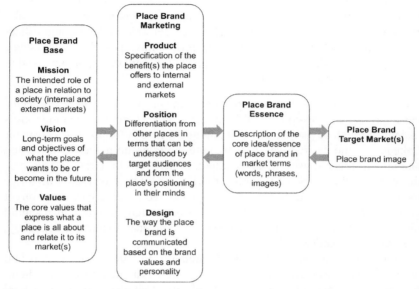

Source: Adapted and redrawn from Gad (2001).

Figure 5.2   'Brand Code' adaptation to place branding

Corporate Brand Identity Models

For corporations and organizations, the product approach has been insufficient and therefore new concepts emerged, revolving around corporate identity. Examples of these models include Brand DNA (Chapman and Tulien, 2010) and the Corporate Brand Identity Matrix (Urde, 2013). Models such as these predominantly take into account the fact that there is an organization behind a brand and that they have at their disposal a much bigger offer (a broad range of products and services) targeted at multiple consumer and business/industrial buyers (B2C and B2B) and multiple non-buyer stakeholders. What is more, they also take into account the organization's mission and vision, its culture and core values, and the key assumptions that show an organization's place in various contexts. Hence, corporate identity presents an internal perspective balanced with an external one. Some also emphasize the need to form relations and the fact that corporations can have multiple identities.

In the corporate models there are also coordinates of brand identity including positioning and execution/communication. These are especially visible in Aaker's (1996) Brand Identity Planning Model (also used for product branding), where the author considers brand identity as consisting of core and extended identity, with the latter, in turn, consisting of: a product, an organization, a person, and a symbol. These are further developed to create a value proposition, build credibility, and foster brand–customer relationships, which together make up a 'brand identity system', whose purpose is to support brand strategists in considering the various brand elements and patterns that can help to clarify, enrich, and differentiate an identity. The brand identity system is followed by a 'brand identity implementation system' which looks at how to position a brand effectively in the mind of the consumer. From there, the brand can identify which brand building programs would be best to implement, and how they should be tracked. The model is therefore complex, and includes branding procedure steps.

Meanwhile, the exact brand identity is the subject of the Brand DNA model. This model assumes that, like a living organism, a brand breathes, moves, evolves, and adapts to its surroundings; in this context, it is a good idea to analyze it because places incorporate these characteristics of openness and dynamics. The model's core genetic structure is composed of elements and attributes unique to a brand's origins and environment. The concept consists of four basic elements that constitute the brand and lead to its DNA: values, style, differentiation, and standards.

Values are the guiding principles that reflect a brand's core ideology and determine all brand activity involving decisions and actions inside and outside the organization. This is particularly important in the case of place brands, where 'core ideologies' are intertwined with *place* brand identity and *people's* place brand identity, as discussed above. Brand values determine two important strategic areas: the brand's reputation, and its ability to build up relations with stakeholders. Brand style refers to brand personality, defines the way of presenting and delivering the seller's, in our case the place's, offerings, and describes relations with clients, staff, and vendors. Differentiators are the unique and distinctive capabilities that enhance a brand to the business and customers, and this is yet another element of particular interest to place branding, given the complexity of 'place' and therefore the many dimensions across which a place can, or cannot, differentiate itself from other places. Finally, brand standards are levels of performance excellence across the internal and external organizational levels, and they refer to four basic elements: employees, customers, processes, and finance. Standards are the most tangible and measurable elements of the Brand DNA concept. Clearly, in a detailed description of the model, reputation plays an important role as it draws on brand values, which is of significance in place branding (see, e.g., Anholt, 2007) as well as in relations with stakeholders.

On the other hand, Urde's (2013) nine elements of the Corporate Brand Identity Matrix define the totality of identity. As shown in the adaptation for place branding in Figure 5.3, its internal component (sender) is described in

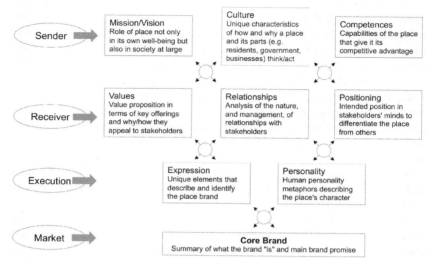

Source: Adapted and redrawn from Urde (2013).

Figure 5.3   *'Corporate Brand Identity Matrix' adaptation to place*
              branding

terms of three characteristics of an organization: its 'mission and vision', its
'culture', and its 'competences'. The external component (receiver) comprises
'value proposition', 'relationships', and 'position'. The model is completed
by two executional elements: 'personality', which describes the corporate
brand's individual character, and 'expression', which defines a brand's verbal
and visual manifestations. The 'brand core' which is at the heart of corporate
brand identity, consists of what it promises to 'be' for a target group(s) and
a summary of the core values that support the promise. As can be seen by
comparison to the 'Brand Code' approach in Figure 5.2, the two models share
several similarities and a similar overall logic. In both cases, elements that
can have greater importance in place instead of corporate branding can, and
should, be expanded on, further defined, and adjusted to fit the particularities
of places.

Destination Brand Identity Models

The models described above have started to be adapted for, and adopted
in, destination branding. We can find here numerous modifications of such
approaches, where usually the 'business product' from mainstream business
models is exchanged for a 'place product' in place branding, where interest

in the place is holistic and incorporates several distinct perspectives, and then for 'destination products' in tourism applications, as in the case of the Brand Wheel or Brand Pyramid models. Furthermore, Konecnik Ruzzier and de Chernatony (2013) and others have posited models specifically developed for destination brands, which are therefore better aligned with the peculiarities of these brands – including the role of internal stakeholders, the presence of multiple types of consumer and non-consumer stakeholders, a complex and diverse tourist product, and the experiential dimension of a destination brand.

A popular approach to destination branding has many common elements with the models discussed so far but is based on the notion of a 'pyramid'. This builds up a brand logically from an assessment of the destination's main attributes to eventually culminate in the essence of what the destination 'is'. A case in point is the Six-Stage Brand Pyramid (WTO, 2009), which consists of (from the bottom up): (1) the objective and measurable attributes that characterize the place; (2) the rational and (3) emotional benefits (or 'emotional take-out') that the place offers to tourists and other visitors; (4) the personality and (5) values of the brand, much like the similar constructs of the models presented above; and (6) the 'brand essence', which, similarly to the 'brand core' and other such constructs discussed earlier, includes perhaps three to four core values that are enduring and which, in combination, comprise the 'destination's DNA'. Of particular relevance to our discussion here, execution of the pyramid is usually very 'marketing-oriented' in nature, while other aspects of place branding, such as value co-creation, are neglected.

There are many modifications of this pyramid approach, introduced by various advisors and consultancy companies depending on the point of reference for the needs (mainly communication needs) of specific destinations. This approach has gained in popularity not only in the context of tourism but also for more comprehensive place branding strategies, most likely due to the logical sequence of the pyramid structure and the deceptive simplicity of applying this model.

Another popular model has been borrowed from product branding, namely: the Brand Wheel (Ted Bates Worldwide, 1980). This bears many similarities to other models, except for the visual way in which it is presented (wheel instead of pyramid, for example), but adds useful emphasis on the distinction between the rational and emotional elements that may comprise a brand. Rational attributes define a destination product and explain what that product 'does' for consumers (functional benefits), while emotional factors identify how a destination makes someone feel about choosing and using it. Bringing these elements together makes it possible to drill down into the core of the brand. The Brand Wheel for destinations model (WTO, 2009) contain five main elements: (1) Values, or what the brand stands for; (2) Brand Personality, or how it is perceived in relation to human characteristic, its style; (3) Substantiators in the form of facts and symbols, which support the brand proposition and may vary from market to market or from one segment to another; (4) Essence, or the true character of the brand; and (5) the destination brand's Proposition, or what makes it unique and better than its competitors. Overall the 'wheel' model does have certain benefits, including the emphasis on the rational–emotional distinction (as well as offering, in the model's full presentation, useful detail on the structure of brand identity), but it also shares several weaknesses with the previous models – particularly in not accounting adequately for the multi-dimensional, relationship-based, dynamic nature, and other aspects that are of key importance to places.

In this context, Konecnik Ruzzier and de Chernatony (2013) propose an interesting framework for developing brand identity, focusing on tourism and considering the issues at the country level (in their work, a case study of Slovenia). Like the 'brand wheel' above, the model is presented in the form of several concentric circles but contains more variables and incorporates general brand identity elements borrowed from one of the authors' brand identity model (de Chernatony, 1999, and its further developments), namely: vision, values, personality, and distinguishing preferences as a key aspect of posi-tioning. The model also includes two further and new elements: a mission to guide a country's future direction, and benefits that enable a country to attract stakeholders and differentiate it from other countries.

Mission and vision give a country brand a clear sense of direction, taking into consideration key macro-environment trends (present or past in the case of mission vs. future in the case of the vision concept). Values shared among influential stakeholders are enduring and derive from a nation's culture, history, and geography. They stimulate behavior while the style of interaction between stakeholders can contribute to a basis for differentiation. Brand personality closely relates to the personality of people who constitute and live the brand. In this regard, personality can include people's main traits and their ways of life. Distinguishing preferences include a place's attractions or attributes which position it as unique in comparison to its main competitors. Place attributes and the benefits that may be derived from them can range from functional to psychological, reflecting unique place characteristics and the rewards people may expect from visiting the place, and mirroring the func-tional/emotional distinction of the Brand Wheel discussed above.

These brand identity elements constantly interact to fulfill visitor expecta-tions through the place brand's functional and emotional values, in order to create a brand promise that emphasizes the experiential dimension of visiting a place, which is sought after by target audiences. Due to the unique charac-teristics of place brands, and unlike other brand identity models, the authors' proposed model treats the relationship among influential stakeholders as a sep-arate, and important aspect in place identity development. Overall, the model contains several elements which argue in favor of its suitability for destination brand identity and perhaps, later on and with suitable adjustments, for place brand identity.

CALL FOR A PLACE BRAND IDENTITY MODEL

In the case of place brand identity, academics have not yet offered a solution that may attract broad agreement. Most probably, a single solution is not possible or even altogether desirable, and yet some consensus on the key elements of such a model is of importance to generating further discussion and searching for optimal propositions.

In the country context, Dinnie (2008) has mentioned key components of nation-brand identity, such as history, territory, sport, icons, and folklore, to represent the enduring essence of a nation. Based on the existing concepts of brand identity, he has made an attempt to present the ways in which nation-brand identity can be transferred and manifested according to the following components (which might be understood as potential components of place brand identity): brand vision, brand scope, brand name, codes of expression, everyday behavior, what makes the brand different, narrative identity, and being an advocate of an ideology.

As for the place branding literature, various authors focus on the implementation perspective of brand identity rather than on what represents it or how to develop it. Therefore, based on the review presented in the chapter, some postulates on the potential elements and key aspects of place brand identity can be put forward in an attempt to fill the existing gap.

Taking into account the peculiarities of places and a place's identity, the internal perspective is key, followed by the related external perspective which comes second. This is because there are people behind a place brand: the inhabitants and other internal stakeholders as well as the interactions between them. They are the 'target groups' and, at the same time, the co-creators of a place for themselves and others. Their involvement is therefore key in both identifying and implementing brand identity. However, a question can be posed whether internal stakeholders should be an element in the structure of place brand identity (as Konecnik Ruzzier and de Chernatony (2013) have suggested), or whether their obligatory and active participation in place branding should be assumed. In this sense, their involvement and influence are simply an obvious part of branding as a comprehensive process and, like all branding steps, identity should be defined in a collaborative manner.

Secondly, each place has a vision which results from the locals' needs and aspirations. Similarly, the mission is related to a specific place's role in the region or broader parts of the world, but still is mostly for the local community. A place's mission and vision should not be disregarded in a place brand identity model because in fact they set the identity's direction and limits. In this context, in their model of Place Branding and Identity Dynamics related to the city of Bradford in the UK, Trueman and Cornelius (2006) used the term 'Lived Identity' for community perceptions, experience, and aspirations for the city.

It also seems that analyzing the attributes and benefits only along a functional and emotional dimension, while valuable and necessary, does not suffice to identify a place's character or uniqueness. The experience dimension now leads the way in which we understand brands, and this is not only for 'place' brands but also for a growing number of commercial products and services. This is why experiential benefits or experiential promise, as Konecnik Ruzzier and de Chernatony (2013) suggested, should make their way to the structure of place brand identity.

Of special importance to place brand identity are culture and heritage, strongly related to the identity of a place and its people. It is hard to qualify culture and heritage as traditional attributes because, especially for the inhabitants, they are more than just potentially attractive features. Rather, they strongly influence a place's values and personality and frequently they are also the key argument for the reasons to believe in place brand essence.

The dilemma posed by the quest for an 'optimal model' also revolves around multiple identity. For example, Anholt (2007) raised doubts about the willingness to make use of a deliberately simplified notion of brand promise or brand essence, which limits the widening of the discourse with multiple target groups. At the same time, as Kotler et al. (1993) have suggested and many have agreed later, place marketers are severely hampered by a series of political pressures as they have to reconcile a welter of interests and establish a place identity acceptable to a variety of public and private actors. In this light, it could be assumed that a brand identity model that captures a place's vision and mission, and that draws on the place's heritage and culture, will provide a broader look at a place brand than just if it considers only particular influence areas (e.g., business, education, tourism etc.) and/or target groups, and will allow considerable flexibility in interpreting actions and communication. Notably, these are decisions related to the right positioning of brand identity.

Finally, every place is an open, constantly changing organism, and for this reason, place brand identity requires a dynamic approach. This is because place represents an open system, constantly changing and evolving together with the relations between people and the environment. Konecnik and Go (2008) argue that a well-developed and controlled brand identity which balances out continuity and change stands a better chance of meeting the challenge of developing brand identity.

As Kavaratzis and Hatch (2013, p. 76) aptly conclude,

there seems to be an agreement that both the place brand and place identity are formed through a complex system of interactions between the individual and the collective, between the physical and the non-physical, between the functional and the emotional, between the internal and the external, and between the organized and the random.

The way of formulating place brand identity needs to consider these dependencies, and therefore it needs to be a multi-component concept.

On the other hand, we should bear in mind that brand identity is always an expression of strategic intent: it will differ in various respects from its actual position and image, and the formulation of a 'desired (or targeted) position' is an essential task of identity management that needs to find a strategic fit between the internal and external elements of 'place' (Urde and Greyser, 2015). Ultimately, the aim for place brand identity is to support the accumulation and communication of distinctive place resources, its features, and its characteristics, to gain an attractive image, strong reputation, and competitive advantage, and to fulfill the aspirations of its people.

REFERENCES

Aaker, D.A. (1996), *Building Strong Brands*, New York, NY: Free Press.

Anholt, S. (2005), What is a nation brand? *Superbrands*, pp. 186–187. Accessed at www.superbrands.com/turkeysb/trcopy/files/Anholt_3939.pdf.

Anholt, S. (2007), *Competitive Identity: The New Brand Management for Countries, Regions and Cities*, Basingstoke: Palgrave Macmillan.

Baxter, J., Kerr, G.M. and Clarke, R.J. (2013), 'Brand orientation and the voices from within', *Journal of Marketing Management*, 29(9–10), 1079–1098.

Berrada, M. (2018), 'Towards a holistic place branding model: a conceptual model proposal', *Chinese Business Review*, 17(5), 223–237.

Blackett, T. and Boad, B. (1999), *Co-branding: The Science of Alliance*, London: Macmillan Press.

Botschen, G. and Mühlbacher, H. (2019), 'Identity-driven design of resonating touch-point experiences', paper presented at the 10th International Research Meeting in Business and Management, 8–10 July, IPAG Business School: Nice, France.

Botschen, G., Promberger, K. and Bernhart, J. (2017), 'Brand-driven identity development of places', *Journal of Place Management and Development*, 10(2), 152–172.

Brown, T., Dacin, P., Pratt, M. and Whetten, D. (2006), 'Identity, intended image, construed image, and reputation: an interdisciplinary framework and suggested terminology', Journal of the Academy of Marketing Science, 34(2), 99–106.

Campelo, A. (2015), 'Rethinking sense of place: sense of one and sense of many', in M. Kavaratzis, G. Warnaby and G. Ashworth (eds), *Rethinking Place Branding: Comprehensive Brand Development for Cities and Regions*, Cham: Springer International Publishing, pp. 51–60.

Chapman, C. and Tulien, S. (2010), *Brand DNA. Uncover Your Organization's Genetic Code for Competitive Advantage*, Bloomington, IN: iUniverse.

Collins, J.C. and Porras, J.I. (1994), *Built to Last: Successful Habits of Visionary Companies*, New York, NY: HarperCollins.
Collins, J.C. and Porras, J.I. (1996), 'Building your company's vision', *Harvard Business Review*, September–October, pp. 65–77.
Csaba, F.F. and Bengtsson, A. (2006), 'Rethinking identity in brand management', in J.E. Schröder and M. Mörling (eds), *Brand Culture*, London: Routledge, pp. 118–135.
da Silveira, C., Lages, C. and Simões, C. (2013), 'Reconceptualizing brand identity in a dynamic environment', *Journal of Business Research*, 66(1), 28–36.
de Chernatony, L. (1999), 'Brand management through narrowing the gap between brand identity and brand reputation', *Journal of Marketing Management*, 15(1–3), 157–179.
de Chernatony, L. (2006), *From Brand Vision to Brand Evaluation: The Strategic Process of Growing and Strengthening Brands*, Oxford: Elsevier Butterworth-Heinemann.
de Fina, A., Schiffrin, D. and Bamberg, M. (2006), 'Introduction', in A. de Fina, D. Schiffrin and M. Bamberg (eds), *Discourse and Identity*, Cambridge: Cambridge University Press.
Dinnie, K. (2008), *Nation Branding: Concepts, Issues, Practices*, Oxford: Elsevier.
Florek, M. and Janiszewska, K. (2013), 'Defining place brand identity: methods and determinants of application', *Actual Problems of Economics*, 12(150), 543–553.
Gad, T. (2001), *4-D Branding*, London: Prentice Hall.
Gioia, D.A. (1998), 'The identity of organizations', in D.A. Whetten and P.C. Godfrey (eds), *Identity in Organizations: Building Theory Through Conversations*, Thousand Oaks, CA: Sage, pp. 40–79.
Gioia, D.A., Schultz, M. and Corley, K.G. (2000), 'Organizational identity, image, and adaptive instability', *Academy of Management Review*, 25(1), 63–81.
Gioia, D.A., Price, K.N., Hamilton, A.L. and Thomas, J.B. (2010), 'Forging an identity: an insider–outsider study of processes involved in the formation of organizational identity', *Administrative Science Quarterly*, 55(1), 1–46.
Giuliani, M.V. and Feldman, R. (1993), 'Place attachment in a developmental and cultural context', *Journal of Environmental Psychology*, 13(3), 267–274.
Gnoth, J. (2002), 'Leveraging export brands through a tourism brand', *The Journal of Brand Management*, 9(4/5), 262–280.
Govers, R. (2011), 'From place marketing to place branding and back', *Place Branding and Public Diplomacy*, 7(4), 227–231.
Govers, R. and Go, F. (2009), *Place Branding: Glocal, Virtual and Physical Identities, Constructed, Imagined and Experienced*, New York, NY: Palgrave Macmillan.
Groote, P. and Haartsen, T. (2008), 'The communication of heritage: creating place identities', in B. Graham and P. Howard (eds), *The Ashgate Research Companion to Heritage and Identity*, Farnham: Ashgate Publishing, pp. 181–194.
Hakala, U., Lemmetyinen, A. and Gnoth, J. (2010), 'Case A: the role of Nokia in branding Finland – Companies as vectors of nation branding', in F.M. Go and R. Govers (eds), *International Place Branding Yearbook 2010*, London: Palgrave Macmillan.
Hatch, M.J. and Schultz, M. (2004), *Organizational Identity*, Oxford: Oxford University Press.
Hernández, B., Martín, A.M., Ruiz, C. and Hidalgo, M.D.C. (2010), 'The role of place identity and place attachment in breaking environmental protection laws', *Journal of Environmental Psychology*, 30(3), 281–288.

Houghton, J.P. and Stevens, A. (2010), 'City branding and stakeholder engagement', in K. Dinnie (ed.), *City Branding: Theory and Cases*, Basingstoke: Palgrave Macmillan, pp. 45–53.

Insch, A. and Florek, M. (2010), 'Place satisfaction of city residents: findings and implications for city branding', in G.J. Ashworth and M. Kavaratzis (eds), *Towards Effective Place Brand Management: Branding European Cities and Regions*, Cheltenham, UK and Northampton, MA, USA: Edward Elgar Publishing, pp. 191–204.

Interbrand (2007), *Building a Powerful and Enduring Brand: The Past, Present, and Future of the ENERGY STAR® Brand*, Interbrand Publication for the U.S. Environmental Protection Agency.

Kalandides, A. (2011), 'The problem with spatial identity: revisiting the "Sense of Place"', *Journal of Place Management and Development*, 4(1), 28–39.

Kalandides, A. (2012), 'Place branding and place identity: an integrated approach', *tafterjournal*, 43, January.

Kapferer, J.N. (1992), *Strategic Brand Management*, New York, NY: The Free Press.

Kapferer, J.N. (2008), *The New Strategic Brand Management; Creating and Sustaining Brand Equity Long Term*, 4th edn, London, UK and Philadelphia, PA, USA: Kogan Page.

Kavaratzis, M. and Hatch, M.J. (2013), 'The dynamics of place brands: an identity-based approach to place branding theory', *Marketing Theory*, 13(1), 69–86.

Keller, K.L. (1998), *Strategic Brand Management: Building, Measuring, and Managing Brand Equity*, Hemel Hempstead: Prentice-Hall International.

Kerr, G. and Oliver, J. (2015), 'Rethinking place identities', in M. Kavaratzis, G. Warnaby and G. Ashworth (eds), *Rethinking Place Branding: Comprehensive Brand Development for Cities and Regions*, Cham: Springer International Publishing, pp. 61–72.

Konecnik, M. and Go, F. (2008), 'Tourism destination brand identity: the case of Slovenia', *Journal of Brand Management*, 15(3), 177–189.

Konecnik Ruzzier, M. and de Chernatony, L. (2013), 'Developing and applying a place brand identity model: the case of Slovenia', *Journal of Business Research*, 66(1), 45–52.

Kotler, P., Haider, H. and Rein, I. (1993), *Marketing Places: Attracting Investment, Industry and Tourism to Cities, States and Nations*, New York, NY: The Free Press.

Kvistgaard, H.-P., Blichfeldt, B.S. and Hird, J. (2015), *In Search of Place Brand Identity: 'How We see Us'*. Accessed at https://doi.org/10.13140/RG.2.1.4434.8644.

Lalli, M. (1992), 'Urban-related identity: theory, measurement, and empirical findings', *Journal of Environmental Psychology*, 12(4), 285–303.

Lewicka, M. (2008), 'Place attachment, place identity, and place memory: restoring the forgotten city past', *Journal of Environmental Psychology*, 28(3), 209–231.

Luque-Martínez, T., Del Barrio-García, S., Ibáñez Zapata, J.A. and Rodríguez Molina, M.A. (2007), 'Modeling a city's image: the case of Granada', *Cities*, 24(5), 335–352.

Mayes, R. (2008), 'A place in the sun: the politics of place, identity and branding', *Place Branding and Public Diplomacy*, 4(2), 124–32.

Morgan, N., Pritchard, A. and Piggott, R. (2002), 'New Zealand, 100% pure: the creation of a powerful niche destination brand', *Brand Management*, 9(4–5), 335–54.

Noordman, T.B.J. (2004), *Culture in City Marketing* [in Dutch], The Hague: Elsevier/ Reed Business Publications.

Paasi, A. (2009), 'The resurgence of the "region" and "regional identity": theoretical perspectives and empirical observations on regional dynamics in Europe', *Review of International Studies*, 35, 121–146.

Peng, J., Strijker, D. and Wu, Q. (2020), 'Place identity: how far have we come in exploring its meanings?', *Frontiers in Psychology*, 11, 294.

Proshansky, H.M. (1978), 'The city and self-identity', *Environment and Behavior*, 10(2), 147–169.

Proshansky, H.M., Fabian, A.K. and Kaminoff, R. (1983), 'Place-identity: physical world socialization of the self', *Journal of Environmental Psychology*, 3(1), 57–83.

Ramos, I.L., Bernardo, F., Ribeiro, S.C. and Van Eetvelde, V. (2016), 'Landscape identity: implications for policy making', Land Use Policy, 53, 36–43.

Ries, A. and Trout, J. (1981), *Positioning: The Battle for Your Mind*, New York, NY: Warner Books – McGraw-Hill.

Scott, S.G. and Lane, V.R. (2000), 'A stakeholder approach to organizational identity', *The Academy of Management Review*, 25(1), 43–62.

Skinner, H. (2008), 'The emergence and development of place marketing's confused identity', *Journal of Marketing Management*, 24(9/10), 915–928.

Skinner, H. (2018), 'Who really creates the place brand? Considering the role of user generated content in creating and communicating a place identity', *Communication & Society*, 31(4), 9–25.

Ted Bates Worldwide (1980), 'The brand wheel', internal document.

Trueman, M. and Cornelius, N. (2006), 'Hanging baskets or basket cases? Managing the complexity of city brands and regeneration', Working Paper No. 06/13.

Tybout, A.M. and Calkins, T. (2005), *Kellogg on Branding*, Hoboken, NJ: John Wiley & Sons.

Upshaw, L.B. (1995), *Building Brand Identity*, New York, NY: John Wiley & Sons.

Urde, M. (2013), 'The corporate brand identity matrix', *Journal of Brand Management*, 20(9), 742–761.

Urde, M. and Greyser, S.A. (2015), 'The Nobel Prize: the identity of a corporate heritage brand', *Journal of Product & Brand Management*, 24(4), 318–333.

Warnaby, G. (2011), 'What about the place in place marketing?' Paper presented at the Academy of Marketing Conference, 5–7 July, Liverpool, UK.

WTO (World Tourism Organization and European Travel Commission) (2009), *A Practical Guide to Tourism Destination Management UNWTO*, Madrid.

6.   From participation to transformation: the multiple roles of residents in the place brand creation process

Alia El Banna and Ioana S. Stoica

PLACE BRAND CO-CREATION

Over the past two decades, and marking an evolution in the branding literature, the meanings associated with brands and their perceived values have been progressively linked to brand 'co-creation' activities (Merz and Vargo, 2009). From a general marketing perspective, brand co-creation is inherent in consumer-generated marketing defined as the process of "brand exchanges created by consumers themselves – both invited and uninvited – by which consumers are playing an increasing role in shaping their own brand experiences and those of other consumers" (Kotler et al., 2013, p. 41). In fact, the image of a brand has shifted from perceptions at the level of the individual (Fournier, 1998) to "a shared reality, dynamically constructed through social interactions" (Ballantyne and Aitken, 2007, p. 365). Referred to as an emerging 'conceptual logic', brands are viewed as an outcome of a collective and collaborative co-creation process that involves all stakeholders (Merz and Vargo, 2009; Hatch and Schultz, 2010) who, often, participate in the brand co-creation and communication process fostering relationships and generating value (Payne et al., 2009).

Place brands are no different, in the sense that a collective approach to promoting places has been highlighted with growing frequency in the current literature (Kavaratzis, 2012; Vallaster et al., 2018; Warren and Dinnie, 2018). Several researchers have adopted the idea of a socially-constructed brand image in the context of place, focusing on the ongoing transformation of place brands to represent meanings and values created through continuous interactions between the place and its stakeholders (e.g., Kotsi et al., 2018). Consequently, the co-creation of place brands, defined as "a discursive social process in which salient stakeholders may directly or indirectly, purposefully or coincidentally interact" (Vallaster and von Wallpach, 2013, p. 1506), acts as a foundation of the creation of place brand images.

Place branding can be seen as an effort to develop a successful communicative platform, or more holistically a combination and interaction between "two mutually supportive" processes, as Therkelsen et al. (2010), put it, which include both the *development* and *communication* of place. Semantically, the authors refer to the processes as the "city of stones", which represents the physical aspects of the place, and the "city of words", which represent "symbolic representation" or communication of the place brand – and further highlight that place branding often fails due to lack of synchronisation between physical and symbolic or place and words.

Furthermore, and until recently, place brands were primarily portrayed as desirable locations by place promotion agencies addressing external target audiences. The involvement of residents in creating and promoting the image of their place, whether towns and cities or regions and countries, has become more pronounced. In fact, it can be argued that residents have always played a primary but behind the scenes role in place-making, until researchers and place marketers and policy makers clued into this fact and contributed to making this role better recognised and more central. Researchers discuss the shifting roles of the residents from only receivers of the message and indirect influencers towards being active proponents of the brand and participants in its creation. More specifically, recent studies have shown that internal place stakeholders are becoming more influential in creating and communicating a place image than place authorities or municipalities (Braun et al., 2018; Kavaratzis, 2004). This group is mainly formed by the local people who are 'living the brand' (Braun et al., 2013) and have become the primary place-makers because of their closer interactions with the place and extensive knowledge about it (Uchinaka et al., 2019).

Research has also shown that, over time, the involvement of residents in place branding can help to reduce discrepancies or mismatches between the promoted and actual image of a place. This inconsistency can ultimately lead to negative place reputation, which is an outcome of brand promises that "exceed the reality of the place" (Molina et al., 2017, p. 30). Tales of places (which shall better remain un-named) that promote themselves, for example, as 'friendly' when they are not or at least are not perceived as such, abound among tourists who come in contact with local personnel in the services sector. As put by Therkelsen et al. (2010), a particularly important challenge here is when there is inconsistency between the message and the actual image of place as perceived by its own inhabitants, local businesses, and communities.

To understand the nature and significance of residents' contribution to place branding, the following sections discuss the main elements that characterise their involvement in and their impact on the co-creation process. Following this introduction, we present a critical overview of the literature on the roles of residents in place brand co-creation and related processes, including, notably, the notion of place brand co-destruction and the contribution of storytelling to place branding. Next, we examine residents, as the main contributors, in the transformation of a place brand by participating in *both* the development and communication of place image. We then summarise the value-added from residents' contribution to place branding. Finally, we draw conclusions and recommendations for future research.

THE ROLES OF RESIDENTS IN THE CO-CREATION OF PLACE BRANDS: A CRITICAL OVERVIEW

Place residents belong to "a multiplicity of groups of people that are bound to have varying and conflicting preferences, desires, or, attitudes" with the place (Braun et al., 2013, p. 25) and are considered as the most important place stakeholders (Freire, 2009; Kemp et al., 2012a) due to their extensive knowledge about the place, their interactions with it, and their ability to have a stronger impact upon its environment. With technological advances and the new dynamics of the network society, there has been a shift in power dynamics; government entities' control over brand messages is today disrupted by place stakeholders' online contribution to co-creating place meaning (González and Lester, 2018).

While research highlights the shifting role of residents towards being primary sources of place-marketing, principal stakeholders of the place, and place-makers themselves through their close interaction with their place surroundings, there is scarce research in place branding that *directly* links residents with the 'co-creation' of the place brand. Rather, the concept of residents' co-creation of place brands has been used interchangeably with the idea of 'participation' (Hereźniak, 2017; Vallaster et al., 2018; Casais and Monteiro, 2019), 'co-production' (Sazhina and Shafranskaya, 2017); and 'engagement' with the place brand (Vollero et al., 2017).

To present a clear picture on the state of research in this area, below we present several central themes and subthemes that emerge from a critical review of both conceptual and empirical research which specifically examines residents' participation and/or attitudes towards participation in the co-creation of the place brand.

Place Brand Co-creation Roles: A Shift of Power

The role of residents as 'co-creators' of their place brands has taken on several forms which reflect the shift in power among actors in place representation. Until recently, place promotion agencies and other local authorities were mostly in charge of 'selling' a place by constructing and promoting a specific narrative. By contrast, today the residents are leaving their position as "passive beneficiaries" and becoming more "active partners and co-producers of public goods, services and policies" (Braun et al., 2013, p. 18). This participation is represented in the literature through three key roles: brand ambassadors, storytellers, and co-destructors of place brands, with existing research having placed less emphasis on the last two roles.

Brand ambassadors

A brand ambassador or brand advocate is a consumer "who says favourable things about a brand or recommends it to others" (Howard and Kerin, 2013, p. 365). Brand ambassadors advocate for a brand, can contribute to its co-creation process through positive word of mouth (WOM) (Kemp et al., 2012a), and may relate their tourism- and product-related experiences with a place, thus becoming advocates of, and being themselves influenced by, both (De Nisco et al., 2017).

Numerous studies highlight the role of residents as place brand ambassadors (e.g., Braun et al., 2013; Uchinaka et al., 2019). Some of these propose that residents become advocates through a brand adoption mechanism (Aitken and Campelo, 2011), which is defined as the "willingness to 'join' and communicate a brand" (Braun et al., 2018, p. 23). For example, in 2012 the public diplomacy team of India's foreign ministry used a YouTube video to encourage people to submit their own videos building on the title 'India is …', and citizens responded by sharing relevant videos and photographs on their personal web pages and social media accounts. Similarly, the town council of Luton in the UK recruited residents to act as the face of the town in its 2018 'Many Voices, One Town' campaign, resulting in social media narratives and photos shared widely on banners and posters. And in a grassroots initiative, the online 'Destination Lund Sweden' campaign was championed and created by local residents to promote their city's unique selling points through videos, downloadable maps, and guides for smartphones.

Residents' willingness to advocate for a brand is influenced by the identity–image match which provides a realistic representation of the place and improves stakeholders' connection with it (Zenker and Petersen, 2014). Residents become ambassadors by aligning place marketing activities with their perception of the place brand. If an alignment exists, residents become more committed to the place branding effort, and in turn become advocates or 'evangelists' of the brand (Kemp et al., 2012b).

In line with social identity theory (Tajfel and Turner, 1986), residents who identify with the place and feel involved in place marketing activities are more inclined to become brand ambassadors and advocates who create positive brand images (Uchinaka et al., 2019). These images are created primarily by communicating messages through online user-generated content (Uchinaka et al., 2019) or WOM (Kemp et al., 2012a), whether directly (e.g., through personal social contacts or as part of public speaking engagements in which brand ambassadors may be involved) as well as indirectly and perhaps even unwittingly (e.g., while it may not be appropriate for an educator to outwardly 'promote' a particular place, one may speak favourably of it in a class if the context allows it). Through user-generated content, place stakeholders become in control of shaping their brand narrative and exert the power to support, repress, or exclude brand messages (Cheong and Miller, 2000), collectively creating diverse dynamic place narratives that are interpretations of the place's identity and its perceived image.

In fact, place brand meanings are "heavily influenced by user-generated content often counteracting official content by public agencies" (González and Lester, 2018, p. 62), which brings to mind the use of 'ambassadors' by major international (and some national) agencies, such as the United Nations and UNESCO, as well as of 'real consumers' in traditional product advertising. A common link among such advocates is that they, and the messages they convey, may be seen by target audiences as less 'formal', more 'relatable', and more 'trustworthy', than formal messaging emanating from the same base sources. Whether such ambassadors are international celebrities or plain 'real-life' consumers relating their views and experiences with a cause or a product, assuming that they and the messages they convey appear credible (and are even seen as coming from 'a friend', a key notion in brand advocacy) they are more likely to be believed and internalised than clearly 'paid advertising' by the source agency or company.

Storytellers

For brands, storytelling is employed as a strategic promotional tool in advertising in which stories "don't always feature the product but rather focus on conveying the brand values through emotion-laden stories" (Laurence, 2018, p. 289). People are compelled by good narratives which carry and transmit emotions to accept and embrace a brand/product. This is what Escalas (2004, 2007) calls the "narration transportation process", which helps consumers make connections from stories to their own experiences, thinking "narratively rather than argumentatively" (Laurence, 2018, p. 289) and further creating brand associations.

Constructed place narratives, real or imagined, are becoming part of a place's identity through their continuous repetition and circulation within society (Warren and Dinnie, 2018). Recently, place branding research appears to have endorsed storytelling as a place promotion tool because of its potential to homogenise conflicting place images into relevant narratives easily observed by wider audiences (Kotsi et al., 2018). As highlighted by Kotsi et al. (2018), "the key to managing multiple stakeholder expectations is bridging the relevance gaps between what the stakeholders perceive to be important by finding, encouraging or generating stories that all parties can relate to" (p. 115).

Residents become more involved in the place brand co-creation process if they themselves engage in 'storytelling their brand' (Braun et al., 2013). Colomb and Kalandides (2010) examined residents' stories as part of the 'Be Berlin' initiative. They found that integrating residents' stories in the branding campaign not only improves civic pride by encouraging social and cultural integration of different parts of the city, but also promotes it to the outsiders by giving "Berliners a voice in shaping [its] external representations" (Colomb and Kalandides, 2010, p. 187). Storytelling can increase the willingness of place stakeholders to be part of, and contribute to, the place branding process if they relate to the stories being promoted and/or to the storytellers (Warren and Dinnie, 2018). On the other hand, 'selective storytelling' that lacks an internal and collective focus can commercialise place and strip it of its key cultural aspects (González and Lester, 2018; Kavaratzis and Ashworth, 2015).

Place stakeholders are more than ever in control of supporting, repressing, and changing place narratives (Cheong and Miller, 2000). Even more so online, storytelling has been shown to promote participation and interaction via social media platforms (online sharing and hashtags) (Kotsi et al., 2018). Residents as storytellers are empowering their communities by giving them voices and reconciling differences through individual or collective stories and shared experiences of place (Hudak and Valley, 2019). Despite this, the role of residents as storytellers in the co-creation of place brands is yet to be further examined in place branding research and is under-utilised in practice.

Co-destructors

Both co-creation and co-destruction of value have been referred to in marketing theory and practice in the context of service encounters associated with Interactive Value Formation (IVF) (Echeverri and Skålén, 2011; Laud et al., 2019; Makkonen and Olkkonen, 2017). An IVF framework manifests in one of three outcomes: co-creation, co-destruction, or no-creation (Makkonen and Olkkonen, 2017). In services marketing, co-destruction has been associated with customers seeking revenge through online engagement with brands as a consequence of bad experiences with customer service (Zhang et al., 2018). In tourism studies, co-destruction has also been related to IVF in which tourists have complained on social media about services provided by airlines (Dolan et al., 2019). The song 'United Breaks Guitars', which went viral globally with over 20 million views after the airline passenger whose guitar was broken in transit posted it on YouTube, is just one case in point: in a broadly interconnected world, consumer/user 'revenge' or even simple 'complaining' can mean entirely different things today as compared to earlier times. In the place branding context, then, co-destruction can be conceptualised as behaviour and actions of residents and other publics and organisations that contribute to diminishing the value of a place's identity, image, and/or brand.

Co-destruction is mainly discussed in services marketing but is considered to be an overlooked concept in the broader marketing literature. Notwithstanding the evidence that supports the value added from co-creative and collaborative place branding processes, there is limited research to uncover potential negative or 'destructive' outcomes for places. Yet while most studies describe co-creation as a 'value formation process' (Laud et al., 2019), a few suggest that it can have detrimental effects by co-destructing the place brand (Echeverri and Skålén, 2011; Vallaster et al., 2018).

Laud et al. (2019) suggest that IVF can benefit the brand when brand practices between the providers and the customers are done congruently, leading to value co-creation. Conversely, when these practices are incongruent, they lead to value co-destruction, which is also referred to as "value co-contamination" by Williams et al. (2016). These authors further suggest that negative outcomes of co-creation occur when collaborators fail to cooperate "*as equal partners*" (p. 708, emphasis added).

Consulting with residents in place branding activities is recognised as a way to "avoid the pitfall of developing 'artificial' brands" (Kavaratzis, 2012, p. 12). As a matter of fact, residents who fear that their place can lose its authenticity in the process of branding can be more supportive only if they are involved in conversations and decisions around place brand initiatives. Capitanio (2018) suggests that residents' participation builds civic capital by reinforcing local values which make the place less liable for controversies and oppositions.

When residents are *not* involved in the official branding activities to communicate or develop the place brand, they may create bottom-up initiatives to oppose the authorities, becoming rather *co-destructors* of the place brand. This co-destruction was evident in the first attempt of the 'I AMsterdam' brand campaign when a group of residents created the 'I AMsterdamned' counter-branding campaign opposing the city's sole focus on attracting investment (Braun et al., 2013). Novy and Mayer (2010) associate this counter-branding campaign with "urban revanchism" or the "culture of control", and noted that it encouraged locals to claim the "right to the city", but regardless of how one may discuss it the reality was that it reflected dissatisfaction and dissent among a noteworthy proportion of residents.

The need for place marketing activities that embrace the residents' perceptions about place is evident in Shafranskaya and Potapov's (2014) study of the Russian town of Perm. The town's unsuccessful branding campaign was mainly attributed to its failure to represent and communicate a credible place image which would meet the needs of the local community, and resulted in residents rebelling against their town brand. As further emphasised by Shafranskaya and Potapov (2014), city branding is an outcome of city quality and "the integral ability to satisfy residents' needs" (p. 128). In fact, residents can "make or break the whole place branding effort" (Braun et al., 2013, p. 23). Vallaster et al. (2018) further associate the co-creation paradigm with the co-destruction of Munich, a town in what they called "refugee crisis". For cities in crisis, co-creation can lead to co-destruction and be a threat to place branding efforts when the promoted place messages contradict the residents' views of the city (Vallaster et al., 2018).

Furthermore, 'brand alienation' may occur and generate controversy when there is a disconnect or mismatch between the promoted brand and the local identity of place (Maiello and Pasquinelli, 2015). One example was the Inuksuk used as the logo of the 2010 Winter Olympic Games held in and near Vancouver in Canada. Inuksuks are iconic stone structures that resemble a human with extended arms, which are traditionally used as landmark directional markers throughout the Arctic tundra of Canada's far north and are considered culturally important symbols among Inuit residents in the area and other Canadians. The logo was rendered as a multi-coloured design and, as with all Olympics, it was meant to represent not just the city but also the country hosting the games. (The relevant Wikipedia (2020) entry provides handy information and images of the structure and links to the Olympics logo.) While generally considered successful, however, it also attracted opposition from Indigenous leaders (who objected to what they saw as the appropriation of a sacred community symbol for purposes unrelated to their culture), Indigenous communities near Vancouver (which felt that a local symbol, such as a Totem pole of the Haida people near the city, would have been more appropriate instead of one from the far away Arctic), non-Indigenous citizens (who wondered why an Indigenous symbol had been chosen to represent the entire country), and others. According to Black (2007), writing about the approved logo in advance of the games, it reflected the "commodified and shallow character of the symbolic representations that come to be associated with global games ... [which are] at best partial and caricatured" (p. 270).

In some cases, residents' co-destruction of the brand is not only attributed to disagreement with how the place brand is promoted but can also be related to the complexity of the place brand itself. On the one hand, basic branding principles make it clear that the more complex a brand is, the harder it is to communicate it effectively – and indeed there are many cases where very 'simple' messages, such as 'Coke adds life' in the product arena and 'I [heart] NY' in place marketing, have been enormously successful. However, working in the context of destination branding, Zenker et al. (2017) suggest that there can also be a misalignment between promotion of an oversimplified place image and the residents' wider knowledge and understanding of their place, leading to disagreements and even campaigns to revoke the brand.

Communication and/or Development of Place Brands

While residents' roles in place branding differ in their communicative or developmental nature, this distinction is not discussed in the literature. In fact, co-creation activities are mostly associated with the notion of 'participation' without a clear understanding of what participatory activities entail and how they impact the co-creation process. As referred to earlier in the introductory section, place stakeholders, in general, can contribute to place branding by engaging in developing and/or communicating the place brand, and the failure of place branding projects is due, in many instances, to the lack of coordination between the actual 'making' of the place brand and actively promoting it (Therkelsen et al., 2010).

Co-creating in a 'communicative' context refers to both the direct and indirect involvement of stakeholders in promoting the meaning of place, respectively in the context of brand advocate or WOM roles in creating brand meaning. As Merrilees et al. (2016) explain, "each resident stakeholder group contributes to creating their own meaning of the city brand by internalizing their specific city brand experience" (p. 7).

Co-creating in a developmental context refers to residents' active involvement in the brand building process (Braun et al., 2013; Kallstrom, 2016; Sazhina and Shafranskava, 2017; Kemp et al., 2012a). However, while engagement in specific consultancy branding projects is developmental in nature, residents who are consulted, to help, for instance, with the visual branding/logo of the place but not in the whole marketing strategy, are not 'actively' involved in the co-creation process (Casais and Monteiro, 2019). The authors further highlight that residents should engage at the early stages of the branding process and that their involvement should not be limited to only participating as consultants in designing the place logo.

Co-creating in communicative or developmental contexts requires a high level of involvement amongst place-brand makers. Hudson et al. (2017) regard co-creation as a process created through three components: recognition, engagement, and transformation. They highlight that active participation is challenging and ultimately transforms the city's unequal power relations, and further describe co-creation as 'superficial' when there is a 'participatory' culture in which people are invited to participate but not given actual control over the activities in which they participate.

This can be further explained by Arnstein's (1969) 'Ladder of Participation', which is of great value to anyone interested in citizens' local participation in the process of shaping their surroundings. The ladder highlights varying degrees of engagement, starting from a minimal level where locals are only informed about changes in place. At higher levels of the ladder, locals are invited to meetings with place authorities to discuss place changes. However, at this stage locals still have no actual power to ensure their views are implemented. As one climbs the ladder further, place authorities agree to 'share' planning activities with locals, and locals eventually achieve ever more decision-making powers over the development and implementation of programs to shape their surroundings. Based on this participation ladder, Arnstein's (1969) 'citizen power' level is achieved with higher participation that can better describe true co-creating in both the communication and development contexts.

RESIDENTS' CONTRIBUTION TO PLACE BRANDING: VALUE ADDED

Residents contribute to place branding, creating new place values or modifying existing ones. While place values are collectively co-created by place municipalities, residents, and local businesses, the residents are the ones who 'produce' these values and test the propositions created by the municipalities by filtering them through their own personal experiences and creating the 'value-in-use' (Kallstrom, 2016). The following sub-sections highlight the key ways through which residents can generate value for places.

Offering Competitive Advantage for Place Differentiation

In an increasingly dynamic global economy where locations compete intensely for investments, talent, tourism, and other inputs, the literature stresses that a place can distinguish itself through the unique culture, values, and characteristics of local people to help create an exclusive presence in their markets of interest.

Residents are in fact considered the 'essence' of place (Govers, 2011): they shape its image, and, when their unique characteristics are embedded in place marketing campaigns, offer it a distinctive character and competitive advantage (Braun et al., 2013). Freire (2009) notes that the perceived friendliness of residents, as an example, is one determining factor in the process of destination evaluation, and further suggests that "much of the place's image is likely to be created by stereotyping the 'typical' local people" (p. 420).

Closing the Gap Between Place Identity and Image

Here the literature suggests that residents' participation in the brand process can alleviate possible conflicts between the brand image promoted by place authorities and the actual identity of the place. As noted earlier, residents may engage in counter-branding against campaigns that do not acknowledge their values and needs, but rather impose an 'artificial' place identity (Capitanio, 2018). To cite another example, the residents of the city of Hamburg created contradictory place images to those promoted through marketing campaigns by the local authorities. While the latter promoted it as a 'city of the waterfront' with many cultural offerings, residents did not identify with the message, creating their own image which was consolidated in a 'Not in Our Name' protest campaign (Oehmke, 2010; Zenker and Bekmann, 2013).

Braun et al. (2013) suggest that the participation of residents is a top priority because their needs and values constitute the local identity of place. Govers (2011) proposes that place branding needs to be co-created with local people to include their preferences and avoid communication which can adversely impact the place brand and its reputation. Baxter et al. (2013) further emphasise that "place marketing strategies may be at risk if the competitive place identity and the place brand identity are unknowingly far removed from the identities held by residents" (p. 1085).

A study of twelve UK towns shows that there are gaps between the identities of the towns promoted by municipalities and the ones experienced by the various communities (Paganoni, 2012). Researchers believe that residents' involvement can be beneficial to diminish this gap (Govers, 2011), and there are numerous studies which suggest that residents can narrow this gap by participating in the policy making and governance of the place (Kangjuan et al., 2017; De Jong et al., 2019); urban planning activities (Hudson et al., 2017; Nyseth et al., 2019); and/or marketing and communication activities (Hereźniak, 2017; Casais and Monteiro, 2019; Rebelo et al., 2020).

Residents' involvement with their place brands leads to a more successful communication of its identity and image (Zenker and Petersen, 2014). They offer legitimisation to the place brand and its messages (Casais and Monteiro, 2019) and create a more sustainable and liveable portrayal of the place (Hereźniak, 2017). Residents further support the brand message transmitted and create their own positive messages of the place, but only if they identify themselves with it (Zenker and Petersen, 2014), by becoming "co-producers of the city's reality" (Hereźniak, 2017, p. 137).

Offering Credibility to the Place Brand

Research on urban planning, place management, and tourism suggests that residents can reinforce and add credibility to place brand messages (Lindstedt, 2015; Kangjuan et al., 2017; Uchinaka et al., 2019). Following this lead, The Turku 2011 Foundation, part of the 'City of Culture' project in Finland, implemented a place branding strategy which created a link between local stakeholders and the municipality and incorporated the residents in the co-creation of the

Turku brand (Lindstedt, 2015). Through this foundation, local stakeholders were empowered to propose, discuss, and refine elements of the 'City of Culture' project. This strategy offered residents the chance to make their voice heard and contribute to the place brand, resulting in an increased credibility of the branding process and an overall successful promotion of the location.

Kangjuan et al.'s (2017) study of the 2010 Shanghai World Expo is yet another effort to examine residents' involvement in place promotion activities. Their findings suggest that if residents are involved in the management, policy making, and official promotion of place, the brand communication becomes more effective and credible, avoiding or at least reducing, mismatches or discrepancies in the messages promoted. Overall, residents tend to add credibility to locations by sharing positive recommendations and feedback on different social media platforms and websites, becoming the primary place brand marketers (Uchinaka et al., 2019).

Improving Destination Images and Creating Sustainable Place Brands

The attractiveness of locations is enhanced through residents who develop strong ties with their communities and participate in the promotion of a destination as part of the "place brand co-ownership" process (Vollero et al., 2017). In this sense, the crux of the issue is not merely how to get residents involved in place branding but how to get them first to identify with their place of residence. As discussed or alluded to in several of the studies mentioned earlier in the chapter, a strong positive place-based identity is a leverageable foundation to achieving place-branding objectives (many – often infamous – leaders throughout history have used this approach for nation-building purposes). Therefore, activities that can increase the relevance and resonance of 'place' among residents may not in themselves be sufficient but clearly are necessary bases to achieve place branding objectives.

The feeling of 'ownership' of a place is also linked with the sustainability of a place brand. Place brands become more sustainable if they involve residents in their branding and promotions (Gajdošík et al., 2018), and research suggests that when residents feel a sense of self-responsibility and ownership in helping to promote their places, they are more likely to engage in sharing positive images through, for example, WOM.

The sustainability of destination brands and residents' responsibility towards them is also discussed by Kemp et al. (2012b) in the long-standing idea of 'civic consciousness'. This emphasises that aligning marketing activities with residents' perceptions of the brand influences them to become committed to the branding effort and encourages them to become advocates or 'evangelists' of the brand which, in turn, strengthens the place's image. Overall, the more residents identify with the destination brand, the more they tend to become WOM advocates who spread positive messages to promote it.

CONCLUSION AND RECOMMENDATIONS

This chapter offers a critical overview of the state of research on residents' contribution to the co-creation process of place brands and their active roles in creating and disseminating authentic and realistic place experiences. The main themes in this discussion highlight the shift in power dynamics associated with residents' contribution to place brand co-creation and focus, more specifically on the key roles of residents in the process, the communicative and developmental nature of co-creation and the value co-created for places by residents' contribution to place branding. Taken together, all the points made so far outline key components as well as further opportunities for researchers and practitioners underlying the co-creation process to build, manage, and implement place brands that are inclusive as well as differentiated from their main competitors.

While residents are considered the 'social milieu' of place and a 'critical dimension' of the place brand (Braun et al., 2013), it is evident that they are more likely to become key supporters of their place brand if they are actively involved in creating it. It also becomes apparent that not all participatory actions involving place brands can be labelled as 'co-creation'. Simply, participation of residents in co-creating their place brands cannot be regarded as a mere formality. Active participation by residents can only be transformative for place brands if their ideas are encouraged and implementation is followed through by place authorities.

Residents take on different roles in building and presenting their place brands. Co-creators, brand ambassadors, storytellers, and co-destructors are key roles discussed in this chapter. While co-creation is mostly associated with positive stakeholder contributions, as represented by place brand advocates or ambassadors, residents' roles as storytellers (in which the positive value created for place brands depends on the narratives shared) or, conversely, as co-destructors of place brands, cannot be ignored. Such thoughts clearly suggest that further examination is needed of residents' collective actions that lead to either positive or negative and even destructive outcomes for places.

This chapter also looks into the nature of residents' co-creation of place brands by engaging in communication or development activities. The literature is not clear in explaining the different roles of residents in these two distinct place building activities. Further research can elucidate the nature of residents' roles in co-creating the place brand. Moreover, as mentioned earlier, the power dynamics in the co-creation process often are not balanced and residents are not given adequate control to actively contribute to shaping their place brand.

It is important, in practice, to implement well-balanced power dynamics that would allow place promotion agencies and authorities to contribute *together* with residents to the co-creation process, and to ascertain which kind of challenges arise and which would need to be overcome in order to co-create successful place brands.

Finally, based on the preceding review of the literature, there is scarce research that examines attitudes towards place brands created by place authorities as compared to those perceived by its residents. Therefore, there is also a need for more empirical studies to gauge residents' commitment to existing place brands by, among others, examining residents' attitudes towards existing place images created by place promotion authorities.

REFERENCES

Aitken, R. and Campelo, A. (2011). The four Rs of place branding. *Journal of Marketing Management, 27*(9–10), 913–933.

Arnstein, S.R. (1969). A ladder of citizen participation. *Journal of the American Planning Association, 35*(4), 216–224.

Ballantyne, D. and Aitken, R. (2007). Branding in B2B markets: insights from the service-dominant logic of marketing. *Journal of Business and Industrial Marketing, 22*(6), 363–371.

Baxter, J., Kerr, G. and Clarke, R.J. (2013). Brand orientation and the voices from within. *Journal of Marketing Management, 29*(9–10), 1079–1098.

Black, D. (2007). The symbolic politics of sport mega-events: 2010 in comparative perspective. *Politikon, 34*(3), 261–276.

Braun, E., Kavaratzis, M. and Zenker, S. (2013). My city–my brand: the different roles of residents in place branding. *Journal of Place Management and Development, 6*(1), 18–28.

Braun, E., Eshuis, J., Klijn, E. and Zenker, S. (2018). Improving place reputation: do an open place brand process and an identity–image match pay off? *Cities, 80*, 22–28.

Capitanio, M. (2018). Participatory place management in the age of shrinkage: the case of Kunitachi within Tokyo's peripheral areas. *Journal of Place Management and Development, 11*(4), 447–462.

Casais, B. and Monteiro, P. (2019). Residents' involvement in city brand co-creation and their perceptions of city brand identity: a case study in Porto. *Place Branding and Public Diplomacy, 15*(4), 229–237.

Cheong, S.M. and Miller, M.L. (2000). Power and tourism: a Foucauldian observation. *Annals of Tourism Research, 27*(2), 371–390.

Colomb, C. and Kalandides, A. (2010). The 'Be Berlin' campaign: old wine in new bottles or innovative form of participatory place branding? In G. Ashworth and M. Kavaratzis (eds), *Towards Effective Place Brand Management*, Cheltenham, UK and Northampton, MA, USA: Edward Elgar Publishing, pp. 173–190.

De Jong, M.D.T, Neulen, S. and Jansma, S.R. (2019). Citizens' intentions to participate in governmental co-creation initiatives: comparing three co-creation configurations. *Government Information Quarterly, 36*(3), 490–500.

De Nisco, A., Papadopoulos, N. and Elliot, S. (2017). From international travelling consumer to place ambassador: connecting place image to tourism satisfaction and post-visit intentions. *International Marketing Review, 34*(3), 425–443.

Dolan, R., Seo, Y. and Kemper, J. (2019). Complaining practices on social media in tourism: a value co-creation and co-destruction perspective. *Tourism Management, 73*, 35–45.

Echeverri, P. and Skålén, P. (2011). Co-creation and co-destruction: a practice-theory based study of interactive value formation. *Marketing Theory, 11*(3), 351–373.

Escalas, J.E. (2004). Narrative processing: building consumer connections to brands. *Journal of Consumer Psychology, 14*(1–2), 168–180.

Escalas, J.E. (2007). Self-referencing and persuasion: narrative transportation versus analytical elaboration. *Journal of Consumer Research, 33*(March), 421–429.

Fournier, S. (1998). Consumers and their brands: developing relationship theory in consumer research. *Journal of Consumer Research, 24*, 343–373.

Freire, J.R. (2009). 'Local people' a critical dimension for place brands. *Journal of Brand Management, 16*(7), 420–438.

Gajdošík, T., Gajdošíková, Z. and Stražanová, R. (2018). Residents' perception of sustainable tourism destination development – a destination governance issue. *Global Business & Finance Review, 23*(1), 24–35.

González, L.R. and Lester, L. (2018). 'All for one, one for all': communicative process of co-creation of place brands through inclusive and horizontal stakeholder collaborative networks. *Communication & Society, 31*(4), 59–78.

Govers, R. (2011). From place marketing to place branding and back. *Place Branding and Public Diplomacy, 7*(4), 227–231.

Hatch, M.J. and Schultz, M. (2010). Toward a theory of brand co-creation with implications for brand governance. *Journal of Brand Management, 17*(8), 590–604.

Hereźniak, M. (2017). Place branding and citizen involvement: participatory approach to building and managing city brands. *International Studies: Interdisciplinary Political and Cultural Journal (IS), 19*(1), 129–142.

Howard, D. and Kerin, R. (2013). A surname brand effect explanation for consumer brand preference and advocacy. *Journal of Product & Brand Management, 22*(5/6), 362–370.

Hudak, K.C. and Valley, P.S.L. (2019). Resident stories and digital storytelling for participatory place branding. *Place Branding and Public Diplomacy, 15*(2), 97–108.

Hudson, C., Sandberg, L. and Schmauch, U. (2017). The co-creation (of) culture? The case of Umeå, European Capital of Culture 2014. *European Planning Studies, 25*(9), 1538–1555.

Kallstrom, L. (2016). Rethinking the branding context for municipalities: from municipal dominance to resident dominance. *Scandinavian Journal of Public Administration, 20*(2), 77–95.

Kangjuan, L., Mosoni, G., Wang, M., Zheng, X. and Sun, Y. (2017). The image of the 2010 world expo: residents' perspective. *Engineering Economics, 28*(2), 207–214.

Kavaratzis, M. (2004). From city marketing to city branding: towards a theoretical framework for developing city brands. *Place Branding, 1*(1), 58–73.

Kavaratzis, M. (2012). From 'necessary evil' to necessity: stakeholders' involvement in place branding. *Journal of Place Management and Development, 5*(1), 7–19.

Kavaratzis, M. and Ashworth, G.J. (2015). Hijacking culture: the disconnection between place culture and place brands. *Town Planning Review, 86*(2), 155–176.

Kemp, E., Childers, C.Y. and Williams, K.H. (2012a). Place branding: creating self-brand connections and brand advocacy. *Journal of Product & Brand Management, 21*(7), 508–515.

Kemp, E., Williams, K.H. and Bordelon, B.M. (2012b). The impact of marketing on internal stakeholders in destination branding: the case of a musical city. *Journal of Vacation Marketing, 18*(2), 121–133.

Kotler, P., Burton, S., Deans, K., Linen, B. and Armstrong, G. (2013). *Marketing* (9th edn). China: Pearson Australia Group.

Kotsi, F., Balakrishnan, M.S., Michael, I. and Ramsoy, T.Z. (2018). Place branding: aligning multiple stakeholder perception of visual and auditory communication elements. *Journal of Destination Marketing & Management, 7*, 112–130.

Laud, G., Bove, L., Ranaweera, C., Leo, W.W.C., Sweeney, J. and Smith, S. (2019). Value co-destruction: a typology of resource misintegration manifestations. *Journal of Services Marketing, 33*(7), 866–889.

Laurence, D. (2018). Do ads that tell a story always perform better? The role of character identification and character type in storytelling ads. *International Journal of Research in Marketing, 35*, 289–304.

Lindstedt, J. (2015). A deliberately emergent strategy – a key to successful city branding. *Journal of Place Management and Development, 8*(2), 90–102.

Maiello, A. and Pasquinelli, C. (2015). Destruction or construction? A (counter) branding analysis of sport mega-events in Rio de Janeiro. *Cities, 48*, 116–124.

Makkonen, H. and Olkkonen, R. (2017). Interactive value formation in interorganizational relationships: dynamic interchange between value co-creation, no-creation, and co-destruction. *Marketing Theory, 17*(4), 517–535.

Merrilees, B., Miller, D. and Halliday, S.V. (2016). Brand-meaning co-creation by stakeholders: an interactive city brand. *Hertfordshire Business School Working Paper.*

Merz, M. and Vargo, S. (2009). The evolving brand logic: a service-dominant logic perspective. *Journal of Academy of Marketing Science, 37*(3), 328–344.

Molina, A., Fernández, A.C., Gómez, M. and Aranda, E. (2017). Differences in the city branding of European capitals based on online vs. offline sources of information. *Tourism Management, 58*, 28–39.

Novy, J. and Mayer, M. (2010). As 'just' as it gets? The European city in the 'Just City' discourse. In P. Marcuse, J. Connolly, J. Novy, I. Olivo and C. Potter (eds), *Searching for the Just City: Debates in Urban Theory and Practice*, Abingdon: Routledge, pp. 103–119.

Nyseth, T., Ringholm, T. and Agger, A. (2019). Innovative forms of citizen participation at the fringe of the formal planning system. *Urban Planning, 4*(1), 7–18.

Oehmke, P. (2010). Stadtentwicklung: Stadt der gespenster [City development: the city of ghosts]. *Der Spiegel, 1*, 94–98.

Paganoni, M.C. (2012). City branding and social inclusion in the glocal city. *Mobilities, 7*(1), 13–31.

Payne, A.F., Storbacka, K., Frow, P. and Knox, S. (2009). Co-creating brands: diagnosing and designing the relationship experience. *Journal of Business Research, 62*(3), 379–389.

Rebelo, C., Mehmood, A. and Marsden, T. (2020). Co-created visual narratives and inclusive place branding: a socially responsible approach to residents' participation and engagement. *Sustainability Science, 15*(2), 423–435.

Sazhina, A. and Shafranskaya, I. (2017). Residents' attitudes towards place marketing: tourism marketing focus. *Almatourism, 8*, 289–297.

Shafranskaya, I. and Potapov, D. (2014). An empirical study of consumer-based city brand equity from signalling theory perspective. *Place Branding and Public Diplomacy*, *10*(2), 117–131.

Tajfel, H. and Turner, J.C. (1986). *The Social Identity Theory of Intergroup Behavior*. In: S. Worchel and W.G. Austin (eds), *Psychology of Intergroup Relations*, Chicago, IL: Hall Publishers, pp. 7–24.

Therkelsen, A., Halkier, H. and Jensen, O.B. (2010). Branding Aalborg: building community or selling place? In G. Ashworth and M. Kavaratzis (eds), *Towards Effective Place Brand Management: Branding European Cities and Regions*, Cheltenham, UK and Northampton, MA, USA: Edward Elgar Publishing, pp. 136–155.

Uchinaka, S., Yoganathan, V. and Osburg, V. (2019). Classifying residents' roles as online place-ambassadors. *Tourism Management*, *71*, 137–150.

Vallaster, C. and von Wallpach, S. (2013). An online discursive inquiry into the social dynamics of multi-stakeholder brand meaning co-creation. *Journal of Business Research*, *66*(9), 1505–1515.

Vallaster, C., von Wallpach, S. and Zenker, S. (2018). The interplay between urban policies and grassroots city brand co-creation and co-destruction during the refugee crisis: insights from the city brand Munich (Germany). *Cities*, *80*, 53–60.

Vollero, A., Conte, F., Bottoni, G. and Siano, A. (2017). The influence of community factors on the engagement of residents in place promotion: empirical evidence from an Italian heritage site. *International Journal of Tourism Research*, *20*(1), 88–99.

Warren, G. and Dinnie, K. (2018). Cultural intermediaries in place branding: who are they and how do they construct legitimacy for their work and for themselves? *Tourism Management*, *66*, 302–314.

Wikipedia (2020). Inuksuk. https://en.wikipedia.org/wiki/Inuksuk, accessed 18 October 2020.

Williams, B.N., Kang, S. and Johnson, J. (2016). (Co)-contamination as the dark side of co-production: public value failures in co-production processes. *Public Management Review*, *18*(5), 692–717.

Zenker, S. and Beckmann, S.C. (2013). My place is not your place – different place brand knowledge by different target groups. *Journal of Place Management and Development*, *6*(1), 6–17.

Zenker, S. and Petersen, S. (2014). An integrative theoretical model for resident-city identification. *Environment & Planning A*, *46*(3), 715–728.

Zenker, S., Braun, E. and Peterson, S. (2017). Branding the destination versus the place: the effects of brand complexity and identification for residents and visitors. *Tourism Management*, *58*, 15–27.

Zhang, T., Lu, C., Torres, E. and Chen, P.J. (2018). Engaging customers in value co-creation or co-destruction online. *Journal of Services Marketing*, *32*(1), 57–69.

7. Peoplescapes and placemaking in a multicultural world: residents' identity, attachment, and belonging

Andrea Insch

INTRODUCTION

> Residential place continues to matter since people feel some sense of "being at home" in an increasingly turbulent world.
>
> (Savage et al., 2004, p. 12)

This chapter discusses the concepts of place identity and placemaking in the context of multicultural societies and explains how the philosophy and practice of placemaking can be applied to foster a sense of belonging and place attachment. Examples of placemaking are detailed and some of the common problems and challenges that can arise are described. Next, the prospects for placemaking in diverse urban communities are identified. To provide the necessary background for examining placemaking in a multicultural world, the chapter begins with an overview of the notion of varying levels of diversity in global cities, driven by the forces of globalisation and the global mobility and transnational connectivity of people.

URBAN COMMUNITIES IN A GLOBAL SOCIETY

The urbanisation of society is a trend that continues to shape life in the twenty-first century. By 2018, more than half the world's population resided in urban areas, with this proportion expected to reach 60 per cent by 2030 (United Nations, 2018). The continuing shift of people moving from rural to urban areas has been driven largely by migration alongside natural population growth, the creation of new urban areas, and the extension of existing ones (International Organization for Migration, 2015). Migrants are less likely to settle in rural locations, preferring urban areas, where their human capital is more highly rewarded (Duncan and Popp, 2017; Price and Benton-Short, 2007a).

Both domestic and international migrants are particularly attracted to cities classified as 'world' or 'global' due to their economic and social significance (Benton-Short et al., 2005; Friedmann, 1986). Specifically, it is estimated that 20 per cent of the world's international migrants live in just 20 global cities – Beijing, Berlin, Brussels, Buenos Aires, Chicago, Hong Kong SAR, China, London, Los Angeles, Madrid, Moscow, New York, Paris, Seoul, Shanghai, Singapore, Sydney, Tokyo, Toronto, Vienna, and Washington DC (Çağlar, 2014) – which are regarded as immigrant gateways. Many immigrants settle outside of these immigrant gateway cities in other global, non-gateway cities, in towns and rural areas (United Nations, 2018). On average, cities are home to about 3.5 per cent foreign-born residents, with some cities significantly exceeding the average. The share of population that is foreign born is 83 per cent in Dubai, 62 per cent in Brussels, 46 per cent in Toronto, and 37 per cent in London (International Organization for Migration, 2015). Overall, it is estimated that 19 per cent of the global population who are foreign-born reside in global cities (International Organization for Migration, 2015).

Auckland, New Zealand's largest city, outranks Los Angeles, Singapore, London, and New York in terms of the proportion of its foreign-born residents (Peacock, 2016). There has been a diversification of the source countries of the city's migrants, as well as a rising proportion of migrants that constitute the city's population, rising to 41.6 per cent in 2018 from 32 per cent in 2001 (Insch, 2018; Statistics New Zealand, 2018). The ethnicity of the city's migrants contrasts with the rest of the country: 46 per cent were born in Asia (compared to 38 per cent in 2001), 19 per cent in the Pacific Islands (versus 14 per cent), and 14 per cent in the UK and Ireland (versus 22 per cent) (Statistics New Zealand, 2018). Auckland is the largest Polynesian city in the world, with 15.5 per cent of the population self-identifying as belonging to a Pacific people's ethnic group (Statistics New Zealand, 2018). The city is also home to the largest urban population of indigenous Māori (McArthur, 2017) and to growing numbers of residents who identify themselves as Asian, at 28 per cent in 2018 compared to 14 per cent in 2001 (Statistics New Zealand, 2018). This aspect of diversity is visible through cultural events staged in the city including the annual Pasifika festival. Even though the aggregate picture of Auckland shows one of increasing ethnic diversity using these broad categories, this picture overlooks differential strata of diversity which are found at the local level, particularly at the level of individual suburbs (Singh, 2015).

As is clear from these statistics, this diversity questions outdated notions of ethnic composition which might otherwise be leveraged to fashion a place identity, and therefore is closely linked to, and affects, the central idea of peoplescapes and placemaking that lies at the core of this chapter. Developing a coherent and stable place-based identity is challenging when the character of its citizens is evolving and in constant flux: locals are key stakeholders in a place, and in those characterised by broad diversity various groups of residents may have yet to develop a strong sense of attachment and belongingness to where they live.

To evaluate and describe cities based on the magnitude, proportion, and diversity of their foreign-born residents, Benton-Short et al. (2005) developed the Urban Immigrant Index (UII). The rankings in this index show the prominence of cities in 'traditional settler societies' such as Australia and North America, as well as the rise in importance of European urban areas as destinations for immigrants.

Another way to understand global cities is through their role as potential gateway destinations for immigrants, which may range from hyper-diverse gateway cities to non-global gateways and bypassed cities (Price and Benton-Short, 2007b). Metropolitan areas in all three categories have a population greater than 1 million, but otherwise differ in their composition and status. 'Hyper-diverse gateways' have at least 9.5 per cent foreign-born inhabitants, have no single country of origin accounting for 25 per cent of their immigrant stock, receive immigrants from all regions, and are frequently cited in global cities literature as economically or politically important. 'Non-global gateways' also have at least 9.5 per cent foreign-born inhabitants, but are not hyper-diverse as the origin of immigrants is concentrated and they are generally overlooked in the relevant literature and not cited as significant global cities. In the third group, 'bypassed global cities' *are* frequently cited as politically and economically important but fewer than 3 per cent of their residents are foreign-born. Examples cited by Price and Benton-Short in 2007 that would still meet the classification criteria today, and would be likely to meet them in the foreseeable future, would include New York, London, Toronto, Sydney, and Amsterdam as hyper-diverse gateways, Las Vegas, Ottawa, Perth, Dubai, and Birmingham as non-global gateways, and Tokyo, Mexico City, Seoul, Cairo, and São Paulo as bypassed global cities.

Clearly, global cities are host to a wealth of diversity among residents, both short and long-term, natives and immigrants, and the latter both international and domestic in their origin. The increased fluidity of movement of people around the world is part of globalisation whereby economic activities have become both dispersed and centralised in an integrated global economy (Hu et al., 2013). Specifically, production and retailing activities have been dispersed, while specialised service functions and control of capital flows have become concentrated in a small number of global cities (Sassen, 1991[2001]), which have risen in standing as "pre-eminent cultural, political, economic and social centres, with emerging command and control characteristics" (Goerzen et al., 2013, p. 430).

Global cities perform a channel role for resource flows (e.g., human, capital, knowledge) around the world, particularly in their region (Beaverstock et al.,

2000). Thus, municipal governments and the firms that power their cities' economies are increasingly more influential than regional or national authorities in influencing migration flows (Duncan and Popp, 2017). On the other hand, local governments are tasked with the responsibilities of attracting and managing the experiences of migrants, as well as existing residents. As part of this responsibility, municipal authorities and other local actors must support migrants transitioning into their new urban environments in order to develop a sense of belonging and place attachment. The process of enabling the inclusion of new residents is often challenging given the increasing diversity of cities, or peoplescapes, as explained by Benton and Ahad (2019, p. 3): "newcomers are heterogeneous in their characteristics and needs, and host societies are hardly harmonious monoliths."

DIVERSITY IN URBAN COMMUNITIES

As discussed above, cities, especially global cities, are places where diversity exists (Insch, forthcoming) and can flourish. In addition to the term 'hyper-diversity', which refers to the variety of countries of origin of immigrants in global cities, the term 'superdiversity' has been coined to provide a more nuanced description of the multi-dimensional nature of diversity in some cities. Such dimensions include gender, religious affiliations and practices, linguistic differences, ethnicity, regional and local identities in places of origin, kinship, clan or tribal affiliation, political parties and movements, migration status and occupation (Vertovec, 2007). In order to make the city meaningful for diverse members of the community, the multiplicity of identities must be given a voice in the public sphere (Nicholls and Uitermark, 2016). According to Fosslien and Duffy (cited in Hoenigman Meyer, 2019, p. 1), "diversity is having a seat at the table, inclusion is having a voice, and belonging is having that voice be heard". To counter barriers to inclusion, in particular those that may affect the sense of place belongingness and identity that is the focus of this chapter, and to encourage community members to engage, individuals with responsibility for city governance "need organizational and discursive strategies that are designed to build voice, to foster a sense of common benefit, to develop confidence among disempowered groups, and to arbitrate when disputes arise" (Friedmann, 2010, p. 161).

BELONGING AND HOME

Community members, both newcomers and those with lengthier connections to a place, feel like valued, legitimate, and accepted community members through gaining a sense of belonging to a place. More broadly, the need to belong is innate and universal (Baumeister and Leary, 1995) and the physical environment, interactions with familiar strangers, and keeping an eye on neighbours can foster familiarity that may grow into a sense of belonging to the neighbourhood (Smets and Hellinga, 2014). This thinking is consistent with social identity theory (Tajfel and Turner, 1986) which refers to that portion of an individual's self-concept that is derived from perceived membership in a pertinent social group (for instance, when a city wins a major sports championship many citizens will bask in the glory even if they had nothing to do with the win).

According to Smets and Hellinga (2014), the concept of belonging is increasingly being applied in analysis in the social sciences. Some authors propose that the concept of belonging can be elaborated in ways which reflect its different aspects and applications. Fundamentally, belonging reflects a feeling of being at home, but the concept can be divided into its two elements: physical (*haven*) and social (*heaven*). A haven is typically a place where people feel safe and comfortable, whereas heaven refers to a place where people feel they can be themselves and are amongst lookalikes (Duyvendak, 2011). Similarly, being attached to a physical place and being attached to a place socially, even though connected, are distinguishable (Smets and Hellinga, 2014). A typical case where the two are linked is the relative anonymity of urban living, which may discourage a sense of community when compared to that achieved by residents of smaller settlements. Having people from multiple backgrounds living in close proximity further compounds the urban challenge by leading to the 'us and them' notions explained by social identity theory.

Understanding how the physical living environment influences people's sense of belonging tends to focus on users' experiences of a place including the design, furnishing, and use of the space (Powell and Rishbeth, 2012). The social attachments to a place that people develop are considered an ongoing process of identification and socialisation in situ. In this way, Savage et al. (2004, p. 12) conceive belonging as an embedded, socially constructed process whereby an individual assesses a place's appropriateness within the context of their "social trajectory and their position in other fields" (e.g., leisure and education).

Building on this notion of belonging, Savage et al. (2004), introduce *elective* belonging to explain how people choose the living environment that fits their identity and life stage and are not tied to a specific community. This refers to a process by which individuals seek to inhabit places inhabited with others that closely resemble themselves, akin to the saying 'birds of a feather flock together'. This has been demonstrated by research into the behaviour of middle class residents in a number of settings in the UK and the US (Watt, 2009). An example of this form of belonging is an informant, in a study by Arp Fallov et al. (2013), living in a village west of Aalborg, Denmark: he and his family chose to move to the village because of their close ties to neighbours as well as the symbolic value of the chosen neighbourhood.

The concept of belonging has also been expanded to include *selective* belonging (Watt, 2009) to describe the process by which individuals may not identify with the entire community, but selectively identify with specific members or sections of their neighbourhood, thereby creating "a gap between themselves and residents from other parts of the neighbourhood" (Smets and Hellinga, 2014, p. 82). Such individuals may attempt to create a bubble for themselves and those they feel comfortable with which seals them off from the perceived undesirable sections of the neighbourhood and members of the community (Atkinson and Flint, 2004). In turn, these neighbourhood places are "made through repeated everyday actions and interventions that work on both the neighbourhood and the individual" (Benson and Jackson, 2013, p. 794). For example, gentrifiers have moved out of suburban England, choosing specific properties in London that match their class status, while simultaneously ignoring and avoiding working-class 'others' who inhabit the locale (Butler, 2003) as well as specific parts of the physical environment of their neighbourhood where they feel uneasy.

Some studies have examined both aspects of place, the physical and the social, in fostering a sense of belonging. For example, Powell and Rishbeth (2012) examine how outdoor places can facilitate or deter migrants' responses to specific places, through their study of first-generation migrants in the English city of Sheffield. Through their analysis of 11 participants' narratives of their everyday walks in their neighbourhood, the authors discuss the importance of several factors that influence the strengthening of place attachment and sense of belonging in a superdiverse neighbourhood. These factors include the potential for social interactions with 'familiar strangers' as well as more familiar contacts, feeling secure and being able to move confidently in the new local environment, perceiving diversity of representation in the built environment, recognising transnational links through cultural activities, and the visual accessibility of social information in the local outdoor environment.

Migrants and refugees, including those compelled to travel to other countries to find safety and economic security, "enter into the challenging process of making 'home' (geographically) far from their original homeland" (Etemaddar et al., 2018, p. 424). They may face many challenges in creating home and settling in their new residence, while sustaining various strong attachments to their original homeland and thus the desire to experience 'moments of home' (Papadopoulos et al., 2017). This can potentially create tensions and the need for the maintenance of hybrid and negotiated cultural identities (Cassim et al., 2020; Cleveland and Xu, 2019; Powell and Rishbeth, 2012), which refer respectively to migrant individuals attached to two or more places and/or who expend effort to rationalise for themselves their choice of belongingness to their home origin, current place of residence, or a combination of these and potentially other places as well (as in the case of a migrant who marries a person from a third origin and develops a degree of attachment to that person's culture).

WHAT IS PLACE AND SENSE OF PLACE?

Place is an elusive concept as it "is both simple (and that is part of its appeal) and complicated" (Cresswell, 2011, p. 128): it is such a part of everyday life that its multiple meanings make its precise definition difficult. A similar challenge applies to the related concepts of sense of place, place attachment, identity, and belonging. Yet, these related concepts can assist to define the concept of place itself. At a basic level, places can be considered as locations "which people have made meaningful" (Cresswell, 2011, p. 132) and in turn have meaning and value for people.

Following the approach of Agnew (1987), Cresswell (2011) outlines three basic components of this meaning: (1) location; (2) locale; and (3) sense of place. The first component is perhaps self-explanatory and refers to the 'where' of place – often, but not always, a set of fixed and objective coordinates on planet Earth. The second component – locale – refers to the material setting for social interactions, and the third – sense of place – is the "subjective and emotional attachment people have to a place" (Cresswell, 2011, p. 133) that is gained through their experiences with the place. In addition to these three elements, places should also be characterised by reiterative social practices, inclusiveness, performability, and a dynamic quality (Cresswell, 2004; Friedmann, 2010). There are often barriers to achieving inclusiveness for those who inhabit and experience a particular place. Some people are excluded from participating in placemaking and become disengaged and even disempowered. In some cases, placemaking may even be seen as a vehicle for selectively redesigning and redefining the place design and its image, which excludes certain voices from being heard, thereby narrowly defining the identity of the urban community (Insch, forthcoming).

Further refining the above definition, Friedmann (2010, p. 154) views place as "a small, three-dimensional urban space that is cherished by the people who inhabit it". Following this definition, place takes a decidedly localised perspective which emphasises the urban neighbourhoods that people inhabit and their everyday interactions. One of the manifestations of the process of creating, maintaining, and contesting place is its naming, which happens at the local level. Like the physical environment which is modified through the actions and interactions of residents and local government officials such as planners, forms of formal and informal place identification such as naming places and the practices of urban branding are co-created through the interactions between local citizens, government officials, and usually those viewed as 'others' such as visitors, and tourists.

There are many instances where cities' names have been changed, particularly in the case of cities subject to colonisation. A case in point is cities in India which had been subject to British colonial rule. For example, Bangalore changed its name to Bengalūru in 2006, although use of the previous Anglicised version appears to be dominant around the world (Anon, 2006) – while on the other hand the change from Bombay to Mumbai seems to have been adopted much more widely. Researchers Stolz and Warnke (2016, p. 50) argue that in the naming and renaming of places, "decolonization does not affect all kinds of colonial toponyms to the same extent" and that it is necessary to comprehensively study the "socio-historic and cultural background of the multilingual societies" to understand how place names change in post-colonial nations (Stolz and Warnke, 2016, p. 52).

Likewise, the representation of place for commercial ends through urban branding strategies and campaigns aims to alter the image of a city, for example, to improve its status and reputation as a global city. In 2009 Brisbane, Australia, embarked on an aspirational strategy to reposition itself as one of the leading global cities in the Asia-Pacific (Insch and Bowden, 2016). Its campaign slogan, 'Brisbane: Australia's New World City', continues to use this re-positioning to promote it as a "thriving multicultural city and successful host of the 2014 G20 Leaders Summit" (Brisbane Marketing, 2017). This aspirational goal of local authorities may not reflect the actual experience of the city's residents since it is the encounters, interactions, and shared experiences of the place that create a shared understanding and endow it with value. In turn, individuals differ in their relationship with a place, as expressed through variations in place identity, attachment, and belonging, in addition to their sense of place. Decoding these concepts assists in understanding the conceptual underpinnings of placemaking and how individuals and groups can differ in their engagement and involvement in this process.

PLACE IDENTITY AND ATTACHMENT

Place identity is centred "on the psychological construct of identity and its relationship with social identity" (Uzzell et al., 2002, p. 29). Proshansky et al. (1983, p. 59) define the concept as a substructure of self-identity, which includes an individual's memories, ideas, feelings, attitudes, values, and preferences about the physical world in which they live. Developing a place identity occurs early in childhood through socialisation and continues throughout an individual's lifetime. In this way, it is a "dynamic, social product of the interaction of the capacities for memory, consciousness and organized construal" (Breakwell 2015, p. 190).

Breakwell's (2015) identity process theory was developed to explain what guides self-identity and, as a part of it, place identity. This theoretical framework has four principles: (1) self-esteem; (2) self-efficacy; (3) continuity over time; and (4) distinctiveness from others. The principle of self-esteem, which relates to the positive evaluation of oneself or with the group with which an individual identifies, suggests that living in a place might be a source of pride for a resident if it boosts their self-esteem. Self-efficacy relates to an individual's belief in their capabilities to meet situational demands and cope with changing circumstances. In the context of place identity, self-efficacy refers to the ways the environment is perceived to facilitate, or at least not to hinder, an individual's everyday lifestyle (Twigger-Ross and Uzzell, 1996). The third principle, continuity of the self-concept, is viewed as a key motive in guiding the formation and maintenance of identity and defining an individual's relationships with places. Individuals seek to ensure the continuity of their self-concept by living in a place that represents their values.

Disruption to the physical environment (e.g., flooding, demolition of homes) and associated social networks might threaten continuity of self, triggering residents to find another place to live (Twigger-Ross and Uzzell, 1996). Change can also be more gradual, such as the case where decisions to modify spatial plans lead to the influx of 'outsiders' (Dixon and Durrheim, 2000). Finally, establishing a sense of distinctiveness is important in the process of acquiring place identity, as individuals seek to identify with those with whom they perceive to share characteristics that are relatively rare and deemed positive in a particular context (Anton and Lawrence, 2014). For example, a resident of a particular neighbourhood or city might use their place identification (i.e., I live in Hackney or I am a Londoner) to differentiate themselves from others (Twigger-Ross and Uzzell, 1996).

Place attachment is considered as a process and an outcome of bonding oneself to an important place (Giuliani, 2003). Low and Altman (1992) define the concept as a psychological process that can develop through cognition and affect, which has been shown to be a prerequisite for attaining a sense of stability, balance, and good adjustment, as well as becoming involved in local activities in the community (Hay, 1998). Individuals might form emotional ties and close bonds with a place through the "steady accumulation of experience with a place" or, alternatively, this process can occur quickly in settings featuring "dramatic landscapes" and places where individuals have had "intense experiences" (Stedman et al., 2004, p. 582). Individuals who are attached to their local area tend to become involved in their local communities through participating in social and sporting clubs and organisations (Anton and Lawrence, 2014). Research has also demonstrated that the longer a person lives in a place, the stronger their place attachment becomes (Kienast et al., 2018).

To clarify understanding of the concept of place attachment, a framework was proposed by Scannell and Gifford (2010) that consists of three dimensions: (1) person – individual experiences in a place create meaning as well as the symbolic meanings of a place shared among a group (i.e., community or a cultural group); (2) process – affective (i.e., happiness, pride, and love), cognitive (i.e., memory, knowledge, schemas, and meaning) and behavioural components of the psychological process of place attachment (i.e., proximity-maintaining and reconstruction of place); and (3) place – characteristics of the place, both social (i.e., social area and social symbols) and physical (i.e., natural and built environment). As the authors note, this framework offers an integrative view of place attachment, which connects "the different types of bonds into a single overarching concept" (p. 7). The overlapping concepts of place identity and place attachment are vital to understanding why and how people form close bonds with places and how a place's symbolic qualities can hold important meaning for people (Insch and Walters, 2018).

This discussion of place and related concepts highlights that *people make a place* and are thus crucial to the process of *placemaking*. The notion of *peoplescape* can be seen as a bridge between the concepts of place and placemaking as people are a fundamental component of shaping the place and also a reflection of this process. In the biological sciences, the term 'peoplescape' has a broad meaning, referring to anthropogenic landscapes, which are complex systems with their own specific rules and feedbacks, where "humans are not only a beneficiary of ecosystem services, but a key influencer of ecosystem dynamics" (Renaud et al., 2018, p. 481).

In the fields of placemaking and tourism, Lew (2017) uses the terms 'peoplescape' and 'ethnoscape' in a more specific way, to refer to both tangible and intangible aspects of a city, including elements such as festivals and special events, street life and local dress, food and drink, types of shops and products for sale, formal and informal entertainment, shop advertisements, and aural and olfactory sensations. In the latter definition, people are an inherent part of the process of creating the socio-cultural artefacts that construct, and at times reconstruct, the place. Through greater involvement in this process, people can form stronger and more intimate bonds with the place, anchoring their attachment and including the place as part of their self-identity.

PLACEMAKING AND ITS ROLE IN URBAN COMMUNITIES

As stressed throughout the preceding discussion, placemaking is a fundamental human activity, which has occurred organically ever since human existence. Formalisation of the concept can be traced to the 1970s when place practitioners and academics (predominantly architects, urban planners, and urban designers) began to formalise ideas about how places can be shaped "to create meaningful experiences (in, of and for) people" (Hes et al., 2020, p. 2). The movement was, in part, a response to modernist architecture and design that was perceived to destroy local identities and focus more on form, rather than on how the public space is used (Hes et al., 2020; Nursey-Bray, 2020).

Figure 7.1 shows the popularity of 'placemaking', as a search term in Google Search on Google Trends. Part (a) of the figure shows the evolution of interest in the concept as a search term over the past 15 years. Part (b) shows the level of interest with regard to the geolocation (city) of Google Searches and illustrates that the highest relative number of searchers were located in two Australian cities – Melbourne and Sydney – followed by Singapore, London, and New York. These are all leading global cities (at least Alpha status in the Globalization and World Cities Research Network (2020) list) and the top three search source cities are located in the Asia-Pacific region.

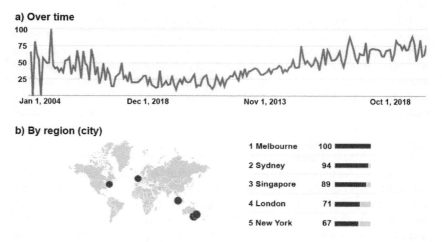

a) Over time

| Jan 1, 2004 | Dec 1, 2018 | Nov 1, 2013 | Oct 1, 2018 |

b) By region (city)

1 Melbourne	100
2 Sydney	94
3 Singapore	89
4 London	71
5 New York	67

Note: According to Google, the values are "calculated on a scale from 0 to 100, where 100 is the location with the most popularity as a fraction of total searches in that location, and a value of 50 indicates a location which is half as popular". A value of 0 indicates that there was not enough data for this term for the location in question. Further, "a higher value means a higher proportion of all queries, not a higher absolute query count" (Google, 2020).
Source: Google Trends, March 2020, https://www.google.com/trends.

Figure 7.1   Interest in 'placemaking' as a search term on Google

Placemaking is an ongoing social process through which individuals, and collectively, groups (including community organisations, government bodies, and companies) engage in actions that "build connection between spaces, people and environment" (Nursey-Bray, 2020, p. 305). Given such a broad conceptualisation of placemaking, it is not surprising that these practices can occur in myriad ways in specific neighbourhoods, communities, and cities. Thus, placemaking has generated much debate in recent years due to the diversity of its conceptualisation and applications.

Some scholars have been critical of placemaking's application in urban places due to the potential for some, or even the majority of, members of the community to be excluded from the process. In some cases placemaking quickly becomes place unmaking (Kalven, 2014) whereby the so-called transformation of a place destroys the place identity of its residents and their physical, social, and emotional connections or fails to achieve the intended results, thus leaving the city in a new situation that may be as bad as before but in a different way (several failed urban renewal projects in the US, UK, and other countries come to mind). Gentrification is a clear example of place unmaking as existing residents become displaced and disconnected from their neighbourhoods (Lew, 2017). Meanwhile, the character and unique identity of the place is irrevocably changed. Such negative consequences of place change can occur under the guise of placemaking when city authorities and other stakeholders place economic and urban development before social equity or ecological sustainability (Hes et al., 2020). Community members can be deliberately excluded from placemaking, thereby abetting their marginalisation and seclusion.

There are many examples around the world where the concept of placemaking has been hijacked to achieve the urban development goals of a select group of commercial interests and government agencies. In this regard, Fincher et al. (2016) are critical of some urban renewal projects in inner metropolitan and outer suburban Melbourne due to their lack of consideration or concern for social equity in the existing community. Placemaking was treated more as short-term revitalisation projects in these locales, and the initiatives that were perceived to achieve greater social equity were limited in scope, such as a small-scale public arts programme. Furthermore, recognition of cultural diversity in these neighbourhoods took more of a commercial leaning, based on the concept of 'cultural precincts' which focused on providing "limited small business assistance schemes and the smallest of re-designed public spaces" (p. 533). The purpose of placemaking was thus not on meeting the needs of the community, but in part to encourage outsiders to visit, spending their time and money in the local retail environment. To this end, local government managers approach placemaking with an eye to redesign the urban community as a place to consume, rather than a place to be (Fincher et al., 2016), or at best as a place in which to do business rather than to live (e.g., the EUR area in Rome, La Défense in Paris, and government-focused cities like Brasilia).

As well as being a vehicle for economic revitalisation and urban regeneration, placemaking is allied with place branding when reimaging and redesigning urban places. Belabas et al. (2020) examined the branding of two superdiverse Dutch cities, Amsterdam and Rotterdam, and argue that migration-related diversity is not taken seriously in either urban planning or city brand communications. Instead, this aspect of these cities' diversity has been depoliticised and reduced to notions of 'cosmopolitanism' and 'international', rather than valuing people's cultural and ethnic diversity. This is in contrast to cities including Barcelona, Leicester, and New York, which, to some extent, cherish their superdiversity and incorporate the needs of diverse communities in their spatial plans, streetscapes, and also in the ways that they collectively celebrate diversity such as through festivals and events (Hassen and Giovanardi, 2018), and communicate this to interested audiences through place branding (Walters and Insch, 2018).

The challenge that remains is how to represent diverse and superdiverse identities through city brands that are meaningful for residents as well as external audiences. Part of this process depends on "optimising the developmental priorities of places through inclusive participation and engagement" (Insch, 2011, p. 153) of community members, so that the change is not driven solely by economic development and marketing communications departments within local governments.

As well as the purpose or focus of placemaking, the manner in which it is executed can also overlook the needs of the community being given priority. One example of attempts at tactical placemaking (Lew, 2017) where the local community was not empowered in the process of reshaping a public space is a project in Dunedin, New Zealand. The project aimed to assess the pedestrianisation of the city's centre – the Octagon – through an initial trial and subsequent full trial entitled the 'Octagon Experience'. The purpose of the closure of streets surrounding the central hub was to evaluate its use if made more pedestrian-friendly. The trials coincided with several major events held in the city which attracted both tourists and residents. During the full trial over the summer months of 2020, and in the earlier partial trial in March 2018 (coinciding with three Ed Sheeran concerts), the public space in the Octagon was modified through the inclusion of temporary street furniture, surface treatments, plants, accent lighting, games, and street food vendors.

Figure 7.2 illustrates the design of the space intended to create a relaxing and family-friendly environment where people would feel comfortable. Reactions from residents, visitors, retail shop owners, tourist operators, and other members of the community were mixed. One of the major criticisms of the project related to the design and execution of the changes to the Octagon and how the local city council authority obtained input and responded to feedback from the public. Overall, there was a lack of agency given to members of the community directly affected by the changes. Some retailers located around the Octagon were concerned that the road closures negatively affected their sales during the trial and restricted some of their customers from travelling to their stores. A major concern for tourism operators and users of the space during the trial was the confusing signage intended to communicate the changes to the space, including 'No Entry' signs at entrance points (Stewart, 2020) and the amateurish redesign.

Figure 7.2   *'Octagon Experience' space design*

Another limitation of the trial was the manner of obtaining feedback, with an optional online survey and feedback form designed to elicit users' reactions. An evaluation of the trials by the city council conceded that, amongst other critiques and challenges:

> Communications and engagement with affected parties could have been better timed and executed with the full range of stakeholders identified from the beginning. Including stakeholders in more timely consultations about the future of the Octagon and the Central City Plan will be vital, as will be balancing the commercial and community interests. It should have started sooner and provided stakeholders with a genuine opportunity to provide input into what was being planned. (Dunedin City Council, 2020)

This was a major weakness of the placemaking process in this context and could have been much better managed and executed. In a similar spirit, the Project for Public Spaces explains that:

> A bike lane is not Placemaking; neither is a market, a hand-painted crosswalk, public art, a parklet, or a new development. Placemaking is not the end product, but a *means to an end*. It is the process by which a community defines its own priorities. This is something that government officials and self-proclaimed Placemakers ignore at their own peril (Project for Public Spaces, 2015).

There are also many examples of urban change that have successfully enabled the philosophy of placemaking, which is articulated in the often cited definition of the Project for Public Spaces (2007). The definition sees the term as referring to "a collaborative process by which we can shape our public realm in order to maximize shared value. More than just promoting better urban design, Placemaking facilitates creative patterns of use, paying particular attention to the physical, cultural, and social identities that define a place and support its ongoing evolution."

Friedmann (2010) describes several cases, in Japan, Canada, and China, where local placemaking efforts have been facilitated through the creation of autonomous neighbourhood institutions that directly engage and activate local residents. In another example of positive placemaking, Nursey-Bray (2020) explains that forms of art such as murals, graffiti, and public exhibitions are 'inherently participative' and thus have the capacity to engage the community as an effective mode of placemaking. Even though this creative placemaking is not devoid of critics, nor is it simple in its application; visual art is a tangible feature of the built environment that can capture attention and has the potential to critically engage with a place's history, memory, geography, and social inequalities.

Efforts involved in making places are everyone's business (Friedmann, 2010) and placemaking is a potentially powerful force for bringing positive change to communities when change takes place, to paraphrase the ubiquitous reference to democratic government, 'for people, by people'. Studies of the benefits of authentic placemaking for the community and its locale report that they are wide-ranging. Hes et al. (2020) divide the demonstrated benefits into three categories: (1) social; (2) ecological; and (3) economic. These three types of benefits are interrelated and many can be placed into more than one category and are listed in Table 7.1.

Table 7.1   *Reported benefits of placemaking in urban communities*

Social Benefits	Ecological Benefits	Economic Benefits
Engendering civic pride	Biodiversity	Increased footfall visitation and length of visit
Inclusiveness and social integration	Health, resilience, and ability to adapt	Reduced public expenditure
Reduced vandalism and crime	Reduced pollution and waste, including impact on – waterways, airways	Increased property value
Enhanced vitality and sociability	Reduced ecological vandalism	Improved economic outcomes – increased revenue, job creation, skill development
Improved social connectedness and sense of belonging	Reduced energy use	
Improved health and reduced depression	Increased participation of the community supporting ecosystem functions	
Fewer accidents	Reduced heat stress	
Improved educational outcomes	Adaptable use of building	
Improved general well-being and sense of place	Local exchange networks	

Source: Based on Carmona (2019) and Hes et al. (2020).

CONCLUSIONS

As Powell and Rishbeth (2012) argue, "the urban environment has a dual role to play in providing both a growing sense of familiarity and in providing diverse opportunities for a process of change: rootedness and transformation" (p. 82). These forces can be complementary but also contradictory, emerging as tensions for those involved in governing local authorities and for individuals negotiating their own place identity and sense of belonging in diverse neighbourhoods and cities. This chapter has identified that the trends of urbanisation and migration are driving changes in the composition of cities around the world. Some cities can be described as superdiverse, or if not, at least as multicultural and diverse. Despite the observed fluidity and mobility of people, there remains an innate human need for belonging – and allied with this requirement is the creation and maintenance of a sense of belonging to a place of residence, or, stated simply: a home.

As well as fostering a connection to the physical place, individuals must develop and grow their social and emotional connections in order to gain this sense of belonging, place identity, and attachment. Those involved in urban governance can apply the concepts and practices of placemaking as an ongoing process of building these interrelationships between people and place, in addition to the organic placemaking that takes place daily. As this chapter has explained, greater integration between different aspects of governing places is needed – most notably between citizen engagement, urban planning, and urban branding – in order to maximise the benefits for community members at the neighbourhood scale and to ensure that place change occurs in positive and equitable ways for the community, including underrepresented and oppressed groups.

REFERENCES

Agnew, J.A. (1987). *Place and Politics: The Geographical Mediation of State and Society*. Boston, MA, USA and London, UK: Allen and Unwin.

Anon. (2006). Leaders: goodbye, Bangalore; place names. *The Economist, 381*(8503), 16.

Anton, C.E. and Lawrence, C. (2014). Home is where the heart is: the effect of place of residence on place attachment and community participation. *Journal of Environmental Psychology, 40*, 451–461.

Arp Fallov, M., Jørgensen, A., and Knudsen, L.B. (2013). Mobile forms of belonging. *Mobilities, 8*(4), 467–486.

Atkinson, R. and Flint, J. (2004). Fortress UK? Gated communities, the spatial revolt of the elites and time–space trajectories of segregation. *Housing Studies, 19*(6), 875–892.

Baumeister, R.F. and Leary, M.R. (1995). The need to belong: desire for interpersonal attachments as a fundamental human motivation. *Psychological Bulletin, 117*(3), 497.

Beaverstock, J.V., Smith, R.G., Taylor, P.J., Walker, D.R.F. and Lorimer, H. (2000). Globalization and world cities: some measurement methodologies. *Applied Geography, 20*(1), 43–63.

Belabas, W., Eshuis, J. and Scholten, P. (2020). Re-imagining the city: branding migration-related diversity. *European Planning Studies*, 1–18. doi:10.1080/09654313.2019.1701290.

Benson, M. and Jackson, E. (2013). Place-making and place maintenance: performativity, place and belonging among the middle classes. *Sociology, 47*(4), 793–809.

Benton-Short, L., Price, M. and Friedman, S. (2005). Globalization from below: the ranking of global immigrant cities. *International Journal of Urban and Regional Research, 29*(4), 945–959.

Benton, M. and Ahad, A. (2019). *Breaking New Ground: Ten Ideas to Revamp Integration Policy in Europe*. Retrieved from: https://www.migrationpolicy.org/ research/ten-ideas-revamp-integration-policy-europe.

Breakwell, G. (2015). *Coping with Threatened Identities*. London: Psychology Press.

Brisbane Marketing (2017). Choose Brisbane. Retrieved from: http://www .choosebrisbane.com.au/contact-us?sc_lang=en-au.

Butler, T. (2003). Living in the bubble: gentrification and its 'others' in London. *Urban Studies*, *40*(12), 2469–86.

Çağlar, A. (2014). *Urban Migration Trends, Challenges and Opportunities*. Background paper for the *World Migration Report 2015: Migrants and Cities: New Partnerships to Manage Mobility*.

Carmona, M. (2019). Place value: place quality and its impact on health, social, economic and environmental outcomes. *Journal of Urban Design*, *24*(1), 1–48.

Cassim, S., Stolte, O. and Hodgetts, D. (2020). Migrants straddling the 'here' and 'there': explorations of habitus and hybrid identities among Sri Lankan migrants in New Zealand. *Journal of Community & Applied Social Psychology*, *30*(2), 185–198.

Cleveland, M. and Xu, C. (2019). Multifaceted acculturation in multiethnic settings. *Journal of Business Research*, *103*(10), 250–260.

Cresswell, T. (2004). *Place – A Short Introduction* (7th edn). Malden, MA: Blackwell.

Cresswell, T. (2011). Defining place. In M. Himley and A. Fitzsimmons (eds), *Critical Encounters with Texts: Finding a Place to Stand* (7th edn, Vol. 12). Boston, MA: Pearson, pp. 127–136.

Dixon, J. and Durrheim, K. (2000). Displacing place-identity: a discursive approach to locating self and other. *British Journal of Social Psychology*, *39*(1), 27–44.

Duncan, H. and Popp, I. (2017). Migrants and cities: stepping beyond World Migration Report 2015. In International Organization for Migration (ed.), *World Migration Report 2018*. Geneva: International Organization for Migration.

Dunedin City Council (2020). *Council Supplementary Agenda*. Dunedin: Dunedin City Council Retrieved from: https://infocouncil.dunedin.govt.nz/Open/2020/06/CNL _20200630_AGN_1313_AT_SUP.htm.

Duyvendak, J. (2011). *The Politics of Home: Belonging and Nostalgia in Europe and the United States*. Basingstoke: Palgrave Macmillan.

Etemaddar, M., Thyne, M. and Insch, A. (2018). A taste of home – choosing a destination wedding. *Anatolia*, *29*(3), 422–432.

Fincher, R., Pardy, M. and Shaw, K. (2016). Place-making or place-masking? The everyday political economy of 'making place'. *Planning Theory & Practice*, *17*(4), 516–536.

Friedmann, J. (1986). The world city hypothesis. *Development and Change*, *17*(1), 69–83.

Friedmann, J. (2010). Place and place-making in cities: a global perspective. *Planning Theory & Practice*, *11*(2), 149–165.

Giuliani, V. (2003). Theory of attachment and place attachment. In M. Bonnes, T. Lee and M. Bonaiuto (eds), *Psychological Theories for Environmental Issues*. Aldershot: Ashgate, pp. 137–170.

Globalization and World Cities Research Network (2020). The world according to GaWC 2020' (updated 21 August 2020). Retrieved from: https://www.lboro.ac.uk/ gawc/world2020t.html.

Goerzen, A., Asmussen, C.G. and Nielsen, B.B. (2013). Global cities and multinational enterprise location strategy. *Journal of International Business Studies*, *44*(5), 427–450.

Google (2020). Google Trends Explore. Retrieved from: https://trends.google.co.nz/trends/explore?date=all&q=placemaking.

Hassen, I. and Giovanardi, M. (2018). The difference of 'being diverse': city branding and multiculturalism in the 'Leicester Model'. *Cities, 80*(October), 45–52.

Hay, R. (1998). Sense of place in the developmental context. *Journal of Environmental Psychology, 18,* 5–29.

Hes, D., Mateo-Babiano, I. and Lee, G. (2020). Fundamentals of placemaking for the built environment: an introduction. In D. Hes and C. Hernandez-Santin (eds), *Placemaking Fundamentals for the Built Environment*. Singapore: Springer Singapore, pp. 1–13.

Hoenigman Meyer, E. (2019). What is diversity, inclusion and belonging? *Nasdaq.com,* 21 October. Retrieved from: https://www.nasdaq.com/articles/what-is-diversity-inclusion-and-belonging-2019-10-21.

Hu, R., Blakely, E.J. and Zhou, Y. (2013). Benchmarking the competitiveness of Australian global cities: Sydney and Melbourne in the global context. *Urban Policy and Research, 31*(4), 435–452.

Insch, A. (2011). Ethics of place making. *Place Branding and Public Diplomacy, 7*(3), 151–154.

Insch, A. (2018). Auckland, New Zealand's super city. *Cities, 100*(80), 38–44.

Insch, A. (forthcoming). Demystifying participation and engagement in the branding of urban places. In D. Medway, G. Warnaby and J. Byrom (eds), *A Research Agenda for Place Branding*. Cheltenham, UK and Northampton, MA, USA: Edward Elgar Publishing.

Insch, A. and Bowden, B. (2016). Possibilities and limits of brand repositioning for a second-ranked city: the case of Brisbane, Australia's 'New World City', 1979–2013. *Cities, 56*(July), 47–54.

Insch, A. and Walters, T. (2018). Challenging assumptions about residents' engagement with place branding. *Place Branding and Public Diplomacy, 14*(3), 152–162.

International Organization for Migration (2015). *World Migration Report 2015: Migrants and Cities: New Parnerships to Manage Mobility.*

Kalven, J. (2014). The unmaking of place. *Invisible Institute*. Retrieved from: https://invisible.institute/news/2014/unmaking-of-place.

Kienast, F., Buchecker, M. and Hunziker, M. (2018). Generating meaningful landscapes for globalized mobile societies: pushing an international research agenda. *Landscape Ecology, 33*(10), 1669–1677.

Lew, A.A. (2017). Tourism planning and place making: place-making or placemaking? *Tourism Geographies, 19*(3), 448–466.

Low, S.M. and Altman, I. (1992). Place attachment: a conceptual inquiry. In I. Altman and S.M. Low (eds), *Human Behavior and Environment*, New York, NY: Plenum Press, pp. 1–12.

McArthur, J. (2017). Auckland: rescaled governance and post-suburban politics. *Cities, 64,* 79–87.

Nicholls, W.J. and Uitermark, J. (2016). Migrant cities: place, power, and voice in the era of super diversity. *Journal of Ethnic and Migration Studies, 42*(6), 877–892.

Nursey-Bray, M. (2020). The ART of engagement placemaking for nature and people in cities. In D. Hes and C. Hernandez-Santin (eds), *Placemaking Fundamentals for the Built Environment*. Singapore: Springer Singapore, pp. 305–326.

Papadopoulos, N., El Banna, A. and Murphy, S.A. (2017). Old country passions: an international examination of country image, animosity, and affinity among ethnic consumers. *Journal of International Marketing, 25*(3), 61–82.

Peacock, A. (2016, 17 January). Auckland a melting pot – ranked world's fourth most cosmopolitan city. *Stuff*. Retrieved from: https://www.stuff.co.nz/auckland/ 75964986/auckland-a-melting-pot---ranked-worlds-fourth-most-cosmopolitan-city.

Powell, M. and Rishbeth, C. (2012). Flexibility in place and meanings of place by first generation migrants. *Tijdschrift voor Economische en Sociale Geografie*, *103*(1), 69–84.

Price, M. and Benton-Short, L. (2007a). Counting immigrants in cities across the globe. Retrieved from: www.migrationpolicy.org/article/counting-immigrants-cities -across-globe.

Price, M. and Benton-Short, L. (2007b). Immigrants and world cities: from the hyper-diverse to the bypassed. *GeoJournal*, *68*(2–3), 103.

Project for Public Spaces (2007). What is Placemaking? Retrieved from: https://www .pps.org/article/what-is-placemaking.

Project for Public Spaces (2015). Equitable placemaking: not the end, but the means. Project for Public Spaces website, 19 June. Retrieved from: https://www.pps.org/ article/equity-placemaking-gentrification.

Proshansky, H.M., Fabian, A.K. and Kaminoff, R. (1983). Place identity: physical world socialization of the self. *Journal of Environmental Psychology*, 3, 57–83.

Renaud, P.-C., de Oliveira Roque, F., de Souza, F.L., Pays, O., Laurent, F., Fritz, H. et al. (2018). Towards a meta-social-ecological system perspective: a response to Gounand et al. *Trends in Ecology & Evolution*, *33*(7), 481–482.

Sassen, S. (1991[2001]). *The Global City*. Princeton, NJ: Princeton University Press.

Savage, M., Bagnall, G. and Longhurst, B.J. (2004). *Globalization and Belonging*. London: Sage.

Scannell, L. and Gifford, R. (2010). Defining place attachment: a tripartite organizing framework. *Journal of Environmental Psychology*, *30*(1), 1–10.

Singh, H. (2015). People: how your neighbourhood will change by 2038, 8 November, *Insights, NZ Herald*. Retrieved from: https://insights.nzherald.co.nz/article/ aucklands-stratified-diversity/#!.

Smets, P. and Hellinga, A. (2014). Belonging and microsettings in a Rotterdam housing complex. In P. Watt and P. Smets (eds), *Mobilities and Neighbourhood Belonging in Cities and Suburbs*. London: Palgrave Macmillan, pp. 80–99.

Statistics New Zealand (2018). 2018 Census place summaries: Auckland Region. Retrieved from: https://www.stats.govt.nz/tools/2018-census-place-summaries/ auckland-region.

Stedman, R.C., Beckley, T., Wallace, S. and Ambard, M. (2004). A picture *and* 1000 words: using resident-employed photography to understand attachment to high amenity places. *Journal of Leisure Research*, *36*(4), 580–606.

Stewart, B. (2020). Lessons from Octagon Experience [Editorial]. *Otago Daily Times*. Retrieved from: https://www.odt.co.nz/opinion/editorial/lessons-octagon -experience.

Stolz, T. and Warnke, I.H. (2016). When places change their names and when they do not. Selected aspects of colonial and postcolonial toponymy in former French and Spanish colonies in West Africa – the cases of Saint Louis (Senegal) and the Western Sahara. *International Journal of the Sociology of Language*, *2016*(239), 29.

Tajfel, H. and Turner, J.C. (1986). The social identity theory of intergroup behavior. In S. Worchel and W. Austin (eds), *Psychology of Intergroup Relations*. Chicago, IL: Nelson Hall, pp. 7–24.

Twigger-Ross, C.L. and Uzzell, D. (1996). Place and identity processes. *Journal of Environmental Psychology*, *16*(3), 205–220.

United Nations (2018). *Sustainable Cities, Human Mobility and International Migration: Report of the Secretary-General.* New York, NY: United Nations Secretary-General. Retrieved from: https://digitallibrary.un.org/record/1472043/?ln =en.

Uzzell, D., Pol, E. and Badenas, D. (2002). Place identification, social cohesion, and environmental sustainability. *Environment and Behavior, 34*(1), 26–53.

Vertovec, S. (2007). Super-diversity and its implications. *Ethnic and Racial Studies, 30*(6), 1024–1054.

Walters, T. and Insch, A. (2018). How community event narratives contribute to place branding. *Journal of Place Management and Development, 11*(1), 130–144.

Watt, P. (2009). Living in an oasis: middle-class disaffiliation and selective belonging in an English suburb. *Environment and Planning A, 41*(12), 2874–2892.

8. The fabric of person–place–time: what metaphors from outer space can teach us in place branding

Mark Cleveland and Nicolas Papadopoulos

INNER SPACE AND OUTER SPACE METAPHORS: THE QUESTION OF SOCIAL IDENTITY

Recent images from the Hubble Space Telescope exposed planetary systems that have baffled astrophysicists, whose marketplace parallels have long fascinated brand managers. Instead of being bound by matter, experts in marketing, social psychology, and other related disciplines have surmised that, while often using different terms to describe them, the gravitational forces holding these systems together for humans are personal and social identities. And unlike most planetary systems which fall under the sway of an all-powerful star, the personal identity object at the center of the human system interacts with its social identity planets in a symbiotic relationship: exerting influence on, while being influenced by, the bodies that surround it. Upon closer scrutiny, most social identity planets are surrounded by dense networks of satellites comprised of products and brands. While some product-brand orbits are relatively stable, others are erratic.

Experts speculate that these wobbly orbits are not only due to perturbations caused by other social loci, but may also be caused by poorly understood ripples in *the fabric of the person–place–time*, perhaps from unspecified situational and consumption contexts. Seen from the surface of each planet, these product-brand satellites appear as gradually shifting consumption constellations.

Centuries ago, a paradigm shift in astronomy witnessed the geocentric model discarded and replaced with a heliocentric view of the solar system. The embrace of concepts like customer-based brand equity (Keller, 1993), the extended self (Belk, 1988), symbolic consumption (Schouten and McAlexander, 1995), and the material self (Bagozzi et al., 2020) testifies to an equivalent movement afoot in marketing, away from a company-centric viewpoint about brands toward one that is truly customer-centric. Brands do not choose their customers. Rather it is the customer that assigns meaning to places and things, and different people assign distinctive subjective meanings. The customer diagnoses and interprets the place-related cues put forth by marketers. Since these meanings evolve as the world changes and as the consumer progresses through life stages, they are temporally bounded. Furthermore, because social identities are malleable and sensitive to the situation, they are also contextually bounded. Understanding how consumers respond to spaces, products, and brands that explicitly or implicitly allude to a place or places requires probing *the fabric of person–place–time*.

This chapter focuses on the social identity side of place and its effects, and, more specifically, on the intersection of consumers' sense of themselves, which is in turn derived in part from place and how this informs their consumption constellations. A key premise in this discussion is that, instead of depicting consumer–brand relationships as relatively independent boxes organized along orthogonal axes, researchers and managers need to see these as complementary constellations arrayed in overlapping orbits, as depicted in Figure 8.1. Therefore, rather than geographic locales, products, and specific brands, we place the consumer at the center of the system (top of the figure). Using space analogies and planetary metaphors, our primary objective is to distill the discourse on social identities as they relate to product/brand dispositions and render this literature into less abstract forms that can be readily grasped. Given this social identity emphasis, we are concerned with the affective and normative effects of place. Sidestepping the fundamental but well-trodden road of cognitive place-based mechanisms – most notably, country-of-origin (COO) effects and the process of place branding – we deliberately avoid concentrating on brand images arising from places that are tangential to consumers' social identities.

This chapter also does not concern itself with those subcultures of consumption that are organized around non-place factors, such as consumer-brand tribes unrelated to place (e.g., Deadheads, the die-hard fans of The Grateful Dead rock group), or subcultures for which place is relevant but peripheral to the brand (e.g., Harley-Davidson motorcycles may be associated with American culture but what connects avid bikers to the brand is mostly the lifestyle it exemplifies), or educational, work, and vacation places – although the ideas expressed could readily be extended to social identities related to them. Finally, we do not go into detailed reviews and descriptions of each component of social identity, which are readily available in many other published works.

A sense of social identity rests on the existence of 'significant others'. Bringing balance to the social identity universe, there can be no ingroups without outgroups. Social identity is learned, not something bestowed by virtue of one's geographical coordinates. There are places, such as North

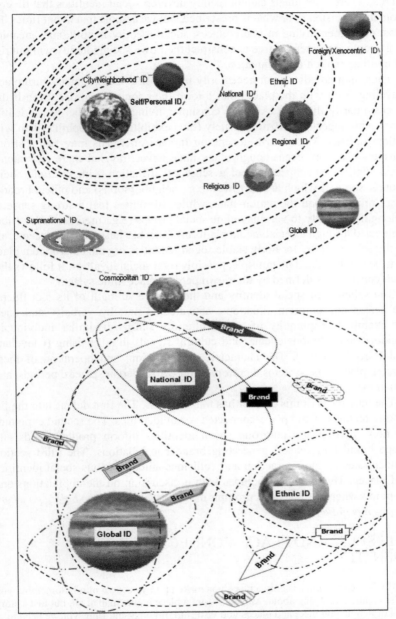

Figure 8.1   *Person–place–time system and consumption constellations example*

Korea, where individuals cannot readily develop social identities that diverge from the mainstream or what is prescribed, but we assume that in our times, for most consumers living in many places, social identity is volitional, meaning that people are generally free to construct their own social identity without risk of inviting explicit condemnation.

Thus, individuals do not necessarily require first-hand contact (birthplace, traveling, etc.) with the places that inform their social identities, even if this is customarily the case. An elite consumer living in Mumbai may identify more with upper-crust British society (thus exhibiting Anglophilia) than with fellow Indians. Most fourth-generation Italian-Americans may feel a strong kinship with Italy even though many have never traveled there and cannot speak Italian. Most people feel a sense of affiliation with multiple social groups, some of which are narrower (e.g., neighborhoods) and others broader (e.g., religion) than the nation-state, while still others feel a strong sense of belonging virtually to various online social groups (e.g., members of a 'tribe' connected through a social media platform). This has hastened the decentering of the self, whereby formerly stable social identities organized around a place or tribe are dislodged by multiple, possibly rival social loyalties. It follows that each consumer is defined by their own person–place–time system.

The salience of social identity and the relative strength of its loci fluctuate across consumption situations, activated in part by verbal/visual cues, for example, propinquity of other culturally similar/dissimilar individuals, holidays and religious events, and cultural signals in advertising (Cleveland and Bartsch, 2019a). The character, configuration, and operation of these person–place–time systems therefore differ across people, places, periods, and situations.

The remainder of this chapter has four sections. The first delves into the literature on the self and place-connected social identities. The second expounds on how ingroup and outgroup social identities inform product needs and shape brand preferences, generating brand constellations. The third section concentrates on the interaction and collisions among various social identities and places. The chapter concludes with a discussion on the applications and pinpoints where, as Star Trek prompts us, researchers need "*to boldly go where no one has gone before*".

THE SELF- AND PLACE-CONNECTED (SOCIAL) IDENTITY

Maybe your country is only a place you make up in your own mind. Something you dream about and sing about. Maybe it's not a place on the map at all, but just a story full of people you meet and places you visit, full of books and films you've been to ...

Hugo Hamilton (2003, p. 295)

Perhaps home is not a place but simply an irrevocable condition.
James Baldwin (1956, p. 88)

As these quotations indicate, consumers not only absorb meaning from places, they are active agents for developing and assigning meaning to them. Credited with coining the term *place identity*, Proshansky (1978) stressed that "there is no physical setting that is not also a social, cultural, and psychological setting" (p. 150). Encapsulating these ideas, researchers generally agree that places reflect symbols which people imbue with meaning that evolves through their continuing interactions with other people, the setting, and other life experiences. The meanings ascribed to different places represent manifestations of personal and social identity. Moreover, the subjective process of place creation also reinforces and shapes personal and social identity, which are used to distinguish ourselves and our groups from other persons and groups.

Social Identity

As our attachment to a place grows, so too does our level of identification with such places, which can involve larger scale entities (e.g., cities and nations) and smaller ones (e.g., neighborhoods or workplaces). Within environmental psychology, place identity has been defined as the person's "incorporation of place into the larger concept of self" (Hauge, 2007, p. 46), and has been characterized as a "pot-pourri of memories, conceptions, interpretations, ideas, and related feelings about specific physical settings, as well as types of settings" (Proshansky et al., 1983, p. 60). In marketing, place identity denotes "the congruency between a consumer's self-identity and a consumption setting" (Rosenbaum and Montoya, 2007, p. 207).

Social identity is a broader concept. It represents people's sense of who they are, based on their group membership(s). Social identity theory circumscribes the group in cognitive terms and deems identification, or self-categorization, to be the psychological instrument of group formation (Tajfel and Turner, 1986). Individuals assign other people to ingroups or outgroups, which may be regarded positively or negatively against a specific reference point. The membership groups that we belong to or might aspire to belong to ('us', or ingroups) are important sources of self-esteem and pride. Such feelings drive people to develop attitudes and engage in behaviors that favor their ingroup, possibly at the expense of others ('them', or outgroups) to which ingroup members will normally affix negative aspects.

Social identity is also a situational concept. Depending on the context, and whether other people are present, different social identity combinations will be central to a person's self-concept, whereas other parts will be dormant. This means that our thoughts and behaviors are more influenced by specific group membership(s) in some circumstances but not in others.

The general drive of consumers to comprehend who they are, and to connect with social category labels, brings forth a wide variety of identity-driven effects having copious practical relevancy. These include heightened sensitivity and attention to identity-related stimuli (Bartikowski and Cleveland, 2017), including attention paid to particular reference groups, behaviors consistent with one's identity (Peñaloza and Gilly, 1999), and focused attention toward autobiographical memories that are consistent with identity-relevant recollections (Reed et al., 2012). Adherence to social values, customs, and behaviors; responding to marketing communications imbued with ethnic icons and other forms of cultural symbolism; and consuming products embodying the particular cultural entity, all are mechanisms for reinforcing allegiance to and solidarity with a particular social group.

Like planets, social identities in the person–place–time system begin as abstract swirling disks of identity-laden particles that gradually accrete into more concrete senses of social awareness. Social identity develops throughout childhood, triggered by the contrasts that children make between their own community and others. This is bolstered by the socializing efforts of parents to infuse in their child feelings of kinship, and is shaped further by other agents of socialization (siblings and extended family members, peers, schools, religious entities, the mass media). A sense of group belongingness is crucial for the formation of a child's self-definition and lays the footing for absorbing cultural values and customs. The importance of social identity to self-esteem grows during adolescence, due to physiological maturation and changes in social expectations.

Social identity is unparalleled as the psychological locus of cultural effects. The delineation of cultures, however, does not always follow the hard edges demarcated by a place's borders. The notion of untainted, perpetual cultural groups is elusive. Intact and pure cultures exist only in the minds of certain people (except perhaps for some isolated tribes, for example in Brazil's Amazon region, that have not come in contact with the surrounding world). Delineating social identities within cultures is thorny due to layers of complexity. The diminished influence of authority figures, and the escalating opportunities to be exposed to outgroup cultures – facilitated by the mobility of people, products, and media across borders – incites some people to identify with several societies, and to procure, observe, or rebuff few or many features from each group (Papadopoulos et al., 2017). Other intricacies include the persistence of distinct regions, ethnic diasporas, religions, and tribes that coexist within or across countries; the cultural discrepancies across generations and other demographic cohorts; and the growing number of people with mixed ethnic heritage. Social identity is therefore best described as a summation of subtypes.

The Gravitational Pulls of Social Identity Planets on Products and Brands

Consumer goods "are a convenient means of storing the memories and feelings that attach to our sense of past" (Belk, 1988, p. 148). Serving as dramaturgical props, consumer objects are part of the extended self and are used by individuals for self-image, personal expression, and to signal solidarity with or apartness from a social group. Social identities are asserted through cultural rituals and by consuming symbolic goods. The projection of culture on consumption reflects the fact that a person's identity is wrapped up in their possessions, known by sociologists as the *Diderot effect* (Cleveland and Laroche, 2012).

As symbols, products and brands denote cultural complexity and transformation, particularly for consumers at the crossroads of cultural narratives. The *looking-glass self*, which is well known to marketing and psychology, refers to the notion that a part of our self-concept comes from our discernment of how we think others see us. Consequently, the meaning of consumer objects is not only the prerogative of the possessor but moreover their impression of how others will appraise these goods. The Veblenian concept of *conspicuous consumption* describes concrete tactics used by consumers for identity signaling and places within social networks. Shrum et al. (2013) differentiated three identity construction motives that are realized through "other signalling": *continuity* (identity-retainment efforts, e.g., purchasing brands from one's homeland and keeping objects as nostalgic markers); *distinctiveness* (enacting rituals to signal distinction, e.g., immigrants wearing traditional attire); and *belonging* (fulfilling the need for affiliation, such as becoming a fan of a local sports team).

Place-related social identity effects are thus more pronounced in conspicuous product categories and for brands conveying a social signaling function. Luxuries, for example, are valued because they communicate social distinctions, wealth, and status, thus helping to uphold consumers' need for self-expression and yearnings for prestige among their peers. *Evaluation-apprehension theory* (Baumeister and Leary, 1995) suggests that consumers sensitive to ingroup norms will be more materialistic to help convey impressions of accomplishment to their ingroup. Similarly, ethnocentric consumers are likely to prefer domestic instead of foreign products to help satisfy their acquisitive needs while complying with ingroup cultural sensibilities and social norms with behaviors that are seen to support the domestic economy.

Consumption Constellations

Englis and Solomon (1996) pioneered describing consumer–brand relationships in cosmic terms, having introduced the concept of *consumption
constellations* to describe 'symbolically-based product complementarity' and
its role in shaping social identities. The ways that social identities and place
associations exert gravity on these constellations – the product/brand satellites
that orbit a given consumer's social identities – fall into the three well-known
components of attitude: cognition (beliefs); affect (feelings, like/dislike);
and conation (behavioral intent). *Cognitive* forces represent the most heavily
researched area, but arguably are perhaps the most peripheral to social identity.
These are connected to intrinsic product characteristics, such as parts, ingredients, and overall quality, and their effects are most felt in cases where a given
place has a strong linkage to a specific product category (Andéhn and L'Espoir
Decosta, 2016), such as the provenance of a wine brand from a protected origin
region.

Affect has a substantial influence on brand attitudes and purchase behavior.
Place is an image attribute that connects consumers, both independently
of and in connection with the products it is associated with, to emotional
benefits including social status, national/place pride, cultural identity, and
feelings of like/dislike of the product regardless of its technical characteristics.
Consumers' affective responses play a critical role in forming, evaluating, and
weighing their beliefs. These responses to explicit or inferred place cues may
encourage or hinder consideration of alternatives and the amount of information that is gathered for decision making.

Conation reflects 'intent to buy' (or not to buy), which draws both on
one's beliefs and affect and also includes one's social identity, which in turn
accounts for one's perception of how a particular behavior may or may not
conform to the social norms of relevant ingroups.

Thus an ethnocentric or nationalistic Canadian consumer may *believe* (cognition) that the taste of Budweiser beer is better, may *like* (affect) the product's
brand name and packaging, but may intend (conation) to become and remain
loyal to a competing domestic product, such as Moosehead beer, because
of a strong normative influence to conform to the social norms of his or her
ingroup that values a strong Canadian identity, harbors similar ethnocentric
views, and feels a close attachment to Canada.

Which brands get captured by a consumer's social identity gravitational
fields(s)? Consider the different advanced alien lifeforms showcased by
the popular Star Trek movies and TV series: Vulcans tend not to be overly
attached to products and brands, upholding an emotional distance; Klingons
tend to be antagonistic toward outgroup societies and their products and
brands; Borgs seek to assimilate alien societies; and Cardassians seek to

subjugate other societies and to colonize their product/brand-scapes. On the other hand, The United Federation of Planets have as their mission "to boldly go where no man has gone before!", being inclined to explore new celestial bodies, much like cosmopolitan consumers who feel comfortable inhabiting multiple 'social identity planets' and revel in learning from novel outgroups and perhaps sharing some of their values.

The above discussion leads to the depiction of various constellations, both overlapping and independent from the point of view of identity, on the bottom of Figure 8.1. Identity pulls brands toward consumers, but brands also exert gravity on each other. For example, binary (trinary, etc.) brands orbit around what NASA calls a 'barycentre', rotating around a common center of mass comprised of two or more identity planets. When a brand(s) becomes part of the consumer's self-concept it may wield influence on one or several identity poles. This is exemplified by such iconic brands as Harley-Davidson and Jeep, high-end brands like Burberry and Gucci, Gap and Tommy Hilfiger for casual apparel, and Apple's iPhone, which succeed in straddling one or more identities that may emphasize 'the national' (for consumers at the brand's place of origin), 'the foreign' (for those who feel a particular connection to a foreign country's products, such as Italian fashion), or 'the global' (consumers with an actual or aspirational global identity).

Ingroup Identity Planets and Gravitational Pulls

Ingroup social identity planets are arrayed along a micro–macro continuum, from the parochial and ethnic, to the global and beyond. The term 'ethnic' denotes any collection of individuals that assert a distinct identity, usually due to a mix of cultural factors including ancestry, history, language, physical features, and possibly religion. *Ethnic identity* is a multidimensional concept, representing the integration of ethnicity into a person's self-concept (Cleveland et al., 2011). It is self-defined and may evolve over time. Given its subjective nature, it is not interchangeable with 'objective' indicators like birthplace or race.

As the idea of the nation-state evolved, beginning in Europe in the 1700s, it led to bringing disparate regions and cities into overarching administrative units. In turn, this led to the formation of national cultures and identities that were constructed from some combination of truth and myth about the area's past (Cleveland and Bartsch, 2019b). Educational, political, religious, media, and other state institutions continue to be central ingredients for nation-building. Interestingly, globalization made trans-border flows easier, even leading to claims that "The World is Flat" (Friedman, 2005) – but while many of the trade liberalization initiatives succeeded and continue to fuel global interchanges, it also generated a considerable backlash that engendered nationalism and protectionism worldwide. As of now, therefore, consumers exist in a paradoxical state where trade and intercultural exchanges indeed create a quasi-global world, while at the personal level nationalism and such movements as 'buy local' are on the rise.

This paradox means that attempting to understand the psychological dispositions of consumers toward any product, whether an Australian bottle of wine bought by a resident of Amsterdam (a cross-national, 'product-from-a-place' issue) or a city government wanting to persuade local residents to adopt a particular initiative (a local, 'place-as-product' issue), was never easy but has recently become exceptionally hard. More than 30 consumer dispositions that have been studied to various degrees in marketing, ranging from ethnocentrism and patriotism to cosmopolitanism and worldmindedness, may interact with each other in complex constellations of consumer orientations whose implications and effects seem near-impossible to unravel (for an inventory and discussion of these dispositions, see Papadopoulos et al., 2018).

The satellites of ethnic and national identity planets are naturally disproportionately comprised of tribal and domestic brands, respectively. Research has shown that many consumers will prefer domestic brands even when they are more expensive, out of a belief that foreign brands are inferior, a desire to protect the national economy, the pride that comes with championing a domestically-produced brand, or to harness the domestic brand for signaling social identity. Religion spans ethnic, national, and other boundaries, is distinct from the respective geographically-rooted identities, and the extent to which individuals observe the tenets of their faith varies (Cleveland and Chang, 2009). Similarly to ethnic and national identities, therefore, religious consumers are liable to spurn global, foreign, or domestic products that are deemed to reflect values that are not in line with their faith (e.g., many Muslim immigrants in Western societies do not conform to Western manifestations in entertainment, food, and other elements of daily life, since these are considered to be improper in relation to their religion).

Consumers are all part of social communities that are considerably smaller than countries and even ethnic groups, and yet there is a paucity of research on local social identities connected to official and informal regions within and astride countries (e.g., Flanders, Texas, Pays-Basque, Kurdistan), cities (and their sports teams), neighborhoods (e.g., 'Quartier Latin' in Paris, 'le Plateau-Mont-Royal' in Montréal), or city blocks and buildings (e.g., 'Billionaire Row' and '15 Central Park West' in Manhattan). We know, from both research and practice, that some people identify themselves more as inhabitants of a particular city or region than of a country. Terms that have been developed to characterize residents' affections for their communities include 'insidedness' and 'rootedness' (Kyle and Chick, 2007), and there is some evidence that these connections are strongest when the residents are perceived as similar to one's self, i.e., "birds of a feather" (McPherson et al., 2001).

Overall, among other effects, the emergence of nation-states in the past and of globalization more recently have engendered feelings of cultural intrusions or economic vulnerability that have prompted many people to renew their commitment toward their local culture (howsoever they may define 'local'), to disdain external influences and associated media/marketing, and to abstain from products and brands 'from outside', even if these are judged to be better than local alternatives.

Gravitational Pulls of Supranational, Global, and Outgroup Planets

The forces of globalization have supplemented the gravitational pull wielded by countries, regions, cities, or towns. Flows of people, money, technology, media, and ideas across borders, coupled with the slackening of nation-state authority, have further led to a distortion of the traditional distinctions and distances between places and scales of identities rooted in place. Supranational identities (e.g., European) springing from historical factors and supranational social units (e.g., European Union) are real and credible, but until recently, rarely studied in marketing. A person may feel a greater kinship with people on the other side of the world than with those living on their own city block. Globalization may be fostering cultures and social identities that transcend national borders. It would be disingenuous to infer the imminent obsolescence of nations and national cultures; however, international marketers need to reconsider the prudence of overreliance upon this unit of analysis and analogous cultural typologies to formulate marketing strategies in this unparalleled period of intercultural mingling.

What planets lie beyond a global identity? One that helps bring harmony to the social identity constellation is cosmopolitanism. In contradistinction to the culturally-emulsifying forces of globalization, cosmopolitanism is indissolubly connected to the local and embraces local, national, and global identities simultaneously by interlacing cultural differences while upholding these dissimilarities. Able to overcome without extinguishing the gravitational pull of the parochial world, cosmopolitans value the variety and type of people with whom they intermingle and see status as bestowed by products from various domestic and international levels. Conversely, outgroup planets or, in our case, outgroup places and their products, may also exert a gravitational pull upon consumers who may feel detached or excluded from, or sense a mismatch with, the values of their ingroup, coupled with a felt connection with an outgroup(s) they like or even admire because of a perceived similarity with its values. Specific to consumption contexts, this can lead to 'xenophilic' or 'xenocentric' behaviors that, respectively, favor all foreign products or those from a specific foreign origin, even when comparable or superior domestic goods are available.

INTERFERENCE, COLLISIONS, AND RIPPLES ON IDENTITY–PLACE RELATIONSHIPS

As is clear from the above, social identities are critically important since they guide people's perceptions, priorities, and actions at any given moment. These identities interact heavily with brand/object place cues. A given social identity exerts a gravitational pull on products and brands that are well matched to the particular identity that is operational. The power of these gravitational waves is intensified when identity and place effects are in sync: the combination leads to a great amplitude (Figure 8.2) that represents a strengthening of brand origin effects. Conversely, when social identity and place effects are countervailing, this may offset these effects, and products that cease to resonate with the target consumers' social identities are spun out of orbit.

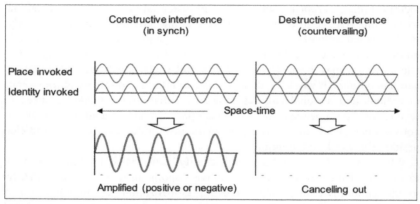

Figure 8.2   Constructive and destructive interference effects

Constructive and Destructive Interference

In physics, interference occurs when two waves superimpose to produce a subsequent wave of greater or lesser amplitude. Applying this to the fabric of person–place–time, *constructive interference* results when the operational social identity is congruent with the place evoked by brand cues associated with the consumption context. The resulting combined effect is greater in magnitude than either the social identity or place independently. Constructive interference can be positive or negative, and can be amplified, respectively, when the person is proud to identify with or feels animosity toward the place. For example, a Thai consumer may be doubly or triply proud of Thai Airlines, because of the brand's embodiment of local imagery (e.g., brand name, staff uniforms, logo, in-flight themes), the airline's global reputation for quality, and the country's positive image as a tourist destination (Winit et al., 2014). In this case, the effect invoked by identity is amplified by that invoked by place. Conversely, *destructive interference* ensues from countervailing social identity and place-evoked phenomena: a patriotic South Korean consumer may react favorably to Sony's well-earned reputation for quality but also unfavorably because it is a Japanese brand, in which case the positive effect elicited by the brand is canceled out by the negative effect of place.

Collisions in Person–Place–Time

The power of various social identity gravitational fields fluctuates across space and time. Like the planetary orbital paths in our solar system, the chances that places and identity positions are always perfectly aligned across protracted time periods (e.g., over the course of a consumer's lifespan) are vanishingly low. Consideration of the shifting orbits of these identity positions can provide a useful framework for understanding consumers' vacillating responses to various places, their peoples, and their products. Social identity collisions are not only possible but natural, resulting in one of at least four distinct – but not mutually exclusive – outcomes.

Emergence of subsidiary social identity positions

A subsidiary social identity is bounded to the gravitational pull of its larger counterpart (a sort of binary planet) – but like the tides caused by the earth's moon, it may emerge and exert an appreciable impact upon its larger cousin. A female Canadian with some Irish ethnic heritage living in Montréal in Canada's French-speaking Québec province may identify first and foremost as a *Québécoise* – but when traveling abroad as a *Canadienne française*, on Saint Patrick's Day as an *Irlandaise*, and during the Stanley Cup ice hockey games as a *pur et dur* (pure and hard) *Montréalaise* supporting the city's Montréal Canadiens team.

A related scenario describes a reciprocating equilibrium established between two or more social identities. China's *yin–yang balance theory* is a complex relational concept which holds that the universe is governed by sets of two opposing and complementary principles or cosmic forces that are observed in nature. *Optimal distinctiveness theory* (Brewer, 1993) is concerned with how individuals achieve homeostasis, or an optimum balance between two opposing motivational forces, which here could represent two or more social identities. Whether viewed from the standpoint of homeostasis or the cosmic duality of yin–yang, this tension stems from a consumer's desire to be inclusive with some social group (the need to assimilate) coupled with their psychological need to be exclusive (the need to differentiate).

Ethnic minorities have long experienced this tension, striving to maintain their uniqueness while integrating into the mainstream society where they live. With globalization and the emergence of global consumer culture (GCC), members of mainstream populations are now finding themselves buffeted by the gravitational pulls of competing social identity planets. The ethnically uniform social groupings and tribal identities of the past are being supplanted by culturally pluralistic civilizations. Some consumers may effortlessly switch between multiple social identities. For others, however, these interwoven identities are inseparable, converging or clashing depending on the setting.

Referring to the paradox we described above, globalization has warped the conventional disjunction between 'home' and 'away' but seems to have made localized forms of identity more important than ever, in large part because of the intensified opportunities for intercultural contact. Rather than swallowing and assimilating unique social identities (Cleveland and Bartsch, 2019a), consumers are concurrently becoming more alike while preserving or even augmenting what makes them culturally distinctive by drawing on local, foreign, and global cultural narratives. For example, researching Greenlandic immigrants to Denmark, Askegaard et al. (2005) revealed manifold and hybridized levels of social identity, including traditional Greenlandic, mainstream Danish, and an identity consistent with GCC, all of which were maintained and remain active through products and consumption rituals. Using products as props to negotiate and signal switching among multiple social identities, consumers shift between multiple brand constellations depending on the role being enacted or suitability to the situation. For instance, some notionally ethnocentric consumers may in fact favor foreign over domestic brands when the former come from countries enjoying a positive reputation in a given product category (e.g., German engineering and Japanese workmanship in the car sector), letting social identity take a backseat to utilitarian or hedonic considerations.

Dominance of principal identities

A dominant social identity may assimilate subordinate ones, as the debris from the latter coalesces into the former, or the subjugated social identity may even be hurled off into the farther reaches of place–time, the memory of it being suppressed.

In this context, *deterritorialization* has been articulated as one of the primary features of GCC, in that it promotes the worldwide dissemination of relatively homogenized consumption preferences. This is what Hannerz (1990) called worldwide "Coca-colonization", in which inter-group cultural differences would inexorably fade and be largely replaced by GCC. However, 'principal' or 'dominant' need not be defined, as in this case, as the global identity, reflecting the highest level of agglomeration in the local–global continuum. In fact, as indicated earlier, globalization brought about a backlash that seems to have strengthened identities defined at lower levels of the continuum.

As noted by Calhoun (2008, p. 429), "neither the interconnectedness [n]or the diversity of the world brings pleasure to everyone". The forces of globalization, while perhaps being welcomed in terms of reducing cross-country barriers and therefore enhancing one's spectrum of options concerning product, information, and other flows, at the same time drive many consumers to reinforce localized values and reiterate national and other restricted forms of identity. Indeed, one tenet of social identity theory is that when confronting complicated social environments, people have a tendency to search out and affiliate with the group with which they feel most at ease (Tajfel and Turner, 1986). Here, having more *options* from within a plethora of foreign goods that are now more widely available does not necessarily mean that all buyers will in fact elect to *buy* them: the perturbations of globalization generate gravitational pushes and pulls that in many cases favor local brands.

Factors ranging from perceived cultural sensitivity and responsiveness on the part of local/domestic products to pride from consuming them, and thereby supporting the national economy as well as one's cultural heritage, are arguably becoming more important for many consumers (Winit et al., 2014). Even within geographically smaller countries like Belgium, Austria, or Switzerland there exist many distinct consumer clusters of lifestyles and brand/product preferences that are not converging at the country level, let alone at continental and global levels. On the other hand, to cycle back to the concept of *deterritorialization* discussed just above, describing GCC as a 'North American' or 'Western' concept is both outdated and misleading. The planet's economic epicenter has been shifting, albeit gradually, from West to East and North to South, creating a globalized world that receives and appreciates a growing amount of inputs from Asia, Latin America, the Indian subcontinent, and Africa. Thus, the resurrection of nationalism and other place-based social identities is a rejoinder to globalization rather than a contradiction of GCC, and is transpiring partly because of GCC. This is akin, perhaps, to a notion with which cosmopolitan consumers are very familiar: embracing cultures and products from around the world, while at the same time including and valuing local ones (Cleveland and Bartsch, 2019b).

Annihilation of place-based social identities

Marginalization (Berry, 1997) may occur for individuals torn between several competing social identities, feeling 'neither here nor there' or identifying as 'neither fish nor fowl'. Consumer marginalization assumes that some people are rejecting or being shorn of territorially-based ethnic, national, or other identities. Researching marginalized rural-to-urban Turkish migrants, Üstüner and Holt (2007) recounted the stigma experienced by consumers that dwelled in the most economically-deprived neighborhoods. This stigmatization drained their ethnic pride, sapping this aspect of their social identity. The authors devised the term 'dominated consumer acculturation' to refer to the two-fold challenges faced by marginalized groups, in terms of their failure to acculturate to the mainstream society, along with being deprived of the solace that accompanies ethnic affili-ation. A subset of marginalized people may instead quench the human need for affiliation by aligning with the close-knit, like-minded, typically counter-culture communities (Kozinets and Handelman, 2004) that are often encouraged by social media.

Creolization

This fourth outcome is the least understood (Cleveland and Laroche, 2007) and, with only a few exceptions (e.g., Cayla and Eckhardt, 2008), is rarely researched. The term originated in the state of Louisiana, where it was (and is) applied to people who were born there, and has come to refer to a long-term process whereby two or more constituent social identity planets comingle and become fused, transmogrifying into a new, creolized social identity planet. In other words, being Creole ('créolité') refers to a new distinct identity planet and does not imply mixed cultural, ethnic, racial, or other origins. Creoles have a propensity to indigenize various aspects of GCC, and vice versa when GCC absorbs local cultural elements which are then re-exported (Cleveland and Bartsch, 2019b). This creolization outcome has parallels with the emergence and evolution of various cultures in the New World. Modern mainstream Mexican culture, fashioned mainly from Spanish and Indigenous elements and shaped over time by political, class, and economic circumstances, is a case in point: one of its sub-national cultures reflects a form of creolization by the Mexico-born descendants of the original Spanish set-tlers. These consumers form the bulk of the urban middle and upper classes in the country and typically exhibit a high degree of *malinchismo* – a disposition similar to xenophilia, which is commonly used as a pejorative by other classes because it favors 'all things foreign', including imported or foreign-owned products and brands, but also disdains 'things local'.

Ripples in Person–Place–Time

Unlike the stability exhibited by physical planetary systems, the fabric of person–place–time is regularly subjected to external shocks that upset the equilibria of the social identity planets and their orbiting product/brand constellations. The after-math of '9-11' showed how globalization can foster jingoism and xenophobia, ingroup sentiments that are ascendant when a given society perceives threats from beyond. Similarly, anger over France's unwillingness to participate in the 2003 invasion of Iraq led to attempts to rename 'French Fries' to 'Freedom Fries' in the United States, even though the product is believed to have originated in Belgium. More generally, elevated levels of ingroup psychological attachment can elicit a motivation to protect the ingroup from perceived external threats and express contempt for outgroups. In turn, this may lead, for example, to increased ethnocentrism, as a means of expressing ingroup pride when the domestic economy is thought to be in peril – especially on the part of consumers at risk of economic dislocation (e.g., due to outsourcing in manufacturing), who have an intrinsic, vested interest in promoting home country products and repudiating foreign goods (Cleveland et al., 2009).

A potentially positive ripple may take the form of brands, which may emerge in the future, that would be connected to out-worldly social identities. Already there are many brands that reference places beyond Earth, from Mars and Milky Way chocolate bars to Quasar electronics, Universal Pictures, Sirius XM radio, Samsung ('three stars' in Korean), and Subaru (the Pleiades star cluster in Japanese, as represented in their logo). The space-to-identity association is likely lost to most consumers who probably see the outer-space references (assuming they understand their meaning) as simple word plays (e.g., Milky Way is probably seen as referring to the milk chocolate rather than the namesake galaxy) – but with that said, true space–identity connections do exist, as in the case of a tiny proportion of extremely devoted fans who identify with being Star Trek's Klingons or Star Wars' Jedi Knights (Office for National Statistics, 2011).

QUANTUM GRAVITY AND DARK MATTER: OF BLIND SPOTS AND UNKNOWN UNKNOWNS

There are ... things we know we know ... [and] we know there are some things we do not know. But there are also unknown unknowns—the ones we don't know we don't know.
Donald Rumsfeld, former US Secretary of Defense (2002)

Researchers have radically advanced our understanding of the fabric of person–place–time. At the frontiers of knowledge, however, much remains tentative or poorly understood. The closing part of this chapter considers things that bind the person–place–time system together but that remain tentative ('known unknowns') or undiscovered ('unknown unknowns').

Physicists have long grappled with reconciling general relativity with quantum field theory, and, likewise, a grand, unifying theory of place-based effects has been elusive. Specialization – the bane of academia – is largely to blame, with research being undertaken principally in silos within individual disciplines and even individual subfields within them. Cross-fertilization has been deficient as a result, producing a disjointed, incomplete picture of the multiplicity and complexity of place-based effects whenever there is an intersection of people, places, and products.

There is still a relative void of knowledge about consumers' shifting, multifarious, and situational social identities, especially in the wake of globalization and the unprecedented flows of people, brands, and messages across borders. As social identity is highly sensitive to situational effects, it can be primed not only by the consumption context but also by cues embedded in the surroundings, including advertising or brand names: an ethnic Korean may not always think about his/ her ethnic identity when evaluating a Japanese brand, but should that identity be primed and salient, it could shift the Japanese brand from the consideration set to the inept (rejection) set.

Once a brand ceases to be relevant it will drift off, out of the consumer's mind-space. Brands that are deemed repellant to a cherished social identity are quickly hurtled out of one's consumption constellation. More work is needed to uncover strategies that will help steer brands that are inextricably intertwined to a given place-identity, in terms of maintaining relevancy as consumers' circumstances evolve. Research is needed to better understand what ruptures in the fabric of person–place–time lead to the jettisoning of once-cherished brands.

The measurement of multiple social identities remains controversial. The potency of social identity is a shorthand indicator for the degree to which the person has absorbed group values and abides with group norms, which in turn guide many consumer behaviors. However, similar to the 'observer effect' bedeviling physics (Scientific American, 1999), merely observing or otherwise measuring social identity (or gauging one particular social identity and not others) alters the state of what is being measured – for example, in terms of priming the consumer – thus distorting its relative influence.

There are several other known-unknown ripples in the fabric of person–place–time that beckon further research. To highlight just a few...

- How do social identities and dispositions evolve over a person's lifetime? How many layers of social identity are incorporated into one's self-concept at various stages? What levels of social identity are incorporated (and disincorporated) and in what sequence? Do these layers eventually merge or remain discrete?
- How do social identity layers combine to affect consumer behavior? For what consumption contexts are these combinations stable (and therefore, anticipated) versus shifting and unpredictable?
- As a counteraction to globalization, which consumers in what situations are prone to stronger identification with their ethnic/city/regional/national culture?
- How are consumers' place-connected identities affected by geopolitical and economic circumstances (e.g., 'buy domestic' campaigns, austerity, recessions) and catastrophic events (COVID-19, 9-11)?
- When and what types of people (e.g., generations) experience nostalgia for a previous social identity, as in the case of members of a subculture in Russia who are in thrall to nostalgia for the former Soviet Bloc era, or of Germany's 'Ossis' (contrasted with the 'Wessies') who are given to 'Ostalgie'?

- Is ethnocentrism among immigrants and minorities who coexist with mainstream society directed to the place of their ethnic ancestry or their adopted place?
- What role is played in consumers' social identities by the images they hold about other places' institutional systems, ethical values, regulatory codes, or legal standards?
- How do individuals resolve the tensions ensuing from simultaneously holding conflicting social identities?
- How do social identities combine with social class, gender-role identity, occupational identity, and personality, to inform consumer behavior, and to what extent are these combinations sensitive to time and place?
- What role do place-connected identities play in how consumers respond to brand extensions, rebranding, and repositioning?
- How do products/brands inform impressions about places for consumers with different combinations of social identities?

And last but not least, concerning 'unknown unknowns' ... As researchers and practitioners we need to humbly accept that, depending on the circumstances, there are likely explanations for person–place–time effects that we have not yet thought of and therefore we cannot specify. Epistemic advances, whether in the form of new conceptualizations, novel methodologies, or measurement improvements, are apt to generate *Eureka!* moments – but we will not get there unless and until we try.

CONCLUSIONS: 'WHEN THE STARS ALIGN'

> When the moon is in the Seventh House. And Jupiter aligns with Mars.
> "Aquarius/Let the Sunshine In", The 5th Dimension

Some scholars have questioned whether product–place associations will persist in the era of transnationalism, global supply chains, and the emergence of GCC (e.g., Miyoshi, 1993; Usunier, 2006). However, it has been clearly demonstrated that such questions have been asked and answered: even in cases when consumers may be unsure about the actual geographic *origin* of a particular brand, their perceptions of brand–place *associations* exert a powerful effect on their brand attitudes, evaluations, and intentions (Papadopoulos, 1993; Magnusson et al., 2011). Accordingly, it is not surprising that firms operating across borders are tempted to manage their customers' perceived origin associations through their branding and communication strategies.

Consumers' perceptions of brand ownership (local vs. foreign) can be confounded by other place aspects, such as the national origin of the retailer selling the good and/or the location of manufacturing, component sourcing, and scope of distribution. These can be managed by marketers in a variety of clever and effective ways, including product positioning, communication of value symbols in brand names and labeling, or appropriate advertising themes, cues, and spokespersons (such as the fictitious Juan Valdez and his trusty donkey for Colombian coffee or the rugged individualist Marlboro Man, or real persons like Catherine Deneuve for French cosmetics).

Perhaps more than ever, social identities are inextricably connected to places. Theorists and managers must recognize that location-related effects in marketing are the consequence of a polygamous marriage of the person–place–time system and the intricate ramifications examined in the preceding discussion along with the questions outlined in the previous section.

Leaving aside, for the moment, key cognitive considerations such as the reputation for excellence in precision manufacturing and technological innovation enjoyed by some places (e.g., Japan and California), the affective attributes conferred by climate and topography (e.g., Italy and Hawaii), or the beauty bestowed by art and architecture (e.g., Paris and New York), this chapter argues that social identities represent a critical *pull* factor governing consumers' product and brand preferences and therefore affecting virtually everything that places do, including the effectiveness, or lack of same, of efforts to brand themselves and to place-associate their product outputs.

Brands are valuable intangible assets to any organization, and therefore need to be judiciously managed. Brand managers peering into a telescope risk miscategorizing customers as segments that revolve around the brand. Instead, it is the brand, ancillary products related to it, and its competitors, each occupying a fraction of the consumer's mind-space, that are subject to the gravitational pulls of various social identities and therefore orbit around consumers as constellations. Seen from this micro perspective, brands are actually the segments, not the consumers or groups of consumers: the manager seeking to capitalize on social identities needs to understand 'how the stars align' and what tools can help bring about that alignment.

REFERENCES

Andéhn, M. and L'Espoir Decosta, P. (2016). The variable nature of country-to-brand association and its impact on the strength of the country-of-origin effect. *International Marketing Review, 33*(6), 851–866.

Askegaard, S., Arnould, E.J. and Kjeldgaard, D. (2005). Postassimilationist ethnic consumer research: qualifications and extensions. *Journal of Consumer Research, 32*(1), 160–170.

Bagozzi, R.P., Ruvio, A.A. and Xie, C. (2020). The material self. *International Journal of Research in Marketing, 37*(4), 661–677.

Baldwin, J. (1956, 2013). *Giovanni's Room*. London: Vintage-Penguin Random House.

Bartikowski, B. and Cleveland, M. (2017). 'Seeing is being': consumer culture and the positioning of premium cars in China. *Journal of Business Research, 77*, 195–202.

Baumeister, R.F. and Leary, M.R. (1995). The need to belong: desire for interpersonal attachments as a fundamental human motivation. *Psychological Bulletin, 117*(3), 497.

Belk, R.W. (1988). Possessions and the extended self. *Journal of Consumer Research, 15*(2), 139–168.

Berry, J.W. (1997). Immigration, acculturation, and adaptation. *Applied Psychology: An International Review, 46*(1), 5–68.

Brewer, M.B. (1993). Social identity, distinctiveness, and in-group homogeneity. *Social Cognition, 11*(1), 150–164.

Calhoun, C. (2008). Cosmopolitanism and nationalism. *Nations and Nationalism, 14*(3), 427–448.

Cayla, J. and Eckhardt, G.M. (2008). Asian brands and the shaping of a transnational imagined community. *Journal of Consumer Research, 35*(2), 216–230.

Cleveland, M. and Bartsch, F. (2019a). Global consumer culture: epistemology and ontology. *International Marketing Review, 36*(4), 556–580.

Cleveland, M. and Bartsch, F. (2019b). Epilogue on global consumer culture: epistemology and ontology. *International Marketing Review, 36*(4), 598–606.

Cleveland, M. and Chang, W. (2009). Migration and materialism: the roles of ethnic identity, religiosity, and generation. *Journal of Business Research, 62*(10), 963–971.

Cleveland, M. and Laroche, M. (2007). Acculturation to the global consumer culture: scale development and research paradigm. *Journal of Business Research, 60*(3), 249–259.

Cleveland, M. and Laroche, M. (2012). Becoming and being a cosmopolitan consumer. In: Melvin Prince (ed.), *Consumer Cosmopolitanism in the Age of Globalization*. New York, NY: Business Expert Press, pp. 51–100.

Cleveland, M., Laroche, M. and Papadopoulos, N. (2009). Cosmopolitanism, consumer ethnocentrism, and materialism: an eight-country study of antecedents and outcomes. *Journal of International Marketing, 17*(1), 116–146.

Cleveland, M., Papadopoulos, N. and Laroche, M. (2011). Identity, demographics, and consumer behaviors: international market segmentation across product categories. *International Marketing Review, 28*(3), 244–266.

Englis, B.G. and Solomon, M.R. (1996). Using consumption constellations to develop integrated communications strategies. *Journal of Business Research, 37*(3), 183–191.

Friedman, T.L. (2005). *The World is Flat: A Brief History of the Twenty-first Century*. New York, NY: Farrar, Straus and Giroux.

Hamilton, H. (2003). *The Speckled People*. London: Fourth Estate.

Hannerz, U. (1990). Cosmopolitans and locals in world culture. *Theory, Culture, and Society, 7*(2/3), 237–251.

Hauge, Å.L. (2007). Identity and place: a critical comparison of three identity theories. *Architectural Science Review, 50*(1), 44–51.

Keller, K.L. (1993). Conceptualizing, measuring, and managing customer-based brand equity. *Journal of Marketing, 57*(1), 1–22.

Kozinets, R.V. and Handelman, J.M. (2004). Adversaries of consumption: consumer movements, activism, and ideology. *Journal of Consumer Research, 31*(3), 691–704.

Kyle, G. and Chick, G. (2007). The social construction of a sense of place. *Leisure Sciences, 29*(3), 209–225.

Magnusson, P., Westjohn, S.A. and Zdravkovic, S. (2011). 'What? I thought Samsung was Japanese': accurate or not, perceived country of origin matters. *International Marketing Review, 28*(5), 454–472.

McPherson, M., Smith-Lovin, L. and Cook, J.M. (2001). Birds of a feather: homophily in social networks. *Annual Review of Sociology, 27*(1), 415–444.

Miyoshi, M. (1993). A borderless world? From colonialism to transnationalism and the decline of the nation-state. *Critical Inquiry, 19*(4), 726–751.

Office for National Statistics (2011). 2011 Census. Office for National Statistics, Government of the UK, accessed 1 June 2020 at http://www.statistics.gov.uk/census2001/profiles/rank/jedi.asp/.

Papadopoulos, N. (1993). What product and country images are and are not. In: N. Papadopoulos and L.A. Heslop (eds), *Product-Country Images: Impact and Role in International Marketing.* Binghampton, NY: The Haworth Press, pp. 1–38.

Papadopoulos, N., El Banna, A. and Murphy, S.A. (2017). Old country passions: an international examination of country image, animosity, and affinity among ethnic consumers. *Journal of International Marketing, 25*(3), 61–82.

Papadopoulos, N., Cleveland, M., Bartikowski, B. and Yaprak, A. (2018). Of countries, places and product/brand place associations: an inventory of dispositions and issues relating to place image and its effects. *Journal of Product & Brand Management, 27*(7), 735–753.

Peñaloza, L. and Gilly, M.C. (1999). Marketer acculturation: the changer and the changed. *Journal of Marketing, 63*(3), 84–104.

Proshanksy, H. (1978). The city and self-identity. *Environment and Behavior, 10*(2), 147–169.

Proshansky, H.M., Fabian, A.K. and Kaminoff, R. (1983). Place-identity: physical world socialization of the self. *Journal of Environmental Psychology, 3*(1), 57–83.

Reed, A., Forehand, M.R., Puntoni, S. and Warlop, L. (2012). Identity-based consumer behavior. *International Journal of Research in Marketing, 29*(4), 310–321.

Rosenbaum, M.S. and Montoya, D.Y. (2007). Am I welcome here? Exploring how ethnic consumers assess their place identity. *Journal of Business Research, 60*(3), 206–214.

Rumsfeld, D. (2002). News transcript: DoD news briefing, U.S. Department of Defense; accessed 20 May 2020 at http://archive.defense.gov/Transcripts/Transcript.aspx?TranscriptID=2636.

Schouten, J.W. and McAlexander, J.H. (1995). Subcultures of consumption: an ethnography of the new bikers. *Journal of Consumer Research, 22*(1), 43–61.

Scientific American (1999). What is the scientific principle stating that the measurement of any object affects that object – that is, that it is impossible to get a perfect measurement? Who came up with this idea, and can it be tested? *Scientific American.* Accessed 25 May 2020 at https://www.scientificamerican.com/article/what-is-the-scientific-pr/ .

Shrum, L.J., Wong, N., Arif, F., Chugani, S.K., Gunz, A., Lowrey, T.M., Nairn, A. et al. (2013). Reconceptualizing materialism as identity goal pursuits: functions, processes, and consequences. *Journal of Business Research, 66*(8), 1179–1185.

Tajfel, H. and Turner, J. (1986). The social identity theory of intergroup behavior. In: S. Worchel and W. Austin (eds), *Psychology of Intergroup Relations.* Chicago, IL: Nelson-Hall, pp. 7–24.

Üstüner, T. and Holt, D.B. (2007). Dominated consumer acculturation: the social construction of poor migrant women's consumer identity projects in a Turkish squatter. *Journal of Consumer Research, 34*(1) 41–56.

Usunier, J.-C. (2006). Relevance in business research: the case of country-of-origin research in marketing. *European Management Review, 3*(1), 60–73.

Winit, W., Gregory, G., Cleveland, M. and Verlegh, P. (2014). Global vs local brands: how home country bias and price differences impact brand evaluations. *International Marketing Review, 31*(2), 102–128.

PART III

'A place is worth a thousand words':
a smorgasbord of country images and effects

9. 'New perspectives welcome': a case for alternative approaches to country of origin effect research

Mikael Andéhn and Jean-Noël Patrick L'Espoir Decosta

INTRODUCTION

The country of origin effect (COO) is a well-researched genre within international marketing (Tan and Farley, 1987; Usunier, 2006), but the theoretical advances in understanding this phenomenon have not been proportional to the significant interest in better circumscribing and understanding it (Bloemer et al., 2009; Samiee, 2011). Yet the significant influence of country image on buyer behaviour has been documented and confirmed repeatedly in numerous studies, thus making the phenomenon of significant interest in both theory and practice.

Consequently, there is an immediate need for new perspectives on COO for the advancement of knowledge in this research stream, and there are numerous recent contributions towards this end. Andéhn and L'Espoir Decosta (2018) outline a range of research priorities that could potentially serve to address the tendency of COO research to be "atheoretical" (see Samiee, 2011) and provide new avenues for understanding COO, while also attempting to redefine the central tenets of this marketing phenomenon. Similarly, Papadopoulos et al. (2018) list a variety of "consumer dispositions" that, when taken together, form a typology of how place-images can influence consumer attitude formation, and by extrapolation, purchase decisions, adding to the foundation from which new knowledge about COO can emerge.

This chapter builds upon an integration of the objectives of these two studies and uses them as examples to propose alternative means to study COO, as well as to provide clarity on the virtues of these approaches.

Norms and Approaches in Country of Origin Research

In order to establish which approaches serve as 'alternatives' to the status quo, it is useful to identify what constitutes the norm of COO research. A cursory examination of the literature reveals that a work employing the term 'COO' to describe itself falls under the rubric of 'consumer behaviour' or 'consumer psychology' (Bilkey and Nes, 1982; Verlegh and Steenkamp, 1999). There is also a certain long-standing premise in COO research that has influenced the core assumptions put forth in studies to this day. For instance, while even early accounts of COO were arguably relatively open-ended, Dichter (1962) suggested that product origin may have an "influence on the acceptance and success of products" (p. 116) without proposing much in terms of *how* or *why* this would happen – essentially making no effort to uncover the premise of the effect. Later studies would, as a rule, construe a linear effect on product eval-uations and/or purchase intentions through cognitive, affective, or normative mechanisms (Verlegh and Steenkamp, 1999).

Although this is rarely stated explicitly in COO studies, the interpretation of COO as having a tangible effect on a continuous variable (such as attitude and/or purchase intention towards a product: Andéhn and L'Espoir Decosta, 2018) conforms to a research paradigm that is positivist and generally employs quantitative methods to produce generalizable findings (Burell and Morgan, 1979). However, well-established alternative approaches to COO, or consumer behaviour and social sciences in general, are also readily available. Following Burell and Morgan (1979), we move away from positivism to the opposite end of the epistemological spectrum towards the interpretivist or anti-positivist research tradition (Goulding, 1999). In consumer research, this tradition is largely dominated by what is known as 'Consumer Culture Theory' (Arnould and Thompson, 2005).

Norms and Approaches in Consumer Culture Theory Research

The premise of the Consumer Culture Theory (CCT) tradition is usually con-sidered to have originated with Veblen's (1899) classical 'theory of the leisure class'. However, in the more specific context of today's marketing scholarship, the premise has a clear lineage from Levy's (1959) argument that consump-tion can be understood as a symbolic enterprise in which "meaning as such" serves as the central constituent of consumer choices. While this proto-CCT scholarship to consumer research has resurfaced from time to time since then, it did not rise to prominence until the 1980s. The CCT label is currently fea-tured in hundreds of papers across nearly a dozen different marketing journals (Arnould and Thompson, 2005). A significant majority of these research contributions share two common characteristics that have to a certain extent become the calling card for the CCT approach to consumption.

First, they almost invariably draw upon, or relate to, the work of Pierre Bourdieu, specifically his opus 'La Distinction, critique sociale du jugement' (1979). This work laid out a theoretical account of capital that, while building upon Karl Marx's (1979) seminal discussion of the relationship between class and capital, rejected the latter's focus on purely economic factors and sought a more nuanced concept of capital by dividing it into three facets: economic, social and cultural. As such, Bourdieu (1979) provided a means of explaining aesthetic tastes as correlating to social classes, which is an obvious premise of most, if not all, consumption choices. Given this focus, it is hardly surprising that his work has been widely used in CCT scholarship. To date, some of the most influential works in this genre have examined topics such as the means of communal belonging (Muniz and O'Guinn, 2001), class relations, and the role of belongings to self-construal (Belk, 1988; Schouten, 1991), all through the lens of consumption in various guises.

The second commonality in CCT scholarship is an exclusive reliance on interpretivist epistemological methodologies that often employ research methods based on interviews or observations and feature some form of immersive consumer ethnography (see Arnould and Wallendorf, 1994). It is noteworthy that, while the number of scholars who identify as belonging to the CCT paradigm has been steadily rising, the moniker 'CCT' itself is something of a misnomer, as it "is not a unified, grand theory, nor does it aspire to such nomothetic claims. Rather, it refers to a family of theoretical perspectives that address the dynamic relationships between consumer actions, the marketplace, and cultural meanings" (Arnould and Thompson, 2005, p. 868). As discussed in this chapter, this orientation renders CCT a particularly powerful tool to meaningfully extend the application of COO research.

CONSUMER CULTURE THEORY AND COUNTRY OF ORIGIN

Extending COO research beyond consumer behaviour or consumer psychology paradigms, and venturing towards CCT and more interpretivist methods, can arguably address its two principal shortcomings. First, this extension will reach beyond the horizons of qualitative methodological approaches and studies that explore marketing phenomena but nonetheless employ positivist epistemological evaluation criteria (that is to say, how the results of a particular study apply beyond its own immediate context, or how a particular finding can be directly deployed to predict the outcome of a particular strategy in a general sense: Lincoln and Guba, 1985). The extended approach can therefore better generate theory through observation and the use of alternative conceptual tools to evaluate rigor and validity (Charmaz, 2006).

Second, the extension expands understanding of the consumption motivations beyond the traditional, continuous, linear, and quantifiable factors that are generally applied, such as purchase intentions or attitudes towards a specific product. This occurs by contextualizing consumption to particular instances, groups, situations or times. Here, the strength of the positivist paradigm to produce generalizable findings across populations and revealing – based on a series of assumptions – how COO influences consumers in general, and not just the particular group under study, also becomes its weakness. Consumption is fundamentally contextual. Consumer preference formation and choices are invariably influenced by a variety of factors (Agrawal and Kamakura, 1999) and do not necessarily align neatly with the conditions of studies claiming to predict consumer behaviour (Bilkey and Nes, 1982).

Rather than trying to resolve this problem, CCT scholarship accepts that strict generalization is not possible and does not strive to achieve it, which presents novel research opportunities. Imagine, for instance, the futility of approaching the work of Scott et al. (2017) with mere quantitative measures relating to the 'consumption' of highly painful experiences through terms such as 'utility' or through a generalized measurement of 'positive attitudes' towards pain as a decontextualized commodity. Similarly, try to imagine the results of an experimental approach to discerning consumers' rationales for preferences between automobiles at the very high and very low ends of a fuel efficiency scale, such as, respectively, a Hummer and a Prius. Then compare the potential findings of such studies to those of Luedicke et al. (2010), who examined and characterized the issue in terms of a broader moral framework of brand-mediated protagonism and antagonism. In our view, this comparison illustrates how the absence of any meaningful overlap in the format of findings speaks to the complementarity of CCT and positivist paradigms, and it is at this point we note that CCT has an underutilized potential to contribute to COO scholarship.

These two studies demonstrate that there are situations in which the positivist paradigm is ill-suited to provide a viable understanding of certain instances of consumption. They also show that there is often a readily identifiable way in which consumer psychology and CCT approaches can facilitate understanding of certain types of consumption in a complementary manner by providing a first step towards appreciating the potential of applying a CCT perspective to COO research. This premise aside, however, there is another reason that CCT is particularly well-poised to make valuable contributions to COO scholarship: the very nature of COO itself.

A central conceptual problem with COO research is evident in its label. COO does not apply exclusively to 'countries'; COO also deals with 'places'

(Van Ittersum et al., 2003) and does not deal strictly with 'origin', but rather with 'association' (Magnusson et al., 2011; Papadopoulos et al., 2018). Indeed, it has been suggested that COO might be more accurately labelled as the 'Place of Association Effect' (Papadopoulos, 1993; Andéhn, 2013, p. 11). This description may still be inadequate, however, as it suggests that the phenomenon can be captured in its entirety under the rubric of an 'effect', which in turn suggests a quasi-linear and quantifiable influence (Andéhn and L'Espoir Decosta, 2018). But even these conceptual 'repairs' to the COO research stream belie the abstraction of places as not only capable of housing meaning but equally capable of transferring meaning to any other conceivable object (including commodities, services, and brands).

As presented by Andéhn and L'Espoir Decosta (2018), there are two central theoretical accounts to explain how this particularity comes into being. The first is provided by Tuan (1977), who elucidates how place comes to be distinct from space through the process of meaning attribution. In this firmly phenomenological approach, the world is revealed to us as space, or 'empty' volume, to gradually become known (to us) as 'place' based on the meaning we attribute to it. The works of Casey (1993; 1997) also outline the relationship between place and object, drawing from Archytas of Tarentum, as 'implacement': a state of co-constitutional relationship in which "[e]verything is somewhere and in place" (Casey, 1993, p. 14).

Consequently, the 'place' draws from space by virtue of housing the object. Taken together, these two philosophical accounts of 'place' provide a firm basis for clarifying what COO entails at a fundamental level; that is, a symbiosis of meanings between place and object, which expands to the understanding and organization of both entities in a direct sense (Andéhn and L'Espoir Decosta, 2020).

Another key factor in furthering the understanding of COO in the context of implacement is to finally part with the notion that consumers respond to 'reality' over their own perceptions (of that reality). To Magnusson et al. (2011), perception topples reality when it comes to 'assigning' origin. If Samsung is perceived as Japanese, it is effectively Japanese for the purposes of COO regardless of where it originated (South Korea) and where it might be manufactured. This association is the critical component and is even variable by degree (Andéhn and L'Espoir Decosta, 2016). In other words, a particular object can be understood by consumers as 'more or less' connected to a particular place.

The potential for breaking from realist epistemologies becomes evident upon further examination of the mythological basis of place (Barthes, 1972). In fact, a diverse set of research traditions argues that 'place' does not strictly require a spatial correlate in order to operate as such (Gao et al., 2012). This is particularly palpable in the COO context. For example, every year millions of children receive gifts that they understand to have originated in Santa's workshop, a place with a highly tenuous relationship to the world in a spatial sense but with an acute mythological presence in Western culture. Perhaps the best way of understanding place as it applies to COO, that is, as place image (Elliot et al., 2011; Papadopoulos et al., 2018), is to concede that it is a 'mythologized' construct. As such, a place cannot be fully and directly experienced in the strictest sense as space can, because it resides exclusively in the realm of meaning, symbols, and mythologies (Casey, 1993).

MYTHOLOGIES IN CONSUMER CULTURE THEORY SCHOLARSHIP

By viewing places as mythological entities, their role within a greater mythology relating to consumption and commodities is clarified. According to Thompson, "[m]ythologies permeate consumer culture. Advertising and mass media freely draw from mythic archetypes and plotlines to create compelling stories, characters, and promotional appeals" (2004, p. 162). This opens up new avenues for understanding how place is employed as a mythological component, not only by consumers but also by marketers. Karababa and Ger (2010) essentially studied an implaced mythology (Ottoman coffee culture in Turkey), not of production but of *consumption*, by highlighting the practices surrounding a particular place–product match mediated by a particular cultural setting. In this example, there are clear venues to illustrate consumption practices of interest, but also to provide inspiration as to how history and culture can intersect and materialize at certain junctures to generate consumption practices. Similarly, there have been contributions drawing from the CCT tradition that have connected national myths with consumption in other ways, such as with Russian vodka (Kravets, 2012), or even implaced myths of political ideologies (Chatzidakis et al., 2012).

At this point, we have only scratched the surface of what can be learned through examining consumption to better understand what it means to be in the world. For example, phenomena such as cosmopolitanism or xenocentrism that have an obvious interrelation with COO can be studied effectively through consumer psychology and consumer behaviour paradigms (Cleveland and Laroche, 2012; Cleveland and Balakrishnan, 2019). However, these approaches are not well suited to capture variations of how these phenomena emerge across divergent contexts. Hence, the question of whether admiration of a particular place (in a particular context) that translates into a preference for certain products entails a form of xenocentrism. For instance, we might be considering Japanese bikers who admire a particular type of American motorcycle, perhaps devoting a significant amount of time and effort to this consumption practice, while they are completely disinterested in other foreign products. In reality, they are only interested in American products from a particular cultural setting and epoch (Porto da Rocha and Strehlau, 2020). In that sense, place and association between commodity and place are clearly the centre of interest and are relevant in the context of understanding international marketing. In fact, generalized measurements and the assignment of trait-like properties would not meaningfully contribute to theoretical development in such situations.

Not only are commodities implaced, but implacement itself is always relational, with meaning shifting as a system across places (Andéhn and L'Espoir Decosta, 2018). Consumers are also invariably situated, which has a profound effect on meaning as well. For instance, with globalization and the perennial streams of global migration, situatedness and places change, and commodities are re-implaced as the process unfolds (Peñaloza and Gilly, 1999). Just as acculturation is a determinant of migrant consumption (Luedicke, 2011), studying consumption practices can shed light on migrants' assimilation of a different culture, such as how migrants from Africa might creatively adopt 'Italianness' to construct a hybrid consumption pattern of their own (Domaneschi, 2018). The consumption patterns of large communities of migrants are not merely theoretical; they require their own market adaptations and invariably warp consumption in places where these changes happen (Peñaloza and Gilly, 1999).

Similarly, we may learn more about how practices such as yoga become transformed after being mythologically 're-implaced' several times over – from India to California and then reappropriated back to India (Askegaard and Eckhart, 2012). Culture is always in flux and constitutes the interface between a commodity's value and its meaning (Holt, 2002). The increasing speed with which information travels across the planet and the seemingly paradoxical convergence of cultures, with a pattern of adjusting cultural expression to one's own context, provide further justification for open-ended studies of how mythologies 'translate' across contexts and are manifested in consumption.

This logic applies to COO research as well. The process of mediating the meaning of a place can be further refined by examining the works of Papadopoulos et al. (2018) and others who have sought to nuance all of the dispositions and means of engagement to place (Strizhakova and Coulter, 2019), as well as their own relative implacement. The mediation itself is a culturally contingent amalgamation of factors that often takes unexpected forms and invariably disciplines and guides consumption practices. In a way, commodities are the manifestation of culture, which Appadurai (1986) termed 'material culture', and even culture is fundamentally anchored in place (Casey, 1993). The arrangement of things into a mediated state of 'implacement' can provide insights that are not readily available through traditional COO research methods. In other words, alternative approaches can account for and begin to rectify an inimical underestimation of the complexity residing at the intersection of place–commodity–culture.

The seminal works of Schooler (1965), Reierson (1967) and Nagashima (1970) served as the cradle of COO research. The American marketing approach to the phenomenon was exclusively teleological in the 1960s, looking to the end result instead of its causes and therefore reporting that consumers at that time perceived products from Asia and South America as bad, products from Europe as good, and products from North America as average. These relationships are organized in a hierarchy, formed by a rational, linear, and easily understandable logic: a country's level of development precipitates its ability (as a monolithic entity) to export products of either high or low quality. This state of affairs is not lost on consumers, who in their capacity as rational utility-maximizing agents evaluate and select products from countries with the 'best' possible image.

Abstraction of the relationships into a generalized hierarchy is a particularly significant problem relating to this perspective. An alternative way of understanding consumers' perceptions is to reject the idea of hierarchy in favour of a 'rhizomatic' network structure, which envisages a learning process that continuously self-replicates and does not have an identifiable beginning or end. This approach views globalization as increased interconnectedness or as a hyper-referential relationship among the meanings of different places and cultural expressions, rather than a tendency towards isomorphism.

The implications for COO research are clear. We are dealing with the discovery of principles relating to place–commodity dyads in general and findings that should be thought of as culturally contextualized and contingent. The most appropriate response to a rhizomatic characterization of global culture and place interrelation is an epistemic shift that is well-suited to the application of CCT, as it focuses on the contextual, the in-depth and the particular (Arnould and Thompson, 2005). Historically, CCT scholarship has effectively considered possible abstractions of the micro-scale ethnographic observations inherent in its methodological orientation, not shying away from more general theorizing (Firat and Venkatesh, 1995).

COUNTRY OF ORIGIN BEYOND INTERNATIONAL MARKETING

There is a dearth of research dedicated to critically deconstructing COO, and conspicuous examples of the omission of potential contributions stemming from the application of interpretivist methods. This is also true for COO research that aims to provide 'up-stream' theoretical advances to its 'genitor' disciplines of anthropology, sociology, and geography. This lacuna is particularly surprising given the longstanding position that "consumer research has a vital moral and political role to play" (Sherry, 2000, p. 278) and the fact that COO research intersects with politically charged issues such as public and cultural diplomacy (Szondi, 2007), trade relations in post-colonial contexts (ibid.), as well as imbalances between 'advanced' and 'developing' economies (Varman and Costa, 2013).

To date, few works examine these issues and relate them to COO in any way. Instead, critiques of COO have almost invariably dealt with the question of whether COO is a relevant factor in marketing (Usunier, 2006; Samiee et al., 2005), with certain exceptions. For instance, O'Shaughnessy and O'Shaughnessy (2000) discuss situations in which COO might apply from a more critical perspective, questioning the overly broad notion that geographical hierarchies can determine the quality of commodities. Similarly, Varman and Costa (2013) relate COO research to global trade and power imbalances, and Andéhn et al. (2020) explore the broader implications of COO as a form of place marketization with often unintended consequences.

There is potential beyond the foregoing studies to further explore COO outside the confines of the implicit fundamental premise of COO literature, which is how commodities can be more effectively marketed. Logical extensions would include building on COO research by contributing directly to its discourse (even in the same journals), as well as extending the study of marketing and consumption to their consequences, contingencies, and broader contexts, but within the boundaries of COO literature. However, simply adopting a CCT approach is insufficient to meet a challenge based on critiques that it is little more than instrumental marketing literature with a thinly disguised neoliberal ethos (Askegaard, 2014).

Indeed, critical researchers often view mainstream CCT as the study of the (frivolous) lifestyles and hobbies of the upper middle classes, without regard for their broader social, environmental, and economic consequences. Such critics believe that CCT serves to valorize such activities without critically and effectively deconstructing them. These attitudes notwithstanding, CCT can indeed fall victim to its unspoken premises and implicit ideologies. Over the years, these have inspired more critical approaches and perspectives that have not truly gained widespread acceptance in marketing as a discipline writ large, at least not to the extent they have in management and organization studies (Burton, 2001). This gap poses a challenge for the quality of marketing scholarship, and also limits opportunities for noteworthy contributions and reimagined approaches that might resolve theoretical stagnation and philosophical impasses.

For instance, the literature contains numerous allusions to the increasingly industrial logic of the production of space (Harvey, 2002). Highly influential works have furthered understanding of the growing prevalence of super-modernist 'nowheres' in our world, embodied in airport lounges and shopping malls (Relph, 1976). This raises a germane question: what is the equivalent of mass production of space for place? In other words, what is the nature of the topogenesis of late capitalism? Andéhn et al. (2020) outline how place meaning is increasingly generated for some commercial end, relating this process to performativity of self, which becomes contaminated by commercial tropes infused with places.

This explanation, however, merely scratches the surface of the overarching issue of the industrial production of place meaning. A relatable parallel may be the example of brand 'flagship' stores that integrate sensory engineering and Tayloristic service-scaping with a brand mythology that forms a 'truly inauthentic' place (Brown et al., 2018). On the other hand, this could be a particularly extreme example of 'placelessness' in which a place loses its unique meaning and becomes a place/space hybrid (Relph, 1976). Indeed, this is a context in which COO research could exemplify a grand historical process while simultaneously presenting the potential for advancement as a research domain through its critical examination.

One notable aspect of place is its ability to warp over time, and studies have shown that place meaning can be confined to a particular time through events. For instance, Giovanardi et al. (2014) outline the warping of social relationships and modes of co-performance and engagement within the confines of the 'right place' during the La Notte Rosa (Pink Night) festival on the north-eastern coast of Italy. Similarly, Hietanen et al. (2016) explore the implications of the so-called Restaurant Day in Helsinki, Finland, during which any member of the public is permitted to serve food for a remuneration. Such public access links the role of the retailer in a particular geography to notions of the 'carnival' (Bakhtin, 1984), which provides insights on how a shift in power relations cannot only 're-order' a place, but also unleash creative energies that can alter situated meaning within a limited time frame (Hietanen et al., 2016).

In the context of COO, a trivial application of the lessons from Giovanardi et al. (2014) and Hietanen et al. (2016) would connect a commodity to the meaning of a place that is temporally contained in 'carnivalesque' suspension, thereby supplanting its everyday meaning. The subsequent outcome is a fundamentally different set of characteristics and mythological implications from the 'everyday place', with the potential to serve as an alternative place–commodity dyad. This is consistent with Bakhtin's (1984) conceptual world represented by the notion of 'chronotopes', which "can be seen as invokable chunks of history that organize the indexical order of discourse" (Blommaert, 2015, p. 105). Thus, for instance, a mere reference to Winston Churchill invokes a historical delineation with a particular valence and set of connotations, all of which are contingent on the context of this invocation. In the case of the Pink Night and Restaurant Day, the shifts in place meaning are recurring and temporary, suggesting that place meaning, if conceptualized in a wave form, takes on an asymmetric oscillation. Thus, the 'space' Rio de Janeiro is always somewhere on a trajectory between 360 days of 'normalcy' and five days of (literal) 'carnival'.

In the context of COO, or indeed marketing in general, this oscillation is not only a way to produce 'spatially effective' meaning; it also provides further evidence that meaning does not need to be derived from 'the now' but can reference specific chronotopes. While a recurring carnival can be understood as something akin to a 'micro chronotope', references to a historical chronotope, such as a 1950s-style American diner in London or a Viking-themed restaurant in Stockholm, are commercially ubiquitous. Chronotopes are widely used in commercial practice in a manner that closely emulates leveraging a COO. However, this falls outside the realm of what COO research becomes once it is memorialized in journal publications.

Similarly, a principal issue related to COO that is conspicuously absent from the literature is how formalization of the right to use a particular indication of origin is the source of various problems. Biénabe and Marie-Vivien (2017) observe that some of these issues can be traced back to how an indication of origin simultaneously acts as a 'public quality standard', thereby constituting a specific piece of intellectual property. Noting that the institutionalization of protected indications of origin is derived primarily from the French system of 'appellation d'origine contrôlée' (AOC), which is in turn based on the concept of 'terroir' (Barham, 2003), we can begin to unravel the asymmetries among the ways in which COO becomes part of a formalized framework, as opposed to what the effect signifies. Barham notes that terroir denotes an "...area or terrain, usually rather small, whose soil and microclimate impart distinctive qualities to food products" (2003, p. 131). As an underlying concept that determines the right to refer to certain products by a particular name, terroir would be especially well-suited to safeguard heritage, uphold certain historically valuable practices, and act as a means for local farmers to remain competitive in an increasingly centralized industrial food production network.

This institutionalization of COO is naturally subject to the trappings of bureaucracy, as well as to being a politically sensitive process (Barham, 2003). There is even potential for an institutionalized COO to be a source of new power imbalances (Mancini, 2013). Marketing scholars, including those in the CCT tradition, could contribute to a nuanced understanding of these challenges, including insights into how places are redefined for commercial ends and how the spatial entity as part of a given place might change when leveraging a certain institutionalized COO.

It would be similarly enlightening to investigate how consumers navigate an objective claim to the particularity of a certain 'terroir' versus the mythological nature of implacement. In their study of the relationship between products and places, L'Espoir Decosta and Andéhn (2018) use the cases of wine in California's Napa Valley and coffee in Colombia's Triángulo de Café to highlight the possibilities for on-site consumption of mythologies of product implacement through *product geography*, a concept they define as "a system of places joined by the commonality of an association to a particular product or category" (p. 16). It follows that a powerful framework, such as a system of intellectual property rights backed by international trade agreements, would restrict producers to certain practices. However, there would be an impetus for a productive resistance against this process, as well as novel forms of adaptation, including "branding from below" (Mancini, 2013).

CONCLUSIONS

In this chapter we endeavoured to demonstrate how COO research could be advanced effectively through the application of a critical perspective. However, we acknowledge the difficulty of doing justice to a broad and multifaceted research stream such as CCT in such a limited context, much less to concurrently extrapolate its full potential. The historical challenges facing COO exemplify a Gordian knot, while an interpretivist approach through a more critical CCT scholarship would represent an 'Alexandrian solution', focusing more on Alexander's act of cutting the knot than on the problem represented by the knot itself. This is, however, not a novel observation. More than thirty years ago, Holbrook and O'Shaughnessy (1988) pointed to the need for further application of interpretivist methods in consumer research. Presumably, it is not only the pronounced tendency of COO literature to be inward looking, or even 'self-referential' (Usunier, 2006), that is its principal shortcoming as a research stream; this combination of idiosyncratic weaknesses has also prevented COO from adopting perspectives that have thrived in adjoining domains of inquiry.

In this regard, however, we advise caution. Alexander may have conquered Western Asia but enjoyed only a brief reign. In other words, when a stream of research congeals, dogma sometimes follows in its wake. Thus, we do not suggest abandoning the mainstream positivist paradigm in consumer psychology and consumer behaviour to fully adopt another epistemology; every methodological approach presents its own inherent shortcomings and idiosyncrasies. Rather, we call for increased plurality of perspectives not only to advance COO research, but to reimagine it towards a more thorough and nuanced understanding of its full potential.

REFERENCES

Agrawal, J. and Kamakura, W.A. (1999). Country of origin: a competitive advantage? *International Journal of Research in Marketing 16*(4), 255–267.

Andéhn, M. (2013). *Place-of-Origin Effects on Brand Equity: Explicating the Evaluative Pertinence of Product Categories and Association Strength.* Stockholm: US-AB.

Andéhn, M. and L'Espoir Decosta, J.-N.P. (2016). The variable nature of country-to-brand association and its impact on the strength of the country-of-origin effect. *International Marketing Review 33*(6), 851–866.

Andéhn, M. and L'Espoir Decosta, J.-N.P. (2018). Re-imagining the country-of-origin effect: a promulgation approach. *Journal of Product & Brand Management 27*(7), 884–896.

Andéhn, M. and L'Espoir Decosta, J.-N.P. (2020) Authenticity and product geography in the making of the agritourism destination. *Journal of Travel Research.* Advance Online Publication. doi: 10.1177/0047287520940796.

Andéhn, M., Hietanen, J. and Lucarelli, A. (2020). Performing place promotion: on implaced identity in marketized geographies. *Marketing Theory 20*(3), 321–342.

Appadurai, A. (1986). *The Social Life of Things: Commodities in Cultural Perspective.* New York, NY: Cambridge University Press.

Arnould, E.J. and Thompson, C.J. (2005). Consumer culture theory (CCT): twenty years of research. *Journal of Consumer Research 31*(4), 868–882.

Arnould, E.J. and Wallendorf, M. (1994). Market-oriented ethnography: interpretation building and marketing strategy formulation. *Journal of Marketing Research 31*(4), 484–504.

Askegaard, S. (2014). Consumer culture theory: neo-liberalism's 'useful idiots'? *Marketing Theory 14*(4), 507–511.

Askegaard, S. and Eckhardt, G.M. (2012). Glocal yoga: re-appropriation in the Indian consumptionscape. *Marketing Theory 12*(1), 45–60.

Bakhtin, M.M. (1984). *Rabelais and his World.* Bloomington, IN: Indiana University Press.

Barham, E. (2003). Translating terroir: the global challenge of French AOC labeling. *Journal of Rural Studies 19*(1), 127–138.

Barthes, R. (1972). *Mythologies.* New York, NY: Hill and Wang.

Belk, R.W. (1988). Possessions and the extended self. *Journal of Consumer Research 15*(2), 139–168.

Biénabe, E. and Marie-Vivien, D. (2017). Institutionalizing geographical indications in southern countries: lessons learned from Basmati and Rooibos. *World Development 98*, 58–67.

Bilkey, W.J. and Nes, E. (1982). Country-of-origin effects on product evaluations. *Journal of International Business Studies 13*(1), 89–100.

Bloemer, J., Brijs, K. and Kasper, H. (2009). The COO-ELM model: a theoretical framework for the cognitive processes underlying country of origin-effects. *European Journal of Marketing 43*(1/2), 62–89.

Blommaert, J. (2015). Chronotopes, scales, and complexity in the study of language in society. *Annual Review of Anthropology 44*, 105–116.

Bourdieu, P. (1979). *La Distinction: Critique Sociale du Jugement.* Paris: Les Editions de Minuit.

Brown, S., Stevens, L. and Maclaran, P. (2018). Epic aspects of retail encounters: The Iliad of Hollister. *Journal of Retailing 94*(1), 58–72.

Burell, G. and Morgan, G. (1979). *Sociological Paradigm and Organizational Analysis.* London: Heinemann.

Burton, D. (2001). Critical marketing theory: the blueprint?, *European Journal of Marketing 35*(5/6), 722–743.

Casey, E. (1993). *Getting Back into Place: Toward a Renewed Understanding of the Place-World.* Bloomington, IN: Indiana University Press.

Casey, E. (1997). *The Fate of Place: A Philosophical History.* Berkeley, CA: University of California Press.

Charmaz, K. (2006). *Constructing Grounded Theory.* London: Sage.

Chatzidakis, A., Maclaran, P. and Bradshaw, A. (2012). Heterotopian space and the utopics of ethical and green consumption. *Journal of Marketing Management* 28(3–4), 494–515.

Cleveland, M. and Balakrishnan, A. (2019). Appreciating vs venerating cultural outgroups: the psychology of cosmopolitanism and xenocentrism. *International Marketing Review 36*(3), 416–444.

Cleveland, M. and Laroche, M. (2012). Becoming and being a cosmopolitan consumer. In M. Prince (ed.), *Consumer Cosmopolitanism in the Age of Globalization,* New York, NY: Business Expert Press, pp. 3–28.

Dichter, E. (1962). The world customer. *Harvard Business Review 40*(4), 113–122.

Domaneschi, L. (2018). Brand new consumers: a social practice approach to young immigrants coping with material culture in Italy. *Cultural Sociology 12*(4), 499–517.

Elliot, S., Papadopoulos, N. and Kim, S.S. (2011). An integrative model of place image: exploring relationships between destination, product, and country images. *Journal of Travel Research 50*(5), 520–534.

Firat, A.F. and Venkatesh, A. (1995). Liberatory postmodernism and the reenchantment of consumption. *Journal of Consumer Research 22*(3), 239–267.

Gao, B.W., Zhang, H. and L'Espoir Decosta, J.-N.P. (2012). Phantasmal destination: a post-modernist perspective. *Annals of Tourism Research 39*(1), 197–220.

Giovanardi, M., Lucarelli, A. and L'Espoir Decosta, J.-N.P. (2014). Co-performing tourism places: the 'Pink Night' festival. *Annals of Tourism Research 44*, 102–115.

Goulding, C. (1999). Consumer research, interpretive paradigms and methodological ambiguities. *European Journal of Marketing 33*(9/10), 859–873.

Harvey, D. (2002). *Spaces of Capital: Towards a Critical Geography.* London: Routledge.

Hietanen, J., Mattila, P., Schouten, J.W., Sihvonen, A. and Toyoki, S. (2016). Reimagining society through retail practice. *Journal of Retailing 92*(4), 411–425.

Holbrook, M.B. and O'Shaughnessy, J. (1988). On the scientific status of consumer research and the need for an interpretive approach to studying consumption behavior. *Journal of Consumer Research 15*(3), 398–402.

Holt, D.B. (2002). Why do brands cause trouble? A dialectical theory of consumer culture and branding. *Journal of Consumer Research 29*(1), 70–90.

Karababa, E. and Ger, G. (2010). Early modern Ottoman coffeehouse culture and the formation of the consumer subject. *Journal of Consumer Research 37*(5), 737–760.

Kravets, O. (2012). Russia's 'Pure Spirit' vodka branding and its politics. *Journal of Macromarketing 32*(4), 361–376.

L'Espoir Decosta, J.-N.P. and Andéhn, M. (2018). Looking for authenticity in product geography. In J.M. Rickly and E.S. Vidon (eds), *Authenticity & Tourism Volume 24: Materialities, Perceptions, Experiences.* Bingley: Emerald Publishing, pp.15–31.

Levy, S.J. (1959). Symbols for sale. *Harvard Business Review 37*(July–August), 117–24.

Lincoln, Y.S. and Guba, E.G. (1985). *Naturalistic Inquiry.* Thousand Oaks, CA: Sage.

Luedicke, M.K. (2011). Consumer acculturation theory: (crossing) conceptual boundaries. *Consumption Markets & Culture 14*(3), 223–244.

Luedicke, M.K., Thompson, C.J. and Giesler, M. (2010). Consumer identity work as moral protagonism: how myth and ideology animate a brand-mediated moral conflict. *Journal of Consumer Research 36*(6), 1016–1032.

Magnusson, P., Westjohn, S.A. and Zdravkovic, S. (2011). 'What? I thought Samsung was Japanese': accurate or not, perceived country of origin matters. *International Marketing Review 28*(5), 454–472.

Mancini, M.C. (2013). Geographical indications in Latin America value chains: a 'branding from below' strategy or a mechanism excluding the poorest? *Journal of Rural Studies 32*, 295–306.

Marx, K. (1979) *Capital*. London: Penguin.

Muniz, A.M. and O'Guinn, T.C. (2001). Brand community. *Journal of Consumer Research 27*(4), 412–432.

Nagashima, A. (1970). A comparison of Japanese and US attitudes toward foreign products. *Journal of Marketing 34*(1), 68–74.

O'Shaughnessy, J. and O'Shaughnessy, N.J. (2000). Treating the nation as a brand: some neglected issues. *Journal of Macromarketing 20*(1), 56–64.

Papadopoulos, N. (1993). What product and country images are and are not. In N. Papadopoulos and L.A. Heslop (eds), *Product-Country Images: Impact and Role in International Marketing*. Binghampton, NY: The Haworth Press, pp. 1–38.

Papadopoulos, N., Cleveland, M., Bartikowski, B. and Yaprak, A. (2018). Of countries, places and product/brand place associations: an inventory of dispositions and issues relating to place image and its effects. *Journal of Product & Brand Management 27*(7), 735–753.

Peñaloza, L. and Gilly, M.C. (1999). Marketer acculturation: the changer and the changed. *Journal of Marketing 63*(3), 84–104.

Porto da Rocha, M.B. and Strehlau, V.I. (2020). Choosing identity in the global cultural supermarket: the German consumption of the Afro-Brazilian Capoeira. *Journal of International Consumer Marketing 32*(3), 194–209.

Reierson, C.C. (1967). Attitude changes toward foreign products. *Journal of Marketing Research 4*(4), 385–387.

Relph, E. (1976). *Place and Placelessness*. London: Pion.

Samiee, S. (2011). Resolving the impasse regarding research on the origins of products and brands. *International Marketing Review 28*(5), 473–485.

Samiee, S., Shimp, T.A. and Sharma, S. (2005). Brand origin recognition accuracy: its antecedents and consumers' cognitive limitations. *Journal of International Business Studies 36*(4), 379–397.

Schooler, R.D. (1965). Product bias in the Central American common market. *Journal of Marketing Research 2*(4), 394–397.

Schouten, J.W. (1991). Selves in transition: symbolic consumption in personal rites of passage and identity reconstruction. *Journal of Consumer Research 17*(4), 412–425.

Scott, R., Cayla, J. and Cova, B. (2017). Selling pain to the saturated self. *Journal of Consumer Research 44*(1), 22–43.

Sherry Jr, J.F. (2000). Place, technology, and representation. *Journal of Consumer Research 27*(2), 273–278.

Strizhakova, Y. and Coulter, R. (2019). Consumer cultural identity: local and global cultural identities and measurement implications. *International Marketing Review 36*(5), 610–627.

Szondi, G. (2007). The role and challenges of country branding in transition countries: the Central and Eastern Europe experience. *Place Branding and Public Diplomacy 3*(1), 8–20.

Tan, C.T. and Farley, J.U. (1987). The impact of cultural patterns on cognition and intention in Singapore. *Journal of Consumer Research 13*(4), 540–544.

Thompson, C.J. (2004). Marketplace mythology and discourses of power. *Journal of Consumer Research 31*(1), 162–180.

Tuan, Y.F. (1977). *Space and Place: The Perspective of Experience.* Minneapolis, MN: University of Minnesota Press.

Usunier, J.C. (2006). Relevance in business research: the case of country-of-origin research in marketing. *European Management Review 3*(1), 60–73.

Van Ittersum, K., Candel, M.J. and Meulenberg, M.T. (2003). The influence of the image of a product's region of origin on product evaluation. *Journal of Business Research 56*(3), 215–226.

Varman, R. and Costa, J.A. (2013). Underdeveloped other in country-of-origin theory and practices. *Consumption Markets & Culture 16*(3), 240–265.

Veblen, T. (1994[1899]). The theory of the leisure class. New York, NY: Penguin Books.

Verlegh, P.W. and Steenkamp, J.B.E. (1999). A review and meta-analysis of country-of-origin research. *Journal of Economic Psychology 20*(5), 521–546.

10. The effects of stereotyping on place/country image perceptions

Peter Magnusson and Stanford A. Westjohn

INTRODUCTION

A stereotype is an oversimplified and overgeneralized belief about a particular category (Cardwell and Marcousě, 1999). Research on stereotyping of people and countries can be traced back almost 100 years (Child and Doob, 1943; Klingberg, 1941). Even earlier, Darton (1790) offered stereotypes of several different places in Europe, which were illustrated by Taras et al. (2016). For example, the latter study described Netherlands and the Dutch as "industrious and hardy, cleanly in their persons, ships, and houses", while, in contrast, the French were stereotyped as "of a changeable disposition, and fond of amusement to excess" (p. 456). Similar stereotypes persist today, and it is probably safe to assume that stereotyping of people and places occurred long before it was recorded in writing.

To make life manageable, consumers often rely on mental shortcuts (i.e., stereotyping). The tendency to rely on heuristic stereotypes has made stereotyping of people and places a central concept in the rich country-of-origin literature and makes it worthy of further consideration. Accordingly, the objective of this chapter is to review and discuss the role of stereotyping on country image perceptions. To do so, we aim to address the following questions: (1) What are stereotypes? (2) How do people stereotype countries and how does it originate? (3) How malleable are country image stereotypes over time? (4) How do country image stereotypes influence consumption behaviors? (5) How can marketing managers use knowledge of country image stereotypes to enhance brand performance? We address these questions through a review of the relevant literature and by highlighting the findings of a longitudinal study that illustrates changes in country image stereotypes between 2008 and 2020.

STEREOTYPES AS MENTAL SHORTCUTS

Social psychologists have long recognized two unique routes that people use to process information. Perhaps most famously, Kahneman (2011) coined the terms *System 1 thinking*, which is fast, intuitive, and emotional, and *System 2 thinking*, which is slow, deliberate, and more logical. Similarly, the elaboration likelihood model distinguishes between the *peripheral route*, which is the low mental effort path with limited elaboration, and the *central route*, which is the high effort, deliberate processing route (Petty and Cacioppo, 1986). Slow, deliberate thinking may seem like the preferred method of processing information, but since people often are "best described as 'cognitive misers' who eschew any difficult intellectual activity" (Petty et al., 1983, p. 136), fast, automatic thinking, with frequent use of heuristics often dominates. A more positive interpretation is that people are often overwhelmed by the endless number of surrounding stimuli in their daily environment. To cope with this information overload efficiently, they simplify the processing of these stimuli by grouping them into sets and creating stereotypes (Zeugner-Roth, 2017). In sum, people are prone to developing stereotypes and "stereotypes play a key role in country image" (Usunier and Cestre, 2007, p. 35).

MACRO AND MICRO COUNTRY STEREOTYPES

Country stereotypes reflect a person's perceptions about the features of a country and are developed through socialization processes and exposure to information about countries (Diamantopoulos et al., 2017). Accordingly, country image is a knowledge structure that synthesizes what we believe about a country. In the country image literature, researchers have taken different approaches to what they believe are the most meaningful country image stereotypes that one should measure. One perspective has taken a very broad view and defined country image as "the total of all descriptive, inferential and informational beliefs one has about a particular country" (Martin and Eroglu, 1993, p. 193). This broad perspective can generally be traced to Nagashima (1970) who offered a broad definition and suggested that country image associations were based on an aggregation of "representative products, national characteristics, economic and political background, history, and traditions" (p. 68).

Most studies appear to have focused on economic and political factors in the measurement of macro country stereotypes. However, some studies have also included a people dimension, which, in our view, is an important additional dimension to consider. Measurements of the people dimension seem to originate with Parameswaran and Yaprak (1987) and similar measurements have also been used by, for example, Knight and Calantone (2000) and Zeugner-Roth et al. (2008).

Other researchers have focused on a narrower product country image emphasizing consumers' stereotypes about the quality of products made in a particular country. This has been labeled product–country image (Papadopoulos, 1993) or micro country image (Pappu et al., 2007). A third perspective advocates an even narrower conceptualization and focuses on a specific industry, for example cars or high-tech electronics (Roth and Romeo, 1992; Usunier and Cestre, 2007). This perspective emphasizes that countries tend to specialize in certain product categories, which may lead to favorable stereotypes for that product category, but it does not necessarily extend to all other product categories. For example, Pappu et al. (2007) suggest that Japan may have a generally favorable overall country image (i.e., macro country image); Japanese cars have a very favorable product country image, but Japanese wine less so.

Furthermore, in addition to the cognitive aspects of country image stereotypes, research has also acknowledged an affective component. This includes affective evaluative judgments such as like/dislike, pleasant/unpleasant, favorable/unfavorable (Heslop et al., 2004). Generally, cognitive and affective evaluations are expected to be congruent, but as evidenced by the consumer animosity (e.g., Harmeling et al., 2015; Klein et al., 1998; Westjohn et al., forthcoming) and country affinity literature (e.g., Oberecker et al., 2008; Papadopoulos et al., 2017), there are multiple exceptions where cognitive and affective evaluations may differ.

As noted by Magnusson et al. (2019), both cognitive and affective measurements have generally examined country stereotypes from a positive–negative valence perspective. For example, product country innovativeness measures have ranged from very innovative to not innovative, workmanship from high to low quality (Roth and Romeo, 1992), and overall country perceptions have, for example, measured perceptions of degree of economic development and technological research capacity (Martin and Eroglu, 1993).

However, not all country stereotypes fall on a more or less favorable continuum. Even though the people dimension has long been recognized as an important part of consumers' country stereotypes (e.g., Parameswaran and Yaprak, 1987), a newer strand of research has found that stereotypes of other countries can also include anthropomorphizing human personality attributes onto countries, which has been labeled country personalities (Cuddy et al., 2009; d'Astous and Boujbel, 2007; Magnusson et al., 2019; Rojas-Méndez et al., 2013). Country personality perceptions often do not fall neatly on a favorability continuum, but they may nonetheless be an important part of consumers' country stereotypes.

HUMAN PERSONALITY STEREOTYPES OF COUNTRIES

Stereotype Content Model

One important human stereotyping framework that has been applied to countries is the stereotype content model (SCM) (Fiske et al., 2007; 2002). The SCM has identified two basic stereotyping dimensions, warmth and competence, which they suggest are able to explain about 80 percent of the variance in perceptions of different social behaviors. Other researchers have opted for different labels, such as communion and agency (Abele and Wojciszke, 2007), morality and competence (Wojciszke, 2005), or intentions and ability (Kervyn et al., 2012), but warmth and competence appear to be the labels most commonly used.

The warmth and competence dimensions are based on two fundamental questions that people ask when encountering out-group members: do they intend to harm me and are they capable of harming me (Fiske et al., 1999)? The two core dimensions of general stereotype content, warmth (e.g., friendly, good-natured, sincere, and warm) and competence (e.g., capable, competent, confident, and skillful), are expected to be able to answer these questions (Cuddy et al., 2009). Groups viewed as competitors are generally stereotyped as lacking warmth, whereas groups viewed as cooperative are stereotyped as warm. In contrast, groups viewed as high status and with high ability are stereotyped as competent, whereas groups viewed as low status are not (Fiske et al., 2002).

The ambivalent nature of stereotypes is a key feature of the SCM, as often groups are viewed as more positive on one dimension and less positive on another. In effect, many groups are stereotyped as either "kind but helpless" or "skillful but cunning" (Cuddy et al., 2009, p. 4). Lack of warmth and low competence seem to be reserved for only traditionally derogated groups, and perceptions of high warmth and high competence seems to be reserved for self-evaluations and in-groups and other (perceived) mainstream social groups.

The ambivalent nature of stereotypes has been found with a variety of target groups, such as occupations, races, religions, gender subtypes, socioeconomic groups, and so on (Fiske et al., 2002; 1999). Importantly, this ambivalence has also been found for country stereotypes. Cuddy et al. (2009) open their article with an illustrative anecdote about German stereotypes of Italians and vice versa. The ambivalent nature of stereotypes is evident by the anecdote that "Germans love Italians, but don't admire them. Italians admire Germans, but don't love them" (Cuddy et al., 2009, p. 2). This sentiment is confirmed in a larger empirical study of European Union countries, which found that

Northern European countries (e.g., UK and Germany) tended to be stereotyped as higher on competence but lower on warmth, whereas Southern European countries (e.g., Spain, Italy, Greece) tended to be stereotyped as higher on warmth but lower on competence.

Outside of Susan Fiske and her colleagues, the ambivalent nature of country stereotypes has also been found by, for example, Chattalas and Takada (2013). However, it should be noted that the ambivalent nature of stereotypes has not always been replicated by other authorship teams. For example, in an examination of Austrian consumers and their explicit and implicit stereotypes of six major countries, the ambivalent nature of warmth and competence did not materialize (Diamantopoulos et al., 2017). Further, Maher and Carter (2011) found a strong positive correlation (r = .51) between consumers' warmth and competence perceptions, which suggests that the ambivalent nature may not always be present. It appears that some countries, despite being perceived as an out-group, may be perceived as both warm and competent, or neither.

Stereotyping Countries on Personality Dimensions

In addition to applying the SCM to countries, a stream of research has emerged over the last decade or so which has attempted to capture the personality stereotypes of countries. This is grounded in psychological trait theory, which naturally is a foundation in the study of human personality. It suggests that traits are aspects of personality that are relatively stable over time and in different situations, influence behavior, and differ between people. One of the most widely accepted conceptions of personality is based on five broad domains which have been shown to define human personality at the highest level of organization (Goldberg, 1990). The Big Five personality dimensions are: (1) agreeableness, described as helpful, trusting, and empathetic; (2) openness to experience, described as curious, having a wide range of interests, and independent; (3) extraversion, described as outgoing and energetic; (4) conscientiousness, described as efficient, organized, and hard-working; and (5) neuroticism, described as sensitive, nervous, and prone to negative emotions (Costa Jr and McCrae, 1992).

The Big Five personality framework has been widely accepted and individual traits significantly predict human behavior. Drawing on the Big Five taxonomy, Aaker (1997) developed a brand personality framework. She defined brand personality as "the set of human characteristics associated with a brand" (1997, p. 347). Aaker further argues that in contrast to product-related attributes, which tend to serve a utilitarian function for consumers, brand personality tends to serve a symbolic or self-expressive function. It is argued that the imbuing of brands with human personality traits serves as a mental shortcut to understand and categorize brands. In effect, ascribing personality attributes to brands are expected to be relatively enduring and can differentiate brands from competitors.

Following this logic, Aaker's (1997) brand personality framework consists of five dimensions: (1) sincerity, described as domestic, honest, and genuine; (2) excitement, described as daring, spirited, and imaginative; (3) competence, described as reliable, responsible, and dependable; (4) sophistication, described as glamorous, pretentious, and charming; and (5) ruggedness, described as tough, strong, and outdoorsy. In comparison with the Big Five personality framework, there is strong overlap between the sincerity dimension and agreeableness, and competence and conscientiousness, while excitement seems to combine aspects of extraversion and openness to experience. However, neither sophistication nor ruggedness seem to have a direct analog to the human personality dimensions. The brand personality framework has since been validated in a variety of contexts (e.g., Clemenz et al., 2012; Sirianni et al., 2013). Combined, the Big Five personality framework and the brand personality taxonomy have led to the emergence of several country personality stereotype frameworks.

Similar to the brand personality framework, country personality stereotypes are based on the idea that human traits provide rich and easily understandable meaning. Human traits are associated with universal mental representations that are easily activated because they have been used previously to characterize people in our environment and predict their behavior. They correspond to easily accessed, abstract cognitions that provide an efficient mechanism for making different types of inferences about objects, including countries (Rojas-Méndez and Hine, 2017). The original definition offered by d'Astous and Boujbel (2007) seems to appropriately capture this concept as they defined country personality as "the mental representation of a country on dimensions that typically capture an individual's personality" (p. 233).

Although, as noted in the introduction, stereotypes about people from different countries have existed for hundreds of years (e.g., Darton, 1790), formal scientific inquiry into country personality stereotypes is more recent. Table 10.1 summarizes several key publications in this stream. As is evident, different country personality dimensions have emerged and authors have used different labels for their dimensions. To help us synthesize the different frameworks, we have attempted to categorize these country personality dimensions based on their degree of overlap with the original Big Five human personality dimensions. This categorization is based on our best judgment, but we acknowledge that the authors of these frameworks or another reader may make a slightly different interpretation.

The first of the country personality stereotyping frameworks was developed by d'Astous and Boujbel (2007). On a sample of Canadian consumers who evaluated seven countries, a framework consisting of six country personality

Table 10.1   Summary of country personality stereotypes literature

Author (Year)	The Big 5 personality dimensions					Other personality dimensions not directly related to the Big 5		
	Agreeableness	Openness to experience	Extraversion	Conscientiousness	Neuroticism			
d'Astous and Boujbel (2007)	*Agreeableness* (amusing, agreeable)	–	–	*Assiduousness* (organized, rigorous, hard at work)	*Unobtrusiveness* (cowardly, wimpy, dependent)	*Wickedness* (immoral, vulgar, decadent)	*Snobbism* (haughty, snobbish, chauvinist)	*Conformity* (religious, spiritual, traditional)
d'Astous and Li (2009)	*Agreeableness* (amusing, agreeable)	–	–	*Assiduousness* (organized, rigorous, hard at work)	*Unobtrusiveness* (cowardly, wimpy, dependent)	*Wickedness* (immoral, vulgar, decadent)	*Snobbism* (haughty, snobbish, chauvinist)	*Conformity* (religious, spiritual, traditional)
Murphy et al. (2007)	*Sincerity* (honest, wholesome, cheerful)	–	*Excitement* (daring, spirited, imaginative)	*Competence* (reliable, intelligent)	–	*Ruggedness*	*Sophistication*	–
Kim et al. (2013)	*Excitement* (humorous, hot, warm, amiable)	*Leadership* (innovative, progressive, dynamic, creative)	–	–	–	*Tradition* (conservative, traditional, authoritarian)	*Sophistication* (sophisticated, noble, dignified)	*Peacefulness* (pure, peaceful)
Rojas-Méndez and Papadopoulos (2012)	*Amicableness* (amicable, welcoming, sincere)	*Resourcefulness* (creative, dynamic, innovative)	*Spirited* (cheerful, charismatic, lively)	–	*Neuroticism* (toughness, tyrannical)	–	–	–
Rojas-Méndez et al. (2013)	*Amicableness* (amicable, welcoming, sincere)	*Resourcefulness* (creative, dynamic, innovative)	–	–	*Self-centeredness* (selfish, obnoxious, narrowminded)	–	–	–
Rojas-Méndez et al (2015)	*Agreeableness*	*Openness to experience*	*Extraversion*	*Conscientiousness*	*Neuroticism*	–	–	–
Rojas-Méndez and Hine (2017)	*Agreeableness*	*Openness to experience*	*Extraversion*	*Conscientiousness*	*Neuroticism*	–	–	–

dimensions emerged: agreeableness, wickedness, snobbism, assiduousness, conformity, and unobtrusiveness. Agreeableness (agreeableness) and assiduousness (conscientiousness) seem to be closely related to their human personality analogs, and unobtrusiveness seems to be similar to neuroticism. The remaining three dimensions are not as easily relatable to the Big Five framework.

Kim et al. (2013) sampled consumers from seven countries who were asked to evaluate the country personality stereotypes for nine different countries. Their framework identified five country personality dimensions. We suggest that excitement seems to relate most closely to agreeableness, and leadership to openness to experience and probably extraversion, whereas sophistication, tradition, and peacefulness do not seem to have a direct human personality analog.

Rojas-Méndez and his colleagues have contributed multiple articles to this literature and different articles have used slightly different country personality dimensions. Most of these articles appear to rely on a large battery (200+) of items of personality traits administered to several different samples. From this large battery of items, they have extracted different personality dimensions. The earliest publications (Rojas-Méndez and Papadopoulos, 2012; Rojas-Méndez et al., 2013) used the labels amicableness (similar to agreeableness), resourcefulness (similar to open to experience), spiritedness (appears similar to extraversion), and self-centeredness (which appears similar to neuroticism). In a more recent article, they have opted to adopt the Big 5 personality dimensions directly (Rojas-Méndez and Hine, 2017).

In sum, significant research has been conducted in the last decade, which has generated many new insights into consumers' country personality stereotypes. However, this literature has not yet reached maturity and a consensus on the relevant country personality stereotypes has not emerged. For example, are the two stereotype content model dimensions sufficient, or do we need a broader and richer personality framework that covers more dimensions? It is interesting to note that the research community appeared quick to adopt Aaker's (1997) brand personality dimensions while not a lot of competing frameworks have gained traction. There is more disparity in terms of country personality dimensions, but perhaps with additional research, the research community can reach (at least close to) consensus on what the relevant dimensions should be.

THE STABILITY OF STEREOTYPES OVER TIME

A key part of the definition of stereotypes is that they are widely held and relatively stable over time. The fact that many people today still hold some of Darton's (1790) country stereotypes serves as a testament to their durability. However, these examples refer to stereotypes of the traits of a country's citizens. Questions remain about how stable product-focused stereotypes are over time.

A well-established stereotype in the country of origin literature is that products from rich, developed markets are perceived more favorably than products from less economically-developed, emerging markets (Verlegh and Steenkamp, 1999). By products 'from rich, developed markets', we mean brands associated with highly developed markets, not necessarily the location of manufacture – for example, Apple's iPhone, although assembled in China, is associated with the US. However, many emerging markets have experienced tremendous economic growth in recent decades, closed the economic gap with the rich, developed countries, and developed highly respected global brands, such as South Korea's Hyundai. Have consumer attitudes been able to keep up with economic developments or are consumer attitudes still outdated? Related research has demonstrated that often consumer stereotypes are based on out-dated information and stereotypes are difficult to break (Rosling et al., 2018). Yet, longitudinal analyses of country image stereotypes are non-existent, to the best of our knowledge. To gain an improved understanding of whether and how country image stereotypes change over time, we are able to combine a new data gathering effort with comparable data from 2008.

Researching Stereotypes across Time: Participants and Procedure

The original data was gathered in the fall of 2008 and was published in *International Marketing Review* in 2011 (Magnusson et al., 2011), and new data was gathered in 2020 representing a 12-year lag between the two data-sets. With the original data, we examined whether the accuracy of perceived brand origin mattered. Our findings indicated that regardless of whether brand origin perceptions were accurate or not (e.g., only 25 percent of respondents thought Samsung was from South Korea), country image perception posi-tively influenced brand attitude. Thus, in our original study, we measured an industry-specific product–country image question: "In general, my attitude toward [product category] from [country] is" on a seven-point scale anchored by 'highly unfavorable' and 'highly favorable'. In 2008, we examined three product categories: high-tech electronics, automobiles, and fashion. In 2020, we chose to replicate the high-tech electronics and automobile categories.

For both the 2008 and 2020 samples, we adopted the data-gathering tech-nique suggested by Bitner et al. (1990), in which students taking a business class were trained in recruitment and data collection procedures and then were asked to identify and contact potential respondents. Each student was invited to complete the survey and recruit a maximum of five other non-student respondents. To verify the integrity of the data, each respondent was asked to provide an email address. One week after the close of the surveys, 10 percent of the respondents were randomly contacted to verify their participation in the research project. No problems were detected. Following the elimination of incomplete surveys and surveys taken by non-US citizens, we had usable responses from 404 participants in 2008 (210 high-tech electronics and 194 automobile industry) and 391 respondents in 2020 (193 high-tech electronics and 198 automobiles). Although the samples were not randomly collected, the demographic characteristics exhibited broad demographic representation and were largely comparable across time periods. Both samples had slightly more females than males, whereas age, education, and income were slightly higher in 2020 than in 2008, as presented in Table 10.2.

Table 10.2   Demographic characteristics

Characteristic	2008		2020	
	Frequency	%	Frequency	%
Gender				
Male	189	46.8	174	44.5
Female	215	53.2	217	55.5
Age				
Average age	37.32		40.37	
SD	14.59		16.23	
Education				
High school diploma	37	9.3	16	4.1
Some college	175	43.0	70	17.9
Bachelor degree	124	30.6	200	51.2
Graduate degree	70	17.1	105	26.9
Household Income (annual, in USD)				
Under $30,000	62	15.3	39	10.0
$30,000–59,999	81	20.0	37	9.5
$60,000–89,999	92	22.7	61	15.6
$90,000–120,000	63	15.6	73	18.7
More than $120,000	106	26.2	176	45.6

Results

In comparing changes in consumer attitudes toward the various countries, there are several noteworthy findings. We reiterate that our measurement is a higher-order favorability question, which presumably incorporates several lower-order beliefs (e.g., cognitive beliefs about product quality) and emotions (e.g., country affinity and animosity), although these are not measured. We present the findings for the automobile industry in Figure 10.1 and for high-tech electronics in Figure 10.2.

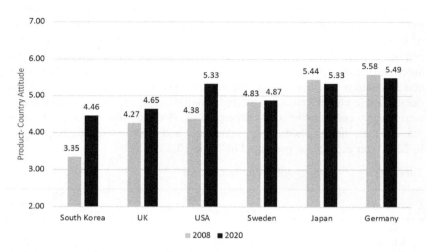

Figure 10.1 *Attitude toward automobiles from various countries in 2008 and 2020*

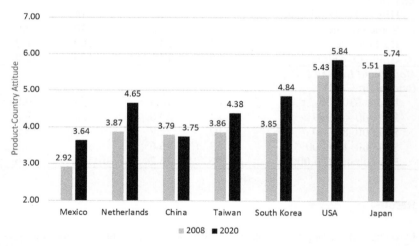

Figure 10.2 *Attitude toward high-tech electronics from various countries in 2008 and 2020*

First, let's examine the findings from 2008. In the automobile industry we measured country favorability stereotypes for six leading countries. The six countries divided into four statistically different groups. A top tier of countries included Japan and Germany, with Sweden perceived slightly less favorably. In the bottom, it was South Korea, statistically less favorable than all other countries, and the USA and UK. It is notable that American consumers rated the domestic auto industry a full point lower than the leading countries at the time.

In the high-tech electronics industry, we measured country favorability for seven leading countries, which are home to most of the major electronics brands in the world. The seven countries divided into three statistically different groups. At the top, the American consumers rated Japan and the USA. A middle tier consisted of the Netherlands, Taiwan, South Korea, and China. In the bottom tier, and statistically less favorable than all other countries, was Mexico, which has a sizable electronic manufacturing industry, but is not the home of any of the world's major brands.

In 2020 in the auto industry, perceptions of the USA have improved, and it has joined Japan and Germany in the top tier, and South Korea has joined the UK and Sweden in the second tier. We included a measure of favorability toward Chinese automobiles in 2020, which we did not collect in 2008. Attitude toward Chinese automobiles is significantly less favorable than all other countries.

In 2020 in the high-tech electronics industry, the top tier still consists of the USA and Japan. South Korea has moved to the top of the middle tier, which also includes the Netherlands and Taiwan. China, on the other hand, has dropped down and joined Mexico in the bottom tier.

There are several noteworthy comparisons between the 2008 and 2020 data. The first one is of significant convergence. Favorability perceptions for the top countries have remained relatively stable (around 5.50), but other countries have significantly closed the gap. The lowest rated country for automobiles in both time periods was South Korea. However, South Korea's rating of 3.35 in 2008 has improved to 4.46 in the new study. Thus, the range from the highest to the lowest was over 2.00 points in 2008, but has shrunk to 1.03 in 2020. The finding is similar for high-tech electronics. The gap between Japan (5.51) and Mexico (2.92) was 2.59 in 2008, but the gap between the highest-rated USA (5.84) and Mexico (3.64) has shrunk to 2.20.

We can conceive two potential explanations for this convergence. It is plausible that the increased consumer awareness of globalization and integration of global supply chains has created confusion. For example, Samsung produces high-quality televisions in many countries around the world, including in China, Hungary, Malaysia, Mexico, Romania, Russia, Slovenia, South Korea, and Vietnam. Thus, the convergence in country favorability ratings may reflect a reduced ability by consumers to discern quality by location. On the other hand, we cannot rule out the possibility of a research design artifact. Although we have attempted to replicate the 2008 study in 2020, the sample is made up of different people. Further, consumers are constantly being asked to fill out surveys and there is evidence that survey overload can make getting accurate responses more challenging.

A second noteworthy finding is that American consumers' perception of their domestic industries has improved considerably. In 2008, American automobiles were rated in the bottom half and more than a full point behind the leading countries. In 2020, the USA has moved into the top tier and in a statistical tie with Germany and Japan. Similarly, the USA was already in the top tier for high-tech electronics, but it has now surpassed Japan to take the top spot (although the difference is not statistically significant). This improvement has coincided with a significant shift toward more nationalist policies in the USA, with a strong emphasis on putting 'America first'.

Third, perceptions of South Korea experienced the most significant improvement, which seems very reasonable. South Korea's leading brands have improved their global brand value significantly over the last decade. Samsung has moved from 21st place to be the world's 6th most valuable brand, Hyundai has moved from 72nd to 36th, and Kia has gone from unranked to 78th. At the same time, South Korea has continued to close the gap with other rich countries and its human development index in 2019 is in the top 'very high human development' category. From our data, it appears that consumer perceptions have improved considerably, and, for automobiles, South Korea has moved from the bottom tier to the middle tier – yet one could probably argue that, based on its brand performances, attitude toward South Korea should perhaps be even higher.

Finally, perceptions of China have moved in the opposite direction. Despite being the manufacturing place for many leading brands for high-tech electronics, notably the iPhone, China has moved from the middle tier to the bottom tier. We did not ask about Chinese automobiles in 2008. In 2020, Chinese auto brands are still not readily available in the USA, and perceptions of Chinese automobiles are significantly lower than toward all other countries. We suggest that this negative attitude toward Chinese products is largely an affective response. USA and China have been embroiled in a trade war, and many American politicians and social commentators have been keen to place blame for the ongoing COVID-19 pandemic on China. The result of this escalating tension is, not surprisingly, a less favorable attitude toward China by American consumers.

THE EFFECT OF COUNTRY STEREOTYPES ON MARKETING STRATEGY

We have discussed two kinds of country stereotypes. The first one relates to stereotype perceptions that are viewed as more or less favorable, which has been the traditional focus of most research in the country of origin sphere. The marketing strategy implications for these kinds of stereotypes are fairly straightforward. If consumers hold favorable perceptions, then this is a potential asset that firms can use to differentiate their brands. German automobile brands (e.g., 'Volkswagen – That's the Power of German Engineering') or Sweden's IKEA, with its blue and yellow stores and strong Swedish influence on product names, are examples of brands that have made heavy use of their country association as a branding tool.

In contrast, brands from countries with weak country image stereotypes must be creative in efforts to dilute the disadvantage. Famous examples include Lenovo's acquisition of the IBM brand name for personal computers. With the help of this co-branding arrangement, Lenovo was able to overcome its negative Chinese image, and is now one of the leading personal computer brands in the world. Hyundai introduced its 10-year warranty in the USA in 1998 to help consumers overcome perceptions of poor Korean workmanship. Since then, Hyundai (and other South Korean brands) have become world-leading brands and the overall country image of South Korea has improved significantly, as evidenced by our longitudinal measurement.

Whereas the marketing implications may be fairly straightforward depending on whether country image stereotypes are positive or negative, how brand managers should use knowledge of country personality stereotypes has not received as much research attention. We are aware of only two studies that have examined this issue, both focused on congruity. The first study, by Rojas-Méndez et al. (2015), examined congruity between the consumer's own personality and a target country's country personality. When the consumer's own personality is more closely aligned with the target country's personality, attitudes and behavioral intentions toward the country improved.

The second study is our own research, which was recently published in the *Journal of International Business Studies* (Magnusson et al., 2019). In that article, we examined alignment between the brand's marketing positioning and the dominant country personality stereotypes. Drawing on a series of studies, we demonstrated that brands benefited from positioning the brand in a way that is more closely aligned with the dominant country personality stereotypes. For example, in a field study at a wine shop, a German wine that was positioned as more 'competent' (aligned with the German country personality stereotype) was rated as tasting better. In comparison, a Spanish wine that was positioned as more 'warm' (aligned with the Spanish country personality stereotype) was rated as tasting better.

Both studies were grounded in a congruity perspective, although each with a somewhat different focus. We do, however, note that research in this area is in its infancy and there should be room for considerable additional research on how countries can assess and use their personality, and how brands can leverage it. We do believe, however, that the growing research on country personality has demonstrated that it is an important aspect of country stereotypes, and that assessing and cultivating a certain country personality seems to be an important step in developing a national brand strategy. Especially for emerging markets, where transitioning from a perception of poor quality and low image to one of high quality can be a slow process (as evidenced by our data on South Korea over a 12-year interval), building and leveraging country personality stereotypes may be an easier path.

CONCLUSION AND FUTURE RESEARCH

In this chapter, we have reviewed and discussed the different types of country stereotypes, their malleability, and how firms and countries may leverage, or attempt to negate, consumer stereotypes. Throughout our review, we have offered a few suggestions for future research. However, we'd like to conclude with a couple of additional suggestions on where research on country stereotypes may go in the future.

One area that has plagued research in this area for some time and received frequent criticism is on the explicitness of a product's origin information in research designs that may have artificially inflated findings by highlighting the origin when consumers might otherwise not be consciously attentive to it. At the same time, some consumers may be reluctant to admit their stereotypical beliefs or they may be unaware of them (Martin et al., 2011). Thus, this requires creative research approaches that are able accurately to identify consumer stereotypes and effects on consumer behaviors – but at the same time they should be developed so as not to inflate findings through unrealistic or artificial designs (Samiee, 2010).

One path that holds promise is the use of implicit measurement approaches, which assess individuals' beliefs and attitudes indirectly through tasks that do not reveal the content of interest (Gawronski and Bodenhausen, 2006). One such example is Diamantopoulos et al. (2017), who used an implicit association test (IAT) to assess consumers' stereotypes of various countries on the stereotype content model dimensions of warmth and competence. More such implicit techniques would be valuable in order to combat challenges that have plagued the literature in this area.

Finally, we focus in the chapter exclusively on country-level stereotypes. Indeed, other chapters in this volume focus on place not only as a country, but supra- or sub-national regions that could just as easily be subject to region stereotypes, for example, America's Southern states or Bavaria in Germany. Less research has been conducted on regions defined by other than national boundaries; however, their findings contribute to our knowledge of place stereotypes, and we encourage more of such research.

In sum, the current trend of increasingly nationalistic attitudes may serve to heighten awareness of the origins of brands and products. Certainly, the increased use of protectionist trade and investment policies reflects the attitude of making a distinction between domestic and foreign brands. The geopolitical climate at the time of writing (trade wars, coronavirus blaming, etc.) also stokes the concept of identifying countries that are friendly and cooperative against those that are seen as adversaries (Papadopoulos et al., 2017). This tendency is likely to be more emotion-based as opposed to cognitive-based; however, in either case it makes the country of origin of brands a more salient characteristic. Given that we still recognize some country stereotypes that are hundreds of years old, consumers may not hesitate to apply age-old stereotypes to be consistent with the emotion they are feeling, positive or negative.

REFERENCES

Aaker, J.L. (1997). Dimensions of brand personality. *Journal of Marketing Research, 34*(3), 347–356.

Abele, A.E. and Wojciszke, B. (2007). Agency and communion from the perspective of self versus others. *Journal of Personality and Social Psychology, 93*(5), 751–763.

Bitner, M.J., Booms, B.H. and Tetreault, M.S. (1990). The service encounter: diagnosing favorable and unfavorable incidents. *Journal of Marketing, 54*(1), 71–84.

Cardwell, M. and Marcousĕ, I. (1999). *Dictionary of Psychology.* Chicago, IL: Fitzroy Dearborn.

Chattalas, M. and Takada, H. (2013). Warm versus competent countries: national stereotyping effects on expectations of hedonic versus utilitarian product properties. *Place Branding and Public Diplomacy, 9*(2), 88–97.

Child, I.L. and Doob, L.W. (1943). Factors determining national stereotypes. *The Journal of Social Psychology, 17*(2), 203–219.

Clemenz, J., Brettel, M. and Moeller, T. (2012). How the personality of a brand impacts the perception of different dimensions of quality. *Journal of Brand Management, 20*(1), 52–64.

Costa Jr, P.T. and McCrae, R.R. (1992). Four ways five factors are basic. *Personality and Individual Differences, 13*(6), 653–665.

Cuddy, A.J.C., Fiske, S.T., Kwan, V.S.Y., Glick, P., Demoulin, S., Leyens, J.-P. and Bond, M.H. (2009). Stereotype content model across cultures: towards universal similarities and some differences. *British Journal of Social Psychology, 48*(1), 1–33.

d'Astous, A. and Boujbel, L. (2007). Positioning countries on personality dimensions: scale development and implications for country marketing. *Journal of Business Research, 60*(3), 231–239.

d'Astous, A. and Li, D. (2009). Perceptions of countries based on personality traits: a study in China. *Asia Pacific Journal of Marketing and Logistics, 21*(4), 475–488.

Darton, W. (1790). *Inhabitants of the World.* London: Publisher unknown.

Diamantopoulos, A., Florack, A., Halkias, G. and Palcu, J. (2017). Explicit versus implicit country stereotypes as predictors of product preferences: insights from the stereotype content model. *Journal of International Business Studies, 48*(8), 1023–1036.

Fiske, S.T., Cuddy, A.J.C. and Glick, P. (2007). Universal dimensions of social cognition: warmth, then competence. *Trends in Cognitive Science, 11*(1), 77–83.

Fiske, S.T., Xu, J. and Cuddy, A.J.C. (1999). Disrespecting vs disliking status and interdependence predict ambivalent stereotypes of competence and warmth. *Journal of Social Issues, 55*(3), 473–489.

Fiske, S.T., Cuddy, A.J.C., Glick, P. and Jun, X. (2002). A model of (often mixed) stereotype content: competence and warmth respectively follow from perceived status and competition. *Journal of Personality & Social Psychology, 82*(6), 878–902.

Gawronski, B. and Bodenhausen, G.V. (2006). Associative and propositional processes in evaluation: an integrative review of implicit and explicit attitude change. *Psychological Bulletin, 132*(5), 692–731.

Goldberg, L.R. (1990). An alternative 'description of personality': the big-five factor structure. *Journal of Personality & Social Psychology, 59*(6), 1216–1229.

Harmeling, C.M., Magnusson, P. and Singh, N. (2015). Beyond anger: a deeper look at consumer animosity. *Journal of International Business Studies, 46*(6), 676–693.

Heslop, L.A., Papadopoulos, N., Dowdles, M., Wall, M. and Compeau, D. (2004). Who controls the purse strings: a study of consumers' and retail buyers' reactions in America's FTA environment. *Journal of Business Research, 57*(10), 1177–1188.

Kahneman, D. (2011). *Thinking, Fast and Slow*. New York, NY: Farrar, Straus and Giroux.

Kervyn, N., Fiske, S.T. and Malone, C. (2012). Brands as intentional agents framework: how perceived intentions and ability can map brand perception. *Journal of Consumer Psychology, 22*(2), 166–176.

Kim, Y.K., Shim, S.W. and Dinnie, K. (2013). The dimensions of nation brand personality: a study of nine countries. *Corporate Reputation Review, 16*(1), 34–47.

Klein, J.G., Ettenson, R. and Morris, M.D. (1998). The animosity model of foreign product purchase: an empirical test in the People's Republic of China. *Journal of Marketing, 62*(1), 89–100.

Klingberg, F.L. (1941). Studies in measurement of the relations among sovereign states. *Psychometrika, 6*(6), 335–352.

Knight, G.A. and Calantone, R.J. (2000). A flexible model of consumer country-of-origin perceptions. *International Marketing Review, 17*(2/3), 127–145.

Magnusson, P., Westjohn, S.A. and Sirianni, N.J. (2019). Beyond country image favorability: how brand positioning via country personality stereotypes enhances brand evaluations. *Journal of International Business Studies, 50*(3), 318–338.

Magnusson, P., Westjohn, S.A. and Zdravkovic, S. (2011). 'What? I thought Samsung was Japanese': accurate or not, perceived country of origin matters. *International Marketing Review, 28*(4–5), 454–472.

Maher, A.A. and Carter, L.L. (2011). The affective and cognitive components of country image: perceptions of American products in Kuwait. *International Marketing Review, 28*(6), 559–580.

Martin, B.A.S., Lee, M.S.W. and Lacey, C. (2011). Countering negative country of origin effects using imagery processing. *Journal of Consumer Behaviour, 10*(2), 80–92.

Martin, I.M. and Eroglu, S. (1993). Measuring a multi-dimensional construct: country image. *Journal of Business Research, 28*(3), 191–210.

Murphy, L., Moscardo, G. and Benckendorff, P. (2007). Using brand personality to differentiate regional tourism destinations. *Journal of Travel Research, 46*(1), 5–14.

Nagashima, A. (1970). A comparison of Japanese and US attitudes toward foreign products. *Journal of Marketing, 34*(1), 68–74.

Oberecker, E.M., Riefler, P. and Diamantopoulos, A. (2008). The consumer affinity construct: conceptualization, qualitative investigation, and research agenda. *Journal of International Marketing, 16*(3), 23–56.

Papadopoulos, N. (1993). What product and country images are and are not. In N. Papadopoulos and L. Heslop (eds), *Product Country Images: Impact and Role in International Marketing* (pp. 3–38). Binghamton, NY: Haworth Press.

Papadopoulos, N., El Banna, A. and Murphy, S.A. (2017). Old country passions: an international examination of country image, animosity, and affinity among ethnic consumers. *Journal of International Marketing, 25*(3), 61–82.

Pappu, R., Quester, P.G. and Cooksey, R.W. (2007). Country image and consumer-based brand equity: relationships and implications for international marketing. *Journal of International Business Studies*, *38*(5), 726–745.

Parameswaran, R. and Yaprak, A. (1987). A cross-national comparison of consumer research measures. *Journal of International Business Studies*, *18*(1), 35–49.

Petty, R.E. and Cacioppo, J.T. (1986). *Communication and Persuasion: Central and Peripheral Routes to Attitude Change*. New York, NY: Springer-Verlag.

Petty, R.E., Cacioppo, J.T. and Schumann, D. (1983). Central and peripheral routes to advertising effectiveness: the moderating role of involvement. *Journal of Consumer Research*, *10*(2), 135–146.

Rojas-Méndez, J. and Papadopoulos, N. (2012). Argentine consumers' perceptions of the U.S. brand personality. *Latin American Business Review*, *13*(4), 329–345.

Rojas-Méndez, J.I. and Hine, M.J. (2017). Countries' positioning on personality traits. *Journal of Vacation Marketing*, *23*(3), 233–247.

Rojas-Méndez, J.I., Murphy, S.A. and Papadopoulos, N. (2013). The U.S. brand personality: a Sino perspective. *Journal of Business Research*, *66*(8), 1028–1034.

Rojas-Méndez, J.I., Papadopoulos, N. and Alwan, M. (2015). Testing self-congruity theory in the context of nation brand personality. *Journal of Product & Brand Management*, *24*(1), 18–27.

Rosling, H., Rosling, O. and Ronnlund, A.R. (2018). *Factfulness: Ten Reasons we're Wrong about the World – and Why Things are Better than You Think* (1st edn). New York, NY: Flatiron Books.

Roth, M.S. and Romeo, J.B. (1992). Matching product category and country image perceptions: a framework for managing country-of-origin effects. *Journal of International Business Studies*, *23*(3), 477–497.

Samiee, S. (2010). Advancing the country image construct – a commentary essay. *Journal of Business Research*, *63*(4), 442–445.

Sirianni, N.J., Bitner, M.J., Brown, S.W. and Mandel, N. (2013). Branded service encounters: strategically aligning empioyee behavior with the brand positioning. *Journal of Marketing*, *77*(4), 108–123.

Taras, V., Steel, P. and Kirkman, B.L. (2016). Does country equate with culture? Beyond geography in the search for cultural boundaries. *Management International Review*, *56*(4), 455–487.

Usunier, J.-C. and Cestre, G. (2007). Product ethnicity: revisiting the match between products and countries. *Journal of International Marketing*, *15*(3), 32–72.

Verlegh, P.W.J. and Steenkamp, J.-B.E.M. (1999). A review and meta-analysis of country-of-origin research. *Journal of Economic Psychology*, *20*(5), 521–546.

Westjohn, S.A., Magnusson, P., Peng, Y. and Jung, H. (Forthcoming). Acting on anger: cultural value moderators of the effects of consumer animosity. *Journal of International Business Studies*.

Wojciszke, B. (2005). Morality and competence in person- and self-perception. *European Review of Social Psychology*, *16*, 155–188.

Zeugner-Roth, K.P. (2017). Country-of-origin effects. In H. Van Herk and C.J. Torelli (eds), *Cross Cultural Issues in Consumer Science and Consumer Psychology: Current Perspectives and Future Directions* (pp. 111–128). Cham: Springer International Publishing.

Zeugner-Roth, K.P., Diamantopoulos, A. and Montesinos, A. (2008). Home country image, country brand equity and consumers' product preferences: an empirical study. *Management International Review*, *48*(5), 577–602.

11. Consumer dispositions and product connections to places: from parochialism to cosmopolitanism and beyond

Mark Cleveland, Nicolas Papadopoulos, and Boris Bartikowski

THE INTERSECTION OF PEOPLE, PRODUCTS, AND PLACES

Every place produces a large variety of outputs, and understanding the antecedents of how and why consumers may view them is essential in marketing. Considering the relevant terms broadly and inclusively, as these are typically defined in marketing, the totality of a place's 'outputs' constitutes the overall 'product' on offer to consumers. Individual 'products' and 'brands' may be commercial goods and services in the traditional sense as well as the 'place' itself, whether it is branded or not. And a 'consumer' or 'buyer' is any type of target individual or organization internationally, nationally, or locally – including purchasers of products associated with the place, residents who may be appealed to for support of initiatives undertaken by place authorities, investors and tourists who may 'buy' it as a preferred location (including local firms and residents who, respectively, may choose to invest in their own city or to explore it instead of vacationing elsewhere), and other target markets.

In all such cases, a common denominator is the presence of a buyer – and a key ingredient to effective marketing is understanding the buyer's culture and its effect on the development of one's self-concept, which in turn depends heavily on one's social identity. In its simplest form, the appropriateness and effectiveness of a '*brand–place*' or '*place–brand*' cue presented by a seller to buyers is determined by how well the brand's positioning fits into the three-dimensional construct that is shown in Figure 11.1 and comprises three distinct vectors:

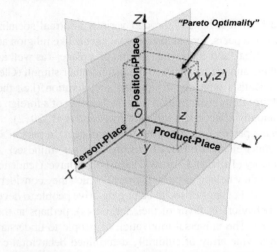

Figure 11.1   The place intersectionality of person–product–position

- Vector X – the '*which*' dimension: *Person–place* hierarchies (i.e., social identities);
- Vector Y – the '*what*' dimension: *Product–place* hierarchies (i.e., place-based levels of meaning associated with the product);
- Vector Z – the '*when*' dimension: *Position–place* hierarchies (i.e., the time-sensitive consumption context, which is situational and may include the presence of other people).

This chapter places special emphasis on the consumer side – that is, the *person–place* hierarchies in Vector X – in order to provide academics and managers with ways of identifying the optimal coordinates of this 3-dimensional roadmap – that is, the 'Pareto Optimality', where no individual condition can be improved without worsening another condition(s) – and thus enhance the ability to predict *Which* consumers will respond favorably to *What* products *When*.

THE ROLE OF CULTURE, SELF CONCEPT, AND SOCIAL IDENTITY

Consumers' perceptions of the world and, in particular, of different specific places in it, are filtered through the lens of culture, which is a primary foundation of consumers' attitudes, behaviors, and lifestyles and is interwoven with nearly every human action. Culture reinforces conventional behavioral expectations by guiding priorities subliminally while consciously invoking social norms. It is not innate but is acquired both first hand – through various informal socialization agents including family and peers, formal institutional agents like religion and education, and the political, legal, and economic systems of a place – as well as vicariously, by watching others and via exposure to media and other stimuli (Cleveland et al., 2009). Social scientists typically distinguish *en*culturation (i.e., the learning of one's home culture) from *ac*culturation (i.e., the learning of a foreign culture), both of which substantially affect one's self-concept (Reed et al., 2012).

Further to one's personal identity (the 'I' component), a person's self-concept includes the distinct element of social identity (the 'we' mindset). According to social identity theory (Tajfel and Turner, 1986), people have a tendency to view the group(s) to which they belong as their 'ingroup', which they consider dissimilar to various 'outgroups'. Feelings of social belonging drive people to develop attitudes and engage in behaviors in favor of their ingroup(s), perhaps at the expense of relevant outgroups. The universal motivation of people to understand who they are brings forth a wide array of culturally determined behavioral consequences, including lifestyles, rituals, tastes, and brand preferences, to name just a few (Reed et al., 2012; Cleveland and Bartsch, 2019). For example, ethnic consumers may patronize grocery stores and restaurants that are congruent with the respective ethnic minority and therefore with their own social identities.

Social identity is the psychological locus of cultural effects, but it is also a temporal and therefore situational concept, which most often leads to the development of several social identities within each person over time, each growing or receding depending on life circumstances. At any given moment, the degree to which one or several social identities are operational depends in part on the context, including the presence and types of other people, and the place in which a particular consumer action is occurring. As indicated by their labels, many social identities are described explicitly in terms of physical places (e.g., Chinese ethnicity) or implicitly in terms of the subjective borders demarcating various social groupings (e.g., 'mainstream' vs. 'minority'). Therefore, place designates not only a physical location, but also something that happens in consumers' minds. In turn, marketing communications may use or trigger social identity – as in the case of the many brands that capitalize on their place of origin, from wines and fashion to cars and electronics.

PLACE VECTORS IN CONSUMER-BASED POSITIONING: PERSON–PRODUCT–POSITION HIERARCHIES

We use the term 'hierarchy' to reflect the fact that consumers' preferences and decision-making are context-dependent. In any given consumption context, they typically juggle a set of social identities which assume greater or receding prominence depending on the time, place, and consumption environment, and the presence and types of other consumers (e.g., ingroup vs. outgroup members). Since consumers have a limited capacity for information processing, their decisions often involve uncertainty and difficult utilitarian and emotional trade-offs, thus developing ever-changing hierarchies of dispositions and objects in their mental schemata. Whether, what, and how product attributes and cues connected to place are attended to and interpreted depends in part on which person–place orientations are operational, and the significance and nature of the consumption context. In other words, the diagnosticity and impact of any place–product cue is not static but assumes greater prominence or recedes into the background across situations.

Importantly, both the psychology-based consumer dispositions and the geography-based place images of products can be related to a wide range of, respectively, 'consumer mind-spaces' and 'product origins', from narrow (e.g., local) to broad (e.g., global). This range makes it possible to develop the person–place and product–place hierarchies, from local to national and global, that are shown in Figure 11.2. The figure is limited in size because of space constraints, but

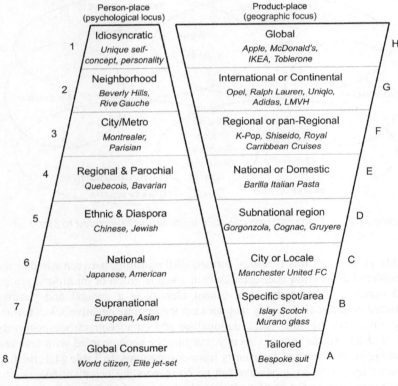

Figure 11.2   Person–place and product–place hierarchies

even so, the basic eight-step scale for each hierarchy it portrays means that juxta-posing the consumer and brand sides results in no fewer than 64 combinations. As will be discussed in the subsections that follow, these combinations are important in two contexts that are critical in both research and practice: understanding con-sumers and positioning products.

Person–Place Hierarchies

Researchers have developed inventories of consumers' social dispositions connected to place and have advanced various typologies to categorize them. Figure 11.3 features a Venn diagram that shows 17 place-related dispositions that are specifically relevant to the present discussion, and distinguishes them on the basis of their ingroup vs. outgroup orientation and the positive vs. negative valence of these orientations in appraising these groups.

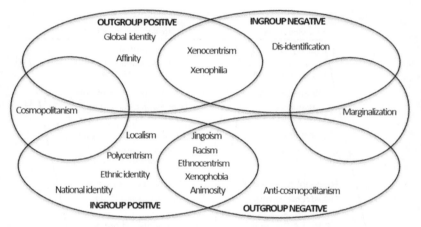

Figure 11.3   Venn diagram of social dispositions connected to place

Table 11.1 refines this typology further, distinguishing between whether the considered disposition is directed toward a single group or multiple ingroups and outgroups. For example, a global identity is a general and positive outward-bound social identity that does not incorporate negative affect toward any group. On the other hand, nationalism and ethnocentrism are positively oriented toward the ingroup society, but may be accompanied with fear and loathing of, or a sense of superiority toward, outgroups. In Table 11.1, the first seven dispositions have positive but no corresponding negative valence, the next seven have a mixture of positive and negative valences, and the last three have negative but no corresponding positive valences.

Table 11.1   *Specificity and direction of consumer dispositions connected to place*

Orientation toward: Disposition	Ingroup(s) Single	Multiple	Outgroup(s) General	Specific
Cosmopolitanism	+	+	+	+
Global Identity			+	
Polycentrism/Mixed Ethnic I.D.		+		
National Identity/Patriotism	+			
Localism/Parochialism	+			
Ethnic Identity	+			
Affinity				+
Xenocentrism	−			+
Xenophilia	−		+	
Jingoism/Nationalism	+	+	−	−
Ethnocentrism	+		−	
Animosity	+			−
Racism	+			−
Xenophobia	+		−	−
Dis-identification	−			
Anti-cosmopolitanism			−	
Marginalization/Deculturation	−	(−)	(−)	−

Notes:
+ positively-valenced orientation.
− negatively-valenced orientation.
(−) possibly, but not necessarily, negatively-valenced orientation.

The paragraphs below describe each of the 17 dispositions shown in Figure 11.2 and Table 11.1. Of these, some refer to consumers' views toward other countries and one's home, while others are more closely related to the social identity construct.

Consumer dispositions toward other countries and home

The 10 dispositions that belong in this group draw on the comprehensive inventory of place-related dispositions by Papadopoulos et al. (2018) toward one's home and other countries, which includes citations to relevant past research for readers who may wish to study them in greater depth.

Cosmopolitanism involves a world-oriented view by high-culture consumers but is also intricately allied to the local narrative. True cosmopolitans span cultural differences while celebrating and safeguarding distinctions between societies, thus embracing local, national, and global identities and having omnivorous consumption patterns pursuing the finest, most authentic experiences available. Consequently, cosmopolitans share with locally-oriented consumers a common objective of preserving cultural diversity, albeit with very different motivations and results, and may embrace multiple social identities, including perhaps temporary ones with cultural outgroups that are not shown separately on the hierarchy in Figure 11.2.

Xenocentrism describes the tendency of a subset of consumers, such as elites in emerging economies, to idealize one or more other cultures while devaluing their own ingroup. Several root causes may induce some individuals to prefer cultural outgroups and absorb their attitudes and norms, including perceived social exclusion and feelings of low self-esteem prevalent amongst low-status societal members (e.g., certain caste, occupation, or gender segments) and/or becoming enamored with a place and its people because of their perceived higher status globally or through first-hand experiences (e.g., tourism). At a consumption level, xenocentrism may translate into preferences for products from one or more specific cultural outgroups over domestic ones.

Xenophilia is similar to xenocentrism but differs in that it refers to consumers who favor foreign outgroups *in general*, while also spurning the domestic ingroup, leading to a preference for foreign over domestic goods overall.

Affinity, unlike the previous two broad dispositions, refers to positive feelings directed at a specific place and does not involve derogation of one's ingroup and culture. Affinity can arise from a variety of factors, including perceived cultural similarity or direct personal experiences (e.g., through family ties) with the external group, and typically extends to positive views of (or even adopting) the cultural values, social norms, and products of the affinity country.

Parochialism is the tendency of people to view their home culture as best, seeking to maintain their own cultural uniqueness without necessarily upholding the cultural integrity of other groups. This disposition points to consumers who are content in their parochial ways of life, prefer local lifestyles and consumption habits, and are likely to choose local products over those from farther afield when the former are available.

Nationalism can be seen as dialectically interconnected to globalization: as the latter advanced over the past few decades, the former has been increasing. Perceptions of potential harm to national interests and national identity have led to many people retreating to their home cultures, as they struggle to recover a sense of constancy, distinctiveness, and even pride. However, while the sibling construct of patriotism is limited to love of one's country (and a willingness to sacrifice for it), nationalism includes feelings of superiority and dislike of external others and is often inflamed by opportunistic politicians, and even by the hosting of global events, such as the Olympic Games, leading to jingoism. Such predispositions frequently engender determined support of domestic products and avoidance of foreign ones.

Ethnocentrism refers to a psychological attachment to an ethnic ingroup, which in the consumer context manifests itself as a general proclivity to prefer domestic products and eschew foreign alternatives. Consumer ethnocentrism is the most widely studied place-based disposition as a predictor of marketplace behavior and one of the most enduring non-tariff barriers to trade. The concept incorporates normative social pressures and perceptions of a moral obligation, leading ethnocentric consumers to, other things being equal, accept economic sacrifices if necessary, in order to support their domestic economy and brands.

Animosity is country-specific, and therefore differs from ethnocentrism in the same way that affinity differs from xenophilia. Animosity refers to strong feelings of dislike, antipathy, and anger, directed at another country as a result of current or past events and disputes in politics, warfare, or economic issues. Importantly, consumers may feel animosity toward a country without necessarily being ethnocentric, since ethnocentrism is not target-specific, but both of these dispositions may affect behavior even if the buyers in each case believe that the foreign goods in question are objectively better.

Xenophobia is the obverse of xenophilia and embodies extreme emotions (distress, fear, hate) and the ensuing negative attitudes (prejudice, hostility) arising from and directed at *all* foreign units. Foreign-made products are likely to be repulsed by xenophobic consumers, regardless of their source.

Racism shares some similarities with other negative dispositions (e.g., animosity) but is unique in being rooted in a specific issue, reflecting a belief that people can be divided into exclusive races and that differences between them give some an inherent superiority over others. The construct and its negative effects are widely documented and well understood, and research shows that higher levels of consumer racism decrease the willingness to buy products or services from the target group(s). We note, however, that racism is as difficult to identify (since it is widely condemned and therefore most often takes subtle forms) as it is important (since racist consumer choices may reflect both actual and symbolic ways of discrimination, such as avoiding providers from the target race, ranging from individual hairdressers, doctors, or teachers to stores in particular neighborhoods).

Types and levels of social identity
The seven dispositions included in this group draw on those described above as well as on other related sources where needed, but focus more on portraying variations in the bases that are related to the development of one's social identity.

Global identity. Until recently, stiff national borders obstructed the flow of people, products, and information, and consumers carried out their everyday lives drawing mostly on local values and customs and in accordance with parochial behavioral expectations. Today, the forces of globalization are stitching together communities around the world, which for some consumers promotes the emergence of a world-minded global identity that recognizes commonalities, rather than stressing differences, and takes interest in global events. The archetypal global consumer switches between global and local and still other identities, taking on one, the other, or a mixture of both when appropriate or beneficial (Bartikowski and Cleveland, 2017).

National identity. The progressive merger of principalities and districts into nation-states over the past few centuries led to the emergence of national societies and identities (Bartsch et al., 2019). Dispositions connected to national identity include patriotism, nationalism, ethnocentrism, animosity, racism, and xenophobia, each of which has dissimilar corollaries for consumer behavior. For instance, while nationalism is assumed to incorporate hostile attitudes toward external others, a strong national identity signifies the inner bond that one has to one's nation, which in turn generates patterns of thinking, feeling, and acting derived from the society's shared conventions and values.

Ethnic identity is a deep-seated and enduring component of social identity whose importance has been exacerbated as contemporary migration waves have made largely homogeneous societies (e.g., France, Spain) more similar to traditionally multicultural ones (e.g., Canada, Australia). One's ethnic identity is instilled early on, as children and adolescents, influenced as they may be by their parents and peers, develop their self-concept as part of their sense of membership of a communal ingroup. Ethnic identity may adapt, transform, and evolve over time (e.g., depending on one's degree of acculturation to mainstream society), and may manifest in people's relations to aspects such as history, language, religion, or geographic region, which vary for different ethnic groups. For example, language is an important aspect of ethnic identity for French Canadians, whereas respect toward elders on the part of younger members of the community plays a major role in shaping Middle Eastern identities (El Banna et al., 2018).

Polycentrism, or the phenomenon of multiple ethnic identities, also results from the growth of immigrant populations from various origins. This creates ethnically diverse societies evolving not only from one's birth and heritage but also from the intermixing of people from different ethnic backgrounds (e.g., through marriage or one's chosen peer ingroups). Persons of mixed ethnicity do not fit snugly into one group but sit astride cultural confines. For instance, a Coptic Christian who emigrates from Ethiopia to Canada, is fluent in English, and marries an Italian-origin Catholic, may see one's self, and/or may be seen by others, as having a polycentric identity comprising some combination of 'Ethiopian', 'African', 'black', 'Christian', 'English-Canadian', 'Italian', or other possible characteristics. Such polycentric identities clearly hold key repercussions for marketing theory and practice, in terms of segmentation, targeting, product positioning, and communication appeals, and word-of-mouth and other interpersonal information exchanges.

Anti-cosmopolitanism. Could there be a concept that reflects a consumer's antagonism toward cultural outgroups in general, without any complementary affability, nor necessarily any acrimony, toward the cultural ingroup? We believe that there could be, although as of yet it has not, to the best of our knowledge, been proposed, at least not in the marketing literature. Such a construct would reflect consumer anxiety about their country being 'swamped' with immigrants, leading to hostility toward outgroup cultures, coupled with a lack of interest and attachment to their own culture or a motivation to preserve it.

Marginalization may be seen as a variant of the notion of anti-cosmopolitanism, where the individual abjures not only national, ethnic, or other localized cultural identities, but also repudiates global and foreign entity modes of social identity. This outright rejection of any social identity forms may be due to acculturative stresses, such as those experienced by immigrants who feel disaffection with their ethnic group, have not successfully integrated with the alternative mainstream group, and perhaps also feel alienated from the global consumer culture (Cleveland and Bartsch, 2019). In such cases, consumer behaviors may be bereft of cultural influences and not driven by a sense of social identity.

Dis-identification refers to consumers who may disavow their own culture, or, at the very least, catalogue themselves as dissimilar from their ingroup, without any corresponding positive attitudes toward other groups. This disposition has only recently been investigated in marketing, but initial evidence suggests that, absent a relevant social identity, it is likely to affect consumer behavior (Josiassen, 2011). For instance, a German who has dis-identified from the 'German' ingroup may elect to buy a Japanese, South Korean, or American car, instead of a German brand, based solely on such utilitarian criteria as price or fuel consumption.

Product–Place Hierarchies

The views that consumers have about places carry over to their perceptions about the products from these places, in many cases invoking social norms. Normative influence reflects the consumer's yearning to enhance his or her impression in the eyes of others they consider relevant. Therefore, most if not all product/place-based inferences are conditional, depending on the social characteristics of the person, as well as the particular context (e.g., the consumption setting, the product category, etc.). For example, the recent (re-)conversion of the Hagia Sofia in Istanbul from a museum to a mosque, and lingering historical tensions (from the Byzantine to the Ottoman empires and beyond to today's Greece and Turkey), are likely to affect how Orthodox, Catholic, and other Christians the world over evaluate Turkey and Turkish products. Similarly, the asymmetric relationship between Canada and the United States palpably affects how Canadians respond to American advertising.

Three social-psychological theories dovetail to explain consumers' place–brand associations. *Associative network memory theory* (Keller, 1993) posits that consumers' thoughts about an attitudinal object (e.g., a brand, whether of a commercial product or a place) comprise interlinked cognitive nodes. Once a brand node is triggered, this spawns the activation of other linked nodes, permitting the recall of brand attributes and semantic associations (e.g., high quality, vibrant city). The link between concepts and objects is conditional upon association strength, which ensues from repeated exposure to these concepts and objects concurrently under varying circumstances. *Self-verification theory* (Swann et al., 2004) suggests that consumers are innately driven to achieve coherence and stability with respect to their identity and, if necessary, will take actions to defend it, such as joining or reinforcing relationships with groups to demonstrate a sense of collective belongingness. *Social identity theory* (Tajfel and Turner, 1986) posits that the social part of an individual's self-concept derives from membership in groups with which one affiliates, and, as mentioned earlier, feelings of social belonging drive people to develop attitudes and engage in behaviors that favor their ingroup(s) over relevant outgroups.

Crucially, these theories converge to predict similar effects/outcomes: that consumers respond more favorably to product, brand, locale, advertising, purchasing environment, and other stimuli that are consistent with their social identity(ies) and tend to repudiate identity-inconsistent stimuli.

Position–Place Hierarchies

Cognition, affect, and conation (behavioral intent), comprising the three mechanisms in the theory of attitude formation, are a good starting point for understanding place-based product effects and the relevant aspect(s) of the '*position*–place' hierarchy that is operational in a given context. *Cognition* encompasses intrinsic product characteristics (e.g., quality, reliability, durability), but also inferences based on product-related place stereotypes (match of place attributes to category beliefs), including its place of origin. In *affect*, place is an image attribute that connects the product to symbolic and emotional benefits, including social status, national pride, and ingroup cultural identity, and helps to determine how beliefs are formed and evaluated as well as their relative valence (strength). *Conation* encapsulates one's purchase intentions based on his or her beliefs and feelings and also incorporates social and personal norms of behavior related to place. For instance, a product may be considered 'objectively' good and emotionally 'liked', but may be purchased or not depending on whether it is thought to be the ethically 'right' or 'wrong' thing to do (e.g., respectively, support for the domestic economy versus products from places seen as involved in objectionable activities currently or in the past, or as having odious politicians or regimes).

Selecting from the person–place and product–place hierarchies in Figure 11.2 in light of these attitude components helps to decide the optimal combination of elements to employ in marketing products and places. When cognition is dominant, the place cue is used to reflect intrinsic product characteristics, and so *product*–place attributes are more critical considerations than *person*–place ones. In other words, the positive or negative biases arising from a consumer's social sense of self are suppressed by product–place considerations. When affect is dominant, place holds symbolic and emotional value to the consumer – for example, as a way of expressing cultural affiliation. Here, *person*–place considerations assume a larger role than product–place concerns in guiding consumption. Finally, because conation includes normative conduct and morality considerations, *person*–place aspects, such as ethnic identity, are apt to overpower product–place aspects, should they conflict with each other.

Perhaps a few anecdotal examples might help to illustrate which mechanism is paramount in a given situation and may predict which place-based social identity aspects are operational, thus pointing to a preferred product–place positioning strategy. At a recent conference in Edinburgh, the first and third co-authors of this chapter, who hail from Canada and France, were at a local pub for evening drinks. Quite naturally, the beverage of choice was Laphroaig 10-year old Islay Single Malt Scotch Whisky. In this case, the combination of the particular production spot (the specific distillery on the island of Islay), and the sub-regional location (Inner Hebrides Islands) and country (Scotland, in the UK), were appropriate given the product, the temporal consumption episode, and the person–place characteristics of the whisky sippers (at that moment, we saw ourselves as cosmopolitan global consumers craving an authentic consumption experience). According to Figure 11.2, these product–place levels are represented by positions B, D, and E, as well as constituted at the consumer level in person–place positions 8, 6, and perhaps also 4 and 1.

As another example, a friend of the lead author has an academic appointment in China. Notwithstanding her patriotism in being Chinese, and her penchant for Chinese brands for many product categories, when it comes to mobile phones her preference is for Apple's iPhone over Huawei, the similarly sophisticated domestic alternative. For her, the iPhone conveys a sense of membership in a global consumer tribe, and because it is assembled in China (yet designed in California), it allows her also to support the domestic economy. Here, the iPhone projects product–place positions H (global image), D (place of design), and E (place of made-in), in order to appeal to the person–place positions 7 (global citizen), 6 (Chinese citizen), and 1 (self-concept).

Another point to draw from Figure 11.2 is that brand positioning can simultaneously employ multiple levels, or emphasize one level to appeal to one group of target consumers and another for a different audience. For example, the leading American beer brand, Budweiser, is presently positioned in the United States as D-domestic, is proudly promoted as both domestic and C-city/locale within its hometown of St Louis, Missouri, and was marketed in the past as H-global, with reference to its then-status as 'the most popular beer in the whole world'. On the other hand, Guinness beer is resolutely Irish in Ireland but is presented as both Irish and global to consumers elsewhere.

Person–place identities interact with individual traits and values, various perceived product–place factors including brand origin, as well as aspects associated with the purchase and/or consumption context. While a full review of the copious

Table 11.2   Place-based dispositions, social risk context, and perceived brand origin

Consumers and Product Context	Consumer Condition		Sample Supporting Studies[a]
	Brand Origin *More* Important	Brand Origin *Less* Important	
Consumer Dispositions			
Ethnic, religious, city or neighborhood, region	High	Low	Cleveland et al. (2011)
National identity and Patriotism	High	Low	Pappu and Quester (2010)
Consumer Ethnocentrism (CET)	High	Low	El Banna et al. (2018)
Consumer Animosity (country-specific)	High	Low	Klein et al. (1998)
Cosmopolitanism (COS)	High	Low	Cleveland and Laroche (2012)
Foreign/Xenocentric identity (XEN)	High	Low	Balabanis and Diamantopoulos (2016)
Global identity	Low	High	Nijssen and Douglas (2011)
Sense of homophily (personal/socio-cultural similarity)	High	Low	Torres (2007)
Perceived similarity of source place to buyer's home	Dissimilar	Similar	Wang and Lamb (1983)
Materialism	High	Low	Cleveland (2015)
Product Context: The Influence of Social Risk			
Conspicuousness of product/brand (visibility to others)	Conspicuous	Inconspicuous	Batra et al. (2000)
Public vs. private consumption	Public	Private	Amine and Shin (2002)
Reference group influence	High	Low	Bearden et al. (1989)
Status vs. non-status product/brand	Status	Non-status	O'Cass and Frost (2002)
Luxury vs. non-luxury product category	Luxury	Non-luxury	Cordell (1991)

Note: [a] To prevent clutter, only a sample of supporting studies is shown in this table. Several of these studies, and additional ones from the main list of references of this chapter (e.g., Bartikowski and Cleveland, 2017; Papadopoulos et al., 2018; Cleveland and Bartsch, 2019), cover one or more of the elements in the first column and can be consulted for further information.

situational elements is beyond the scope of this chapter, a partial list of these elements is summarized in Table 11.2.

'SO WHAT?': SELECTED NOVEL INSIGHTS AND IMPLICATIONS FOR RESEARCHERS AND MANAGERS

The previous sections of this chapter have added a unique perspective to existing research by highlighting a large number of implications that arise from specific consumer dispositions and the potential effects of social identity. Rather than revisiting those concept-specific implications, this discussion focuses on a handful of key novel insights that flow from our depiction of the place intersectionality of person–product–position and are relevant to both research and practice. We use such terms as outputs, products, brands, and consumers in the broad sense specified in the introduction and in line with how they are viewed in marketing, letting the context define the exact meaning as necessary, and believe that these are relevant to both managers and researchers and to both commercial products and services as well as places.

Consumer Dispositions Matter

The ways that persons, products, and positions can be intertwined are many and complex, and this complexity is exacerbated by the scope and variety of factors that affect these relationships. What is more, the 17 consumer dispositions presented above were selected in relation to the three hierarchies that are of specific interest to this chapter, and therefore tell only part of the story. Of the two studies that have offered relevant inventories and taxonomies to date, one focused specifically on 19 *positive* dispositions toward *foreign countries* only (Bartsch et al., 2016), one reported on 32 *positive and negative* orientations toward *foreign and domestic goods* (Papadopoulos et al., 2018) – and both indicated that even more dispositions can be identified through in-depth study dedicated to developing an exhaustive catalogue.

Neither research nor practice can reasonably account for all the possible permutations, but a small handful of examples can illustrate why both need to do so where feasible. Taking the consumer affinity construct as one case in point, it has only been examined in a small handful of studies at the country level – yet its relevance is perhaps even greater at the subnational place level: other things being equal, one may expect that people may feel a greater degree of affinity toward compatriots living in nearby towns than to those in other countries. Might this lead, for example, to more positive views toward products or investment from those towns, or inter-city collaborations in promoting regional tourism? The construct concept says 'yes', but we do not know since this perspective has not been studied and is unlikely to have been used in practice.

A similar comment can be made about consumer ethnocentrism. We know that communities that span national borders (e.g., Basques, Kurds) or lie within a larger sovereign nation-state (e.g., Quebecois, Catalans, Scots) can be very nationalistic – but are they also ethnocentric? If so, how strongly, and either way does *this* (as opposed to nationalism) affect their purchase behavior? Likewise with racism: marketing research on places tends to consider them fairly homogeneous, but is this construct and its effects considered when cities with multi-racial populations put forth place branding initiatives, and if so, how? Lastly, when considering parochialism versus cosmopolitanism, do we account for places like New York City, whose citizens love it and have a very strong preference for the 'local' lifestyle and customs (very parochial) in large part because the 'local cultural capital' is rich enough to satiate one's needs for cultural diversity (very cosmopolitan)?

A quick answer to such questions must be, once again, twofold: we do not know, which means we need more research; and we badly need to know, for practitioners to be more effective and successful at what they do.

Layers of Place Above and Below that of the Nation-state

In the country-of-origin literature, the image of various origins and its effects on buyers has been studied at the level of the nation-state. However, this unit of analysis is ill-suited for uncovering market segments above and below the nation-state threshold (Cleveland et al., 2011). Places at any level are not merely positions on a map but denote physical and mental spaces that may be sub-places within a larger entity (e.g., neighborhoods in a city) or extend across two or more entities (e.g., 'Asia-Pacific'). For example, many products today are marketed as 'Made in the EU' or have some version of 'Euro/European' in their brand name, while on the other hand 'Farm to Fork' has become a major trend for food products among co-called 'locavore' consumers. Such developments respectively expand or narrow the definition of what is 'domestic', as reflected, respectively, in the strategies of such brands as the cross-nationally positioned Alberto Européen hair shampoo or the locally-focused Farmboy, a chain of food markets in Ontario, Canada, that heavily promotes its product sourcing from farms in each store's area where possible.

Is 'Glocal' Better or Worse than Either Global or Local?

With respect to *glocalization*, which is often heralded as the optimal solution (Cleveland and Bartsch, 2019) in terms of how managers should 'think global, act local', one caveat is in order. The intermingling of local elements with foreign or global components can elicit negative emotions and defensive reactions if this mixing is sensed as degrading, sullying, or otherwise threatening the strength or integrity of the local culture. As just one case in point, the 'glocal' strategy used by Starbucks famously backfired in China, attracting protests and being decried for desecrating traditional Chinese culture over their coffee shop in Beijing's Forbidden City (which was forced to close). Shifting the perspective to 'place' as the product, a similar effect could be encountered if a city advertised itself to residents or others as combining, for example, 'local heart' with 'global vision'.

Tangible Goods vs. Intangible Services vs. Places

Within the international marketing literature, discussions surrounding the optimal degree of standardization of the marketing mix have long centred on brands of tangible goods. That focus has recently begun to shift to include services, which contribute the bulk of GDP in most industrialized nations and may represent the biggest opportunities for international marketers, since the globalization of services has lagged that of goods and since several emerging countries still have considerable room for growth in this sector. However, such opportunities face additional challenges due to the four unique characteristics of services (intangibility, perishability, inseparability, and particularly, variability) which often interact with cultural characteristics and thus with place-related social orientations (Laroche et al., 2004).

Outgroup ownership is often an asset in service-dominated exchanges. For example, in financial services, foreign ownership may reduce risk perceptions in such emerging markets as Peru, where stable foreign banks, like Canada's Scotiabank, reduce 'tangibility' risk, much like the grand masonry banking temples of the late nineteenth century served to allay consumers' apprehensions about possible bank failure. At the same time, because services are often characterized by a high degree of consumer involvement with personnel and facilities, they consequently require a high level of sensitivity to the local culture.

Cultures vary with respect to behavioral norms, which affect consumers' service expectations and perceptions of service quality. This could impact banks just as it could a city's tourism office located in a major target market, since customers in different places are accustomed to evaluating services differently and to holding different expectations about optimal encounters. Foreign-based service brands can easily hire domestic front-line service providers, to resonate and bond with local customers. In this way, global service providers can position themselves as 'glocalizers' or 'best-of-both worlders' that offer the quality and prestige associated with being global, while at the same time being sensitive and responsive to local customs and peculiarities.

Disguised, Fictitious, or Exaggerated Brand Provenance and Place Branding

The association (or not) of oneself with desirable (or not) identity images figures prominently amongst the impressions that people try to construct and communicate. In this light, examination of the person– and product–place hierarchies in Figure 11.2 shows why some brands seek to promote their place identity based on objective and observable characteristics – while others exaggerate it, generate fictitious versions of it, disguise it, or hide it altogether (Papadopoulos, 1993).

For example, most US consumers are probably unaware that the 'all-American' Budweiser beer brand is foreign-owned, a characteristic that may not be attended to for habitual purchases where affective factors, in this case the 'place of association', may be more important. Some brands avoid identification with their origin so as to project a global image (e.g., Coca-Cola, Adidas); others seek to benefit from 'borrowed' place cues that invoke positive place associations (e.g., Häagen-Dazs ice-cream from Brooklyn Heights, New York, uses a Danish-sounding name, and Brazil's A Marca Bavaria beer was positioned in Canada in relation to a place associated with a long tradition of high-quality beers); and still others opt for branding that relies on invoking a *type* of place instead of a specific origin (e.g., the 'valley' of Hidden Valley salad dressing could technically be anywhere, but the brand denotes an ersatz bucolic place).

In all such cases, successful marketing is not just a matter of 'creating a brand image' but, more importantly, of the extent to which that image matches the product's actual characteristics and is in line with the target buyers' social identities. In this context, Häagen-Dazs may have greater appeal to cosmopolitan than parochial consumers, and the premium positioning of A Marca Bavaria backfired when it was reported that it was a 'poor man's beer' in Brazil (Holloway, 2006).

Turning to the marketing of places, modest 'puffery' in positioning and advertising seems to be considered 'okay' and is frequently used, but higher levels may also backfire in at least three instances: if the presented image is greatly at odds with actual place characteristics (e.g., in tourism claims of 'friendly locals' often do not materialize in the personal experiences of visitors, potentially creating negative word of mouth); if a campaign aiming to raise civic pride among residents exaggerates significantly ('we are the best city in the world!'), thus misrepresenting how they view their own place; and if, perhaps as a function of typically constrained budgets, a place promotes itself to all targets in the same way, even though the promoted image may be at variance with the social identity of some markets (e.g., what makes the Cote d'Azur or Las Vegas very attractive to some may be viewed as immoral by others).

CONCLUDING REMARKS: INDIGENIZATION, SHOCKS TO THE SYSTEM, ODD PARTNERS, AND MORE

The above subtitle might have been rendered better as, 'How little we know and how much we need to know'. In traditional research, the research 'gaps' that scholars attempt to close are reasonably clear and specific; for example, of the 17 dispositions above, some have been studied a lot but still leave room for in-depth investigations (e.g., ethnocentrism) and some very little, calling for much more attention (e.g., xenocentrism, and even more so, xenophilia). Combined, addressing such gaps can keep researchers busy for a long time – but there is much more to be said, or better, to be researched, for questions that are not typically part of traditional studies.

One clear example is the case of 'shocks to the system', which can take such forms as the recent COVID-19 pandemic, the massive migrant waves from the Middle East and North Africa toward (mostly) Europe, Brexit, or the threat of major war following the border standoff and military skirmishes between India and China. Thinking about and researching their potential consequences on consumer dispositions is hard. We do know, in the abstract, that events of this magnitude change how people think – but what are their implications specifically for consumers? Might those in place X become more ethnocentric or less because of event Y? Do global events, such as the pandemic, unite people to fight against it and make them more worldminded, or do they encourage countries to incubate different varieties of global consumer culture, or is it more likely that consumers will turn to parochialism?

Global consumer culture is indigenized by specific cultures, as with clearly global 'Hollywood' becoming localized in India's *Bollywood* and Nigeria's *Nollywood* – but, ironically, if 'globalization' and its associated culture may fall off the radar for some time, might people become less hostile and reactive, and might this diminish their motivation to preserve the uniqueness of their local culture?

What kind of culture is the so-called *Korean Wave* or *K-pop* phenomenon, which took the world by storm for over a decade? First, it is not *Korean* but *global* consumer culture with a strong *Korean seasoning*. Second and more intriguing, what kinds of dispositions does it trigger, for example, in places that formerly dominated Korea, such as Japan and China, where it resonates because it expresses global consumer culture, or because people can relate to and identify with its origin, or for any number of other reasons that have yet to be researched?

And what of 'authenticity', that characteristic that flows from a place's unique features, is of high value to many consumers, and offers a competitive advantage since it cannot be readily copied – does it apply only within its 'comfort zone' of localness at the town or regional levels, or might it also be relevant at the national and global levels? Is Gouda cheese a product of the city of Gouda itself or of the Netherlands? Can a product like Coca-Cola, which does not involve much originality or craftsmanship, claim to be 'authentically global' because of its worldwide distribution and of marketing strategies such as its 'I'd like to teach the world to sing' campaign?

To deliver on the 'More' in the heading of this section, it goes without saying that many other factors not reviewed in this chapter also contribute heavily to a person's identity, his or her behavioral inclinations in the marketplace, and the products that he or she actually favors and buys. In a nutshell, 'all of the above' represent fruitful variables for researchers to incorporate into future investigations of the place intersectionality of person–product–position. As Papadopoulos (1993, p. 17) put it, "The available evidence suggests that, if anything, the higher the level of globalization, the greater the significance of [product–place associations]"; in other words, it is exactly because of globalization that the significance of place in marketing contexts is intensifying rather than waning. As more and more markets have gone global, consumers are progressively able to select from multiple identities, adopt various different dispositions, and consider a large variety of global, foreign, and local options for many product categories – which provides enough food for thought to keep researchers and managers busy for some time to come.

REFERENCES

Amine, L.S. and Shin, S.H. (2002). A comparison of consumer nationality as a determinant of COO preferences. *Multinational Business Review*, *10*(1), 45.

Balabanis, G. and Diamantopoulos, A. (2016). Consumer xenocentrism as determinant of foreign product preference: a system justification perspective. *Journal of International Marketing*, *24*(3), 58–77.

Bartikowski, B. and Cleveland, M. (2017). 'Seeing is being': consumer culture and the positioning of premium cars in China. *Journal of Business Research*, *77*(August), 195–202.

Bartsch, F., Riefler, P. and Diamantopoulos, A. (2016). A taxonomy and review of positive consumer dispositions toward foreign countries and globalization. *Journal of International Marketing*, *24*(1), 82–110.

Bartsch, F., Cleveland, M., Ko, E. and Cadogan, J. (2019). Facts, fantasies, foundations, formations, fights, and fallouts of global consumer culture: an introduction to the special issue. *International Marketing Review*, *36*(4), 514–523.

Batra, R., Ramaswamy, V., Alden, D.L., Steenkamp, J.-B.E.M. and Ramachander, S. (2000). Effects of brand local and nonlocal origin on consumer attitudes in developing countries. *Journal of Consumer Psychology*, *9*(2), 83–95.

Bearden, W.O., Netemeyer, R.G. and Teel, J.E. (1989). Measurement of consumer susceptibility to interpersonal influence. *Journal of Consumer Research*, *15*(4), 473–481.

Cleveland, M. (2015). *Wanting Things and Needing Affiliation: Ethnic Consumers and Materialism*. In: A. Jamal, L. Peñaloza and M. Laroche (eds), *Routledge Companion on Ethnic Marketing*, London: Routledge, pp. 147–182.

Cleveland, M. and Bartsch, F. (2019). Global consumer culture: epistemology and ontology. *International Marketing Review*, *36*(4), 556–580.

Cleveland, M. and Laroche, M. (2012). *Becoming and Being a Cosmopolitan Consumer*. In: M. Prince (ed.), *Consumer Cosmopolitanism in the Age of Globalization*. New York, NY: Business Expert Press, pp. 51–100.

Cleveland, M., Papadopoulos, N. and Laroche, M. (2011). Identity, demographics, and consumer behaviors: international market segmentation across product categories. *International Marketing Review*, *28*(3), 244–266.

Cleveland, M., Laroche, M., Pons, F. and Kastoun, R. (2009). Acculturation and consumption: textures of cultural adaptation. *International Journal of Intercultural Relations*, *33*(3), 196–212.

Cordell, V.V. (1991). Competitive context and price as moderators of country of origin preferences. *Journal of the Academy of Marketing Science*, *19*(2), 123–128.

El Banna, A., Papadopoulos, N., Murphy, S.A., Rod, M. and Rojas-Méndez, J.I. (2018). Ethnic identity, consumer ethnocentrism, and purchase intentions among bi-cultural ethnic consumers: 'divided loyalties' or 'dual allegiance'? *Journal of Business Research, 82*, 310–319.

Holloway, A. (2006). More beer from Brazil. *Canadian Business*, 24 April. Accessed 28 September 2020 at: https://www.canadianbusiness.com/business-strategy/more-beer -from-brazil/.

Josiassen, A. (2011). Consumer disidentification and its effects on domestic product purchases: an empirical investigation in the Netherlands. *Journal of Marketing, 75*(2), 124–140.

Keller, K.L. (1993). Conceptualizing, measuring, and managing customer-based brand equity. *Journal of Marketing, 57*(1), 1–22.

Klein, J.G., Ettenson, R. and Morris, M. (1998). The animosity model of foreign product purchase: an empirical test in the People's Republic of China. *Journal of Marketing, 62*(1), 89–100.

Laroche, M., Ueltschy, L.C., Abe, S., Cleveland, M. and Yannopoulos, P. (2004). Service quality perceptions and customer satisfaction: evaluating the role of culture. *Journal of International Marketing, 12*(3), 58–85.

Nijssen, E.J. and Douglas, S.P. (2011). Consumer world-mindedness and attitudes toward product positioning in advertising: an examination of global versus foreign versus local positioning. *Journal of International Marketing, 19*(3), 113–133.

O'Cass, A. and Frost, H. (2002). Status brands: examining the effects of non-product-related brand associations on status and conspicuous consumption. *Journal of Product & Brand Management, 11*(2), 67–88.

Papadopoulos, N. (1993). What product and country images are and are not. In N. Papadopoulos and L.A. Heslop (eds), *Product–Country Images: Impact and Role in International Marketing* Binghampton, NY: The Haworth Press, pp. 1–38.

Papadopoulos, N., Cleveland, M., Bartikowski, B. and Yaprak, A. (2018). Of countries, places and product/brand place associations: an inventory of dispositions and issues relating to place image and its effects. *Journal of Product & Brand Management, 27*(7), 735–753.

Pappu, R. and Quester, P. (2010). Country equity: conceptualization and empirical evidence. *International Business Review, 19*(3), 276–291.

Reed II, A., Forehand, M.R., Puntoni, S. and Warlop, L. (2012). Identity-based consumer behavior. *International Journal of Research in Marketing, 29*(4), 310–321.

Swann Jr, W.B., Polzer, J.T., Seyle, D.C. and Ko, S.J. (2004). Finding value in diversity: verification of personal and social self-views in diverse groups. *Academy of Management Review, 29*(1), 9–27.

Tajfel, H. and Turner, J.C. (1986). The social identity theory of intergroup behavior. In: S. Worchel and W.G. Austin (eds), *Psychology of Intergroup Relations*. Chicago, IL: Hall Publishers, pp. 7–24.

Torres, I.M. (2007). A tale of two theories: sympathy or competition? *Journal of Business Research, 60*(3), 197–205.

Wang, C. and Lamb, C.W. (1983). The impact of selected environmental forces upon consumers' willingness to buy foreign products. *Journal of the Academy of Marketing Science, 11*(2), 71–84.

12. Country of origin cues in advertising: theoretical insights and practical implications

Fabian Bartsch and Katharina Petra Zeugner-Roth

INTRODUCTION: THE USE AND PROCESSING OF COUNTRY OF ORIGIN CUES

The global advertising market amounted to US$532.5 billion in 2019 (Imarc Group, 2020), and estimates suggest that, on average, consumers are confronted with 4,000 to 10,000 advertising messages every day (Forbes, 2017). Naturally, competition for consumer attention is fierce, with advertisers seeking to communicate their brand messages to an increasingly skeptical audience (Isaac and Grayson, 2016). Beyond the obvious differences in the types of advertising channel (i.e., online, offline, video, magazine, billboard, radio, TV, etc.), advertisers also need to decide on brand-specific messages along with a range of communication cues that will inform consumers about their market offerings (e.g., Alden et al., 1999; Herz and Diamantopoulos, 2013a). From an information theory perspective (Olson and Jacoby, 1972), products and brands are conceived to consist of both intrinsic (e.g., taste, color, design) and extrinsic (e.g., price, brand name, country-of-origin) cues. Each cue provides a basis for evaluating products.

One extrinsic cue that has received considerable attention, especially in the international marketing literature, is a product's country of origin (COO). There is an impressive stream of research that demonstrates that COO (alone as well as along with other extrinsic or intrinsic cues) impacts consumers' product quality evaluations, risk perceptions, buying intentions, as well as willingness to pay (for recent reviews, see Lu et al., 2016; Zeugner-Roth, 2017). However, and surprisingly, only few studies (i.e., Hornikx et al., 2020; Verlegh et al., 2005; Zeugner-Roth and Bartsch, 2020) address whether and how advertising can adopt and use COO cues in eliciting favorable responses from consumers. This is despite the fact that a favorable COO provides brands with an external, essentially free, non-brand specific signal of credibility that consumers use in decision making (Magnusson and Westjohn, 2011). Relying on a favorable COO in advertising, thus, should be an obvious choice that comes with only few downsides, if any.

This chapter focuses on how COO cues are used in advertising, how consumers process them, and how additional COO and product-related information shapes consumer responses. Based on the elaboration likelihood model (Petty and Cacioppo, 1986), we develop a conceptual model that combines the literature on COO effects with insights from the literature on the processing of advertising cues to develop a comprehensive overview of how COO cues affect consumer responses. Integrating theory with practical insights, we discuss the conceptual link between COO cues and product-related responses via two processing routes: central and peripheral processing of COO cues. Apart from consumers' product-country knowledge that determines the processing route, various extraneous factors such as origin, product ethnicity, consumer characteristics, and differences in market contexts affect the COO cues–product response relationship (see Figure 12.1, overleaf). These factors are discussed in more detail below.

COUNTRY OF ORIGIN CUES

The COO effect is rooted in consumers' images of countries (i.e., country images) as well as the image of products from that country (i.e., product-country images; c.f. Papadopoulos and Heslop, 2014). These images are formed based on actual product experience, but also on information gathered through advertising and other communication tools such as press articles and word-of-mouth (Verlegh et al., 2005). Previous research has examined the composition of country images and product-country images (for a review of the literature, see Roth and Diamantopoulos, 2009), and how consumers use COO as a cue for forming their product evaluations and purchase intentions. Table 12.1 (p. 215) summarizes how COO cues can be used in advertisements.

Cognitive Cues

Traditionally, the COO of a product or brand has been used as a signal of overall product quality and quality-related attributes such as reliability and durability (Verlegh and Steenkamp, 1999), which is also the predominant function of COO in extant literature (Zeugner-Roth and Žabkar, 2015). Advertisements employing COO as a cognitive cue typically demonstrate the superior nature of a product or brand from a certain COO. A well-known example is Audi's slogan 'Vorsprung durch Technik', meaning 'Being Ahead

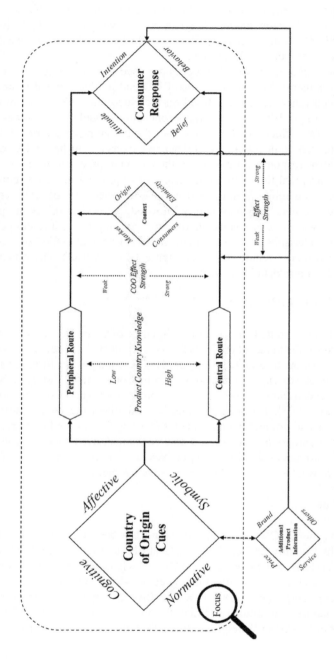

Figure 12.1   Country of origin cues in advertising

Table 12.1   *Examples of the use of cognitive, affective, symbolic, and normative COO cues in advertising*

COO Cue	Description	Example
Cognitive	COO of a product or brand as a signal of overall product quality and quality-related attributes such as reliability and durability (Verlegh and Steenkamp, 1999)	*Volkswagen*'s slogan 'Das Auto' *Ikea*'s slogan 'Design and Quality of Sweden'
Affective	COO as an image attribute that links the product to emotional benefits and feelings (Verlegh and Steenkamp, 1999)	*Tim Horton*'s 2017 campaign celebrating 150 years of Canada (e.g., the Canada 150 menu) *Havaianas*' 2017 campaign 'Made of Brazilian summer'
Symbolic	COO satisfies symbolic needs such as those for self-expression, social status, and prestige (Bhat and Reddy, 1998)	*L'Oréal Paris*' slogan 'Because you're worth it' *Tissot*'s logo and slogan 'Legendary Swiss watches since 1853'
Normative	Social and personal norms related to certain COOs (Verlegh and Steenkamp, 1999)	*Ford*'s 'Built for America' campaign *SPAR supermarket*'s 'Two strong partners' campaign advertising its cooperation with Austrian regional farmers

through Technology' (Audi, 2020). The German-language tagline is a fundamental element in the marketing communication of Audi in many European countries, Latin America, Oceania, Africa and parts of Asia including Japan.

Affective Cues

The affective use of COO as an image attribute links the product to emotional benefits and feelings (Verlegh and Steenkamp, 1999; Laroche et al., 2005). In advertising messages, COO could be linked to the joy of using/owning/buying a product from a certain COO and/or feeling of nostalgia and national pride. For example, brands using COO as an affective cue in advertisements are Dolce & Gabbana presenting their perfume in a typical Italian family dinner situation or Havana Club showing a typical Cuban woman at a colorful Havanan bar offering the rum (Zeugner-Roth and Bartsch, 2020).

Symbolic Cues

Similar to brands, COO can also be used to satisfy symbolic needs such as those for self-expression, social status, and prestige (Bhat and Reddy, 1998). Luxury watches, for example, typically highlight the Swiss origin of their brand on the product and in the advertisement. This is even true for hybrid products such as Louis Vuitton watches, where the brand originates from France, but 'made in Switzerland' is highlighted on certain watch models.

Normative Cues

COO can also have a normative value for consumers. Consumers hold social and personal norms related to certain COOs, and these can impact their attitudes and behavior (Verlegh and Steenkamp, 1999). The normative role of COO is usually studied in connection with consumer ethnocentrism and national identity (e.g., Fischer and Zeugner-Roth, 2017; Verlegh, 2007), where the purchase of domestic products is seen as the right way of conduct to support the domestic economy. Fabindia, an Indian apparel brand, for instance, stresses in its ads that the purchase of their products supports rural artisans and helps to preserve India's rich cultural heritage and traditions (Fabindia, 2020). In recent years, the normative function of COO has been expanded to green consumption behavior, where COO is viewed as a cue to signal the green image of a source country (e.g., Chan, 2000).

CONSUMER PROCESSING OF COO INFORMATION

To explain how cues such as COO used in advertising are processed by consumers, as well as to evaluate the importance given to such information in consumer responses, extant research (e.g., Bloemer et al., 2009) draws on the Elaboration Likelihood Model (ELM) of Petty and Cacioppo (1986). The ELM model proposes that the effect strength of cues will depend on different processing routes. A *central processing* route relates to a high level of personal relevance concerning the advertised brand or product; hence the cue takes on a prominent role in forming consumers' responses. A *peripheral processing* route relates to low levels of personal relevance concerning the advertised brand or product; hence the cue does not strongly influence consumer responses.

Applying the ELM model in a COO context, Bloemer et al. (2009) develop the COO ELM model. Drawing on earlier models of COO processing such as the halo and summary construct model (Han, 1989; Knight and Calantone, 2000), the processing route (central/peripheral) of COO information is determined by consumers' product country knowledge, that is, the extent of "internally stored knowledge about a country's products (i.e., the product [country] image)" (Bloemer et al., 2009, p. 65). In addition to the processing route, the COO ELM model also acknowledges the availability of additional, non-COO-related information in the evaluation process. This information refers to any non-COO-related cues that help consumers to make informed decisions and judgment about a product or brand. Typically, this would include the brand itself (i.e., brand image), the price–performance expectations, service promises, as well as other factors that help in making an assessment (Liefeld et al., 1996).

If the processing of the COO cue takes a central route, consumers deem the value of the COO information as relevant and have confidence in their knowledge about products from the country in question. Due to their high product country knowledge and their confidence in this knowledge, the COO image will function as a *summary construct* (Han, 1989), in which the COO image "may serve to summarize beliefs about product attributes, directly affecting brand attitude" (Knight and Calantone, 2000, p. 130). Consumers are thus not very likely to invest cognitive effort in identifying additional information cues but rather rely on their existing knowledge about the COO. Hence, the COO effect is supposed to be direct and of substantial significance (Bloemer et al., 2009).

In contrast, if consumers perceive product-country knowledge is low or moderate, COO cues are likely to be of less importance, and thus processing will take a peripheral route. Because of consumers' lower levels of product-country knowledge and confidence about their knowledge, COO cues will be less diagnostic for inferring product attributes, and, hence, consumers are more likely to include additional product information in the evaluation process. Overall, the COO effect is only at an intermediate to moderate level, but the total effect is supposed to be stronger because of the explicit consideration of COO cues plus additional information. Depending on the importance given to the additional information, research distinguishes three different scenarios for the processing of COO cues following a peripheral route (Bloemer et al., 2009).

The *halo effect* (Han, 1989) corresponds to a process where additional product information is missing or disregarded. The impact of the COO cue on consumer responses is indirect through consumers' product-related beliefs and rather weak. Depending on the timing of the processing of additional information, Bloemer et al. (2009) further distinguish between the *default heuristic* and the *attribute model*. According to the former, COO-related information is presented together with additional information at the time of purchase, there is reciprocal interaction between the two, and both will jointly and equally contribute to product responses. Finally, the *product attribute approach* assumes that COO-related information is given to consumers at a later point of time than additional information, and both contribute to product and brand responses independently of each other, with more importance given to additional cues for the evaluation because of the time delay.

CONTEXTUALIZING CONSUMER RESPONSES TO COUNTRY OF ORIGIN CUES

The effect of COO cue processing on consumer responses should not only vary according to their product-country knowledge and the processing of additional product cues, but also based on other product- and consumer-related factors that may influence responses. In what follows, we focus on four significant factors whose impact has been empirically confirmed by current research, allowing managers to make informed decisions about how determining COO cues are for their products and brands. Specifically, we focus on a brand's origin, a brand's degree of product ethnicity, key consumer characteristics that shape COO-related brand responses, and differences between developed and developing market contexts.

Product Origin

One of the factors that is likely to moderate the impact of the COO cue on consumers' responses is the domestic (versus foreign) origin of a product or brand. In most cases, COO cues featuring a domestic origin will amplify the positive relationship between COO and consumers' product and brand-related responses (Balabanis and Diamantopoulos, 2004; Verlegh, 2007). Also known as domestic country bias or home country preference, this form of in-group bias reflects "a systematic tendency to favor one's own group" (Pettigrew, 2004, p. 827) over others. Rooted in social identity theory (Tajfel and Turner, 2004), it is assumed that people will seek to strengthen their perceived in-group identity, which is typically associated with one's home country – the place where people grow up, have family, and have strong cultural and social ties. For these reasons, consumers typically favor domestic over foreign products and brands, as these are better suited to strengthen in-group identification with their home countries.

Zeugner-Roth and Bartsch (2020) examine the use of COO in advertising claims and find that domestic products and brands are more likely to use COO in their advertising in both a developed and developing market context. The literature discusses several ways in which domestic country bias can be leveraged in advertising campaigns. First, COO can be related to cognitive reasons related to the perceived superior quality of domestic products (e.g., 'You know what you get from your home country'). Second, emotional reasons, including feelings of pride and responsibility for the home country, can lead consumers to prefer products and brands of domestic origin (Fischer and Zeugner-Roth, 2017; Verlegh, 2007). Third, normative, that is, morally imposed reasons, could be the cause of a strong home-country bias, including ethnocentric justifications (Shimp and Sharma, 1987), or even environmental concerns (Elliott and Cameron, 1994).

Product Ethnicity

Another product-related factor that is acknowledged in extant research to strengthen the effect of COO cues on consumer responses relates to the degree to which a COO is globally known for, and has expertise in, producing products in a specific product category (e.g., Germany for cars, Italy for leather goods, Brazil for coffee). Also known as product ethnicity (Usunier and Cestre, 2007) or product–country matches (Roth and Romeo, 1992), this phenomenon is formally defined in the literature as a "stereotypical association of a generic product with a particular country-of-origin" (Usunier and Cestre, 2007, p. 36). It is a form of typicality (Rosch and Mervis, 1975) that consumers may use in making inferences about product performance. Consequently, COO information that is in line with consumers' expectations of prototypical features of a product category will have a more substantial positive effect on consumer responses compared to COO information that is not in line with prototypical features of the category. Some scholars (e.g., Samiee, 2010) even argue that product ethnicity is a necessary precondition for strong COO effects to occur. Zeugner-Roth and Bartsch (2020) investigate the usage of product ethnicity in advertising claims made by national manufacturers in two cultural contexts. They find that although product ethnicity is an important argument for consumers, not all brands originating from a COO with a high product ethnicity use it in their advertising claim in both a developed and developing market context.

Consumer Characteristics

The international marketing literature provides a plethora of consumer character- istics that influence the impact of COO cues on brand responses (see Bartsch et al., 2016b and Papadopoulos et al., 2018 for detailed reviews). These are further classified into country-*specific* consumer characteristics such as emotions people hold towards a specific origin (consumer affinity and consumer animosity), and more *general* consumer characteristics measuring domestic country bias (con- sumer ethnocentrism), positive dispositions to foreign countries, products, and brands (cosmopolitanism), or positive dispositions towards globalization (global identity). Conceptually rooted in theories related to individuals' identities (see Bartsch et al., 2016b for an overview), often a distinction between in-groups and out-groups is made, assuming that people are favorably biased towards members and products of their in-group (Mackie and Smith, 1998). We provide an overview of these consumer dispositions and their likely impact on product responses below.

Consumer affinity is formally defined as a "feeling of liking, sympathy, and even attachment towards a specific foreign country" (Oberecker et al., 2008, p. 26) and captures positive country-specific emotions. In the case of consumer affinity, a foreign country has become part of a consumer's in-group, for instance, due to prior experience with this country or due to normative exposure (Oberecker et al., 2008). Thus, consumers develop positive feelings about products and brands representative of this in-group. Oberecker and Diamantopoulos (2011) show that feelings of affinity reduce risk perceptions towards the affinity country, while also increasing purchase intentions for affinity country products. Recent studies extend these findings in the context of origin misclassifications and find that consumer affinity can have a detrimental effect on brand evaluations and purchase intentions if the true origin is not an affinity country (Cakici and Shukla, 2017). Consequently, the effect of COO cues is likely to be more substantial for ads from countries for which consumers hold such a country-specific affinity.

In contrast, *consumer animosity*, defined as "remnants of antipathy related to previous or ongoing military, political or economic events" (Klein et al., 1998, p. 90), captures consumers' negative emotions towards a specific country forged in past or ongoing military and economic conflict (Barbarossa et al., 2018). The detrimental effect of consumer animosity on responses towards products from a specific foreign country is well documented in extant research (see Riefler and Diamantopoulos, 2007 for a review). Apart from the negative direct effect on purchase intentions documented by Klein et al.'s (1998) seminal paper, recent findings of Heinberg (2017) provide evidence that foreign region-related animosity also strengthens consumer willingness to pay for domestic products. Cakici and Shukla (2017) empirically confirm that in cases of brand origin misclassifications, animosity for the real and the assumed COO significantly affects brand judgment negatively and reduces purchase intentions. Hence, consumer animosity is likely to reduce the presumed positive effect of the COO cue on product and brand response. In fact, depending on the strength of animosity towards the country, the processing of COO cues could even lead to a total rejection of the foreign product or brand, regardless of the processing of additional (positive) product information.

Unlike consumer animosity that is country-specific, a more general consumer characteristic that is likely to evoke negative responses to foreign COO cues is *consumer ethnocentrism*. Defined as "beliefs held by … consumers about the appropriateness, indeed morality, of purchasing foreign-made products" (Shimp and Sharma, 1987, p. 280), consumer ethnocentrism captures a unique economic version of ethnocentrism according to which the purchase of foreign products is considered to be morally wrong because it may hurt the domestic economy (Verlegh, 2007). Current literature provides ample evidence that consumers high on ethnocentrism will interpret foreign COO cues as negative, and domestic COO cues as positive and thus adjust responses accordingly (see Shankarmahesh, 2006 for a review). Thus, similar effects are expected for the processing of COO cues in advertising.

Cosmopolitanism is defined as a "specific set of qualities held by certain individuals, including a willingness to engage with the other (i.e., different cultures), and a level of competence towards alien culture[s]" (Cleveland and Laroche,

2007, p. 252). It captures consumers' positive disposition to foreign products and cultures for self-validation purposes to strengthen consumers' self-concepts. Cosmopolitan consumers are drawn towards elements of foreign consumer cultures to enlarge their perceived cultural horizon (Cleveland et al., 2009). In the context of processing COO-related advertising cues, it is likely that for cosmopolitan consumers, information about foreign origins will have a high degree of object relevance as it signals a pathway for an identity strengthening mechanism through foreign product and brand consumption. Hence, information about a foreign COO is likely to strengthen this effect. At the same time, the literature acknowledges that cosmopolitans do not reject domestic products (Zeugner-Roth et al., 2015). Instead, cosmopolitan consumers were found to prefer local over industrialized and mass-produced products (Cannon and Yaprak, 2002).

Finally, consumers' *global identity*, defined as "mental representations in which consumers believe in the positive effects of globalization, recognize the commonalities rather than dissimilarities among people around the world, and are interested in global events" (Tu et al., 2012, p. 36), may also contextualize the effect of COO cue processing on brand and product-related responses. Consumers with high levels of global identity identify with and own products and brands that serve as symbols of global consumer cultures (Bartsch et al., 2016a). Foreign products and brands can serve as such proxies (Alden et al., 1999). Thus, foreign COO cues should be of higher value for consumers high on global identity compared to those that are not. However, such an effect is likely to be more pronounced for consumers originating from developing countries (e.g., Batra et al., 2000).

Market Differences

The relationships specified above are further influenced by the market context in which they are analyzed. Prior research shows that products and brands with a developed COO achieve higher quality evaluations and purchase intentions than products from an emerging COO for consumers in both developed and developing markets (Klein et al., 2006; Pappu et al., 2007). At the same time, for emerging markets, normative (e.g., consumer ethnocentrism) and affective (e.g., patriotism, nationalism) reasons increasingly come into play: Chinese consumers, for instance, show similar levels of ethnocentrism as consumers in developed markets (Klein et al., 2006). This is also reflected in the advertising practices of companies. Zeugner-Roth and Bartsch (2020) find that companies from both developed and developing markets are more likely to use COO for domestic products. In emerging markets, this is specifically the case for products with a high product ethnicity, such as home-grown spices and clothes reflective of local lifestyles.

Differences between market contexts are also expected with respect to the importance and meaning given to COO information in developed versus developing markets. In Europe, for instance, roughly one-third of all advertisements contain at least some kind of COO information in them (Hornikx et al., 2020). On the other hand, the COO cue is much more pronounced in emerging markets such as India where about two-thirds of all ads analyzed were found to use it, whereas in European countries COO is most often used for hedonic products: in emerging markets it is associated with status and prestige and has a predominantly symbolic function (Zeugner-Roth and Bartsch, 2020).

DISCUSSION AND CONCLUDING THOUGHTS

This chapter summarizes current knowledge on the usage of COO cues in advertising and discusses their effects on consumer responses to products and brands. We integrate the existing literature into a conceptual model that highlights: (a) different types of COO cues; (b) different processing mechanisms relating to brand and product responses; (c) the impact of additional information in this process; and (d) key factors derived from previous research that are likely to amplify or attenuate the COO effect on product and brand responses.

COO cues in advertising are of a cognitive, affective, symbolic, and/or normative nature. Based on the premises of the ELM model, depending on consumers' product-country knowledge, COO cues are processed either *centrally* – their impact is substantial and strong – or *peripherally* – their impact is less pronounced, and additional product information contributes substantially to the evaluation process.

Regardless of the type of processing route, a set of product and consumer characteristics may further moderate the relationship between COO cue processing and product/brand-related responses. A domestic product origin should strengthen the COO effect due to consumers' home country bias. A strong product–country match will also increase the signaling strength of COO cues for product responses. Furthermore, individual differences among consumers may substantially shift their reliance on COO cues as diagnostic signals for product and brand evaluation. Finally, we highlight that the processing of COO cues in advertising potentially differs according to the degree of market development. The presumed home country bias may not be as pronounced in developing markets compared to developed markets (Batra et al., 2000). Existing research further indicates a dominant use of COO cues in advertising for symbolic products in such markets compared to hedonic products in developed markets (Zeugner-Roth and Bartsch, 2020).

We can envision several future research directions that could empirically advance our conceptual summary. At the same time, this discussion provides potentially fruitful food for thought for practitioners in both business, where the primary interest is in COO-based brand marketing, and the management of countries and other places, where consultants and various public agencies work to advance the image and reputation of the origin places themselves. First, despite the proliferation of COO research and its multiple applications in international marketing, comparatively few works have investigated the actual use of COO cues in advertising. Abundant studies examine: (a) how consumer characteristics shape responses to foreign and domestic product and brands (e.g., Papadopoulos et al., 2018); (b) different types of COO image variables (e.g., Roth and Diamantopoulos, 2009); or (c) differences in misperceptions of COO information including its overall relevance for decision making (e.g., Balabanis and Diamantopoulos, 2011). However, there is limited work that directly investigates the usage of COO cues in advertising (e.g., Zeugner-Roth and Bartsch, 2020), despite the contribution this may make to the discussion on the relevance of the COO cue (e.g., Samiee, 2010; Usunier, 2006) and its important theoretical and managerial implications.

Second, both the halo and summary construct models of Han (1989) put the main emphasis on the processing of COO-related information, with additional cues being either (a) missing, or (b) disregarded, or (c) summarized in product beliefs. In advertising, consumers need to process various sources of information at the same time, including the brand, design, and color of the product – hence a design putting COO at the center of research is not realistic and might face the problem of omitted variable bias (Clarke, 2005). Thus, an ecologically sound assessment of the impact of COO-related advertising should account for the impact of additional product cues in making an informed assessment about the strength and importance of COO cues in advertising (Samiee, 2010; 2011). In a similar manner, a fruitful direction for future research would also empirically investigate the most likely pathways in how consumers process COO cues in advertising, centrally or peripherally.

Third, the ELM aims to explain the cognitive processing of information. However, extant literature on both advertising (e.g., Batra and Ray, 1986) and COO images (e.g., Laroche et al., 2005; Zeugner-Roth and Žabkar, 2015) strongly suggests that such cues may also be processed affectively. In other words, in non-directed purchase decisions both cognitive and emotional responses to COO cues contribute to product responses (Herz and Diamantopoulos, 2013b) – a finding that is of interest to both academic researchers and practicing managers. In addition, the theory of reasoned action (Fishbein and Ajzen, 1975) assumes that norms impact behavior directly and independently of attitudes. Hence, country-related norms could have a more immediate impact on product response than the processing of cognitive, affective, and symbolic COO cues. To date, with few exceptions, research remains scarce in studying such complementary processing mechanisms.

Fourth, beyond the type of processing, future research should also investigate, and managers should consider, how advertisements make reference to the COO. The literature indicates that country-specific inferences can be made explicitly or implicitly (Herz and Diamantopoulos, 2013a). Explicit references in advertisements directly refer to the COO (e.g., country name, capital cities, flags, etc.), while implicit references employ imagery to refer to it indirectly (e.g., important landmarks, national characters, landscapes, etc.). These differences in COO usage are likely to trigger different responses in different situations. For instance, the impact of explicit or implicit categorizations of COO cues may depend on the decision context. Spontaneous decisions favor implicit processing of COO cues, while more involved decisions favor explicit processing of COO cues (Diamantopoulos et al., 2017). To date, more work is needed to disentangle the complex interactions of implicit and explicit cues, their processing and consumers' product responses.

Finally, empirical evidence from a content analysis of advertising claims in two countries supports the theoretical notion that COO is most often used for products with a high ethnicity (Zeugner-Roth and Bartsch, 2020). However, drawing from the stereotype content model (Cuddy et al., 2008), country stereotypes capture elements of both competence (i.e., expertise) and warmth (i.e., feelings of friendliness). Product ethnicity captures the former while neglecting the latter. Since COO is mostly used for hedonic products in developing markets, a holistic assessment of COO usage in advertising should thus also include elements of country warmth. Furthermore, more research is needed to investigate the duality of warmth and competence in contributing to consumers' responses to COO information in advertising.

REFERENCES

Alden, D.L., Steenkamp, J.-B.E.M. and Batra, R. (1999). Brand positioning through advertising in Asia, North America, and Europe: the role of global consumer culture. *Journal of Marketing*, *63*(1), 75–87.

Audi (2020). Vorsprung durch Technik. Accessed 10 November 2020 at https://www.audi.com/en/company/history/vorsprung-durch-technik.html.

Balabanis, G. and Diamantopoulos, A. (2004). Domestic country bias, country-of-origin effects, and consumer ethnocentrism: a multidimensional unfolding approach. *Journal of the Academy of Marketing Science*, *32*(1), 80–95.

Balabanis, G. and Diamantopoulos, A. (2011). Gains and losses from the misperception of brand origin: the role of brand strength and country-of-origin image. *Journal of International Marketing*, *19*(2), 95–116.

Barbarossa, C., De Pelsmacker, P. and Moons, I. (2018). Effects of country-of-origin stereotypes on consumer responses to product–harm crises. *International Marketing Review*, *35*(3), 362–389.

Bartsch, F., Riefler, P. and Diamantopoulos, A. (2016b). A taxonomy and review of positive consumer dispositions toward foreign countries and globalization. *Journal of International Marketing*, *24*(1), 82–110.

Bartsch, F., Diamantopoulos, A., Paparoidamis, N.G. and Chumpitaz, R. (2016a). Global brand ownership: the mediating roles of consumer attitudes and brand identification. *Journal of Business Research*, *69*(9), 3629–3635.

Batra, R. and Ray, M.L. (1986). Affective responses mediating acceptance of advertising. *Journal of Consumer Research*, *13*(2), 234–249.

Batra, R., Ramaswamy, V., Alden, D.L., Steenkamp, J.-B.E.M., Ramachander, S. and Rachmander, S. (2000). Effects of brand local and nonlocal origin on consumer attitudes in developing countries. *Journal of Consumer Psychology*, *9*(2), 83–95.

Bhat, S. and Reddy, S.K. (1998). Symbolic and functional positioning of brands. *Journal of Consumer Marketing*, *15*(1), 32–43.

Bloemer, J., Brijs, K. and Kasper, H. (2009). The CoO-ELM model: a theoretical framework for the cognitive processes underlying country-of-origin effects. *European Journal of Marketing*, *43*(1/2), 62–89.

Cakici, N.M. and Shukla, P. (2017). Country-of-origin misclassification awareness and consumers' behavioral intentions: moderating roles of consumer affinity, animosity, and product knowledge. *International Marketing Review*, *34*(3), 354–376.

Cannon, H.M. and Yaprak, A. (2002). Will the real-world citizen please stand up! The many faces of cosmopolitan consumer behavior. *Journal of International Marketing*, *10*(4), 30–52.

Chan, R.Y.K. (2000). The effectiveness of environmental advertising: the role of claim type and the source country green image. *International Journal of Advertising*, *19*(3), 349–375.

Clarke, K.A. (2005). The phantom menace: omitted variable bias in econometric research. *Conflict Management and Peace Science*, *22*(4), 341–352.

Cleveland, M. and Laroche, M. (2007). Acculturation to the global consumer culture: scale development and research paradigm. *Journal of Business Research*, *60*(3), 249–259.

Cleveland, M., Laroche, M. and Papadopoulos, N. (2009). Cosmopolitanism, consumer ethnocentrism, and materialism: an eight-country study of antecedents and outcomes. *Journal of International Marketing*, *17*(1), 116–146.

Cuddy, A.J.C., Fiske, S.T. and Glick, P. (2008). Warmth and competence as universal dimensions of social perception: the stereotype content model and the bias map. *Advances in Experimental Social Psychology*, *40*, 61–149.

Diamantopoulos, A., Florack, A., Halkias, G. and Palcu, J. (2017). Explicit versus implicit country stereotypes as predictors of product preferences: insights from the stereotype content model. *Journal of International Business Studies*, *48*(8), 1023–1036.

Elliott, G.R. and Cameron, R.C. (1994). Consumer perception of product quality and the country-of-origin effect. *Journal of International Marketing*, *2*(2), 49–62.

Fabindia (2020). Fabindia: Serving India. Accessed 10 November 2020 at https://www.fabindia.com/.

Fischer, P.M. and Zeugner-Roth, K. (2017). Disentangling country-of-origin effects: the interplay of product ethnicity, national identity, and consumer ethnocentrism. *Marketing Letters*, *28*(2), 189–204.

Fishbein, M. and Ajzen, I. (1975). *Belief, Attitude, Intention and Behavior: An Introduction to Theory and Research*. Reading, MA: Addison-Wesley.

Forbes (2017). Finding brand success in the digital world. *Forbes*, 25 August. Accessed at https://www.forbes.com/sites/forbesagencycouncil/2017/08/25/finding-brand-success-in-the-digital-world/#3be090f2626e.

Han, C.M. (1989). Country image: halo or summary construct? *Journal of Marketing Research*, *26*(2), 222–229.

Heinberg, M. (2017). Outbreaks of animosity against the West in China: effects on local brand consumption. *International Marketing Review*, *34*(4), 514–535.

Herz, M. and Diamantopoulos, A. (2013a). Activation of country stereotypes: automaticity, consonance, and impact. *Journal of the Academy of Marketing Science*, *41*(4), 400–417.

Herz, M. and Diamantopoulos, A. (2013b). Country-specific associations made by consumers: a dual-coding theory perspective. *Journal of International Marketing*, *21*(3), 95–121.

Hornikx, J., van Meurs, F., van den Heuvel, J. and Janssen, A. (2020). How brands highlight country of origin in magazine advertising: a content analysis. *Journal of Global Marketing*, *33*(1), 34–45.

Imarc Group (2020). Global advertising market to reach US$ 769.9 billion by 2024, strengthened by the proliferation of digital media. Accessed 10 November 2020 at https://www.imarcgroup.com/global-advertising-market-grew-at-a-cagr-of-4-during-the -last-five-years.

Isaac, M.S. and Grayson, K. (2016). Beyond skepticism: can accessing persuasion knowledge bolster credibility? *Journal of Consumer Research, 43*(6), 895–912.

Klein, J.G., Ettenson, R. and Krishnan, B.C. (2006). Extending the construct of consumer ethnocentrism: when foreign products are preferred. *International Marketing Review, 23*(3), 304–321.

Klein, J.G., Ettenson, R. and Morris, M.D. (1998). The animosity model of foreign product purchase: an empirical test in the People's Republic of China. *Journal of Marketing, 62*(1), 89.

Knight, G.A. and Calantone, R.J. (2000). A flexible model of consumer country-of-origin perceptions. *International Marketing Review, 17*(2), 127–145.

Laroche, M., Papadopoulos, N., Heslop, L.A. and Mourali, M. (2005). The influence of country image structure on consumer evaluations of foreign products. *International Marketing Review, 22*(1), 96–115.

Liefeld, J.P., Heslop, L.A., Papadopoulos, N. and Wall, M. (1996). Dutch consumer use of intrinsic, country-of-origin, and price cues in product evaluation and choice. *Journal of International Consumer Marketing, 9*(1), 57–81.

Lu, I.R.R., Heslop, L.A., Thomas, D.R. and Kwan, E. (2016). An examination of the status and evolution of country image research. *International Marketing Review, 33*(6), 825–850.

Mackie, D.M. and Smith, E.R. (1998). Intergroup relations: insights from a theoretically integrative approach. *Psychological Review, 105*(3), 499–529.

Magnusson, P. and Westjohn, S.A. (2011). Is there a country-of-origin theory? In S.C. Jain and D.A. Griffith (eds), *Handbook of Research in International Marketing*. Cheltenham, UK and Northampton, MA, USA: Edward Elgar Publishing, pp. 292–316.

Oberecker, E.M. and Diamantopoulos, A. (2011). Consumers' emotional bonds with foreign countries: does consumer affinity affect behavioral intentions? *Journal of International Marketing, 19*(2), 45–72.

Oberecker, E.M., Riefler, P. and Diamantopoulos, A. (2008). The consumer affinity construct: conceptualization, qualitative investigation, and research agenda. *Journal of International Marketing, 16*(3), 23–56.

Olson, J.C. and Jacoby, J. (1972). Cue utilization in the quality perception process. In M. Venkatesan (ed.), *Proceedings of the Third Annual Conference of the Association for Consumer Research*. Chicago, IL: Association for Consumer Research, pp. 167–179.

Papadopoulos, N. and Heslop, L.A. (2014). *Product-country Images: Impact and Role in International Marketing*. Binghampton, NY: Routledge.

Papadopoulos, N., Cleveland, M., Bartikowski, B. and Yaprak, A. (2018). Of countries, places and product/brand place associations: an inventory of dispositions and issues relating to place image and its effects. *Journal of Product & Brand Management, 27*(7), 735–753.

Pappu, R., Quester, P.G. and Cooksey, R.W. (2007). Country image and consumer-based brand equity: relationships and implications for international marketing. *Journal of International Business Studies, 38*(5), 726–745.

Pettigrew, T.F. (2004). Review of ethnocentrism: Theories of conflict, ethnic attitudes and group behavior. In K. Kempf-Leonard (ed.), *Encyclopedia of Social Measurement*. San Diego, CA: Academic Press, pp. 827–831.

Petty, R.E. and Cacioppo, J.T. (1986). The elaboration likelihood model of persuasion. *Advances in Experimental Social Psychology*, *19*, 123–205.

Riefler, P. and Diamantopoulos, A. (2007). Consumer animosity: a literature review and a reconsideration of its measurement. *International Marketing Review*, *24*(1), 87–119.

Rosch, E. and Mervis, C.B. (1975). Family resemblances: studies in the internal structure of categories. *Cognitive Psychology*, *7*(4), 573–605.

Roth, K.P. and Diamantopoulos, A. (2009). Advancing the country image construct. *Journal of Business Research*, *62*(7), 726–740.

Roth, M.S. and Romeo, J.B. (1992). Matching product category and country image perceptions: a framework for managing country-of-origin effects. *Journal of International Business Studies*, *23*(3), 477–497.

Samiee, S. (2010). Advancing the country image construct: a commentary essay. *Journal of Business Research*, *63*(4), 442–445.

Samiee, S. (2011). Resolving the impasse regarding research on the origins of products and brands. *International Marketing Review*, *28*(5), 473–485.

Shankarmahesh, M.N. (2006). Consumer ethnocentrism: an integrative review of its antecedents and consequences. *International Marketing Review*, *23*(2), 146–172.

Shimp, T.A. and Sharma, S. (1987). Consumer ethnocentrism: construction and validation of the CETSCALE. *Journal of Marketing Research*, *24*(3), 280–289.

Tajfel, H. and Turner, J.C. (2004). The social identity theory of intergroup behavior. In J.T. Jost and J. Sidanius (eds), *Political Psychology*. New York, NY: Psychology Press, pp. 276–293.

Tu, L., Khare, A. and Zhang, Y. (2012). A short 8-item scale for measuring consumers' local–global identity. *International Journal of Research in Marketing*, *29*(1), 35–42.

Usunier, J.-C. (2006). Relevance in business research: the case of country-of-origin research in marketing. *European Management Review*, *3*(1), 60–73.

Usunier, J.-C.C. and Cestre, G. (2007). Product ethnicity: revisiting the match between products and countries. *Journal of International Marketing*, *15*(3), 32–72.

Verlegh, P. (2007). Home country bias in product evaluation: the complementary roles of economic and socio-psychological motives. *Journal of International Business Studies*, *38*(3), 361–373.

Verlegh, P. and Steenkamp, J.-B.E.M. (1999). A review and meta-analysis of country-of-origin research. *Journal of Economic Psychology*, *20*(5), 521–546.

Verlegh, P.W.J., Steenkamp, J.-B.E.M. and Meulenberg, M.T.G. (2005). Country-of-origin effects in consumer processing of advertising claims. *International Journal of Research in Marketing*, *22*(2), 127–139.

Zeugner-Roth, K. (2017). Country-of-origin effects. In H. Van Herk and C.J. Torelli (eds), *Cross-cultural Issues in Consumer Science and International Business*. New York, NY: Springer International Publishing, pp. 111–128.

Zeugner-Roth, K.P. and Bartsch, F. (2020). COO in print advertising: developed versus developing market comparisons. *Journal of Business Research*, *120*(11), 364–378.

Zeugner-Roth, K.P. and Žabkar, V. (2015). Bridging the gap between country and destination image: assessing common facets and their predictive validity. *Journal of Business Research*, *68*(9), 1844–1853.

Zeugner-Roth, K.P., Žabkar, V. and Diamantopoulos, A. (2015). Consumer ethnocentrism, national identity, and consumer cosmopolitanism as drivers of consumer behavior: a social identity theory perspective. *Journal of International Marketing*, *23*(2), 25–54.

13. Cross-border acquisitions and offshoring strategies: the effects on country/place image and reputation

Michela Matarazzo

CROSS-BORDER ACQUISITIONS, OFFSHORING, AND CONSUMERS' PERCEPTIONS

Over the last two decades scholars have been focusing on the topic of international acquisitions, as the increase in foreign direct investment in industrialized countries since the mid-1980s has largely come about through cross-border M&As. In most cases, a merger is initiated and led by a dominant firm, reflecting an acquisition rather than a merger as such, and the theory as well as practical implications for both types of inter-corporate arrangements are very similar in both cases. This chapter focuses on cross-border acquisitions (CBA), defined as linkages involving an acquirer firm and a target firm whose headquarters are located in different home countries (Shimizu et al., 2004), and their potential effects on consumers. (Note: to prevent clutter, 'acquisition' and 'consumer' or 'customer' (and their related terms) are used here to refer to all types of corporate arrangements and buyers, unless the context points to a specific meaning of the generic term and/or an alternative expression is called for, such as, respectively, 'international joint ventures' and B2B 'customers'.)

CBAs are a common practice for multinational companies augmenting their brand portfolio through acquisitions in other countries, which means that managers need to make decisions in a global context. Existing research has focused on international acquisitions at different levels: country, firm, the 'deal' itself, and the consumer.

One important research stream is on CBA performance, aimed at defining and suggesting good practices and reducing the number of failures of such operations. Nevertheless, the question of what determines the international success or failure of international acquisitions has not been answered conclusively and is still under investigation today.

The success of a company mainly depends on consumers' willingness to buy its products. Therefore, managers involved in a CBA should also implement a marketing-oriented strategy directed to consumers, instead of focusing only on financial and strategic outcomes. Nevertheless, the acquisition literature on the consumer perspective remains limited, and a lack of focus on this perspective may be a contributing factor to a CBA's failure (Heinberg et al., 2016).

Research into consumers' dispositions toward a CBA could shed more light on its prospects, thus representing a critical factor affecting its success. Furthermore, understanding the role of consumers could assist companies in better segmenting and targeting international markets. One of the most important organizational and marketing questions arising in the CBA field is to what extent this managerial decision influences consumers of the target company. In this regard, Bekier and Shelton (2002) stated that there is considerable risk of losing consumers in CBAs because managers are strongly focused on internal issues at the expense of customer-related tasks such as product, service quality, and assortment.

Homburg and Bucerius (2005, p. 107) demonstrate that "market-related performance (e.g. customer loyalty, market share) is a much more important driver of financial performance after the merger or acquisition than are cost savings". The basic principles of CBAs are largely similar to those of their domestic counterparts. Indeed, as with domestic acquisitions, acquiring an existing foreign business allows the acquiring firm to rapidly obtain its resources, such as its knowledge base, technology, and human resources, internalize an activity to reduce or avoid transaction costs, and expand its market share (Shimizu et al., 2004). However, owing to their international nature, CBAs also involve unique challenges, as countries have different economic, institutional (i.e., regulatory), and cultural structures (Hofstede, 1994), and above all they have a different image. These differences are perceived by individuals, managers, employees, and consumers of the acquired firm, affecting company internationalization in numerous ways (Ellis, 2007).

CBAs and the Discrepancy in Country Images

Country-based factors play an important role in CBAs especially for those products that can benefit from a favorable product–country match, that is, when the important dimensions for a product category are also associated with the main dimensions for a country's image (Roth and Romeo, 1992). French and Italian fashion, Swedish crystals, and Swiss watches are some cases in point. A CBA or an international joint venture with a partner from an unfavorable match country might be detrimental for the brand image especially when the consumer's product evaluation depends also on the detailed facets of country-of-origin, such as where the products were actually made, and where their parts or ingredients came from. Indeed, in this case the perceived authenticity of the product can be compromised because of the ownership transition to a foreign country with an unfavorable country/product match.

The scant literature on CBAs from the consumer's perspective has investigated the effect of a change in the country of company (COC) on consumers' perception toward the product/brand from various different points of view. These include the relationships between:

1. consumer ethnocentric tendencies (CET), brand image fit, and post-CBA brand attitudes (Lee et al., 2011; Shi et al., 2017);
2. country of origin (COO), post-CBA brand attitudes (Chang et al., 2015a; Heinberg et al., 2016; Fang and Wang, 2018), and consumers' brand ownership (Chung et al., 2014);
3. consumer animosity and consumer attitude toward a product launched by a foreign firm's subsidiary established through a CBA (Fong et al., 2015);
4. acquirer's corporate reputation and post-CBA consumers' repurchase intentions (Fong et al., 2013; Matarazzo et al., 2018), as well as the interaction effects of acquirer's corporate reputation and country image on host country consumer's repurchase intentions (Matarazzo et al., 2020) and psychic distance (Resciniti et al., 2020).

These studies suggest that a transition in corporate ownership via a CBA can increase consumers' uncertainties about the new entity even when the brand and the target company remain unchanged. Indeed, the acquiring company has its own reputation and identity, which differ from the target firm and can affect the brand image by giving an impression that the brand is no longer operated by the original heritage. Drawing on Woo et al. (2019), who make a distinction between downward and upward offshoring in the apparel sector, it is possible to extend these two tendencies to the context of CBAs.

Another source of uncertainties for consumers is the country of the acquirer that can have a more positive or more negative image compared to the country of the target company, respectively in upward and downward international acquisitions. The critical question raised by the acquisition is related to the sudden and unexpected separation between country of brand (COB) and COC, that is, the country of brand and country of acquired company, which may cause changes in the way consumers perceive the brand after the acquisition as a result of the impact of the new COC on the previous COB.

Offshoring Strategies and the Decomposition of COO

Another common practice in companies' international expansion is moving the whole production process or some parts of it to one or more facilities in countries other than, and potentially very different from, the producer's own. This is a natural consequence of globalization and the vertical dis-integration of global value chains that are two remarkable characteristics of the modern age. In literature the offshoring strategies have been studied in connection to three main objectives: efficiency (low cost-seeking strategies); exploration (resource and technology-driven strategies); and exploitation (development of foreign markets). Whatever a company's motivation and however legitimate it may be, it is important to consider consumers' reactions to the offshoring transfer of production. Indeed, as with CBAs, in the case of offshoring there is a separation between country of manufacture and country of brand origin that may affect consumers' perceptions of the brand. The fragmented effects of COO due to the dis-integration of the global value chain have been studied extensively in the marketing literature.

COO is a multifaceted and complex construct that can be decomposed into country of manufacture (COM), country of design (COD), country of parts (COP), and country of assembly (COA) (Hamzaoui-Essoussi et al., 2011). As a consequence, brands of hybrid products may be related to several places – which very often results in brands being associated with 'origins' different from their own. For example, the brand origin of BMW is Germany despite BMW's biggest production plant currently being in the United States (located in Spartanburg, SC), where the X3, X4, X5, and X6 models are manufactured (Felix and Firat, 2019). The specific consequence of such offshoring strategies is a split between consumer perceptions of the country with which a product/ brand is identified and its country of manufacture. This fragmentation of global value chains due to offshoring strategies is a phenomenon involving many industries, from apparel to food, furniture, automotive, and so on.

Although some scholars argue that in the current globalized world 'where' a product is actually manufactured is irrelevant (Phau and Prendergast, 2000), a great majority of scholars posit that COO continues to be very important today and perhaps even more so than in earlier times. A recent conceptual paper by Papadopoulos et al. (2018) highlights the persistent significance of company and/or brand 'origin images' in the global era, elaborates in detail on the psychological dispositions that make 'origin' important and relevant to consumers, and discusses the factors that make the construct both intriguing, as well as challenging to study in research and apply in practice. Accordingly, recent research has demonstrated the effect of COO on important outcome variables such as communication of country-specific associations and brand choice, product evaluations, brand quality, attitudes toward the brand, willing-ness to pay, purchase intentions, and actual purchases (see, for example, Herz and Diamantopoulos, 2013).

To analyze the effects of offshoring on consumers' reactions, Woo et al. (2019) observed two opposite tendencies, downward and upward offshoring, particularly in the apparel sector. The first reflects the low-cost-seeking strategies of many companies that subcontract to factories in low-wage countries such as China, but also to such countries as Romania, Serbia, Bosnia, and Turkey. In this case it may happen that by sourcing production in low-wage countries, which typically are at an emerging or developing stage and often have unfavorable country images, firms may save costs but also invite negative product evaluations by consumers and, consequently, see their brands' value reduced. Consequently, there is a trade-off between lower costs and potential consumers' response that must be considered before an offshoring decision. The second, and more recent, tendency is the reverse: upward offshoring to countries with a stronger image than the brand's original home (e.g., Chinese companies making their products in Italy), aimed at improving the global visibility of the brand. Given the general growth of offshoring, the authors also stress that a distinction must be made between upscale and mid- or low-market brands, since the effect of downward or upward strategies may be different depending on the nature and status of the product.

CONSUMER REACTIONS TO TRANSITIONS IN COUNTRY IMAGES: SOME THEORETICAL EXPLANATIONS

Changes in country of company or of brand, such as those being discussed here, can be explained and better understood by drawing on several relevant theories, which are highlighted in this section.

Cognitive Dissonance Theory

Cognitive dissonance theory (Festinger, 1957) argues that consumers feel a motivational state of dissonance that arouses psychological discomfort after being exposed to an incoming cognitive stimulus about an object that is not consistent with their existing cognitions about the object. As consumers try to avoid discomfort, they tend to modify their perception toward the object by accepting the new cognitive element coming in. Applying cognitive dissonance theory to the context of offshoring, a discrepancy between the brand's original country image and the new location image created by offshoring could evoke cognitive dissonance in consumers' brand perceptions, thus resulting in adjustment in brand perceptions and brand attitudes (Chung et al., 2014).

Balance Theory

Balance theory (Heider, 1958) argues that people tend to show behaviors characterized by a cognitive coherence over time in decisions and thought, to reach intimate wellness and harmony. People experiencing a cognitive imbalance must face a discrepancy between what they think (cognitive reality) and what they perceive from the external environment (perceived reality). When a person is in an imbalanced state of mind, cognitive coherence is restored by managing the determinants of behavior and perception. Balance theory can be explained as a logic–mathematics relational system in which each person is connected to several entities through preference relations that can be positive or negative. The coherence of the whole relational system occurs when the result of multiplying all valences (positive or negative) of all the relations is positive, in which case there is a balanced state. For example, in the case of three entities, a balanced state exists if all three relations are positive or if two are negative and one is positive.

In the context of acquisitions, a third player is added to the prior relationship between the consumer and the acquired firm, that is, the acquiring firm toward which the consumer can have a positive or negative preference relationship. In the specific case of CBAs and offshoring strategies, not only firm-based factors need to be considered but also country-based ones. Consequently, the relational system involves at least three entities represented by the consumer's relationship with: (1) the acquired firm; (2) the acquiring firm; and (3) the acquiring firm's country. An imbalanced state occurs when, for example, the consumer has a positive attitude toward the acquired brand and the acquirer, and a negative attitude toward the acquirer's country.

Information Integration Theory

One's existing knowledge and stock of information can be portrayed as a network of nodes that are stored in memory and connected by linkages whose strength is caused by the strength of the associations among the nodes. When a person codes new external information, or he or she recovers previous information internally, a relevant node is activated that in turn can prompt other connected nodes to act. Integration Information Theory (Anderson, 1981) argues that people change their attitudes after having integrated a new element with another one and with previous attitudes.

In the light of this theory, the attitude of a person toward a CBA or an offshoring strategy comprises new information stored in a new node. For example, a consumer finds out about an acquisition or an offshoring strategy by reading a report, keeps in mind a new message as a consequence of his or her interpretation of the information received, and integrates it with pre-existing beliefs related to the acquirer's reputation.

Psychological Reactance Theory

The theory of psychological reactance (Brehm, 1966) assumes that when people's behavioral freedom is restricted through elimination, or threat of elimination of alternative choices, they experience an unpleasant motivational state of arousal (reactance) that induces them to preserve and retain the lost or threatened behavior, that is, their personal freedoms. According to this theory, individuals can restore or re-establish their threatened freedom through cognitive reorganizations – for example, by an increase in the attractiveness of the constrained behavior and a decrease in the evaluation of the source of the restriction. By engaging in the free-will behavior of devaluing their attitudes toward the acquirer brand, or the brand of the company employing offshoring strategies, consumers can re-establish some of their personal freedom. In CBAs, however, customers of the target brand have few behavioral options other than either to accept the CBA, which means also accepting the new COC and thus becoming customers of the new (acquirer) brand, or not to accept the reality of the CBA and switch to another brand.

Social Identity Theory

Research has used social identity theory to explain in-group favoritism, favorable evaluations, and the preferential treatment of people perceived as belonging to the same in-group. Working with various co-researchers, Tajfel (e.g., Tajfel et al., 1971) developed this theory when he observed that people tend to identify with certain groups and not with others, respectively termed in-groups and out-groups. One consequence is social comparisons that strengthen positive feelings of identifying with a perceived higher status group. Members belonging to a lower status group will acknowledge the superiority of a relevant out-group in trying to achieve positive group distinctiveness. In contrast, individuals will tend to distance themselves from an out-group that they do not find relevant to themselves (e.g., "I am not a dancer, and that group has no motivational implications for me"). Dissociative groups are out-groups with which people try to avoid being associated. Applying social identity theory to the context of CBAs implies that the target consumers encounter new corporate owners from foreign countries and, as a result, they might dis-identify with an acquirer from a country that reflects a discrepancy between current COC and original COB. The same thing can be stated for the context of offshoring where the discrepancy is connected to the COB and COM.

DOWNWARD AND UPWARD CBAS AND OFFSHORING: UPSCALE VERSUS MIDMARKET BRANDS

The image of a country is a key macro-level variable that influences consumers' attitudes and purchase intentions toward the products of firms from that country (Papadopoulos, 1993). Thus, country image influences consumers' decisions and could have positive consequences on their behavior. The substantial impact of a country's image on consumer brand perception is well documented in the marketing and branding literature (Pappu et al., 2007).

In line with the theory of social identity discussed above, consumers may dis-identify with a brand and its new corporate owners if the acquiring company reflects a country that presents a discrepancy between the current COC and original COB. This is especially true today, since many companies from emerging countries actively engage in downward CBAs in order to expand into international markets but also very often to strengthen their position within their domestic markets. Indeed, given that the domestic market is of paramount importance for many local companies in countries like China or India, through cross-border M&As they send a strong signal to domestic consumers that their products are of high quality and have a prestigious image (Fang and Wang, 2018).

Recent literature suggests that consumers' expectations and reaction toward a company associated with a particular country (COC) can differ by the brand's status because of the differing levels of identification that consumers put into the original country association of the brand (COB). As a consequence, it is important to make a distinction between luxury and mass-market brands. The fashion industry, where brand tier is more important than in many other sectors, serves as a good context for this discussion. For instance, do consumers assign the same level of importance to whether Versace's corporate ownership is still in Italy, or Guess's is still in the United States?

It was not an accident that, after the acquisition of Versace by the American Capri Holdings of Michael Kors, many Versace brand lovers complained that the brand's identity was no longer the same, or that the merger with the American brand changed its market positioning – and some comments showed feelings of disappointment, anger, and betrayal. The explanation of such a reaction rests on the fact that the home country is an integral part of the perceived value of a luxury brand (Kapferer and Bastien, 2012). Indeed, the luxury industry has its geographical origin in, and long histories related to, European countries (Brun and Castelli, 2013), and most craftspeople who have expertise in this industry also reside in Europe. Therefore, a luxury brand's European origin can be a crucial pillar in its heritage, reflecting its history and authenticity through its connection to a certain country over time. Even those researchers who have critiqued the relevance of a product's COO in today's global markets would be likely to accept and confirm that consumers make strong associations between luxury brands and their home countries (Aiello et al., 2009).

Homans' (1958) social exchange theory has been used in past research to demonstrate that consumers' expectation and reaction toward a brand can differ by the brand's status, mainly because of the differing levels of investment that consumers put into the exchange. According to the theory, consumers naturally expect benefits that are comparable to the costs they expend in social exchanges. Based on this concept, they are likely to expect a higher level of gains from a luxury brand's authenticity and consistency in the brand's origin country. Conversely, their expectations of brand-to-country consistency for mass-market brands would be lower since their level of investment in the exchange (e.g., cost, time, involvement, number of consideration sets, etc.) would be much lower. For example, the fact that Valentino was acquired by a Qatari company might cause consumers' disappointment because it is no longer an Italian company, and they might feel that the brand does not deserve its high price compared to its new country of association. On the other hand, however, the fact that a mass-market Italian brand like Motivi has moved to a foreign country might not be perceived as important by consumers relative to the luxury brand's transition, since they do not invest as much deliberation into the purchase.

It is also important to take into account the feelings of psychological ownership about a brand that may make people resistant to unexpected changes (Chang et al., 2015b) when an investor from a foreign country acquires the brand. A luxury brand is a case in point since very often it is a part of consumers' extended self (Belk, 1988) and reflects consumers' emotions, personality, social status, cultural values, and vision of the world. Feelings of psychological ownership toward a brand trigger a greater sense of loss for consumers when it is acquired by a company from a foreign country, as something that was 'theirs' can be seen as 'stolen'. Consistent with the theory of reactance discussed above, this sense of loss may lead to a negative emotional state, along with a sense of frustration that becomes even stronger when the acquisition involves a dissociative reference group or, in this case, country (Cleveland, 2015).

The extant literature shows similar consumer reactions in the case of offshoring, suggesting that consumers frequently express feelings of anger and frustration toward this practice and are willing to punish, with such means as negative word-of-mouth and intentions to boycott firms that carry out offshoring activities (Hoffmann, 2013). Consumers formed an online activist forum against Prada, for example, considering its strategic choice to offshore unacceptable as well as unfair in light of the brand's high price level.

It is expected that these negative reactions might be even stronger when the acquiring firm is from a country with which consumers would rather not identify. Accordingly, some studies have shown that higher levels of brand ownership negatively affect consumers' post-acquisition brand attitudes and undermine their intentions to purchase the product when a company from a dissociative country acquires the brand (Chang et al., 2015a). On the other hand, when it comes to mass-market brands, consumers are less emotionally invested and tend to show a lower level of ownership toward them, and are therefore less likely to consider them as a part of their extended self. Consequently, they are also less likely to experience a sense of loss no matter who takes the ownership of the brand.

According to balance theory one can predict that, after an acquisition, consumers may experience an imbalanced state of mind, changing their perception of the acquired brand because of the new relationship between it and the acquirer company's country. It is important to make this distinction between the before and after mind-states, because imbalance can arise when consumers had a favorable attitude toward the brand before the acquisition but an unfavorable attitude toward the new country, or the other way round. Indeed, in the first case, in order to restore the balance consumers will develop a more negative attitude toward the acquired brand if the new country has an inferior image compared to the home country's image. In the opposite situation, consumers' brand attitude will be affected favorably to restore balance. The two distinct imbalance states reflect the above-mentioned two opposite directions, downward and upward, of both acquisitions and offshoring strategies. Finally, if a consumer has a favorable attitude toward the brand before the CBA, there will be no change in her or his brand attitude because her or his pre-existing favorable attitude toward the brand and the new country are well balanced.

In this regard, Italy is a case in point as many of its fashion and design brands were acquired by the two most prominent French groups, Louis Vuitton (which acquired Bulgari, Fendi, and Loro Piana, among others) and Kering (Gucci, Bottega Veneta, Brioni, and Pomellato, and other such brands). In this case, it is likely that not much changed in terms of consumer perceptions after the acquisitions, because there is a condition of country-to-brand fit. Bluemelhuber et al. (2007, p. 433), who introduced the concept of COO fit, defined it as "the consumer's perception of the overall compatibility of the two countries of origin involved in the brand alliance", and showed significant positive effects of this fit on attitudes toward cross-border brand alliances. Lee et al. (2013) found that in high COO fit conditions, when both brands enjoyed favorable COO perceptions, attitudes toward both the host and partner brands were enhanced after the alliance.

THE ROLE OF THE ACQUIRER'S CORPORATE REPUTATION

The literature has recognized the critical role of corporate reputation in customers' buying behavior. Authors of marketing studies on reputation state that the better the firms' reputations, the better their financial performance (Roberts and Dowling, 2002), and, directly of interest to this discussion, perceived product quality (Weigelt and Camerer, 1988), customer satisfaction and loyalty (Bartikowski et al., 2011), and word-of-mouth reputation (Walsh and Bartikowski, 2013). Several scholars consider corporate reputation as an intangible asset that can contribute to a competitive advantage in the marketplace of goods and services (Brønn and Brønn, 2015).

Given that people react to signals they are exposed to in line with rationality and risk aversion principles, signaling theory (Erdem and Swait, 2001), which relates to associative network memory models, is also highly relevant in this context. This theory argues that those who receive a signal tend to make a cognitive effort to interpret information in order to mitigate their sense of uncertainty. This theory is particularly suitable to contexts characterized by imperfect information, for example within firms, when the attributes of a product are latent or difficult to observe. The prerequisite of the credibility of the signal is that it includes sunk costs for the sender, which cannot be recovered if the promise inside the signal is not kept. In light of this theory, reputation can be interpreted as a signal sent by a firm to reduce the uncertainty perceived by consumers in the pre-purchase stage, when consumers' expectations are shaped. Specifically, the quality of products manufactured by the firm in the past becomes a positive signal of the current and future quality of its products. The sunk costs within the signal sent by the firm are compensated by a premium price that the consumer is willing to pay and by customer loyalty, both of which are positive feedback to the signal sent.

The marketing literature has highlighted spillover effects linked to signals that can be transferred, for example, to a new product as in the case of umbrella branding (Wernerfelt, 1988), or to its association to a specific country image (Papadopoulos and Heslop, 2002), in the B2B context when a product is sold to a business customer (e.g., a retailer) with a high reputation (Helm and Salminen, 2010). In this case, the established signal reduces the uncertainty of the new signal. This occurs when the launch of a new product generates positive quality expectations if the firm has a favorable reputation (established signal) even if in actuality the product is of lower quality than the average of that firm's products. According to this theory and the related spillover effects, a CBA can be interpreted as a signal able to either increase or reduce consumer expectations on product quality from the acquiring/acquired firms.

The effective management of corporate reputation should be treated as a key element in the successful implementation of CBAs, particularly given the amount of confusion and uncertainty that tends to surround such events. Balmer and Dinnie (1999) and other researchers have indicated that many CBAs failed to produce the synergistic benefits that were expected by them, and this could be attributable to corporate identity and communication issues. As these authors note, in a CBA context, the participating firms are creating a new corporate identity that must be nurtured in order to allow their consumers to identify with the new organization.

In general, it is more common for acquisitions to change rather than retain the name and/or symbol of the acquired company (Ettenson and Knowles, 2006) so that it can be associated more readily with the (stronger) acquirer. On the other hand, the acquirer may not want to create a new identity if the acquired firm has strong brand equity and a local heritage that needs to be preserved so that its brands remain recognizable by consumers. An acquisition can create uncertainty for consumers, and therefore a good reputation on the part of the acquired company could reduce it.

Consumers may have concerns regarding the acquirer's ability to maintain the quality or image of the acquired firm after the CBA. Consumers perceiving a firm to have a good reputation are more likely to believe that it is competent, acts honestly in daily operations, and considers the interests of others in the relationship when making decisions. Additionally, according to Lafferty and Goldsmith (1999), corporate reputation has a significant influence on consumers' purchase intentions. Recent studies on CBAs from the consumer's perspective have shown that corporate reputation is positively related with stronger repurchase intentions by customers (Matarazzo et al., 2018, 2020).

Considering the issue from the perspective of open systems theory, Lopez et al. (2011) argue that a firm is linked to its environment and that changes in the latter may influence the firm and vice versa. However, environmental factors may also influence the formation of corporate image, with country image being one of the most important of these factors. Thus the two constructs, the corporate reputation of a firm and the image of its country, are linked to each other.

In the COO literature, only a few authors look at the relationship between country and corporate image, even though Bernstein (1984) showed early on that the former can affect and shape the latter. Dowling (1993) argues that corporate image is often part of a hierarchy, with itself being a 'subordinate' to the country's 'super' image. Vidaver-Cohen et al. (2015), for example, predict better reputation for firms headquartered in the United States and Northern Europe than for those based in Latin American and Southern European countries. Their study noted that the literature suggests that COO has an effect on all of the key organizational competencies driving reputation (product/service quality, innovation orientation, workplace climate, governance procedures, community citizenship, leadership practices, and financial performance). Thus, it is likely that consumers will use the reputation of a firm in association with the country's image as a means of evaluating the firm and gathering information about its behavior, history, values, prestige, and trustworthiness in international markets.

CONCLUSION

In the current scenario, the construct of COO is very relevant in the context of CBAs and offshoring, especially in the downward direction, since many multinational firms from emerging countries are acquiring firms from developed ones. This chapter illustrates the state of the art within the COO stream of research, specifically in relation to the context of CBAs and offshoring, by investigating the effect of: (1) the transition in country-of-company after a CBA; (2) the decomposition of COO after an offshoring strategy; as well as (3) the effect of the acquiring firm's corporate reputation on consumers' behavior toward the post-acquisition organization.

Furthermore, following Woo et al. (2019), the chapter stresses the importance of making distinctions related to: (1) the downward and upward strategic direction of CBAs and offshoring and (2) the social status of brands along the luxury to mass-market dimension. For reference, Figure 13.1 summarizes the relevant points of that study and the present discussion. In this context, that study showed two surprising results related to offshoring strategies that could be extended to CBAs, even though there is no specific research evidence on this parallel application. One is related to upward strategies, where brand perceptions did not improve, as hypothesized, when offshoring to, or merging with, firms in a foreign country with a better image than that of the initiating firm. The second is related to mass-market brands, where it was found that downward offshoring affects both them as well as upscale brands, with the direction of offshoring (downward vs. upward) emerging as a more critical variable than the brand's tier. While these results are labeled as 'surprising', it is important to note that they find their justification in the five psychological theories discussed in the 'theoretical explanations' above as well as the additional explanatory models and theories mentioned in this and other pertinent sections of the chapter (see Figure 13.1).

As discussed above, the growth in downward and upward CBAs and offshoring strategies also has important implications for corporate reputation. Indeed, several of the studies highlighted earlier (Resciniti et al., 2020) have shown that the acquirer's corporate reputation influences consumer response. With regard to offshoring, in 2010 Prada launched the project 'Made in Prada', a capsule collection represented by iconic fashion items of four countries diff-

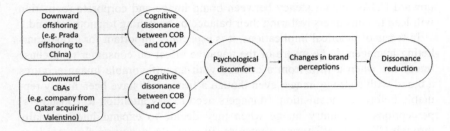

Source: Based on and adjusted from Woo et al. (2019).

Figure 13.1   Cognitive dissonance in downward CBAs and offshoring

erent from Italy: Scotland for kilts, India for needlework, Japan for jeans, and Peru for alpaca wool. The project aimed to assure its customers that regardless of where the products are manufactured, behind them there is always the company and its reputation to guarantee the products' excellence.

Regarding CBAs, Matarazzo et al. (2018) showed that in the food sector stronger intentions to repurchase the products of the post-CBA target are associated with a more favorable acquirer's corporate reputation even though they are weaker in the case of an unfavorable COC. Conversely, that study found that weaker repurchase intentions are associated to a poor acquirer's corporate reputation, despite a favorable COC. According to balance theory (see Figure 13.2), if the acquirer in a downward CBA has a good corporate reputation, consumers may restore their balance by decreasing their post-acquisition loyalty and perhaps switching to another brand after the acquisition, because of the emerging triadic relationship among a positive brand image, a positive acquirer corporate reputation, and a negative COC. In the opposite case of

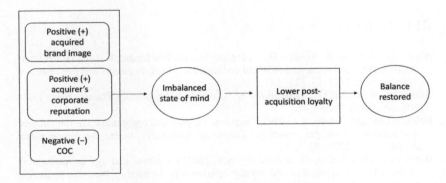

Figure 13.2   Imbalanced state of mind in downward CBAs

upward CBAs, inconsistency between brand image and corporate reputation will lead to consumers restoring their balance by switching to another brand.

In terms of practical implications, it is especially important for global marketing managers to be aware of the negative effect on consumer repurchase intentions when a firm from a country with an unfavorable image acquires a brand with a strong image, even though a firm might have been highly reputable before the acquisition. Managers need to pay attention to consumers' perceptions of country image when they decide to expand internationally through CBAs or offshoring strategies. In sum, the acquiring firm needs to manage COC and COM to ensure that consumers will remain loyal to the acquired firm.

In CBAs, some firms can de-emphasize the ownership change to avoid possible negative reactions from consumers. Furthermore, managers could communicate that the foreign acquirer wants to preserve and strengthen the heritage of the local firm. In doing this, managers could even introduce the brand of the local firm to other countries if possible, thus enforcing its visibility and brand awareness worldwide and benefiting the acquired firm's country. In this way, they may try to strengthen the connection between host country consumers and their country in order to avoid association with the unfavorable COC. To do so, they would have to actively communicate that the acquired firm's values and beliefs remain in agreement with the value system of its country.

It seems appropriate to conclude the above discussion and this chapter with reference to an official communication to Versace's customers, on Twitter by Donatella Versace, the day after her namesake Italian brand was acquired by the American Michael Kors in September 2018: "I also want to reassure you that Versace will remain ITALIAN and Made in Italy and that it will keep its GLAMOUR, DARING and INCLUSIVE attitude that have made you all love it".

REFERENCES

Aiello, G., Donvito, R., Godey, B., Pederzoli, D. and Wiedmann, K. (2009). An international perspective on luxury brand and country-of-origin effect. *Journal of Brand Management*, 16(5–6), 323–337.

Anderson, N.H. (1981). *Foundations of Information Integration Theory*. New York, NY: Academic Press.

Balmer, J.M. and Dinnie, K. (1999). Corporate identity and corporate communications: the antidote to merger madness. *Corporate Communications: An International Journal*, 4(4), 182–192.

Bartikowski, B., Walsh, G. and Beatty, S.E. (2011). Culture and age as moderators in the corporate reputation and loyalty relationship. *Journal of Business Research*, 64(9), 966–972.

Bekier, M.M. and Shelton, M.J. (2002). Keeping your sales force after the merger: merging companies should look to their revenues, not just their costs. *The McKinsey Quarterly*, Autumn, 106–116.

Belk, R.W. (1988). Possessions and the extended self. *Journal of Consumer Research*, 15(2), 139–168.

Bernstein, D. (1984). *Company Image and Reality: A Critique of Corporate Communications*, Abingdon: Taylor & Francis.

Bluemelhuber, C., Carter, L. and Lambe, C.J. (2007). Extending the view of brand alliance effects: an integrative examination of the role of country of origin. *International Marketing Review*, 24(4), 427–443.

Brehm, J.W. (1966). *A Theory of Psychological Reactance*. New York, NY: Academic Press.

Brønn, C. and Brønn, P.S. (2015). A systems approach to understanding how reputation contributes to competitive advantage. *Corporate Reputation Review*, 18(2), 69–86.

Brun, A. and Castelli, C. (2013). The nature of luxury: a consumer perspective. *International Journal of Retail & Distribution Management*, 41(11–12), 823–847.

Chang, H., Zhang, L. and Xie, G.X. (2015a). Message framing in green advertising: the effect of construal level and consumer environmental concern. *International Journal of Advertising*, 34(1), 158–176.

Chang, H., Kwak, H., Puzakova, M., Park, J. and Smit, E.G. (2015b). It's no longer mine: the role of brand ownership and advertising in cross-border brand acquisitions. *International Journal of Advertising*, 34(4), 593–620.

Chung, K., Youn, C. and Lee, Y. (2014). The influence of luxury brands' cross-border acquisition on consumer brand perception. *Clothing and Textiles Research Journal*, 32(4), 219–234.

Cleveland, M. (2015). Wanting things and needing affiliation: ethnic consumers and materialism. In A. Jamal, L. Peñaloza and M. Laroche (eds), *Routledge Companion on Ethnic Marketing*, London: Routledge, pp. 147–182.

Dowling, G.R. (1993). Developing your company image into a corporate asset. *Long Range Planning*, 26(2), 101–109.

Ellis, P.D. (2007). Paths to foreign markets: does distance to market affect firm internationalisation? *International Business Review*, 16(5), 573–593.

Erdem, T. and Swait, J. (2001). Brand equity as a signaling phenomenon. *Journal of Consumer Psychology*, 7(2), 131–157.

Ettenson, R. and Knowles, J. (2006). Merging the brands and branding the merger. *MIT Sloan Management Review*, 47(4), 38–49.

Fang, X. and Wang, X. (2018). Examining consumer responses to cross-border brand acquisitions. *European Journal of Marketing*, 52(7/8), 1727–1749.

Felix, R. and Firat, A.F. (2019). Brands that 'sell their soul': offshoring, brand liquidification and the excluded consumer. *Journal of Marketing Management*, 35(11/12), 1080–1099.

Festinger, L. (1957). *A Theory of Cognitive Dissonance*. Stanford, CA: Stanford University Press.

Fong, C.M., Lee, C.L. and Du, Y. (2013). Target reputation transferability, consumer animosity, and cross-border acquisition success: a comparison between China and Taiwan. *International Business Review*, 22(1), 174–186.

Fong, C.M., Lee, C.L. and Du, Y. (2015). Consumer animosity and foreign direct investment: an investigation of consumer responses. *International Business Review*, 24(1), 23–32.

Hamzaoui-Essoussi, L., Merunka, D. and Bartikowski, B. (2011). Brand origin and country of manufacture influences on brand equity and the moderating role of brand typicality. *Journal of Business Research*, 64(9), 973–978.

Heider, F. (1958), *The Psychology of Interpersonal Relations*. New York, NY: John Wiley.

Heinberg, M., Ozkaya, H.E. and Taube, M. (2016). A brand built on sand: is acquiring a local brand in an emerging market an ill-advised strategy for foreign companies? *Journal of the Academy of Marketing Science*, 44(5), 586–607.

Helm, S. and Salminen, R.T. (2010). Basking in reflected glory: using customer reference relationships to build reputation in industrial markets. *Industrial Marketing Management*, 39(5), 737–743.

Herz, M.F. and Diamantopoulos, A. (2013). Country-specific associations made by consumers: a dual-coding theory perspective. *Journal of International Marketing*, 21(3), 95–121.

Hoffmann, S. (2013). Home country bias in consumers' moral obligation to boycott offshoring companies. *Journal of Marketing Theory and Practice*, 21(4), 371–388.

Hofstede, G. (1994). Management scientists are human. *Management Science*, 40(1), 4–13.

Homans, G.C. (1958). Social behavior as exchange. *American Journal of Sociology*, 63(6), 597–606.

Homburg, C. and Bucerius, M. (2005). A marketing perspective on mergers and acquisitions: how marketing integration affects postmerger performance. *Journal of Marketing*, 69(1), 95–113.

Kapferer, J.N. and Bastien, B. (2012). *The Luxury Strategy: Break the Rules of Marketing to Build Luxury Brands.* London: Kogan Page.

Lafferty, B.A. and Goldsmith, R.E. (1999). Corporate credibility's role in consumers' attitudes and purchase intentions when a high versus a low credibility endorser is used in the ad. *Journal of Business Research*, 44(2), 109–116.

Lee, J.K., Lee, B.K. and Lee, W.N. (2013). Country-of-origin fit's effect on consumer product evaluation in cross-border strategic brand alliance. *Journal of Business Research*, 66(3), 354–363.

Lee, H.M., Lee, C.C. and Wu, C.C. (2011). Brand image strategy affects brand equity after M&A. *European Journal of Marketing*, 45(7/8), 1091–1111.

Lopez, C., Gotsi, M. and Andriopoulos, C. (2011). Conceptualising the influence of corporate image on country image. *European Journal of Marketing*, 45(11–12), 1601–1641.

Matarazzo, M., Lanzilli, G. and Resciniti, R. (2018). Acquirer's corporate reputation in cross-border acquisitions: the moderating effect of country image. *The Journal of Product & Brand Management*, 27(7), 858–870.

Matarazzo, M., Resciniti, R. and Simonetti, B. (2020). Cause-related marketing for successful cross-border post-acquisition performance. *International Marketing Review*, 37(4), 695–712.

Papadopoulos, N. (1993). What product and country images are and are not. In N. Papadopoulos and L.A. Heslop (eds), *Product-Country Images: Impact and Role in International Marketing*. Binghampton, NY: The Haworth Press, pp. 1–38.

Papadopoulos, N. and Heslop, L.A. (2002). Country equity and country branding: problems and prospects. *Journal of Brand Management*, 9(4/5), 294–314.

Papadopoulos, N., Cleveland, M., Bartikowski, B. and Yaprak, A. (2018). Of countries, places and product/brand place associations: an inventory of dispositions and issues relating to place image and its effects. *Journal of Product & Brand Management*, 27(7), 735–753.

Pappu, R., Quester, P.G. and Cooksey, R.W. (2007). Country image and consumer-based brand equity: relationships and implications for international marketing. *Journal of International Business Studies*, 28(5), 726–745.

Phau, I. and Prendergast, G. (2000). Conceptualizing the country of origin of brand. *Journal of Marketing Communications*, 6(3), 159–170.

Resciniti, R., Matarazzo, M. and Baima, G. (2020). Consumers' reactions to cross-border acquisitions: the role of psychic distance and acquirer's corporate reputation. *British Food Journal*, 122(2), 655–677.

Roberts, P.W. and Dowling, G.R. (2002). Corporate reputation and sustained superior financial performance. *Strategic Management Journal*, 23(12), 1077–1093.

Roth, M.S. and Romeo, J.B. (1992). Matching product category and country image perceptions: a framework for managing country-of-origin effects. *Journal of International Business Studies*, 23(3), 477–497.

Shi, T., Li, J. and Lim, C.L.(2017). Host country consumers' brand attitudes after cross-border acquisitions. *Journal of Product & Brand Management*, 26(6), 559–572.

Shimizu, K., Hitt, M.A., Vaidyanath, D. and Pisano, V. (2004). Theoretical foundations of cross-border mergers and acquisitions: a review of current research and recommendations for the future. *Journal of International Management*, 10(3), 307–353.

Tajfel, H., Billig, M.G., Bundy, R.P. and Flament, C. (1971). Social categorization and intergroup behavior. *European Journal of Social Psychology*, 1(2), 149–178.

Vidaver-Cohen, D., Gomez, C. and Colwell, S.R. (2015). Country-of-origin effects and corporate reputation in multinational firms: exploratory research in Latin America. *Corporate Reputation Review*, 18(3), 131–155.

Walsh, G. and Bartikowski, B. (2013). Exploring corporate ability and social responsibility associations as antecedents of customer satisfaction cross-culturally. *Journal of Business Research*, 66(8), 989–995.

Weigelt, K. and Camerer, C. (1988). Reputation and corporate strategy: a review of recent theory and applications. *Strategic Management Journal*, 9(5), 443–454.

Wernerfelt, B. (1988). Umbrella branding as a signal of new product quality: an example of signaling by posting a bond. *The Rand Journal of Economics*, 19(3), 458–466.

Woo, H., Jin, B.E. and Papadopoulos N. (2019). Does the direction of offshoring matter? Comparison of downward and upward offshoring strategies in changing consumers' brand perception by brand tiers. *The Journal of the Textile Institute*, 111(6), 795–807.

PART IV

'Here, there, and everywhere': advances,
adversities, applications, and associations in
'country' and 'place' marketing

14. The role of advertising in place branding

Rick T. Wilson

ADVERTISING IN THE PLACE BRANDING CONTEXT

Advertising is an important marketing function within place branding, and it is also perhaps one of its most visible forms. In addition to various specific objectives, overall it can raise a location's profile and situate it within a decision maker's consideration set. Yet advertising is frequently criticized, with some researchers and practitioners noting that some place managers often put too much emphasis on creating logos and slogans or crafting place identities that are vastly different from its reality (e.g., Ashworth and Kavaratzis, 2009; Govers, 2013). Other criticism highlights that place managers often possess unrealistic expectations or confusion about the role of advertising in place branding (Wells and Wint, 2000). Despite these denunciations, place managers spend a great amount of time, effort, and expense in promoting their locations through advertisements and websites to different communities of interest, which include tourists, investors, residents, and other key stakeholders.

The purpose of this chapter is not to review the criticism levied against place advertising, but rather to introduce and discuss a strategic process that managers of places can use when developing advertising campaigns to promote the attractiveness of a location to its chosen target markets. In particular, the Place Branding Advertising Model is presented as a tool to help researchers and practitioners design, execute, and evaluate advertising strategy in a place branding context. Prior to introducing the Place Branding Advertising Model, the definition of advertising, the principal actors involved in place branding, and their associated contexts are reviewed.

Definition of Advertising

Advertising is defined by two necessary attributes: "a message from an advertiser, and the intention to persuade" (Thorson and Rodgers, 2019, p. 4). This definition is broader in scope than older and more traditional ones. Due to the emergence of digital technology and new methods to promote brands, several attributes have been dropped, such as advertising being a paid form of promotion, from an identified sponsor, and mass mediated. The increasing importance of brand-owned media, such as interactive websites and social media accounts, has negated it being defined as paid. The proliferation of shared brand information through social media and word-of-mouth means that now people cannot always discern the sponsor. Digital technology has also enabled the development and use of highly individualized messages rather than a single message distributed to the masses. Accordingly, this chapter adopts the above broader definition.

Advertising and Place Branding

As outlined in other chapters of this book, there are three main contexts in which advertising can be used within place branding: tourism, economic development, and urban planning. In tourism, advertising is used by destination marketing organizations (DMOs), such as convention and visitors' bureaux, tourism boards, and tourism agencies, to attract tourists. In economic development, it is used by governmental and quasi-governmental investment promotion agencies (IPAs) to attract corporate investors interested in establishing or purchasing a business within a location's borders. Finally, in urban planning, governmental agencies or departments use a variety of promotional tools to attract and retain residents. While the initiating organization, their intended targets, and even what their promotional endeavors are called may vary across place branding contexts, the underlying advertising strategy and theory are consistent.

PLACE BRANDING ADVERTISING MODEL

From a promotional perspective, places have often been compared to corporations as both are more complex than traditional consumer products (Hankinson, 2007; Kavaratzis, 2009). Like corporations, places are rooted in multiple disciplines, have numerous stakeholders, and possess attributes that are highly complex and frequently intangible. Yet, places are often faced with greater diversity of both public and private stakeholders than are corporations, thus making it difficult for them to adopt a single identity (Kavaratzis, 2009).

In this light, the Place Branding Advertising Model, which is presented next, integrates traditional advertising models (e.g., Vakratsas and Ambler, 1999) with other place branding models (e.g., Hankinson, 2004; Kavaratzis, 2004) to facilitate the strategic development of advertising programs for places. The model applies traditional advertising strategy to the unique attributes of places across all three place branding contexts. As found in Figure 14.1, the Place

Branding Advertising Model is comprised of four areas: attributes, strategy, advertising, and outcomes. The model highlights the promotional outcomes likely to result from the advertising of places, which is dependent on thoughtful marketing strategy and the identification of salient place attributes that are designed and executed with the respective target markets in mind.

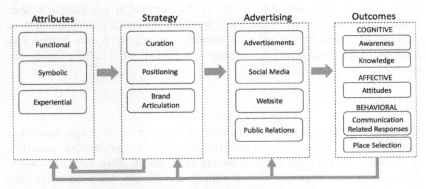

Figure 14.1   Place Branding Advertising Model

Attributes

The development and execution of place advertising requires long-term and strategic planning (Dinnie, 2008). It begins with a thorough assessment of a location's attributes. These attributes form the identity of a place and are derived from many of its intrinsic features and history (Govers and Go, 2005; Kavaratzis and Hatch, 2013; Kotler and Gertner, 2002). Place identities are not static, and they evolve over time and are continuously influenced by culture and how others view the place in what is referred to as place image (Papadopoulos, 1993; Hatch and Schultz, 2002; Kavaratzis and Ashworth, 2005). Place attributes can be functional, symbolic, or experiential, which Hankinson (2004) refers to as a place's personality, and Kavaratzis (2004) generally refers to as landscape and infrastructure in their respective models. Place attributes form the identity of a place and influence its image (Kavaratzis and Hatch, 2013).

Functional attributes are tangible, utilitarian, and environmental in form and include such items as beaches and hotels for tourism; knowledge resources and transportation infrastructure for economic development; and schools and shopping facilities for urban planning. Symbolic attributes are intangible, extrinsic, and correspond with an individual's need for social approval, personal expression, or outer-directed self-esteem (Keller, 1993). From a place branding perspective, consumers, investors, and/or residents may value the prestige, exclusivity, or standing it may bestow on their self-concept, or brand-concept, to visit, live, or establish a business in a particular location. Finally, experiential attributes refer to what it feels like to visit, live, or work in the location and include such items as the hospitality of service workers for tourism; ease in doing business for economic development; and friendliness of local residents for urban planning. While place attributes vary from location to location and by whether the location is a nation, region, or city, Table 14.1 (opposite) presents a general list of these attributes organized by type and place branding context, which were derived from a review of the place branding literature (e.g., Stylidis et al., 2016; Wilson and Baack, 2012).

Strategy

Effective advertising campaigns for places are based on reality, where the desired image for a place, as portrayed in advertisements and other promotional materials, is consistent with a place's actual identity (Hankinson, 2004; Kerr and Oliver, 2015). To ensure congruency between image and identity, place managers must actively and continuously manage their place's identity, coordinate with key stakeholders, and evaluate the strengths and weaknesses of their place attributes with respect to competition (Hanna and Rowley, 2015). These tasks form the basis of marketing strategy, which, as outlined in Figure 14.1, consists of curation, positioning, and brand articulation. These marketing strategy tasks not only shape downstream advertising strategy, but they can also reinforce existing place attributes or influence the development of new ones as shown in the feedback loop in the figure.

Curation

Managing a place's identity requires curation: coordinating with stakeholders, making investments to maintain and develop place attributes, and facilitating the effectiveness of the place's governing structure. Researchers have suggested that stakeholders are the most important component of place branding as these individuals and organizations can both directly and indirectly influence place identities and images (Hankinson, 2007; Kavaratzis and Hatch, 2013). Stakeholders comprise several groups including the intended targets for place branding (i.e., tourists, investors, and residents), the public and private organizations directly involved in managing place identities (e.g., visitors' bureaux and investment promotion agencies), and other organizations and individuals who share similar goals in promoting a place (e.g., suppliers, local businesses, the community, etc.; Hankinson, 2009; Houghton and Stevens, 2010; Stubbs and Warnaby, 2015).

While all stakeholders are important, Stubbs and Warnaby (2015) argue that residents can be one of the most important, given that many place marketing

Table 14.1 Place attributes

Attributes	Tourism	Investment Promotion	Urban Planning
Functional	• Infrastructure – public transportation, internet, mobile • Facilities – shopping, dining, accommodation, cultural entertainment • Recreation – parks, outdoor activities, historic sites, museums, natural attractions • Environment – cleanliness, general appearance, safety, road traffic, architecture • Climate	• Knowledge resources – availability of local partners and synergistic assets; proximity to knowledge-intensive industries and spatial clusters; availability of skilled/professional labor; presence of competitive/related firms • Market attractiveness – proximity to regional markets; large and growing domestic market; access to different consumer demands and preferences • Economic governance – macroeconomic policies and institutional competence of host government; government restructuring of economic activities; IPA promotional activities • Infrastructure – quality of infrastructure; ease in processing/transporting output • Natural resources – quality and quantity of resources	• Infrastructure – public transportation, internet, mobile • Facilities – shopping, dining, cultural entertainment, schools • Services – police, health, government • Economy – job opportunities • Housing – quality and variety of housing, cost of living • Recreation – parks, outdoor activities, historic sites, museums, natural attractions • Environment – cleanliness, general appearance, safety, road traffic, architecture • Climate
Symbolic	• Self-concept – destination reflects on the traveler's sense of self, such as being viewed as a foodie, adventurer, free-spirit, sophisticated, etc.	• Brand identity – location provides a unique set of associations that build on the company's core values, such as innovativeness, entrepreneurialism, egalitarianism, etc. • Legitimacy – locating a business in a place to establish credibility in an industry or market	• Self-concept – location reflects on the resident's sense of self, such as being viewed as wealthy, sophisticated, frugal, cultured, prestigious, etc.
Experiential	• Friendliness, diversity, and character of local residents	• Local management style • Character of local workers • Ease in doing business	• Friendliness, diversity, and character of local residents • Quality of life

programs are underfunded and so advertising by itself is often not enough to build place images. Residents can not only provide insight into important place attributes for inclusion in advertising, but as engaged and supportive partners, they can also act as ambassadors both at home and abroad. Other place branding organizations representing the same location but from a different place branding context can also be an important stakeholder. Wilson (2018) highlights an example where Scotland created the Scotland Brand Working Group to facilitate discussion and coordination among the country's several place marketing organizations, including Visit Scotland, Scottish Enterprises, Universities Scotland, Creative Scotland, and Talent Scotland, to ensure a common narrative in advertising that is authentically Scottish.

An additional function of curation is for place managers to continually nurture and invest in the place attributes that make a location unique or attractive to tourists, investors, and residents. For tourism, DMOs may encourage government and private business to upgrade sports facilities, the quality of accommodation, or public transportation (Wise and Perić, 2017). For investment promotion, IPAs may lobby other governmental agencies to develop and maintain sound national and economic policies (Wells and Wint, 2000). For urban planning, this may include maintaining and upgrading infrastructure and organizing and hosting larger scale and quality events (Dragin-Jensen et al., 2016; Stylidis et al., 2016). Lastly, in what Kavaratzis (2004) calls administrative structure, curation also involves place managers ensuring that their respective governmental agencies and departments are structured to facilitate efficient decision-making and servicing in support of tourists, investors, and residents.

Positioning
Once place managers have taken inventory of their place attributes and invested in its curation, they can begin to work with their stakeholders to assess how their location's place attributes are superior or inferior and unique or undifferentiated from its peers. Managers should identify attributes that are highly valued by the intended targets and which the place does well in providing. Not all attributes need be completely differentiated; some may simply signal to potential tourists, investors, or residents that the location meets the basic requirements for initial consideration.

There are generally six positioning strategies discussed in marketing (Aaker and Shansby, 1982) that are similarly applicable to places. These strategies act to situate the place in the minds of its targets with respect to other places under consideration. First, places may be positioned based on one or a group of functional, symbolic, or experiential attributes. Second, places may be differentiated based on price for a given level of quality associated with highly desired attributes, for example, cost of a beach vacation. Third, places can be positioned based on how a location is expected to be used or applied by targets, such as selecting a place based on its ease of exporting to adjacent markets. Fourth, positioning can also occur based on the type of user a place is seeking to attract, for example, extreme sports enthusiasts.

Fifth, places can be categorized into different classifications of locations and positioned as such, for example, a 'green' economy. Finally, places can be positioned either explicitly or implicitly with respect to other competing places, such as being "the most stable economy in the region". While not required in advertising, slogans and headlines are often representative of a place's positioning strategy and its unique selling proposition (Richardson and Cohen, 1993; Wilson, 2021), and examples pulled from research and organized by branding context are presented in Table 14.2 to further elucidate the aforementioned positioning strategies.

Table 14.2   Competitive positioning examples

Positioning Strategies	Tourism	Investment Promotion	Urban Planning
Attribute	"Arkansas: The natural state" or "Parks, resorts, and golf", Oklahoma	"Business friendly Bahrain" or "Ireland, knowledge is in our nature"	"Art deco city", Napier City, New Zealand or "City of water and light", Invercargill City, New Zealand
Price–quality	"Seven emirates, one destination", UAE	"Save money by thinking: France offers 50% research tax credit" or "Ensure your profits with Malaysia's vibrant business environment"	
Use or application	"Find yourself here", California	"We build industry", Lesotho or "Safe haven for Africa's shipping", Cabinda, Angola	
Product user	"Divers' paradise", Bonaire	"Ireland, innovation comes naturally"	"Young heart, easy living", Palmerston North City, New Zealand or "Keep Austin weird", Austin, Texas
Product class	"Home of adventure and entertainment", Nevada or "In the Southern Caribbean. Real. Different.", Curaçao	"Europe's west coast", Portugal or "Towards a green and self reliant economy", Bhutan	
Competitor	"Massachusetts, take a real vacation" or "Panama – the road less traveled"	"World's number one reformer", Georgia or "New business haven in Europe", Macedonia	

Source: Florek et al. (2006), Galí et al. (2017), Lee et al. (2006), Miller and Henthorne (2006), and Wilson (2021).

Brand articulation

A final strategic consideration before development of an advertising strategy can commence is to articulate the place branding elements that are likely to be included in advertising (Hanna and Rowley, 2015). These include nomenclature and visual and verbal elements, and are used to accurately, consistently, and uniquely represent the place in advertisements and online communications (He and Balmer, 2007; Wilson, 2018). Nomenclature refers to all aspects of the place's name inclusive of its actual name, nickname, earlier references to its name, abbreviations of it, and any other references to it in URL addresses. While the nomenclature for most places is unlikely to change, Hankinson (2001) noted several towns along England's Yorkshire coast that created a new regional name (Yorkshire Coast) to jointly promote investment and tourism. From a heritage perspective, some locations, like Istanbul, may reference their former name (Constantinople) to signal its rich history and culture to tourists (Wilson, 2018).

Visual and verbal elements act to hasten recognition and promote more efficient message processing. Visual elements include items such as logos, colors, and any other graphics or symbols consistently paired with the place in communications. Verbal elements refer to items that are written and spoken, such as slogans, jingles, or other prominently placed verbiage in advertising. For these elements to be impactful and avoid being viewed as superficial, their meaning should be taken from the culture, history, or current reality of a place (Dinnie, 2008; Kerr and Oliver, 2015). Meaning can be derived from territorial symbols, such as flags, boundary maps, colors, flora/fauna, and emblems, as well as from cultural symbols, such as famous people, landmarks, architecture, heritage, and recreational and business activities. Warnaby and Medway (2010) and Wilson (2018; 2021) discuss this and provide examples for how territorial and cultural symbols can be incorporated effectively into logos and slogans.

Of all the branding elements, logos and slogans seem to receive the majority of attention from both practitioners and academics. It is worth repeating that logos and slogans are not required for advertising programs, but they tend to be used more frequently in place branding than in other business fields (Wilson, 2021) and are some of the most visible forms of place branding (Govers, 2013). While researchers have provided evidence that too much emphasis, time, and budget is often allocated to their development and use, often ignoring or marginalizing other marketing and curation strategies (Ashworth and Kavartzis, 2009), thoughtful creation of differentiated logos and slogans grounded in relevant place attributes can confer legitimacy, credibility, and professionalism onto the place and its managing agency (Hildreth, 2013; Wilson, 2021).

Advertising

The next process in the Place Branding Advertising Model involves advertising, which includes advertisements, public relations, social media, and websites (Balmer, 2002; Kavaratzis, 2004; Thorson and Rodgers, 2019). While places continue to use traditional advertising media like television and print, there is growing evidence that a larger share of their promotional budgets are moving toward digital media, including online advertising, social media, and websites (El Banna et al., 2016; Hanna and Rowley, 2015; Wilson, 2018). Indeed, industry associations emphasize that in today's digital world, places must have a website that is informative, easy to navigate, and contain branding elements that uniquely identify and actively sell a place to potential targets and stakeholders (WAIPA, 2019).

Whether in advertisements or on websites, a place's promoted image, through its articulated attributes, support arguments, and crafted branding elements, must be consistent with the place's identity or it will ultimately not be accepted as true by the target audience (Kerr and Oliver, 2015). Kavaratzis (2004) describes this needed consistency between the reality of a place's identity and its perceived image using three distinct types of communication. Primary communications represent a place's features and actions as previously discussed in the attributes and curation sections of the Place Branding Advertising Model, respectively. Secondary communications are purposeful communications represented by the advertising portion of the Place Branding Advertising Model and form the primary focus of this chapter. According to Kavaratzis (2004), primary and secondary communications influence tertiary communications, which refer to the word-of-mouth of targets and other stakeholders, further reinforced by media and competitors' communications. Tertiary communications are not directly controllable by place managers, which is why advertising strategy must be based on reality lest it be viewed as inauthentic or propaganda.

Outcomes

It can easily be argued that most, if not all, decisions of where to visit, work, or live are high involvement decisions given the amount of time and money that goes into evaluating choices and their consequences in making an incorrect selection (Kerr and Oliver, 2015). Tourists can potentially lose substantive amounts of money on airfare and accommodation and wasted vacation time if the trip does not live up to expectations. Businesses can lose years of planning and potentially major parts of their budget in acquisition or construction costs or missed sales if managers misjudge location decisions or if the local investment and economic climates change drastically. Residents, too, can lose time and money in moving expenses or buying and selling a home if they later determine the decision to live in a particular location is not what they expected. While the location choice is a high involvement decision, place advertising serves multiple functions, and tourists, investors, and residents may not always be in a highly involved state when encountering advertisements. As such, the outcomes resulting from place advertising are not always the selection of a destination but may be incremental steps in the decision-making process that ultimately lead to selection.

In general, advertising outcomes are broadly grouped into three areas: cognitive, affective, and behavioral (Vakratsas and Ambler, 1999). These areas are applicable to place branding and are outlined in Figure 14.1. The cognitive outcome is concerned with information transfer and ensures the target market remembers the advertisement and the place name, or learns something about the place's functional, symbolic, or experiential attributes. Affective outcomes are concerned with consumer or managerial liking, feelings, emotions, and preferences provoked by advertisements and other promotional tools. Behavioral outcomes can be categorized as either communication-related responses or place selection. Communication-related responses are behaviors that are something short of deciding to visit, live, or work in a location and include such items as visiting a website, following a place on social media, or word-of-mouth communication. In a place branding context, place selection includes visiting a destination, buying a home or renting an apartment in a location, or purchasing or establishing a business in a location.

The success or failure of advertising campaigns not only inform the general business strategies for places, but they can also alter or reinforce earlier decisions made with respect to advertising strategy, marketing strategy, and place attributes as shown in the feedback loops in Figure 14.1. While a number of assessment methods are available to measure advertising campaign success across all outcome areas, self-report methods like surveys and interviews are the most widely used, especially in place branding (Morgan et al., 2012). Newer technologies, such as electroencephalography (EEG), eye tracking, and facial analysis, are used widely elsewhere in advertising and are beginning to be used in place branding as well (McDuff, 2017; Scott et al., 2019). To help place managers assess the effectiveness of their advertising programs, a summary of the primary outcome measures and suggested assessment methods is found in Table 14.3.

Table 14.3   Place branding advertising outcome measures and methods

Outcome	Measures	Methods
Cognitive		
Awareness	Attention to the overall ad, branding elements, images, and copy	Surveys, interviews, tracking studies, eye tracking
	Recognition, aided recall, or unaided recall of ad or place name	Surveys, interviews, tracking studies
Knowledge	Recognition, aided recall, or unaided recall of place attributes, ad arguments, or copy	Surveys, interviews, tracking studies
Affective	Attitude toward the ad, place, or place attributes	Surveys, interviews, tracking studies, social media listening, and sentiment analysis
	Emotional response	Electroencephalographic (EEG), pupil dilation, facial testing, dial testing
	Intent to visit, live, or invest	Surveys, interviews, tracking studies
Behavioral		
Communication-related	Visit a website	Page visits, page views, visit duration, cookies, surveys, interviews, tracking studies
	Visit a DMO, IPA, or government office	Surveys, interviews, people counts, visit duration, surveys, interviews, tracking studies
	Inquiries	Emails, call counts, call duration, surveys, interviews, tracking studies
	Download a mobile app	App installs
	Follow a place on social media	Likes, posts, shares, follows, surveys, interviews, tracking studies
	Word-of-mouth (write a review or talk about the place)	Surveys, interviews, tracking studies, content analysis of online reviews
Place selection	Visit, live, or invest in a location	Surveys, interviews, tracking studies

THE ROLE OF ADVERTISING IN PLACE BRANDING

The role of advertising in destination marketing and investment promotion has been studied more extensively than it has been in the urban planning context. In both destination marketing and investment promotion, evidence suggests advertising does not greatly influence the core location decision but rather influences other aspects of the decision-making process leading up to the destination choice.

Destination Marketing

From a destination marketing perspective, Stienmetz et al. (2015) and Choe et al. (2017) find that tourism advertising is more likely to influence the choice of attractions, restaurants, and hotels at the tourist destination than the actual destination decision. Advertising may also increase the length of stay at the destination (Pratt et al., 2010). While tourism advertising may not lead to destination selection in the short run, research suggests that it may raise a location's profile through top-of-mind awareness and create a positive image for the destination that may ultimately lead to destination choice in the long run (Kim et al., 2005). Assuming advertisements' primary function within destination marketing is to increase top-of-mind awareness and encourage consumers to request additional information, a study of five different media – TV, magazines, newspapers, internet, and radio – found that only TV advertising was related to top-of-mind awareness and only magazines were similarly related to requesting information (Kim et al., 2005). Given the prevalence of digital media today, results are likely to be different especially for younger consumers, but research in this area is just beginning to build.

Investment Promotion

In investment promotion, advertising is thought to influence stages three and four of the five-stage site selection process (World Bank, 2006), and advertising strategy varies in early versus later stages of decision-making (Papadopoulos et al., 2016). In the first two stages, managers identify a need to expand the business to another location and then define the location characteristics or criteria used to evaluate potential locations. In stage three, managers identify a long list of 8 to 20 locations for consideration, and advertising at this stage serves as an image-building function that can increase top-of-mind awareness and situate a location in a firm's initial consideration set (Wilson and Baack, 2012). Stage four involves evaluating potential locations in greater detail and frequently includes site visits. However, due to the high cost and effort of in-depth assessment and location visits, typically no more than five locations are evaluated at this stage. Here, advertising can serve as an investment-servicing function by providing costly and difficult-to-find location information in advertisements or by directing managers to visit the investment promotion agency's website for market-specific information or contact the agency for additional assistance

(Harding and Javorcik, 2012; Wells and Wint, 2000; Wilson, 2021; Wilson and Baack, 2020a). The fifth and final stage is the selection of the location for building or acquiring a local business.

Most studies of advertising within investment promotion have centered on print advertisements. Wilson and Baack (2012; 2020a) performed content analyses of traditional advertisements and advertorials, respectively, as found in US business magazines where countries were promoted for foreign investment. The investigation of traditional, single-page advertisements found evidence of nearly all place attributes highlighted in Table 14.1 but noted that individual ads did not include all attributes, nor did ads go into great detail when these attributes were presented (Wilson and Baack, 2012). The authors surmised the primary purpose of these image-building ads were to raise country awareness and encourage investors to contact the country's investment promotion agency or visit its website for more detailed information. The examination of advertorials found a greater presence of place attributes with respect to depth and breadth due in great part to the ad's multipage format (Wilson and Baack, 2020a). The investment promotion advertorials mimicked editorial content and provided comprehensive information on nearly all relevant country attributes.

In comparing the two studies, the 2012 analysis showed greater differentiation among countries with respect to content, branding, and positioning, which is expected given that advertorials in the 2020 analysis by definition do not contain branding. Yet, Wilson and Baack (2020a) also noted that many of the advertorials were produced by a handful of communication agencies, which made many advertorials appear formulaic and lacking in competitive differentiation with respect to mentioned place attributes.

Taking a subset of the aforementioned advertisements, Wilson and his colleagues presented several advertisements to site selection managers and demonstrated, with as little as one exposure, that investment promotion advertising could influence advertising outcomes. In particular, one study showed that ads could change managerial attitudes and beliefs about place attributes and increase the likelihood managers would seek additional information, contact the investment promotion agency, or recommend the location for investment (Wilson et al., 2014). Additionally, managers, who believed the investment promotion advertisements presented to them were highly creative (Baack et al., 2016) or from a country perceived to be more trustworthy or experts in foreign direct investment (Wilson and Baack, 2020b), found the ads to be more effective in changing attitudes and behavioral intentions.

Beyond print, investment promotion research has also investigated online communications and more specifically, agency websites. From an advertising strategy perspective, a World Bank (2012) report stressed the importance for investment promotion websites to appear professional, contain branding, and provide detailed investor-related information that is easily accessible. Despite this recommendation, many websites failed to adhere to these recommendations. A content analysis of 22 national-level investment promotion websites representing IPAs on all continents found that the comprehensiveness of included attributes and sophistication of website design varied greatly from website to website (El Banna et al., 2016). In some instances, this research noted that several countries had multiple websites promoting foreign investment with conflicting messaging and an apparent lack of coordination among them.

Another content analysis of investment promotion websites representing 181 countries assessed the presence and competitive differentiation of branding elements (Wilson, 2021). Although this study found that 88 percent of websites contained logos and many incorporated territorial and cultural symbols in their construction, a large number of graphically designed logos were comprised of symbols that were too abstract for the average investor to recognize and comprehend and therefore were unlikely to influence perceptions (Warnaby and Medway, 2010). The Wilson (2021) study also found that only 21 percent of websites had slogans, and that these were overwhelming generic, undifferentiating, and unlikely to be meaningful to investors. While research on investment promotion websites is small, available research does appear to indicate that for all the time and expense place managers are reported to spend on developing logos and slogans, there is considerable opportunity for improvement.

CONCLUSION

Advertising can be an important part of place branding, but it should not be viewed as a panacea for all that afflicts a location nor is advertising just a logo or slogan. Advertising is a strategic process that involves the identification of important and differentiated place attributes, the curation of these attributes, and using these attributes to position a place vis-à-vis its competitive peers through nomenclature, visual, and verbal branding elements. Only then should place managers commence the development of advertising campaign strategy using advertisements, social media, public relations, and websites. The Place Branding Advertising Model can be used by academics to frame place branding research where advertising and promotion is a topic of interest and to assist with analyzing case studies in practice. The model can also support practitioners by providing a framework to guide the promotional planning process and to set expectations for the role of advertising in place branding.

REFERENCES

Aaker, D.A. and Shansby, J.G. (1982). Positioning your product. *Business Horizons*, 25(3), 56–62.

Ashworth, G. and Kavaratzis, M. (2009). Beyond the logo. Brand management for cities. *Brand Management*, 16(8), 520–531.

Baack, D.W., Wilson, R.T., van Dessel, M.M. and Patti, C.H. (2016). Advertising to businesses: does creativity matter? *Industrial Marketing Management*, 55, 169–177.

Balmer, J.M.T. (2002). Of identities lost and identities found. *International Studies of Management and Organizations*, 32(3), 10–27.

Choe, Y., Stienmetz, J.L. and Fesenmaier, D.R. (2017). Measuring destination marketing: comparing four models of advertising. *Journal of Travel Research*, 56(2), 143–157.

Dinnie, K. (2008). *Nation Branding: Concepts, Issues, Practice*. Oxford: Butterworth-Heinemann.

Dragin-Jensen, C., Schnittka, O. and Arkil, C. (2016). More options do not always create perceived variety in life: attracting new residents with quality- vs. quantity-oriented event portfolios. *Cities*, 56, 55–62.

El Banna, A., Hamzaoui-Essoussi, L. and Papadopoulos, N. (2016). A comparative cross-national examination of online investment promotion. *Journal of Euromarketing*, 25(3–4), 131–146.

Florek, M., Insch, A. and Gnoth, J. (2006). City council websites as a means of place brand identity communication. *Place Branding*, 2(4), 276–296.

Galí, N., Camprubí, R. and Donaire, J. (2017). Analysing tourism slogans in top tourism destinations. *Journal of Destination Marketing & Management*, 6, 243–251.

Govers, R. (2013). Why place branding is not about logos and slogans. *Place Branding and Public Diplomacy*, 9(2), 71–75.

Govers, R. and Go, F.M. (2005). Projected destination image online: website content analysis of pictures and text. *Information Technology & Tourism*, 7(2), 73–89.

Hankinson, G. (2001). Location branding: a study of the branding practices of 12 English cities. *Brand Management*, 9(2), 127–142.

Hankinson, G. (2004). Relational network brands: towards a conceptual model of place brands. *Journal of Vacation Marketing*, 10(2), 109–121.

Hankinson, G. (2007). The management of destination brands: five guiding principles based on recent development in corporate branding theory. *Journal of Brand Management*, 14(3), 240–254.

Hankinson, G. (2009). Managing destination brands: establishing a theoretical foundation. *Journal of Marketing Management*, 25(1–2), 97–115.

Hanna, S.A. and Rowley, J. (2015). Rethinking strategic place branding in the digital age. In M. Kavaratzis, G. Warnaby and G.J. Ashworth (eds), *Rethinking Place Branding: Comprehensive Brand Development for Cities and Regions*. Cham: Springer, pp. 85–100.

Harding, T. and Javorcik, B.S. (2012). Investment promotion and FDI inflows: quality matters. *CESifo Economic Studies*, 59(2), 337–359.

Hatch, M.J. and Schultz, M. (2002). The dynamics of organizational identity. *Human Relations*, 55(8), 989–1018.

He, H. and Balmer, J.M.T. (2007). Identity studies: multiple perspectives and implications for corporate-level marketing. *European Journal of Marketing*, 41(7/8), 765–785.

Hildreth, J. (2013). The joys and sorrows of logos and slogans in place branding. *Place Branding and Public Diplomacy*, 9(2), 217–222.

Houghton, J.P. and Stevens, A. (2010). City branding and stakeholder engagement. In K. Dinnie (ed.), *City Branding: Theory and Cases*. Basingstoke: Palgrave Macmillan, pp. 45–53.

Kavaratzis, M. (2004). From city marketing to city branding: towards a theoretical framework for developing city brands. *Place Branding*, 1(1), 58–73.

Kavaratzis, M. (2009). Cities and their brands: lessons from corporate branding. *Place Branding and Public Diplomacy*, 5(1), 26–37.

Kavaratzis, M. and Ashworth, G.J. (2005). City branding: an effective assertion of identity or a transitory marketing trick? *Tijdschrift voor Economische en Sociale Geografie*, 96(5), 506–514.

Kavaratzis, M. and Hatch, M.J. (2013). The dynamics of place brands: an identity-based approach to place branding theory. *Marketing Theory*, 13(1), 69–86.

Keller, K. (1993). Conceptualizing, measuring, and managing customer-based brand equity. *Journal of Marketing*, 57(1), 1–22.

Kerr, G. and Oliver, J. (2015). Rethinking place identities. In M. Kavaratzis, G. Warnaby and G.J. Ashworth (eds), *Rethinking Place Branding: Comprehensive Brand Development for Cities and Regions*. Cham: Springer, pp. 110–118.

Kim, D., Hwang, Y. and Fesenmaier, D.R. (2005). Modeling tourism advertising effectiveness. *Journal of Travel Research*, 44(1), 42–49.

Kotler, P. and Gertner, D. (2002). Country as a brand, product, and beyond: a place marketing and brand management perspective. *Brand Management*, 9(4/5), 249–261.

Lee, G., Cai, L.A. and O'Leary, J.T. (2006). WWW.Branding.States.US: an analysis of brand-building elements in the US state tourism websites. *Tourism Management*, 27(5), 815–828.

McDuff, D. (2017). New methods for measuring advertising efficacy. In S. Rodgers and E. Thorson (eds), *Digital Advertising: Theory and Research*. New York, NY: Routledge, pp. 327–342.

Miller, M.M. and Henthorne, T.L. (2006). In search of competitive advantage in Caribbean tourism websites. *Journal of Travel & Tourism Marketing*, 21(2/3), 49–62.

Morgan, N., Hastings, E. and Pritchard, A. (2012). Developing a new DMO marketing evaluation framework: the case of Visit Wales. *Journal of Vacation Marketing*, 18(1), 73–89.

Papadopoulos, N. (1993). What product and country images are and are not. In N. Papadopoulos and L.A. Heslop (eds), *Product-Country Images: Impact and Role in International Marketing*. Binghampton, NY: The Haworth Press, pp. 1–38.

Papadopoulos, N., Hamzaoui-Essoussi, L. and El Banna, A. (2016). Nation branding for foreign direct investment: an integrative review and directions for research and strategy. *Journal of Product & Brand Management*, 5(7), 615–628.

Pratt, S., McCabe, S., Cortes-Jimenez, I. and Blake, A. (2010). Measuring the effectiveness of destination marketing campaigns: comparative analysis of conversion studies. *Journal of Travel Research*, 49(2), 179–90.

Richardson, J. and Cohen, J. (1993). State slogans: the case of the missing USP. *Journal of Travel & Tourism Marketing*, 2(2/3), 91–110.

Scott, N., Zhang, R., Le, D. and Moyle, B. (2019). A review of eye-tracking research in tourism. *Current Issues in Tourism*, 22(10), 1244–1261.

Stienmetz, J.L., Maxcy, J.G. and Fesenmaier, D.R. (2015). Evaluating destination advertising. *Journal of Travel Research*, 54(1), 22–35.

Stubbs, J. and Warnaby, G. (2015). Rethinking place branding from a practice perspective: working with stakeholders. In M. Kavaratzis, G. Warnaby and G.J. Ashworth (eds), *Rethinking Place Branding: Comprehensive Brand Development for Cities and Regions*. Cham: Springer, pp. 110–118.

Stylidis, D., Sit, J. and Biran, A. (2016). An exploratory study of residents' perception of place image: the case of Kavala. *Journal of Travel Research*, 55(5), 659–674.

Thorson, E. and Rodgers, S. (2019). Advertising theory in the digital age. In S. Rodgers and E. Thorson (eds), *Advertising Theory*. New York, NY: Routledge, pp. 3–17.

Vakratsas, D. and Ambler, T. (1999). How advertising works: what do we really know. *Journal of Marketing*, 63(1), 26–43.

WAIPA (2019). *Overview of Investment Promotion: Report of the Findings from the WAIPA Annual Survey of 2018*. Geneva: The World Association of Investment Promotion Agencies.

Warnaby, G. and Medway, D. (2010). Semiotics and place branding: the influence of the built and natural environment in city logos. In G.J. Ashworth and M. Kavaratzis (eds), *Towards Effective Place Brand Management: Branding European Cities and Regions*. Cheltenham, UK and Northampton, MA, USA: Edward Elgar Publishing, pp. 205–221.

Wells Jr, L.T. and Wint, A.T. (2000). Marketing a country: promotion as a tool for attracting foreign investment, revised edition (Occasional Paper 13), The International Finance Corporation, the Multilateral Investment Guarantee Agency, and the World Bank. Accessed at http://www.fias.net.

Wilson, R.T. (2021). Slogans and logos as brand signals within investment promotion. *Journal of Place Management and Development*, 14(2), 163–179.

Wilson, R.T. (2018). Transforming history into heritage: applying corporate heritage to the marketing of places. *Journal of Brand Management*, 25(4), 351–369.

Wilson, R.T. and Baack, D.W. (2012). Attracting foreign direct investment: applying Dunning's location advantages framework to FDI advertising. *Journal of International Marketing*, 20(2), 95–115.

Wilson, R.T. and Baack, D.W. (2020a). An exploration of advertorials used to attract foreign direct investment. *Journal of Current Issues & Research in Advertising*, 41(1), 36–53.

Wilson, R.T. and Baack, D.W. (2020b). How the credibility of places affects the processing of advertising claims: the case of investment promotion advertising. In S. Sar (ed.), *Proceedings of the 2020 Conference of the American Academy of Advertising*. American Academy of Advertising.

Wilson, R.T., Baack, D.W. and Baack, D.E. (2014). Foreign direct investment promotion: using advertising to change attitudes and behaviors. *Marketing Management Journal*, 24(2), 108–123.

Wise, N. and Perić, M. (2017). Sports tourism, regeneration and social impacts: new opportunities and directions for research, the case of Medulin, Croatia. In N. Bellini and C. Pasquinelli (eds), *Tourism in the City: Towards an Integrative Agenda on Urban Tourism*. Cham: Springer International, pp. 311–320.

World Bank (2006). *Investment Promotion Agency Performance Review 2006: Providing Information to Investors – A Report of Global IPA Performance Results.* Washington, DC: The World Bank Group.
World Bank (2012). *Global Investment Promotion Best Practices 2012.* Washington, DC: The World Bank Group.

15. Place branding as an instrument in strategic spatial planning: insights from urban regions in Western Europe and North America

Eduardo Oliveira and Anna M. Hersperger

PLACE BRANDING AND PLACE IMAGE IN TODAY'S ENVIRONMENT

Literature substantiates that place branding – the application of the principles and methods of branding to the promotion of the environmental and non-environmental qualities of places – is widespread among planners, place managers, and policymakers (Kavaratzis, 2018). This is because countries, regions, and cities across the world are in competition for private investments, business ventures, sporting and cultural event hosting, as well as for new residents and workforce in general and highly qualified ones in particular (Warnaby and Medway, 2013). Inter-regional competition has indeed become a global challenge especially in urban regions (Papadopoulos et al., 2017).

Urban regions, also defined as metropolitan regions, are some of the most dynamic territories worldwide and play a key role in promoting the development of local and regional economies and in ensuring a sustainable future (Acuto et al., 2018). A first response of governments to inter-regional competition was to launch tax incentives, but these soon proved to be relatively ineffective in channelling investments (Rainisto, 2003). Developing and implementing place branding strategies, similar to those that companies apply to market their products or services, turned out to become the most popular approach of municipal and regional governments. As a result, governments started to implement branding with various objectives to reinforce the chief goal of positioning themselves on the inter-regional competition stage (Li and Cai, 2019).

Previous studies extensively outline how, or through which means, urban regions develop and implement branding strategies. At the present time, these strategies primarily take advantage of the quality and distinctiveness of the places' urban features (or non-environmental qualities), and landscape amenities (or environmental qualities) (e.g. Boisen et al., 2017; Kavaratzis et al., 2017).

Urban features are described as the quality of transport infrastructure, availability, and affordability of housing, existing creative, technological, or other industries, and the quality of educational facilities and health, such as research institutes and hospitals (Anholt, 2007). Large transportation infrastructures or mega urban projects also 'feed back' into branding strategies, and hence attract additional investment and talented workforces whilst helping to enhance the branding strategies themselves (Choplin and Franck, 2010; Flyvbjerg, 2007). Museums, concert halls or opera houses, built heritage, the overall built environment that constitutes a city's urban fabric, the availability of sport venues, and the quality and diversity of tourism facilities, are also promoted as urban features on which branding strategies are anchored (Kavaratzis et al., 2017).

For example, in a recent comparative study Vuignier (2017) outlines that urban features are important factors for attracting companies and investments to Western Switzerland (the French-speaking part of the country). The Spanish urban regions of Barcelona and Bilbao capitalize on existing cultural built heritage or cultural facilities in their branding narratives as *Gaudi Barcelona* and *Guggenheim Bilbao*, respectively (Evans, 2015). The business-to-business service agency of the Greater Zurich Area promotes the existing technological ecosystem, composed of firms and research institutions, to attract new investment and a talented workforce to several Swiss cantons and cities through the *Greater Zurich–Where Tech Invests* publicity campaign.

A few urban areas frame environmental qualities in general (Mondal and Das, 2018) and landscape amenities in particular in place branding strategies (San Eugenio Vela et al., 2017). Landscape amenities are valuable strengths of such areas in terms of their recreational and aesthetic values. They include agricultural land (Sayer et al., 2013), forest land, and wildlife habitats (McGranahan, 2008) as well as natural conservation areas, wetlands, recreational open spaces, and urban parks and gardens, together with such culturally significant elements as old trees (Lin and Su, 2019; Blicharska and Mikusinski, 2014). For example, the city of Minneapolis in the United States has used its landscapes amenities to create the image of *City by Nature* (Meet Minneapolis, 2014). Singapore's authorities promote this city-state in Southeast Asia as a business location through the branding strategies *Singapore the Garden City* aligned with the brand *Enterprise Singapore* (Wang et al., 2019).

An interesting example of focusing on sustainability for positioning an urban region is the city of Vancouver in Canada, which has ambitiously implemented its *Greenest City Action Plan* in order to stay at the leading edge of urban sustainability. The rather audacious claim of being the greenest city (without easily identifiable references to whether the superlative compares it locally, regionally, or globally) has been supported through planning and strategic thinking. For instance, one novel component in Vancouver's initiative is their *Regional Food System Strategy*, in which the city proposes the development of an agro-tourism strategy that identifies opportunities for producers to diversify their farm operations, create a brand, and sell more products directly to urban dwellers (Metro Vancouver, 2011).

In parallel with the increasing use of place branding strategies by governments, strategic spatial planning (SSP) was introduced as a method for developing a coordinated vision to guide the medium- to long-term development of urban regions (Hersperger et al., 2020). It is reasonable, therefore, to expect that spatial planning and place branding have overlapping and related interests concerning the use, organization, and meaning of space and place (Vanolo, 2017; Oliveira, 2016).

In this chapter we argue that place branding can be considered an SSP instrument. We begin with a review of prior research on both fields as a background for the discussions that follow on the linkage between place branding and SSP and the role of strategic spatial planners in place branding, without neglecting the possible intervention of place branding experts in SSP. The empirical assessment presented in this chapter was gathered from a content analysis of the strategic plans currently in force in 16 West European and North American urban regions. The methodology and results are described in the case analysis section later in this chapter. We conclude by sketching a practice-oriented agenda, which paves the way for highlighting possibilities for place branding as an instrument of strategic spatial planning in support of achieving sustainable spatial development.

STRATEGIC SPATIAL PLANNING

For those less familiar with spatial planning theories, a brief definition of strategic spatial planning will certainly be helpful here. Spatial planning and SSP are often perceived as tautological concepts; however, the evolution of the latter term clarifies that not all spatial planning is strategic. The practice which emphasizes the 'strategic' part gained popularity at the beginning of the 1990s and seemed to offer an alternative to traditional approaches; the turn to strategy in spatial planning discourse is a response to the shortcomings of an incremental planning style by projects (cf. Pagliarin et al., 2019). In order to embrace the complexity of spatial developments, the strategic element of the process was positioned at the critical junction between the need for a comprehensive vision of the future and the impossibility of predicting possible interfering factors (Oliveira and Hersperger, 2018). The current practice of strategic spatial planning reflects a shift from government, as a single actor, towards a multi-actor and community-based governance. Several researchers have noted that SSP is not a single concept, procedure, or tool, but rather, it is a set of concepts, procedures, and tools that must be tailored carefully to different spatial contexts (Albrechts, 2010).

Strategic spatial planning is thus selective and oriented to issues that really matter. Albrechts (2013) interprets it as a tool, able to support a strategic-oriented change and thus to socially and economically improve places by using different instruments. Urban regions often employ SSP as a response to economic and social changes, as well as to support structural shifts from, for example, an industry-based to a service-oriented urban region.

The outputs of an SSP process are the plans, consisting of a written report and often a cartographic representation of the envisioned spatial development. Key strategic domains within plans are typically threefold. First, how much growth is expected and/or desired to fulfil the urban region's need for economic development and housing. Second, where distinct types of urban development (e.g., dense housing, mixed uses, industrial facilities) should be located. And third, identifying areas/land parcels that should be protected in order to assure the long-term persistence of natural and cultural assets. Indeed, in recent years, sustainable development and environmental concerns have become important objectives in strategic plans (Hersperger et al., 2020).

THE LINKAGE BETWEEN PLACE BRANDING AND STRATEGIC SPATIAL PLANNING

Both place branding and SSP bring into focus urban priorities, provide the motivations for preserving urban features and landscape amenities, and request the engagement of civic society and key place actors. Indeed, thirty years ago, Ashworth and Voogd (1990) stressed that place branding links well with spatial policy and governance systems. In this line of thought, place branding, as an SSP instrument, lends itself to a spatial consciousness of branding places, thus making it more environmentally responsible and effective in supporting economic and social development. By considering place branding as an instrument in SSP, the initiative is more than just catchy slogans, colourful logos, star architects, or bidding for 'City of Talent' or 'Region of Innovation' status, which have been applied as solutions regardless of place-specific features, landscape amenities, and governance settings. However, it is only recently that place branding has noticeably broadened its scope to include a wide range of other socio-spatial and spatial-economic issues, and in doing so, it is drawing closer to practices of SSP. A place-branding framework for cities and urban regions proposes that place branding, aligned with SSP, would contribute to envisioning alternative futures through the participation of key actors from the public and private sectors as well as citizens (Oliveira, 2016). Furthermore, flexibility and adaptability to circumstances of strategic planning could be an advantage when strengthening place branding narratives further (Deffner et al., 2020).

Examples from both theory and practice help to illustrate the linkage between branding and planning. For example, Grenni et al. (2020), through a case study in Finland, contend that place branding is not just what a place is about in the present time, but also about joint efforts to make it better and adapted to evolving challenges. They conclude that in a scenario of spatial development, place branding is the co-creation of cultural narratives that support sustainable perspectives for the future. Through their case study of the Region of Ruhr in Germany, Asprogerakas and Mountanea (2020) concluded that branding activities were integrated into a spatial strategy in order to construct new identities based on existing ones. Lucarelli and Heldt Cassel (2020) devote attention to the roles of place branding in regional planning processes in Sweden. Porter (2020) reflects on place branding in support of landscape planning in the English Lake District National Park.

Two examples from practice would also be useful here. The *Strategic Development Plan for Edinburgh and South East Scotland 2016* aims to ensure that communities are involved in the design and shaping of development at an early stage, using a variety of tools to engage local people in conversations about what Edinburgh and South East Scotland should be like (SESPlan, 2016). In Edinburgh, for instance, placemaking or the renewal of urban and rural built environments is set to play a fundamental role in attracting investment and supporting economic growth, promoting healthy lifestyles, and providing a sense of identity and community. The *City of Helsinki Strategic Spatial Plan* provides the bases for its economic development strategy. Additionally, it serves as a blueprint for the development, implementation, and marketing of the proposals of the plan (Helsinki City Planning Department, 2009).

THE CONTRIBUTION OF STRATEGIC SPATIAL PLANNERS TO PLACE BRANDING

If one understands place branding as an SSP instrument, planners need to play a role in it. Cities and urbanized regions have been promoted in a manner similar to that developed for commercial products in the business sector, and while these places have reiterated that their intention was not to call into question the expertise, capabilities, or integrity of those dealing with branding and promotion in the context of places, their actions do raise a number of questions for spatial planning. As Ashworth and Voogd (1999) underlined early on, "[if marketing and branding] is to be part of public sector planning then it must be exercised, or at the very least its capabilities and results understood, by public sector planners" (p. 156).

More recently, Ginesta et al. (2020) debated the implications that place branding has for regional public management, through their case study of the city of Vic in Catalonia. The city promoted itself as "*Vic, a city with a human dimension*" through a place-based branding project commissioned by the city council and carried out by a local university. Dealing with the challenges of branding places, according to Ginesta and colleagues, requires a combination of vision, intuition, organization, and determination. Thus, spatial planners must strengthen their creativity to respond proactively to the complex issues faced by places (cf. Albrechts, 2010).

Indeed, the role of strategic spatial planners goes beyond the technicality of land-use plans, territorial zoning, or spatial regulations. Specialists in this area are also strategic navigators, trying to work out future potentialities. They also need to consider competitive agendas, place-based innovation, and transnational learning processes, as well as dealing with private capital.

According to Healey (2006), there is an imaginative power in SSP: the making of the plan and its end result, the plan itself, can be imagined as a vision of the future of a place. The anticipated role of place branding is to construct and convey a preferred image of a place, and to formulate a concept that resonates with a specific group of potential participants, be they external visitors, potential investors, or present inhabitants. It is paramount that the planners discuss and maintain the needs and hopes of the community at the core of all spatial interventions and spatial strategies. A successful place branding initiative, at the urban regional scale, that is able to integrate the stories of communities at the heart of the branding narrative in a participative-oriented approach, is likely to enhance the perceived value of SSP and the role of spatial planners.

Place branding experts can also provide a valuable contribution to SSP. In many places, spatial planning never has been an influential field, while in some European countries, such as the UK, the Netherlands, or Poland, the former centralized planning systems have lost much of their power due to legal and political reforms (Niedziałkowski and Beunen, 2019; Gunn and Hillier, 2014; Allmendinger and Haughton, 2013). In those situations, where existing forms of planning are not effective or lack institutional support, place branding experts can enrich the search for new strategic planning approaches. For example, when investigating three regions – Tuscany, Italy; Missouri; and northern Minnesota in the US – Van Assche and Lo (2011) noted that a strong place brand allows for robust spatial planning interventions (as in the case of Tuscany). Another interesting example is the *Joint Planning for Berlin and Brandenburg* (Ministry of Infrastructure and Agriculture, 2012). This plan emphasizes that, through the course of spatial strategies targeting industrial redevelopment, several cultural values in an aesthetic sense were created based on the shared history of the States of Berlin and Brandenburg. This is in line with Van Assche et al. (2020), who stress that SSP could use the insights in place-based value creation stemming from place branding, while place branding can offer more realistic strategies if it includes insights on how places might actually be changed or preserved through coordinated interventions.

Furthermore, it is important to realize that place branding is neither a magic solution nor a one-size-fits-all approach. Place branding narratives are only effective if the place works, and a place 'only works' if planned with a view to the needs of its users and governed with the support of participatory methodologies (Ripoll González and Gale, 2020). In this context, local residents and a range of stakeholders would need to take an active role in the design of place branding strategies (Ginesta et al., 2020). At the same time, spatial planners are encouraged to shift away from rigid, conventional approaches towards a more proactive way in order to bring structural issues into the political agenda and to give substance to the instruments and transformative practices that are needed to address the challenges (Albrechts, 2010). In conclusion, to implement place branding as an SSP instrument, spatial planners, place managers, and policymakers and local stakeholders need to jointly develop place branding, to counteract environmental and social issues whilst supporting local economies.

SELECTED CASE STUDIES ON BRANDING IN SPATIAL PLANNING STRATEGIES

The goal of the case study analysis was to shed light on how place branding has been integrated and narrated (or not) in the plans or related strategic initiatives of selected urban regions of Western Europe and North America. The complete database of regions and the documents used to analyse them, from which instructive illustrations are discussed below, included Amsterdam (the Netherlands), Barcelona (Spain), Berlin-Brandenburg (Germany), Cardiff, London, and Edinburgh (United Kingdom), Copenhagen (Denmark), Dublin (Ireland), Edmonton and Vancouver (Canada), Helsinki (Finland), Oslo (Norway), Pittsburgh and Portland (United States), Stockholm (Sweden), and Vienna (Austria). A total of 80 strategic plans and related spatial-based documents currently in force were analysed, for an average of roughly five documents per case.

The empirical evidence was generated through a content analysis of these documents. The content analysis methodology is a form of scientific inquiry that has commonly been regarded as a useful method for social science research. This method, often grouped under the term 'discourse analysis', has been applied to qualitative or textual forms of data such as written documents (e.g., reports and plans) or visual materials (e.g., photographs and videos), and has been widely used in spatial planning research.

Only a few of the assessed plans specifically refer to the place branding narrative. Instead, we identify three interconnected, and often overlapping, narratives that focus on place attractiveness, place promotion, and place branding. Their interconnectedness relates to (1) a common competitiveness-driven goal, and (2) gaining the attention of a target audiences (people and/or businesses) – albeit often with different meanings.

The place attractiveness narrative sums up the efforts of urban regions in using their urban features and other amenities to attract people in general, but in particular a qualified workforce, and investments in the form of business ventures or infrastructures (Kotler et al., 1993). The attractiveness narrative is chiefly about the expression of intentions, for instance, the intention of attracting new investors aiming at supporting a structural change, from a traditional industrial region to one in which knowledge-intensive activities become the backbone of the productive sector.

The place promotion narrative aids in operationalizing these intentions. This narrative is difficult to grasp; putting it simply, it is essentially about marketing communication. Although it dates back to early conceptualizations of local governments' approaches to address the challenge of inter-regional competition and promoting *governance* over *government* (Brenner, 2004), it overlaps extensively with the place attractiveness and place branding narratives. The first episodes of place promotion are described through many historical cases in Gold and Ward (1994), who defined this narrative as "the conscious use of publicity and marketing to communicate selective images of specific geographical localities or areas to a target market" (p. 2). Place promotion is mainly focused on targeting audiences such as new residents, visitors, or investors, through messages intended to increase their knowledge of what the place has to offer in terms of urban features, landscape amenities, governance settings, and tax incentives (Boisen et al., 2017).

The place branding narrative assumes that place brands are crucial for the way in which places are experienced by residents, visitors, and investors. This narrative differs from the two others because of its long-term framework under which actions of different stakeholders can complement and reinforce each other and collectively produce the desired result, that is, to position a place internationally and thus gain a competitive advantage. Place branding narratives shape the expectations people have of a place and thus their experience, which, in turn, is thought (or at least hoped) to lead to increased satisfaction that people derive out of such an experience (Kavaratzis et al., 2015). Contrary to the 'hit-and-run' type of communication of often ad hoc messages typical of the place promotion narrative, the place branding narrative is planned into the future; it is an iterative effort to sustain and/or improve the reputation of the place. That said, it overlaps with the two other narratives as its mandate is one of image orchestration, which put emphasis on being able to influence both coordinated place promotion and the operationalization of intentions to attract specific audiences. The ultimate goal of a place branding narrative has been achieved when the targeted audience holds a favourable image of the place over longer times.

Below we provide a summary of insights and observations, drawing on selected findings from the database.

Place Attractiveness Narrative

Place attractiveness is a dominant narrative across many of the plans we studied. For example, Amsterdam's *Structural Vision* aims to keep the green spaces or 'green wedges' around the city, improve their accessibility, utilize them for the purification of water and the supply of clean air, and make them more attractive for recreational use. This document underlines the goal of economic sustainability and the importance of urban features and nature-based amenities securing the city's development into an attractive metropolis, one where people will also be able to reside, work, and spend leisure time comfortably, in 2040 (Lauwers et al., 2011).

Similarly, Copenhagen's *Finger Plan 2015 – A Strategy for the Development of Greater Copenhagen* (Ministry of the Environment, Denmark, 2015) stands out in comparison to the strategic plans at other urban regions because of its strong reliance on urban-green amenities (such as urban wedges), along with other urban qualities, to attract investors and future residents. Conservation of landscape amenities, therefore, is a key strategy of Copenhagen, along with attractiveness related to its knowledge institutions and infrastructure improvements.

Other metropolitan areas use similar approaches in general but highlight their own perceived aspects of place attractiveness. The *Joint Planning for Berlin and Brandenburg* (Ministry of Infrastructure and Agriculture, 2012) underpins the strengths of the area's urban features such as excellent research and science landscape, a flexible and innovative economy, as well as internationally popular cultural offers, as attractive factors for businesses and people. In Vancouver, Canada, in addition to their 'greenest city' campaign mentioned earlier, place attractiveness appears as an anchor domain linked to its economic competitiveness (Greater Vancouver Regional District Board, 2017). A little farther south in the United States, the *Metro 2040 Growth Concept* in Portland, Oregon, states that it is the stability of its urban growth boundary that makes the city attractive for investment (Metro Council – Oregon Metro, 2000). The urban growth boundaries provide a framework for how growth will be concentrated, focusing on efficient land use, protecting natural areas and farmland, and promoting a multi-modal transportation system.

Place Promotion Narrative

References to place promotion are common across the cases we studied and are primarily linked to economic positioning or restructuring. For example, the *Cardiff Local Development Plan 2006–2026* (Cardiff Council, 2006) prioritizes the promotion of the city as a major tourist destination, including the provision of the development of a variety of high-quality tourist facilities and visitor accommodations as a response to evidenced economic challenges currently facing the urban region. In Germany, the *Strategy Report: Metropolitan Region Berlin-Brandenburg* (State of Brandenburg, 1999) proposes active promotion of various city centres across the region. The establishment of urbanized centres with high-quality urban environmental and living conditions is a key condition to new residential and working areas in the urban region so that Berlin-Brandenburg can become 'decentrally concentrated' and spatially organized based on sustainability principles.

An integrative approach to SSP in which place promotion is considered is also emphasized in the *Regional Planning Guidelines for The Greater Dublin Area 2010–2022* (Dublin Regional Authority and Mid-East Regional Authority, 2010). These planning guidelines stress that the success of Greater Dublin depends on balanced development integrated with prioritized investment; high-quality forward planning; adaptability to environmental, societal, and economic changes; and strong promotion of urban facilities across the domains of housing, transportation, and businesses. The guidelines set out a strong framework for the promotion of regional development with a particular focus on investment. The vision articulated in these guidelines is that by 2022, Greater Dublin will be an economically vibrant, active, and sustainable international gateway region, with strong connectivity across the metropolitan area as well as nationally and worldwide, and a region which fosters communities living in attractive, accessible places well supported by community infrastructure including leisure facilities, green corridors, active agricultural lands, and protected natural areas.

The promotion of global economic competitiveness and regional prosperity of the place is also one of the guiding principles of Edmonton, the capital city of Alberta in Canada, articulated in the *Edmonton Metropolitan Region Growth Plan* (Capital Region Board, 2016). Coordinating and optimizing regional infrastructure, investing in transit, and planning complete communities to attract workers, are all part of the Edmonton's place promotion principle.

Likewise, Pittsburgh in the US is planning for its future on many fronts, with a range of approaches to ensure that the people who live, work, and learn in this part of western Pennsylvania are engaged in shaping the urban region. *Pittsburgh's Comprehensive Plan* includes guidelines for the promotion of historic and cultural features to residents and visitors intended to involve them in planning towards the future (City of Pittsburgh – Department of City Planning, 2012).

Place Branding Narrative

In the same city, the *Strategic Plan for Downtown Pittsburgh 2012–2016* (Pittsburgh Downtown Partnership, 2012) underlined the importance of the downtown urban area to the region's brand as a centre of business, sustainability, and innovation practices. In its quest to help improve the city in different domains, the plan proposes aligning place branding for business attraction based upon regional cluster and industry targets (e.g., technology start-ups and healthcare companies). Even though place branding is not explicitly mentioned in the spatial plans assessed for Portland, a *Managing Directorate* document stressed that 'developing a world-class place branding practice' is a priority in the city's agenda.

Moving from North America to Europe, the vision statement of the *Regional Development Plan for the Stockholm Region 2010* (Stockholm City Council, 2010) was broader, aiming to develop Stockholm as Europe's most attractive metropolitan region. A key strategic element of this plan was to develop the social content of the Stockholm brand and the marketing of the region, both internally and externally (cf. Lucarelli and Heldt Cassel, 2020). To achieve this, the plan explicitly notes that a sense of community is necessary in order to strengthen cohesion in the region. This plan also underlines that if the region does not succeed in strengthening its international profile, it will end up missing the chance to position itself favourably amongst other growing knowledge regions in Europe.

One of the major challenges identified in *Barcelona's Metropolitan Strategic Reflection* (Àrea Metropolitana de Barcelona, 2015) in the economic area is the consolidation of the 'Barcelona brand' throughout the whole territory of the city's broader Metropolitan Area. This shows the presence of spatial strategic thinking in both place branding efforts and urban development, which, one could argue, reflects a rooted tradition on the linkage between planning and branding. The case of Barcelona, whose initial strategic plan goes back to 1988, involved a process of spatial transformation and reorganization. The city council was able, both before the 1992 Olympic Games and after, to implement planning strategies that served to reinforce the narrative that the region offers quality urban features for business, tourism, and cultural and sportive activities. The area was branded as an urban region with favourable conditions in which to live, visit, and invest, and the brand has been anchored in SSP and civic engagement (cf. Pareja-Eastway et al., 2013).

The strategic dimension of the plan recognizes the importance of aligning the 'Barcelona brand' narrative with SSP to increase economic leadership, both in terms of international scope, to attract foreign investment, and in the development of a model of quality tourism, in which local businesses also play an important role. The document *Barcelona Vision 2020* (PEMB, 2010) strengthens further the brand's narrative by stressing that the city's goal can only be attained if all productive, social, and natural sectors are aligned within the values the place brand holds and promotes, thus mirroring a preoccupation to planning Barcelona strategically and within multi-level governance arrangements.

CONCLUSIONS

This chapter has examined the phenomenon of place branding and its links with the strategic spatial planning (SSP) approach, including an analysis of how SSP endeavours of 16 urban regions in Western Europe and North America deal with place branding. Among other findings, we identified three interrelated narratives. The assessed plans employ a place attractiveness, a place promotion and a place branding narrative. The dominant narratives are place attractiveness and place promotion. These are focused in promoting urban features aiming at attracting talent, trade, investment, and visitors, which altogether are expected to strengthen the economy and provide new development opportunities. Results show that only a few plans refer explicitly to place branding as a collectively defined vision encompassing strategic interventions aiming not only at spatial development but also fostering social cohesion and authenticity, among others.

Drawing on the preceding discussion, we conclude this chapter with a six-point practice-oriented agenda, intended to further develop place branding as a future-oriented effective strategy that supports cities and metropolitan areas, together with SSP, to reach long-term social, economic, and ecological goals of sustainability.

First, there is a need to align place branding practice with place-specific qualities through tailor-made and context-sensitive initiatives. This would enable place branding to overcome the pitfalls of the one-size-fits-all approach, which still prevails in most of practice. *Second*, there is a need to align place branding with spatial-development plans and strategic spatial-planning goals of a place, thus improving the overall spatial condition of a territory towards sustainability. *Third*, place branding practice needs to incorporate strategic thinking, to enable structural change and economic and social transformation in a place, thus responding to the contemporary challenges such as weak economic confidence and environmental degradation. *Fourth*, there is a need for co-production in place branding practice to ensure that place branding narratives are collectively defined and thus represent often conflicting interests and perspectives. *Fifth*, place branding practice must be aligned with the envisioning process of devising desirable futures, thus harmonizing the expectations people hold in their minds with the actual reality of the place in the present and with the aspirational future. And *sixth*, place branding practice should be considered as a possible route to reinvigorating spatial identities and 'a sense of place' among residents – with these two objectives being among the most commonly discussed in the place branding literature, but seldom considered in its practice.

Aligning place branding practice with SSP has the potential to support the operationalization of the United Nations' *Sustainable Development Goal Number 8*, which is entitled "Decent work and economic growth", and also possibly link to *Goal Number 3*, "Good health and well-being", and *Goal Number 11*, "Sustainable cities and communities" (UN, 2019). Place branding as an instrument in SSP can foster the economic and socio-spatial logic of a country, city, or region, as well as reshaping responses to contemporary sustainability challenges faced by urban regions. For example, place branding can contribute to support the protection of the natural landscape-amenities discussed earlier in this chapter.

It is the contention of this chapter that place branding in strategic spatial planning can help the field become more embedded as an instrument for the attainment of strategic goals in urban regions. It can also help to shape envisioned shared futures, contribute to improving the socio-spatial and spatial-economic conditions, and make a significant contribution to sustainable spatial development.

ACKNOWLEDGEMENTS

We would like to thank the editors for their helpful comments on an early version of this chapter. The content analysis included in this chapter was undertaken in the context of the CONCUR project (grant number BSCGIO_157789) at the Swiss Federal Research Institute WSL, Switzerland (2016–2018), supported by the Swiss National Science Foundation. The writing stage was undertaken in the context of the MIDLAND project (grant number 677140), funded by the European Research Council under the European Union's Horizon 2020 at the University of Louvain, Belgium (2019–2020).

REFERENCES

Acuto, M., Parnell, S. and Seto, K.C. (2018), Building a global urban science. *Nature Sustainability*, 1, 2–4.
Albrechts, L. (2010), More of the same is not enough! How could strategic spatial planning be instrumental in dealing with the challenges ahead? *Environment and Planning B: Planning and Design*, 37 (6), 1115–1127.

Albrechts, L. (2013), Reframing strategic spatial planning by using a coproduction perspective. *Planning Theory*, 12 (1), 46–63.

Allmendinger, P. and Haughton, G. (2013), The evolution and trajectories of English spatial governance: 'neoliberal' episodes in planning. *Planning Practice and Research*, 28 (1), 6–26.

Anholt, S. (2007), *Competitive Identity: The New Brand Management for Nations, Cities and Regions*. Basingstoke: Palgrave Macmillan.

Àrea Metropolitana de Barcelona (2015), *Metropolitan Strategic Reflection: Building the Barcelona Metropolitan Area: Strengthening the Local World*, AMB.

Ashworth, G.J. and Voogd, H. (1990), *Selling the City: Marketing Approaches in Public Sector Urban Planning*. London: Belhaven Press.

Asprogerakas, E. and Mountanea, K. (2020), Spatial strategies as a place branding tool in the region of Ruhr. *Place Branding and Public Diplomacy*, 16, 336–347.

Blicharska, M. and Mikusinski, G. (2014), Incorporating social and cultural significance of large old trees in conservation policy. *Conservation Biology*, 28, 1558–1567.

Boisen, M., Terlouw, K., Groote, P. and Couwenberg, O. (2017), Reframing place promotion, place marketing, and place branding – moving beyond conceptual confusion. *Cities*, 80, 4–11.

Brenner, N. (2004), *New State Spaces: Urban Governance and the Re-scaling of Statehood*. Oxford: Oxford University Press.

Capital Region Board (2016), *Edmonton Metropolitan Region Growth Plan*, accessed 17 June 2020.

Cardiff Council (2006), Cardiff Local Development Plan 2006–2026, accessed 17 June 2020.

Choplin, A. and Franck, A. (2010), A glimpse of Dubai in Khartoum and Nouakchott: prestige urban projects on the margins of the Arab world. *Built Environment*, 36 (2), 192–205.

City of Pittsburgh – Department of City Planning (2012), Pittsburgh's Comprehensive Plan, accessed 17 June 2020.

Deffner, A., Karachalis, N., Psatha, E., Metaxas, T. and Sirakoulis, K. (2020), City marketing and planning in two Greek cities: plurality or constraints? *European Planning Studies*, 28 (7), 1333–1354.

Dublin Regional Authority and Mid-East Regional Authority (2010), *Regional Planning Guidelines for the Greater Dublin Area 2010–2022*, accessed 17 June 2020.

Evans, G. (2015), Rethinking place branding and placemaking through creative and cultural quarters. In: M. Kavaratzis, G. Warnaby and G.J. Ashworth (eds), *Rethinking Place Branding – Comprehensive Brand Development for Cities and Regions*. Cham: Springer International Publishing, pp. 135–158.

Flyvbjerg, B. (2007), Policy and planning for large-infrastructure projects: problems, causes, cures. *Environment and Planning B: Planning and Design*, 34 (4), 578–597.

Ginesta, X., San Eugenio Vela, J., Corral-Marfil, J.-A. and Montaña, J. (2020), The role of a city council in a place branding campaign: the case of Vic in Catalonia. *Sustainability*, 12 (11), 4420.

Gold, J.R. and Ward, S.V. (eds) (1994), *Place Promotion: The Use of Publicity and Marketing to Sell Towns and Regions*. Chichester: John Wiley Publishers.

Greater Vancouver Regional District Board (2017), *Metro Vancouver 2040 Shaping Our Future*, accessed 17 June 2020.

Grenni, S., Horlings, L.G. and Soini, K. (2020), Linking spatial planning and place branding strategies through cultural narratives in places. *European Planning Studies*, 28 (7), 1355–1374.

Gunn, S. and Hillier, J. (2014), When uncertainty is interpreted as risk: an analysis of tensions relation to spatial planning reform in England. *Planning Practice and Research*, 29 (1), 56–74.

Healey, P. (2006), Transforming governance: challenges of institutional adaptation and a new politics of space. *European Planning Studies*, 14 (3), 299–320.

Helsinki City Planning Department (2009), *The 'City of Helsinki Strategic Spatial Plan'*. Douglas Gordon, Rikhard Manninen and Olavi Veltheim (eds), Helsinki : City of Helsinki.

Hersperger, A.M., Bürgi, M., Wende, W., Bacau, S., Grădinaru, S.-R. (2020), Does landscape play a role in strategic spatial planning of European urban regions? *Landscape and Urban Planning*, 194, 103702.

Kavaratzis, M. (2018), Place branding: are we any wiser? *Cities*, 80 (October), 61–63.

Kavaratzis, M., Giovanardi, M. and Lichrou, M. (eds) (2017), *Inclusive Place Branding: Critical Perspectives in Theory and Practice*, London, UK and New York, NY, USA: Routledge.Kavaratzis, M., Warnaby, G. and Ashworth, G.J. (2015), *Rethinking Place Branding: Comprehensive Brand Development for Cities and Regions*, Cham: Springer International Publishing.

Kotler, P., Haider, D. and Rein, I. (1993), *Marketing Places: Attracting Investment, Industry and Tourism to Cities, States and Nations*, New York, NY: The Free Press.

Lauwers, C., Ponteyn, B. and Van Zanen, B. (2011), *Economically Strong and Sustainable Structural Vision: Amsterdam 2040*, accessed 17 June 2020.

Li, Q. and Cai, X. (2019), Regional brand development from the perspective of brand relations spectrum: taking Changle as an example. *Proceedings of the 2019 International Conference on Management, Education Technology and Economics* (ICMETE 2019), Paris, France and Amsterdam, the Netherlands: Atlantis Press.

Lin, J.C. and Su, S.J. (2019), Taiwan's geoparks. In: *Geoparks of Taiwan: Geoheritage, Geoparks and Geotourism*, Cham: Springer.

Lucarelli, A. and Heldt Cassel, S. (2020), The dialogical relationship between spatial planning and place branding: conceptualizing regionalization discourses in Sweden. *European Planning Studies*, 28 (7), 1375–1392.

McGranahan, D.A. (2008), Landscape influence on recent rural migration in the US. *Landscape and Urban Planning*, 85 (3–4), 228–240.

Meet Minneapolis (2014), *City by Nature Basics*, accessed 17 June 2020.

Metro Council – Oregon Metro (2000), *2040 Growth Concept*, accessed 17 June 2020.

Metro Vancouver (2011), *Regional Food System Strategy*, accessed 17 June 2020.

Ministry of Infrastructure and Agriculture (2012), *Joint Planning for Berlin and Brandenburg*. Joint publication between the Ministry of Infrastructure and Agriculture and the Senate Administration for Urban Development and Environment, Berlin and Potsdam, Germany.

Ministry of the Environment, Denmark (2015), *The Finger Plan 2015: A Strategy for the Development of Greater Copenhagen*, accessed 17 June 2020.

Mondal, B. and Das, D.N. (2018), How residential compactness and attractiveness can be shaped by environmental amenities in an industrial city? *Sustainable Cities and Society*, 41 (August), 363–377.

Niedziałkowski, K. and Beunen, R. (2019), The risky business of planning reform: the evolution of local spatial planning in Poland. *Land Use Policy*, 85 (June), 11–20.

Oliveira, E. (2016), Place branding in strategic spatial planning: a content analysis of development plans, strategic initiatives and policy documents for Portugal 2014–2020. *Journal of Place Management and Development*, 8 (1), 23–50.

Oliveira, E. and Hersperger, A.M. (2018), Governance arrangements, funding mechanisms and power configurations in current practices of strategic spatial plan implementation. *Land Use Policy*, 76 (July), 623–633.

Pagliarin, S., Hersperger, A.M. and Rihoux, B. (2019), Implementation pathways of large-scale urban development projects (lsUDPs) in Western Europe: a qualitative comparative analysis (QCA). *European Planning Studies*, 28 (6), 1242–1263.

Papadopoulos, N., El Banna, A. and Murphy, S.A. (2017), Old country passion: an international examination of country image, animosity, and affinity among ethnic consumers. *Journal of International Marketing*, 25 (3), 61–82.

Pareja-Eastway, M., Chapain, C. and Mugnano, S. (2013), Success and failures in city branding policies, in: S. Musterd and Z. Kovács (eds), *Place-making and Policies for Competitive Cities*. Chichester: Wiley-Blackwell, pp. 150–171.

PEMB – La Estratègic Metropolità de Barcelona (2010), *Pla Estratègic Metropolità/ Barcelona Visió 2020*, accessed 17 June 2020.

Pittsburgh Downtown Partnership (2012), *The Strategic Plan for Downtown Pittsburgh 2012–2016*, accessed 17 June 2020.

Porter, N. (2020), Strategic planning and place branding in a World Heritage cultural landscape: a case study of the English Lake District, UK. *European Planning Studies*, 28 (7), 1291–1314.

Rainisto, S.K. (2003), *Success Factors of Place Marketing: A Study of Place Marketing Practices in Northern Europe and the United States*. Doctoral dissertation, Helsinki University of Technology, Institute of Strategy and International Business.

Ripoll González, L. and Gale, F. (2020), Place branding as participatory governance? An interdisciplinary case study of Tasmania, Australia. *SAGE Open*, 10 (2), 1–12.

San Eugenio Vela, J., Nogué, J. and Govers, R. (2017), Visual landscape as a key element of place branding. *Journal of Place Management and Development*, 10 (1), 23–44.

Sayer, J., Sunderland, T., Ghazoul, J., Pfund, J.L., Sheil, D., Meijaard, E., Venter, M. et al. (2013), Ten principles for a landscape approach to reconciling agriculture, conservation, and other competing land uses. *Proceedings of the National Academy of Sciences of the United States of America*, 110 (21), 8345–8348.

SESPlan (2016), *Strategic Development Plan for Edinburgh and South East Scotland*, accessed 17 June 2020.

State of Brandenburg (1999), Ministry of Agriculture, Environmental Protection and Regional Planning of the State of Brandenburg. *Strategy Report: Metropolitan Region Berlin-Brandenburg*, accessed 17 June 2020.

Stockholm City Council (2010), *Regional Development Plan for the Stockholm Region 2010*, accessed 17 June 2020.

UN – United Nations (2019), *Sustainable Development Goals.*, accessed 17 June 2020 at https://sdgs.un.org/goals.

Van Assche, K. and Lo, M.C. (2011), Planning, preservation and place branding: a tale of sharing assets and narratives. *Place Branding and Public Diplomacy*, 7 (2), 116–126.

Van Assche, K., Beunen, R. and Oliveira, E. (2020), Spatial planning and place branding: Rethinking relations and synergies. *European Planning Studies*, 28 (7), 1274–1290.

Vanolo, A. (2017), *City Branding: The Ghostly Politics of Representation in Globalising Cities*. London, UK and New York, NY, USA: Routledge.

Vuignier, R. (2017), Place branding and place marketing 1976–2016: a multidisciplinary literature review. *International Review on Public and Nonprofit Marketing*, 21 (12), 125014.

Wang, G., Li, H., Yang, Y., Jombach, S. and Tian, G. (2019), "City in the park", Greenway network concept of high-density cities: adaptation of Singapore Park connector network in Chinese cities. *Proceedings of the Fábos Conference on Landscape and Greenway Planning*, 6 (1), 13.

Warnaby, G. and Medway, D. (2013), What about the "place" in place marketing? *Marketing Theory*, 13 (3), 345–363.

16. Popular culture and place-associated products in country image

Candace L. White

INTRODUCTION

This chapter argues that popular culture and place-associated products serve as a mediator variable that can mitigate perceptions, positive or negative, about the place or country with which they are associated. The chapter is written from a US perspective, and the word 'country' is used broadly as a synonym for nation/state. It is understood the two terms do not mean the same to everyone, and recognized there are cultural regions within nation/states that can be considered different countries; however, the geopolitical complexity of the differences is beyond the scope of this chapter, so country is used for the sake of brevity. The chapter focuses on perceptions of country image rather than on the deliberative actions that constitute place marketing and nation branding. Nation branding and place marketing are something that people within a country do. An image is something a country has.

Popular culture, which includes entertainment and media exports as well as iconic brands, plays a significant role in determining perceptions about a country's image (Dinnie, 2008). According to Fiske (2010), popular culture is not only about the consumption of goods, but it also includes the social process of generating and circulating meanings within a social system. As a variable in the process of country image formation, popular culture is dynamic and impossible to 'manage'. Popular culture can elicit positive associations and/ or mitigate negative associations with a country, or have the opposite effect, depending on how the popular culture of a country is viewed by people outside the country. When viewed positively, popular culture can contribute to a country's image and soft power.

CONCEPTUALIZING POPULAR CULTURE

Popular culture is contemporary culture. It is different from high culture, which is associated with elite arts and music, and from traditional (folk) culture, which is associated with artifacts and traditions of bygone eras. Popular culture is characterized by commodities that are commercially produced and include those of the commercial entertainment industries such as movies, music, video games, television programs, and books. While entertainment commodities are ubiquitous sources of popular culture, other commodities such as fashion, food, trends, and iconic brands and place-associated products can also become popular culture artifacts. The term 'popular culture' carries meaning beyond the purchase and use of products and commodities. Fiske (2010) differentiated between the products and commodities produced by industries in a society, and the concept of popular culture as the ways people *use* the products to create their own meanings, transforming commodities into part of their personal or group identity. Thus, the concept of popular culture can be viewed both through a social lens and through an economic lens.

Viewed through a social lens, popular culture is about the interests of people who use the commodities associated with popular culture and the meanings they ascribe to them. Kidd (2007) noted, "the clothing we wear, the music we listen to, and the television we watch not only constitute our identities, but also help to separate our identity categories from others" (p. 76). Iconic brands such as Levi jeans become cultural artifacts that have social meaning and can create a sense of identity for the wearer, but also can convey shared meaning in a social system.

Components of popular culture often are widely appropriated by people in other countries, from modes of dress to preferences in music. Hirschman (1988) referred to how people in other countries learned the ideology of consumption from watching syndicated episodes of *Dallas* and *Dynasty* on television. Suh et al. (2016) found cultural appropriation, which refers to the adoption of parts of a culture of another country, impacted attitudes about a foreign country and its brands and products in a positive direction. Schneider (2006) noted that the cultural appropriation of hip-hop music around the world, as well as the popularity of Muslim musicians such as Sami Yusuf among non-Muslim audiences, shows that popular culture is a universal language. Commodities of popular culture become part of cultural identity, and appropriation of a foreign culture is positively correlated with stronger positive attitudes about the country with which the commodity is associated. An affinity for products and entertainment of a country may mitigate negative dispositions about other aspects of the country.

Viewed through an economic lens, popular culture is a commercial culture, or a "set of commodities produced through capitalistic processes driven by a profit motive and sold to consumers" (Kidd, 2007, p. 72). Most, if not all, of the commodities associated with popular culture are not necessary for human survival, but are consumed for entertainment, identity, status, or aesthetic purposes. Such commodities have cultural as well as functional value (Kidd,

2007). Fiske (2010) argued that culture, however industrialized, can never be adequately described in terms of the buying and selling of commodities. He believes the concept of popular culture falls somewhere between production and consumption. The artifacts of popular culture become part of the identity of the consumer.

Historically, popular culture has been associated with the products of the commercial entertainment industry (Bayles, 2014). In the United States in the early twentieth century, movies were used to exert political power through cooperative agreements between the film industry and the US government. The Congressional Committee on Public Information, known as the Creel Commission, exercised tremendous power over Hollywood movies through the US War Trade Board, which approved films for export (Fraser, 2008, p. 208). The film industry was used to promote President Wilson's vision of a world peace and democracy, and Mickey Mouse was used as symbol of patriotism. Hollywood movies provided a soft power component to the Marshall Plan as part of a two-pronged strategy of economic aid and cultural exports to Europe. Hollywood studios received roughly $10 million in direct subsidies as part of the US European Recovery Plan, and in return "were obliged to export movies that portrayed American life and values in a positive manner as part of the Truman administration's Cold War soft power campaign in Europe" (Fraser, 2008, p. 211).

Today, however, the commodities that contribute to popular culture are produced in the US by the private sector in a free market with no association with the government beyond the minimal rules of regulatory agencies such as the Federal Trade Commission and Federal Communications Commission. Little control can be exerted over external portrayals of a country in popular culture produced by the private sector in a free market economy. Positive or negative national stereotypes may be endlessly repeated (Bayles, 2014).

POPULAR CULTURE AND SOFT POWER

Nye's (2004) concept of soft power is based on a country's attractions that include its values and culture. The assessment of the soft power of a country is in the eyes of the beholder. While soft power emanates from three basic sources, culture, politics, and foreign policy, Nye (2011) noted the caveats. Culture contributes to soft power only in places where it is attractive to others. Foreign policies and political values are only attractive when others see them as legitimate and when a country lives up to its own values. As he put it, "Attraction and persuasion are socially constructed. Soft power is a dance that requires partners" (Nye, 2011, p. 84).

Sources of soft power include education systems, popular culture and the media, science and technology, and brands and products. In the United States, examples range from entertainment exports like Hollywood movies to popular consumer goods that have become iconic and strongly associated with its culture (White, 2010). According to Bohas (2006), conceptualizations of soft power underestimate the powerful influence of popular culture. A fundamental component of soft power may be the cultural molding that is formed from consuming American brands and watching US television programs that show a slice of American life, resulting in a diffusion of the American way of life that becomes integrated into the everyday lives of people around the world (Bohas, 2006; De Zoysa and Newman, 2002). Fullerton et al. (2007) reported that while most subjects in their study in Singapore held slightly negative opinions of Americans, watching American-produced media fostered positive feelings toward Americans. Elasmar (2007) found a positive correlation between watching American entertainment media and positive attitudes toward the United States.

Nes et al. (2014) found that culture, music, and entertainment are significant drivers that stimulate affinity for another country, which has implications for popular culture as a component of soft power. A proposition of the study was that affinity and animosity are different and distinct constructs rather than bipolar opposites of the same construct. The study, using Norway and the United States as objects of affinity or animosity, found that

> appraisals of events related to culture/landscape and music/entertainment stimulate positive feelings (affinity) or no emotions, but seldom negative emotions. Appraisals of events related to economics or military/war stimulate negative emotions (animosity) or no emotions, but seldom positive emotions. Appraisals related to the people dimension and the politics dimension stimulate positive emotions (affinity), negative emotions (animosity) or no emotions. (p. 782)

According to the authors, "people who develop affinity toward a foreign country may do so because they identify with the country's culture, they consider the country to be one of their in-groups because they find it attractive, or they find that their identification with the country contributes to their social identity" (p. 774). Thus, affinity related to components associated with popular culture (culture, music, entertainment) is conducive to positive understanding.

In a study designed to uncover how images and attitudes about the United States are constructed, White (2010) found that while respondents believed the United States imposes its culture and foreign policies on other countries and acts unilaterally for its own political interests, "admiration of American popular culture and positive beliefs about the United States that were inculcated at an early age, primarily from television and movies served to temper attitudes" (p. 119). When asked what affected their perceptions about the US the most, television was the predominant influence. American-produced television programs provided the images they most readily recalled, the majority of which were positive. The study found that US products and brands also contributed to their attitudes about the United States, usually in a positive way. However, there were critical viewpoints related to popular culture as well. Respondents recalled that when they were young, they loved the *idea* of going to McDonald's, but at the same time did not like having a McDonald's in their community. They thought the food was unhealthy and they were afraid the American corporation would hurt local business. Some respondents were resentful of the pervasiveness of American entertainment media, as well as critical of superficial and materialistic values they felt were perpetuated by popular culture and US-led consumerism (White, 2010).

How popular culture from the United States is perceived depends on the cultural worldview of the receiver and how congruent it is with their own and US cultural values. Soft power depends on willing receivers and shared values to attract followers (Nye, 2004). The mediating effect of popular culture is sometimes in a negative direction. DeFleur and DeFleur (2003) found that images in Hollywood films and programming containing violence, sex, and crime teach young people in other countries to hate Americans. The differences in their findings and the more positive finding above are likely to reflect the values of the respondents in the study. Wike et al. (2017) noted that in the six Muslim-majority nations surveyed by the Pew Research Center in its Global Attitudes Survey, a median of just 40 percent of respondents find American pop culture appealing. Thus, the role of popular culture as a component of soft power depends on how messages are received and the extent to which people in other countries share the values that are communicated. Furthermore, popular culture is a dynamic variable that can elicit both negative and positive feelings simultaneously. As a European colleague told the author of this chapter, "we always criticize the American way, but we always live it".

Popular Cultural Imperialism

Cultural imperialism is the assertion of the values and customs of a more powerful group over less powerful groups. The influence of the United States is evident in its military and economic strength, and its cultural influence is pervasive around the world not only in popular culture but in modes of dress and the use of American phrases and slang. English as the lingua franca may be of British origin, but the internet, social media, and American media exports solidified the effect. However, the 'Americanization' that is felt around the world evokes mixed feelings. Kidd (2007) noted that popular culture is an element of capitalism that, at times, has negative consequences.

White (2010) found that US products and brands as well as popular culture contributed to positive beliefs about the country, but also found concerns about cultural imperialism. Respondents were somewhat resentful of the pervasiveness of American entertainment media, as well as critical of superficial and materialistic values they felt were perpetuated by US-led consumerism. When asked how early perceptions of the United States were formed, many interviewees in the study mentioned American brands and products such as McDonald's, Pizza Hut, Disney, and Apple, which held an iconic status and represented ways to experience a bit of American life. At the same time, the study found evidence of resistance to American cultural imperialism. An interviewee in the study said, "We are losing our identities. The problem is we are watching American people, American shows, American movies and we are getting the negative factors of America. We're even getting fatter." Another said, "Suddenly it becomes very scary to have American stuff everywhere. Suddenly you realize, hmm, we don't like their philosophy, but we have so much American stuff" (White, 2010, p. 133).

Kohut and Stokes (2006) wrote that "most non-Americans consider globalization and Americanization to be one and the same phenomenon" (p. 141), and noted that many anti-globalization demonstrations are almost indistinguishable from anti-American protests. The Pew Research Center's survey (Wike et al., 2017), mentioned above, found that the public in most nations do not think it is good that American ideas and customs are spreading to their country. Among the ten European countries surveyed, the survey found no majorities supporting Americanization, and there was even less support for the spread of American ideas and customs in Latin America and the Middle East. However, despite concerns about the pervasiveness of American ideas and exports, products and goods from the United States are popular around the world. Nearly 70 percent of Hollywood box office revenue comes from abroad, as do the majority of profits for Coca Cola, Apple, McDonald's, and a host of other American brands. It is in fact ironic that people with animosity toward the United States use American social media platforms like Facebook and Twitter to express their animosity.

COUNTRY IMAGE

Country image is the aggregate of perceptions, attitudes, and beliefs of people outside the country, based on a variety of cultural, economic, aesthetic, and political variables, all of which have multi-faceted components that are filtered through cultural lenses. Scales used to measure country image include items about cultural and social appeal as well as exports (cf. Anholt, 2007; Buhmann and Ingenhoff, 2015; Passow et al., 2005), which encompass components of popular culture. The process through which assessments about another country are made is normative, cognitive, conative, and/or affective, but the affective component may be the strongest mediator (White et al., 2019).

The image one has of another country is dynamic, and is based on a complex arrangement of assessments, which are filtered through a person's cultural worldview. Thus, it is impossible to describe a country's image in universal terms, because the image exists in the eyes of multiple beholders. The complexity of the formation of country image helps explain why the same person may have an overall unfavorable image of a country, but still have a favorable image of products or entertainment produced by that country. Movies that are violent may be admired for their special effects and cinematography. Explicit content in films or television can be offensive to some viewers, but the viewers may, at the same time, admire the freedom from censorship that the content represents.

As noted above, popular culture includes more than products of the entertainment industries. Other commodities such as place-associated brands and products are components of popular culture that may also be seen as positive or negative, depending on different worldviews. American trends may be seen as innovative, but also as contributing to waste and over-consumption. A person can hold negative cognitive beliefs about capitalism, and at the same time have admiration (affective beliefs) for commercial products produced by capitalist countries. A paradox about American culture is that it is admired and held in contempt in equal measure by many people around the world (Kohut and Stokes, 2006).

Brand America

The country image of the United States is in decline and its brand is eroding. Polls including Gallup, Pew Research, Country RepTrak, and the Good Country Index show plunging rankings for the United States. The Good Country Index (Anholt, 2020), which ranks countries based on their contributions to the common good of humanity, shows the United States in 40th place.

Based on data from the Global Attitudes Survey by the Pew Research Center (Wike et al., 2017), between 2016 and 2017 favorable views of the United States fell by double digits in seven European countries, which was part of a larger global pattern: the image of the United States declined across most of the 37 nations polled, in what the authors of the study called a "a dramatic turn for the worse" in terms of negative attitudes. The 2019 Global Attitudes Survey found favorable views up by a few points in some countries, but the slight increase still indicated double-digit declines since the end of Barak Obama's presidency (Wike et al., 2020). The decline of the US image abroad has been driven in large part by negative perceptions of US leadership under Donald Trump, accompanied by mixed views about the US form of democracy, as well as opposition to the spread of American ideas and customs around the world.

The continuing backlash to American cultural imperialism, which Fiske (2010) calls McDomination, would suggest an erosion of the influence of American popular culture – but data from around the world show otherwise. For most people around the world, movies, music, and television produced in the United States are still popular aspects of the American brand. The Pew research data found that most people around the world like American entertainment: half or more of the public in 30 of 37 nations surveyed say they like US cultural products, which has held true in most countries since the question was first asked in 2002. As reported by the study's authors (Wike et al., 2017), the data show "a broad affection for American pop culture" even when other attitudes related to politics, leadership, and foreign policy are very negative.

It appears that popular culture may contribute to US soft power when other factors are in decline, and has a mediating effect on overall image. The 2019 Soft Power 30 report ranks the United States in fifth place (*The Soft Power 30*, 2020). The country has dropped down one spot each year for the past three consecutive years. However, since the inception of the index, the United States has ranked as first in culture every year, defined as the global reach and appeal of a nation's cultural outputs, both pop-culture and high-culture. The report notes that "American pop culture is more globally pervasive than any other country's comparable outputs, and that is unlikely to change anytime soon."

BRANDS AND COUNTRY IMAGE

Brands and products that are strongly associated with a country or place can be components of popular culture and contribute to the formation of country image. Product–country image relationships, studied in what is known as the product–country image (PCI) or country-of-origin (COO) effect, is one of the most researched topics in international marketing (Papadopoulos, 2019). The concept of a COO effect assumes people have predetermined evaluations about places (Newburry and Song, 2019). The original premise of COO studies was that a favorable reputation and image of a country, particularly in terms of its economic, technological, and/or artistic development, positively reflects on products produced in it and can increase buying intentions. Positive attributes of the country have a halo effect that extends to perceived attributes of products made in the country (Han, 1989). Negative country images affect product assessments and buying intentions in a negative direction.

Verlegh and Steenkamp (1999), in a meta-analysis of 41 previous COO studies, found a complexity of cognitive, affective, and normative reasons for associating products and countries. Factors including personal experience, emotional connection to the country of origin, and perceptions of a country's economy and culture impact country of origin assessments. The majority of COO research has examined the effect of country image on consumers' perceptions of quality and purchasing behaviors of foreign products. COO studies have looked at countries and nation/states as places of product origin, but also include studies that consider place of origin of a product at the region or city level.

However, in the globalized marketplace it is increasingly difficult to find products that are 'made-in' one country. Many products are designed in one country, acquire materials from several other countries, which are shipped to a different country for assembly, then shipped again for distribution, making it difficult to identify a country of origin. Nonetheless, most well-known brands are still associated with a country as their place of origin, regardless of where the product is made. Nes (2019), acknowledging the global supply chain, defined origin as the country of origin *associated* with the product, not the legal country of origin where products are manufactured (p. 33, italics added). According to Papadopoulos (2019), "what matters is the relationship between products and countries and the image that results from it" (p. 13). It is the place of association that impacts product evaluation. Iconic brands are associated with the home country of the corporations that produce them, even if they are not made in the country with which they are associated. While some researchers assert that globalization has made at least parts of the 'country of origin' premise irrelevant, almost 30 years ago Papadopoulos (1993) noted that this reflects a narrow view of 'origin' and that "the available evidence suggests that, if anything, the higher the level of globalization, the greater the significance of PCI" (p. 17). More recently, that author and his colleagues have stressed that "what matters is the relationship between products and countries and the image that results from it", and that the key today is the place with which products are *associated* by their producers and consumers (e.g., Papadopoulos et al., 2012, 2018; Papadopoulos, 2019). Such is the case of Apple, for example, whose iPhones are manufactured in China, but no one thinks of them as a Chinese brand, and even in implied associations with places that have nothing to do with the product, as with 'Alpenweiss' wine made in Canada or French-named wines made in California.

Roth and Diamantopoulos (2009) noted that the focus of COO research has gradually shifted from evaluating preferences based on the national origin of a product to a more complex construct, namely the *country* image (CoI) of the countries under consideration. Newburry and Song (2019) contend that, "product-country images refer to country images regarding a particular type of product, and as such can be viewed as a component of an overall country image" (p. 51). Nes et al. (2014), in their previously mentioned study about the effect of feelings toward a country on buying intentions, found that country image is a mediating variable between affinity toward a country and buying intentions of the country's products. Their findings indicated that affinity for a country has a positive impact on demand for products from the country.

Corporate Brand as Nation Brand

Strong place-associated brands can become part of a nation brand. Ralph Lauren is an iconic American brand that purposely associates its products with the United States, and even incorporates the US flag into some of its clothing. The company uses well-known geographic areas of the country in its advertising – the Rocky Mountains and Wild West images, Nantucket beaches and lighthouses, Southern magnolias, American family campsites, and a range of other iconic imagery – that evokes Americanism. According to the company's website (Ralph Lauren, 2020), the Polo shirt has become "an icon of American style". Ralph Lauren markets its wares with the slogan *Style Made in America*, which evokes the country of origin, 'made-in' notion. The fact that most of the company's products are manufactured in the Philippines, Taiwan, China, and Italy, among other places, is beside the point in terms of association with a country, since the slogan refers to the products' 'style' rather than 'place of manufacture'.

Just as Ralph Lauren incorporates blue stars and red and white stripes into its products and American imagery into its marketing, IKEA incorporates blue and yellow, the color of the Swedish flag, into its corporate persona. Its advertising features stereotypical Swedes, Swedish meatballs are sold in its stores, and it uses Swedish language brand names for its products along with Swedish cultures and traditions in its marketing. In terms of product–country association, it does not matter that IKEA's headquarters are in the Netherlands (and before that, Denmark), or that most of its products are manufactured in China and countries other than Sweden. Its corporate brand has appropriated the nation brand of Sweden, and the effects have been reciprocal. Olle Wästberg, former director of the Swedish Institute, credits IKEA for doing more for the image of Sweden than all of Sweden's government efforts (Wästberg, 2009).

Inverse Country of Origin Effect

Product image and country image are a reciprocal two-way street whose parts can foster each other (Nes et al., 2014). Country image can affect perceptions and attitudes about products produced in a country, but brands can also affect country image. Lee et al. (2008) found that consumption of products from South Korea, particularly electronics, caused people to associate the reputation of the country with high technology and an advanced economy. Well-regarded brands can contribute to a favorable national reputation, which is an inverse COO effect.

White (2012) examined the COO model in the opposite direction to see if brand image affects perceptions of the country in which the product is made. The study found that when subjects had a favorable view of a brand, the halo effect extended to the country of origin. Using pre- and post-tests, subjects who had a favorable view of Red Bull energy drinks had a more favorable view of Austria, the country where Red Bull originated, after watching a stimulus video that linked the product to the country. Furthermore, participants who knew Red Bull was a product of Austria before seeing the stimulus video rated the image of Austria higher in the pre-test than those who did not know. Similarly, the country image of Estonia changed significantly in a positive direction after subjects learned that Skype was developed there. The inverse COO effect was found for all product–country associations in the study.

A country's brands and products, when they are viewed positively and accepted by people in other countries, can make a positive contribution to the overall image of a country. When people wear, use, and listen to products from a foreign country and appropriate them into their daily lives, the country of origin of the products – or at least the country that is associated with the product – is held in higher esteem. Suh et al. (2016) purported that cultural appropriation is separate from the COO effect itself, and acts primarily as an influence on the image of the country of origin, which also suggests an inverse COO effect. The halo moves from the products to the country.

POPULAR CULTURE DIPLOMACY

US popular culture is consistently viewed favorably by people in most countries (Wike et al., 2017). Even when the political values and foreign policies are viewed critically, the people and culture of the United States are viewed more favorably. In surveys across decades, respondents in the Pew Global Attitudes Survey differentiated among the American people and way of life, on the one hand, and the political administration and foreign policies of the United States, on the other, and consistently have had more positive attitudes toward people and culture. Music and entertainment, which are key components of popular culture, are significant drivers of affinity for a country (Nes et al., 2014).

An irony is that the United States, whose top export is cultural products and whose popular culture permeates the world, is struggling to define itself (Schneider, 2006). In a time of polarized political discourse and negative views about the politics and foreign policies of the country, popular culture may provide the only neutral and unified voice and serve as a much-needed instrument of soft power. Popular culture transcends and outlasts any particular political administration, and Dinnie (2008) argued that "negative perceptions connected with a country's political regime or military profile may be offset by more positive associations with the same country's contemporary culture" (p. 72).

The concepts of affinity for popular culture and cultural appropriation have implications for cultural diplomacy and nation branding. The essence of public diplomacy is the "attempt to favorably influence public opinion in other countries to bring about an understanding of a nation's ideas and ideals, institutions and culture" (Tuch, 1990, p. 3), which is the cultural aspect of diplomacy. Cultural understanding about a country that leads to attraction often comes from popular culture, and Schneider (2006) argued that popular culture is the greatest untapped resource in the cultural diplomacy arsenal. Bayles (2014) argued that America's image has been entrusted to the entertainment industry because of cutbacks to governmental public diplomacy, and that budget cuts to US public diplomacy have left popular culture as America's de facto ambassador, which may not be a bad thing. In most parts of the world, public diplomacy initiatives are more effective if they are perceived to be separate from any goal of advancing foreign policy, particularly when the foreign policies are unpopular.

The Soft Power Dance

Cultural exports such as movies and music, as well as iconic consumer goods produced by the private sector, become strongly associated with a country and help create soft power. A component of US soft power is the early shaping of taste, collective imagery, symbols, and ideas that come from popular culture, and which constitutes a form of cultural molding (Bohas, 2006). Fraser (2008) said American soft power is usually situated within a neoliberal approach, from a theoretical perspective, which emphasizes the role of non-state actors and the importance of ideas and values: "The export of American values and lifestyles via Hollywood and satellite TV indeed fits neatly into neoliberal models" (p. 207). However, the soft power effect of popular culture depends on the degree to which countries share the values that are communicated through popular culture exports and on how they are interpreted. As mentioned earlier, the soft power dance requires partners (Nye, 2011).

The nature of popular culture is that it is dynamic and uncontrolled. It is produced and exported by the private sector for profit rather than for diplomatic motives. Its representation of the United States is raw and unfiltered, and for some people, downright offensive. According to Bayles (2014), contemporary American movies portray a culture possessed by the pursuit of sex, money, and power, and movies and video games create the impression that the United States is much more violent than it is (p. 62). She wrote, "when our fellow human beings look at America through the screen of our entertainment, what they see most darkly is a rejection of tradition, religion, family, and every kind of institutional restraint, in favor of unseemly egotism and libertinism" (p. 258).

The dilemma, according to Schneider (2006), is that the United States' largely profit-driven popular culture is understood by much of the world to 'represent' the United States. She noted that countries such as those in the Middle East, in which the lines between the public and the private sector are blurred, "have difficulty reconciling their cultural climates with the idea that the images of sex and violence in American film and music are fictitious, emanate purely from the private sector, and do not reflect a government communication strategy" (p. 201). However, in other areas of the world, the disassociation between popular culture representations and US governmental strategic representations is an advantage. It allows people to hold one set of attitudes about US popular culture while holding different attitudes about the US government.

Mark (2009) contended that to be most effective, cultural diplomacy should be free to operate from government control in independent models that allow cultural diplomacy "to show a country in its brilliance, vitality, and madness" (no page number). Culture is not just art, performance, and other forms of high culture, but as all aspects of a nation's cultural composition including popular culture. In this light it can be said that US popular culture is honest and represents freedom of expression. American movies, along with sex and violence, portray good over evil and victorious underdogs, which are themes that resonate with people around the world. Regardless of content, the artistic and technical aspects of the American film industry are widely admired. Schneider (2006) noted, "although Hollywood can inspire admiration, envy, or disgust, it still is the gold standard" (p. 198).

CONCLUSION

The literature reviewed in this chapter gives evidence to the proposition that popular culture and place-associated products can have a mediating effect on country image. Country image, in turn, affects perceptions of business practices of the country as well as purchase behaviors of foreign consumers for products produced and exported from the country. Suh et al. (2016) established the relevance of cultural appropriation beyond its use for predicting purchase intentions. They noted that countries often invest in initiatives designed to promote a positive COO effect such as the sponsorship of major sporting events, and argued that promotion of popular culture would appear to be a more cost-effective approach, which "raises the possibility for companies whose products are not influenced positively by any COO effect to look to benefit instead from cultural appropriation effects" (p. 2728). Cultural initiatives, they contended, can modify a stereotype or image of a country and its outputs.

To the question, 'Does popular culture reflect the values and customs of a culture?', the answer is yes. Even when aspects of popular culture are perceived as negative, they are part of the representation of what is relevant and contemporary in a country. "Popular culture is a living, active process: it can be developed only from within, it cannot be imposed from without or above" (Fiske, 2010, p. 83). Thus, popular culture cannot be viewed as an independent variable in the process of place marketing or nation branding, but as a mediator variable in the formation of country image, viewed through different cultural lenses. It contributes to a country's soft power, but as Nye (2004) said, soft power requires willing receivers.

REFERENCES

Anholt, S. (2007). *Competitive Identity: The New Brand Management for Nations, Cities and Regions.* New York, NY: Palgrave Macmillan.

Anholt, S. (2020). The Good Country Index. *The Good Country*, accessed 14 September 2020 at https://www.goodcountry.org/index/results/.

Bayles, M. (2014). *Through a Screen Darkly: Popular Culture, Public Diplomacy, and America's Image Abroad.* New Haven, CT: Yale University Press.

Bohas, A. (2006). The paradox of anti-Americanism: reflection on the shallow concept of soft power. *Global Society*, 20(4), 395–414.

Buhmann, A. and Ingenhoff, D. (2015). The 4D model of country image: an integrative approach from the perspective of communication management. *International Communication Gazette*, 77(1), 102–124.

DeFleur, M.L. and DeFleur, M.H. (2003). *Learning to Hate Americans: How U.S. Media Shape Negative Attitudes Among Teenagers in Twelve Countries.* Spokane, WA: Marquette Press.

De Zoysa, R. and Newman, O. (2002). Globalization, soft power, and the challenge of Hollywood. *Contemporary Politics*, 8(3), 185–202.

Dinnie, K. (2008). *Nation Branding: Concepts, Issues, Practice*, Oxford: Taylor & Francis Group.

Elasmar, M.G. (2007). *Through their Eyes: Factors Affecting Muslim Support for the U.S.-led War on Terror.* Spokane, WA: Marquette Books.

Fiske, J. (2010). *Understanding Popular Culture*, 2nd edn. London, UK and New York, NY, USA: Routledge (Taylor & Francis Group).

Fraser, M. (2008). American pop culture as soft power: movies and broadcasting. In Y. Watanabe and D.L. McConnell (eds), *Soft Power Superpowers: Cultural and National Assets of Japan and the United States.* London, UK and New York, NY, USA: Routledge, pp. 205–220.

Fullerton, J.A., Hamilton, M. and Kendrick, A. (2007). U.S. produced entertainment media and attitude toward Americans. *Mass Communication & Society*, 10, 171–187.

Han, C.M. (1989). Country image: halo or summary construct? *Journal of Marketing Research*, 26, 222–229.

Hirschman, E.C. (1988). The ideology of consumption: a structural-syntactical analysis of 'Dallas' and 'Dynasty'. *Journal of Consumer Research*, 15(3), 344–359.

Kidd, D. (2007). Harry Potter and the functions of popular culture. *The Journal of Popular Culture*, 40(1), 69–89.

Kohut, A. and Stokes, B. (2006). *America against the World.* New York, NY: Henry Holt.

Lee, S., Toth, E.L. and Shin, H. (2008). Cognitive categorization and routes of national reputation formation: US opinion leaders' view on South Korea. *Place Branding and Public Diplomacy*, 4(4), 272–286.

Mark, S. (2009). A greater role for cultural diplomacy. *Clingendael Discussion Paper in Diplomacy*, June, No. 114.

Nes, E.B. (2019). The role of country images in international marketing: country-of-origin effects. In D. Ingenhoff, C. White, A. Buhmann and S. Kiousis (eds), *Bridging Disciplinary Perspectives of Country Image, Reputation, Brand, and Identity*. New York, NY, USA and London, UK: Routledge (Taylor & Francis Group), pp. 33–48.

Nes, E.B., Yelkur, R. and Silkoset, R. (2014). Consumer affinity for foreign countries: construct development, buying behavior consequences and animosity contrasts. *International Business Review*, 23(4), 774–784.

Newburry, W. and Song, M. (2019). Nation branding, product-country images, and country rankings. In D. Ingenhoff, C. White, A. Buhmann and S. Kiousis (eds), *Bridging Disciplinary Perspectives of Country Image, Reputation, Brand, and Identity*. New York, NY, USA and London, UK: Routledge (Taylor & Francis Group), pp. 49–68.

Nye Jr, J.S. (2004). *Soft Power: The Means to Success in World Politics*. Cambridge, MA: Public Affairs (Perseus Books Group).

Nye Jr, J.S. (2011). *The Future of Power: Its Changing Nature and Use in the Twenty-First Century*. New York, NY: Public Affairs.

Papadopoulos, N. (1993). What product and country images are and are not. In N. Papadopoulos and L.A. Heslop (eds), *Product-Country Images: Impact and Role in International Marketing*. Binghampton, NY: The Haworth Press, pp. 1–38.

Papadopoulos, N. (2019). Country, product-country, country-of-origin, brand origin or place image? Perspectives on a perplexing theme: place-product associations and their effects. In D. Ingenhoff, C. White, A. Buhmann and S. Kiousis (eds), *Bridging Disciplinary Perspectives of Country Image, Reputation, Brand, and Identity*. New York, NY, USA and London, UK: Routledge (Taylor & Francis Group), pp. 11–32.

Papadopoulos, N., El Banna, A., Murphy, S.A. and Rojas-Méndez, J.I. (2012). Place brands and brand-place associations: the role of 'place' in international marketing. In S. Jain and D.A. Griffith (eds), *Handbook of Research in International Marketing*, 2nd edn. Cheltenham, UK and Northampton, MA, USA: Edward Elgar Publishing, pp. 88–113.

Papadopoulos, N., Cleveland, M., Bartikowski, B. and Yaprak, A. (2018). Of countries, places, and place-based product and brand associations: an inventory of dispositions and issues relating to place image and its effects. *Journal of Product and Brand Marketing*, 27(7), 735–753.

Passow, T., Fehlmann, R. and Grahlow, H. (2005). Country reputation – from measurement to management: the case of Liechtenstein. *Corporate Reputation Review*, 7(4), 309–326.

Ralph Lauren (2020). Corporate website, accessed 14 September 2020 at www .ralphlauren.com.

Roth, K.P. and Diamantopoulos, A. (2009). Advancing the country image construct. *Journal of Business Research*, 62(7), 726–740.

Schneider, C.P. (2006). Cultural diplomacy: hard to define, but you'd know it if you saw it. *The Brown Journal of World Affairs*, 13(1), 191–203.

Suh, Y.G., Hur, J.Y. and Davies, G. (2016). Cultural appropriation and the country or origin effect. *Journal of Business Research*, 69(8), 2721–2730.

The Soft Power 30 (2020). USC Center on Public Diplomacy, accessed 14 September 2020 at https://www.uscpublicdiplomacy.org/users/softpower30.

Tuch, H.N. (1990). *Communicating with the World: U.S. Public Diplomacy Overseas.* New York, NY: St Martin's Press.

Verlegh, P.W.J. and Steenkamp, J.-B.E.M. (1999). A review and meta-analysis of country-of-origin research. *Journal of Economic Psychology*, 20(5), 521–546.

Wästberg, O. (2009). The symbiosis of Sweden and IKEA. Association of Public Diplomacy Scholars at University of Southern California, *PD Magazine*, 'Middle Powers: Who They Are; What They Want', Summer. Accessed 14 September 2020 at https://nation-branding.info/2009/07/08/brand-symbiosis-sweden-ikea/.

White, C. (2010). Anti-American attitudes among young Europeans: the mitigating influence of soft power. *American Journal of Media Psychology*, 3(3–4), 119–140.

White, C. (2012). Brands and national image: an exploration of inverse country-of-origin effect. *Place Branding and Public Diplomacy*, 8(2), 110–118.

White, C., Kiousis, S., Buhmann, A. and Ingenhoff, D. (2019). Epilogue. In D. Ingenhoff, C. White, A. Buhmann and S. Kiousis (eds), *Bridging Disciplinary Perspectives of Country Image, Reputation, Brand, and Identity.* New York, NY, USA and London, UK: Routledge (Taylor & Francis Group), pp. 289–300.

Wike, R., Stokes, B., Poushter, J. and Fetterolf, J. (2017). The tarnished American brand. Pew Research Center. Accessed 14 September 2020 at https://www.pewresearch.org/global/2017/06/26/tarnished-american-brand/.

Wike, R., Poushter, J., Fetterolf, J. and Schumacher, S. (2020). Trump ratings remain low around globe, while views of U.S. stay mostly favorable. Accessed 14 September 2020 at_https://www.pewresearch.org/global/2020/01/08/trump-ratings-remain-low-around-globe-while-views-of-u-s-stay-mostly-favorable/.

17. Understanding 'public diplomacy', 'nation branding', and 'soft power' in showcasing places via sports mega-events

Nina Kramareva and Jonathan Grix

INTRODUCTION

The study of the use of sports mega-events (SMEs) for various purposes by states of all political hues is relatively new. Commentators attempting to explain the rationale behind governments hosting such major, expensive and expansive sporting spectacles have drawn on traditional concepts (e.g., 'diplomacy', 'propaganda') and much newer ones such as 'place' and 'nation' branding and 'soft power'.

The purpose of this chapter is to unpick and assess three key concepts that appear to provide the most traction on understanding the motivations of why states host SMEs. The extant literature often uses these concepts interchangeably, conflates them, or misuses them. The intention below is to indicate not only how these concepts differ and where they overlap, but to show how they can be applied to empirical examples of a variety of countries with different political regimes and levels of economic development – liberal and non-liberal, advanced capitalist, and emerging – and their hosting strategies. First, we discuss 'public diplomacy', and how it differs from propaganda, before introducing 'sport diplomacy', that is, the use of sport as diplomatic means. Second, we address the question of why SME hosts view their events as opportunities for 'place' or 'nation' branding. Finally, we turn to 'soft power', the concept around which academic literature has grown exponentially in the recent decade.

We look at how many commentators from the media, academic, and political spheres increasingly use the term 'soft power' to explain everything from sport diplomacy, to nation branding through the political use of sport, and to 'sportswashing', or the use of sports to divert attention from various misdeeds or potential problems. Such a broad-brush approach has, as we shall see, led to confusion surrounding the labelling of motives behind the hosting of SMEs, compounded as it is by the number of different regime types using sport with often multiple aims. For example, Russia has been criticised for not optimising soft power gains from its double hosting of the *2014 Winter Olympics* in Sochi and the *2018 FIFA World Cup* (WC). One could argue that this was not their primary intention (Grix and Kramareva, 2016), but, rather, that they sought to bolster nation-building and national identity, and not to burnish their image abroad.

We conclude this chapter with a number of examples which serve to categorise different uses of the Olympic Games, ranging from what we term the 'propaganda Games', through to 'branding Games' and to 'soft power Games'. In so doing, we are attempting to clarify how states foreground specific motives when hosting mega sporting spectacles, and highlight that these motives need to be understood within their political, economic, and historical context.

PUBLIC DIPLOMACY AND SPORT

Public diplomacy, which arguably has grown in importance among the majority of states throughout the world since 9/11, 2001, is as much a contested concept as 'soft power'. There are several competing definitions of public diplomacy, some of which give greater emphasis to the role of private individuals and groups in its practice, rather than of governments (Gilboa, 2008). Public diplomacy studies differentiate between the 'old' modus operandi via 'hierarchical state-centric structures' and the 'new' model of a 'network environment' in which several actors, of which the state is but one, undertake public diplomacy (Melissen, 2005; Hocking, 2005). However, the state, usually the Foreign Ministry, still plays a central role in managing the network and funds many of the 'arm's length' organisations that comprise it. The 'new' public diplomacy is consequently seen as involving an array of non-state actors, including sporting bodies such as FIFA (*Fédération Internationale de Football Association*) and the IOC (*International Olympic Committee*) at the international level, and National Sports Organisations (NSOs) at the national level.

Sport has long been used as part of a state's diplomatic armoury and has, fairly recently, spawned its own branch of study ('sport diplomacy': Murray and Pigman, 2014; Rofe, 2016). Interestingly, states previously well-known for their use of political propaganda were among the first to turn to the Olympics as a means to re-integrate into the international order. For example, the Rome (1960), Tokyo (1964), and Munich (1972) Olympics were attempts at using the biggest global sporting spectacle as a vehicle to show the world that the respective countries had changed from aggressors to reliable international partners (Collins, 2007; Horton and Saunders, 2012; Guthrie-Shimizu, 2013). Indeed, the hosting of the Olympics by former axis powers shows that they were amongst the first to understand that public diplomacy is not 'propaganda' or 'government diplomacy' but 'diplomacy of public opinion, that is, the projection of the values and ideas of the public onto the international sphere' (Castells, 2008, p. 91).

There is a clear difference between propaganda and public diplomacy in the use of SMEs. The *1936 Summer Olympic Games* in Berlin represent the most striking example of sport used for propaganda purposes. Of note was the unprecedented level and cost of ideological augmentation, which was designed to lure 'regions and states that were politically, militarily and geo-strategically interesting more deeply into the sphere of German influence' (Bonde, 2009, p. 1460), and which set the precedent for international 'cultural propaganda by totalitarian states' (p. 1459). It could also be argued that the 1936 Games was the start of what we now know as a sports 'mega-event', due to its bombastic nature and attempts to showcase Germany and the Nazi regime.

During the Cold War it was traditionally understood that public diplomacy was practised in the West, whereas the Soviets spread propaganda (Cull, 2010). However, both propaganda and public diplomacy strive to achieve a comparable result. The fundamental difference between the two concepts lies in the treatment of the foreign audience, the targeted level of public engagement, and accordingly, the methods and instruments adopted (Evans and Steven, 2010). In contrast to propaganda, which is traditionally a one-dimensional proclamation of self-contained politicised truths habitually divorced from reality, the messages of governments engaged in public diplomacy allegedly come from listening to their publics. The central point here is that public diplomacy not only mirrors the standpoint and intent of an interested party, it also takes into account the opinions, aspirations, and values of its audience (Cowan and Arsenault, 2008). This also implies that dialogue and cooperation are the modes of communication (Cull, 2010) that have succeeded the one-dimensional monologue, which was the only palpable way of addressing foreign publics under propaganda (Nickles and Paull, 2003). What sets public diplomacy apart from 'propaganda, lobbying, and public relations', in the main, is 'a focus on relationship building at every level' (Cowan and Arsenault, 2008, p. 11).

With the USSR joining the Olympic Movement, the 1952 Olympic Games in Helsinki is sometimes identified as the first dramatic ideological confrontation of the Cold War, which cemented the world's division into two blocs (Riordan, 1974). The political role of athletes at that time, unequalled in history, has been embraced by the term 'diplomats in tracksuits' (Holzweissig, 1981; Balbier, 2009). The term refers to East German athletes, who were seen as 'soldiers of sport', whilst elite sport was understood on both sides of the Atlantic as a modern form of 'psychological warfare' (Riordan, 1974, p. 322).

Public diplomacy from that time onwards has called for sport's assistance for two major reasons. The first is to engender rapprochement and resolve impasses in official relations between countries by appealing to the universal apolitical human values encompassed by sport (Cha, 2013). This was a popular tactic during the Cold War, exemplified by several high-profile cases of so-called 'ping-pong diplomacy' between China and the USA during 1971 (Wang, 2003), and an attempt to repeat its success through 'baseball diplomacy' between the USA and Cuba (Carter and Sugden, 2012).

These classic examples of sport diplomacy can be understood as events in which sport acted as an 'ice-breaker', effectively opening dialogue. After the USA table tennis team had visited China in 1971, President Nixon lifted a 20-year trade embargo; thus the initial sporting contacts led to more formal discussions and negotiations, which were intensified following a basketball competition between the two countries one year later. The idea was to facilitate communication after a long freeze in relations. The fact that the Chinese were clearly superior in ping-pong and the Americans in basketball was designed to rob sport temporarily of one of its core attractions: its unpredictability (i.e., spectators do not know who will win). In such cases, sport is simply the means to an end: the opening of long-stalled diplomatic relations.

The second reason is to demonstrate the denunciation of a hostile political and ideological worldview, most vividly illustrated by the US-led boycott of the 1980 Olympics in Moscow, with the Kremlin returning the favour at the 1984 Games in Los Angeles (Moretti, 2013; Balbier, 2009).

Ultimately, public diplomacy differs from propaganda in that it is not as state-based or as strictly censored. It was made possible fundamentally by developments in communication technologies and the growth of participation of the general public in politics (Melissen, 2005). Seminal examples of SMEs used for public diplomacy purposes include the three 'Asian' Olympic Games in Tokyo, Seoul, and Beijing. As Horton and Saunders stress (2012, p. 890), "all three festivals were immersed in political diatribe, and were heavily driven by public diplomacy". Yet it is the *1988 Seoul Olympics* that deserves particular attention. Considering the geostrategic dissolution of the communist bloc in 1991, these games could be appraised as a theatrical performance of the Cold War's closing chapter, which, by triggering South Korea's diplomatic rapprochement and commercial cooperation with the USSR and its satellites, expedited the impending triumph of democratic ideals and a market economy (Black and Van der Westhuizen, 2004).

The widely recognised success of the 1988 Games, and the ensuing graduation of South Korea to the club of advanced states, was accompanied by a key geopolitical legacy (Radchenko, 2012): rather than taking the side of the Pyongyang (i.e., North Korean) regime, and thus keeping the Cold War fires burning, the socialist bloc allowed pragmatism to prevail instead of, for example, boycotting the Games, which might have further discredited the Olympic Movement or potentially turned the simmering confrontation into a real conflict. Not only did they participate in the Seoul Olympics: they also eagerly welcomed a thaw in relations with South Korea, thus sanctioning the final political isolation of North Korea (Manheim, 1990). South Korea's hosting of the 2018 Winter Olympic Games once again highlighted the diplomatic side of sport. This more recent case came after a sustained period of heightened tension between North Korea and the USA and acted as a filter through which tensions were eased, leading to the first visit to North Korea by a South Korean president shortly thereafter (Council on Foreign Relations, 2014). A comparison between this (2018) 'sport diplomacy' example and the so-called 'ping-pong diplomacy' case (1971) reveals a similar role for sport acting as a catalyst to restarting stalled or easing strained relations between states.

PLACE AND NATION BRANDING

The majority of experts tend to endow SMEs with the power to substantially increase a host destination's brand image and contribute to its brand equity (Grix, 2013; Horne and Houlihan, 2014). A problem within this tendency, however, is that many academics, readily followed by practitioners, have started substituting the notion of 'image promotion' with 'place branding' (Anholt, 2008; Fan, 2010). Given that the concept of 'image promotion' is itself contentious (Ståhlberg and Bolin, 2016), this has not necessarily led to clarity. First, a brand image, in its simplified form, is a set of associations, beliefs, and attitudes relating to a particular name or symbol in the mind of a consumer (as Kotler et al., 1999, put it, images are a 'product of the mind').

Therefore, a country's image could be considered to be a fusion of the acquired knowledge about a country's art, music, history, politics, famous residents, geography, and climate, and other objective and subjective perceived characteristics (Endzina and Luneva, 2004). Due to information asymmetry and individual national mentality, different people hold varying images about one and the same country, which may not correspond to objective reality (Morgan et al., 2002). What differentiates place image promotion from conventional branding is that the former always has to deal with a set of established ideas and stereotypes, whereas branding does not necessarily envisage repositioning (Anholt, 2008).

For example, in 2012, Britain was faced with the challenge of addressing the image of a dwindling empire with antiquated traditions. The *2012 London Olympic Games* were thus envisaged to transform Britain from a "backward-looking and hidebound, arrogant and aloof" state (Leonard, in Zhong et al., 2013, p. 395), as it was perceived in some parts of the world, to a country spearheading modernity (Oettler, 2015). According to Zhou et al. (2013), those who designed, promoted, and delivered the Games carried out what was seen as a stellar job in emphasising Britain's past successes along with its creativity and contributions to such areas as sport and music, which seems to have worked and went down well with the public – whereas other national features which, according to these authors also featured prominently, such as "innovation, technology, entrepreneurship, knowledge (i.e., science and research), and ... green initiatives" (p. 872) did not strike a chord internationally (Arning, 2013).

As indicated above, an image defies the direct control of the producer, which in this case is either a city or a state. It is formed within the mind of a person and, contrary to widespread belief, this is not achieved through advertising and promotion, but rather through consumers' mental interpretations of their contact with the brand – including but certainly not limited to advertising, logos, and other such. In other words, an image in this sense is formed in the eye of the beholder, which complicates endeavours to provide a coherent unified umbrella brand image, one that would simultaneously secure buy-in from the local community as well as from the international public (Fan, 2010). In the end, Britain's Olympics succeeded in repositioning it through a combined take on tradition juxtaposed with a celebration of its modern-day pop culture icons. A notable and memorable example of this rather unorthodox approach was the appearance of James Bond alongside Queen Elizabeth during the opening ceremony (Park and Tae, 2016).

In this context, Kotler and Gertner's (2002) idea that a country's image can not only be evaluated and measured, but might also be influenced by marketing managers, is accurate to the extent that a particular visual and/ or textual expression can be produced and promoted. Indeed, Knott et al. (2017, p. 902) recently argued that SMEs "should be included in the list of nation brand identity 'communicators', as [they] possess the potential to aid the development or re-positioning of a nation brand image". If the images are to change the way a host is perceived, however, they have to be credible or at least correspond to reality. That is, if a country wishes to showcase a changed, reformed, or modernised version of itself, it has to live up to its promises. Therefore, the spectacular Olympic façade should not be seen as an opportunity to conceal invidious sides of a society or cover the underbelly of a political system, but rather to represent meaningful efforts to change that place's image for the better, capitalising on the various different indicators that form a country's umbrella brand and, hopefully, concomitant changes to the place itself (Anholt, 2008).

While national identity and national brand identity are interrelated, an important distinction exists between the two concepts. The former develops naturally through the course of time and exists irrespective of whether or not individuals are consciously aware of it (Anholt, 2008; Kavaratzis, 2004). National brand identity, on the other hand, is developed by brand specialists in pursuance of definite economic or political objectives (Fan, 2010; Anholt, 2010). China's brand identity in the context of the 2008 Olympics, for example, was seen as the 'New Beijing, Great Olympics', and was based on the principles of a "Green Olympics, High-Tech Olympics and People's Olympics" (Li, 2017, p. 256). This portrayed the threefold nature of China's Olympic objectives, enabling Beijing to forefront its efforts to change for the better with regard to sustainable development, thereby addressing Western criticisms on air pollution and broader environmental issues. This also placed the main source of its competitive advantage, namely its technological genius, in the limelight. However, most significantly, it emphasised its focus on nation building through the Olympics.

In contrast, the *2012 London Olympics* demonstrated the quintessential Britishness of the twenty-first century (Bryant, 2015), thereby presenting Britain as "a nation secure in its own post-empire identity" (Hepple, 2012). Such representations are part and parcel of what both Britain and China are and want to be; however, they are not all that there is to these nations. National brand identity is, therefore, based on the constituents of national identity and the most distinctive, enduring, and representative traits of a particular nation (Kotler et al., 1999; Papadopoulos and Heslop, 2002), which differentiate it from other nations and positively resonate with the target audience. However, as the examples above show, national brand identity is not only context- and time-dependent, it also lends itself to various modifications and interpretations subject to stakeholders' requirements and strategic interests.

Thus, while national identity is relatively permanent and fairly resistant to change, national brand identity is more flexible; it therefore lends itself to be tailor-made for specific occasions. For example, Germany's identity in the context of the *2006 FIFA World Cup* became the 'Land of Ideas', whereas China, among other things, forefronted its commitment to peace through its 'One World, One Dream' motto). The link between national

identity and national brand identity, therefore, is that the latter is a deriva-
tive of the former or an adapted simplification.

Although national identity is at the heart of nation branding, the concept
does appear to be more applicable to an analysis of SMEs in the 1990s.
According to Tagsold (2010, p. 291), with particular reference to the 1964
Tokyo Games:

> Since the Olympic Games have turned into highly merchandised events, key-
> words such as 'place promotion' and 'managing spectacle' seem to be most
> appropriate in describing the stakes for urban planners. But urban planners
> before the 1984 Los Angeles Olympic Games had different notions. This was
> especially the case in cities such as Tokyo, where symbolic politics and the
> burdens of history called for image management not simply in order to enhance
> marketing opportunities but to reconstruct national identities.

Besides signalling the return of a repentant Japan, the Tokyo Games were
envisaged to fulfil an overarching agenda, namely, to map out the country's place in modernity while allowing for the maintenance of national
distinctiveness. This hybrid path, where sport played a pivotal role, thereby
constituted Japan's new evolving identity (Niehaus and Tagsold, 2013).
Japan was determined to show the world its commitment to peaceful,
Western-style technological and economic development, while adhering
to its cultural values (Horton and Saunders, 2012). In this respect, the
country's actions in WWII were something to be reconciled with, rather
than negated or erased from national memory. In doing so, during the first
satellite telecast of the Olympics, the official narrative juxtaposed Japan's
ultra-modern infrastructure, such as the *Shinkansen* bullet train and other
cutting-edge urban achievements and sporting facilities, with traditional
symbolic architecture, such as the Meiji Shrine, the figure of the Emperor,
and the *hinomaru* ('Rising Sun' flag) (Tagsold, 2010).

There are two factors that all three Asian Olympic Games have in
common which, arguably, make the Asian Olympic discourse stand
out from that of other advanced states. These were nationwide, almost
'state-of-emergency' mobilisations of resources, coupled with the seminal
role played by civic (inclusive) nationalistic sentiments and a surge of
national pride and patriotism associated with hosting the Games (Finlay
and Xin, 2010). As Horton and Saunders (2012) put it, "these events [were]
a 'coming-out party' ... for the international community and for their own
people ... predicated on the need for each of the host nations to shed an
old skin or perhaps an unsavoury visage, if not to induce a total national
metamorphosis" (p. 903).

Japan's and South Korea's experiences are remarkable: in view of the
circumstances, it was necessary for these countries to assume new iden-

tities in a limited timeframe. The synthetic nature of Japan's post-WWII and South Korea's post-Cold War identities, which represented simplified interpretations of their cultural DNA adopted primarily for the West's consumption, instantaneously became enduring and economically lucrative national brand identities. In this respect, the Olympic Games became a part of modern mythology and helped to ingrain these new identities in the national psyche, reducing the cognitive distance between them. Yet the complexity of the concepts of national identity and national brand mean that it remains difficult to transmit a coherent unified message to different target groups across different markets (Anholt, 2010).

SOFT POWER AND SMES

In the research focusing on SMEs – and in particular on the 'legacies' they are said to produce – 'soft power' and international prestige are among the areas most often studied. In the context of these developments, states themselves have started to attribute great importance to the successful staging of SMEs such as the FIFA WC and the Olympics (Manzenreiter, 2010). SMEs, in turn, have been praised for their ability to attract an unprecedented global audience and to command attention over an extended period of time. Given the high fluidity and congested nature of the modern media landscape, SMEs provide a host state with a unique opportunity to propel itself to the forefront of the news and, therefore, to dominate global discourse at least for the period of the event. As we show below, the 'soft power' concept has become part of politicians' rhetoric, and the aim of increasing a state's international prestige and political attractiveness to foreign publics through hosting SMEs has caught the attention of all types of political regimes and levels of economic development.

In previous work we have critiqued the term 'soft power', first coined in 1990 by Joseph Nye, but came to the conclusion that he "clearly put his finger on something when coining [that] concept— there has evidently been a shift in attempts to manipulate the 'politics of attraction' in international affairs among states of all political hues" (Grix et al., 2015, p. 463). One of the key reasons behind the proliferation of usage of the concept and the popularity of soft power strategies is that hard power strategies – military might, war, and economic sanctions – are either not available to many states or are understood as a less attractive prospect in today's world.

For Nye (2002), the 'power' side of the concept denotes one's ability to reach outcomes one wants without recourse to coercion. For twenty-first-century leaders, Nye (1990) suggests political outcomes can be achieved through an amalgamation of both 'hard' and 'soft' power strategies. On the one hand, states may draw upon forms of 'hard power', through, for example, military force or punishing economic measures; on the other, they may choose to adapt the political agenda indirectly in such a way that it shapes the preferences of others through, for instance, emulating one's 'intangible assets': attractive culture, innovative ideologies, and/or credible and commendable institutions, values, and policies.

It is this latter approach that Nye calls 'soft power': "the ability to achieve goals through attraction rather than coercion" (Keohane and Nye, 1998, p. 98). Such attraction converts into power outcomes when those on the receiving end of the soft power strategy look to the state producing it for affirmation, guidance, and leadership, or seek to imitate their domestic and/or international achievements. Recent years have seen an increase in the use of the soft power concept by scholars and commentators attempting to explain why states seek to acquire various forms of cultural and political attraction. However, within mainstream scholarship in the international relations, political science, and sport studies literature, an ongoing debate is concerned with what actually constitutes soft power, how national leaders and states go about acquiring it, and the success of soft power in both the short and long term.

For the purpose of this chapter we point to the overlaps between 'soft power', 'public diplomacy', and 'nation branding' that are often behind the confusion in debates on the use of SMEs by states. 'Soft power' clearly encapsulates elements of both 'public diplomacy', with its focus on influencing 'foreign publics', and 'nation branding', with its focus on showcasing the nation. This is important because many commentators often use 'soft power' to mean any or all of these concepts. Such a broad-brush approach to a wide variety of states hosting SMEs means that the subtle differences between liberal and non-liberal, advanced and emerging nations, federal and central governance are lost. We take this further in the section below where we seek to 'categorise' some of the most important Olympic Games held since 1936 (Berlin).

Central to Nye's 'soft power' concept is the notion of persuading, influencing, but also enticing and attracting 'foreign publics' and impacting positively on their opinion of a state. Central also to public diplomacy is the notion of attempting to influence other foreign publics' opinions of states. Public diplomacy, of course, uses traditional diplomatic channels and is generally understood as a tool for securing foreign policy interests, whereas 'soft power' strategies typically do not. 'Nation branding', on the other hand, has turned to using the tools of marketing to project a state's image abroad. There appears some overlap of the 'old' and 'new' types of public diplomacy, blurring the role of the state in public diplomacy and branding. While the lines between 'nation branding' and 'public diplomacy' are less clear-cut than perhaps they were previously, the central role of the state in using sport to achieve non-sporting goals is apparent in the vast majority of cases.

Thus, 'sport diplomacy' efforts are still undertaken by high-level government officials (cf. our 'ping-pong' example above) and 'nation branding' pulls in a series of other actors, including national tourism boards and business. Australia, for example, projected a national image of a 'sporting nation' before, during, and after the Sydney Olympics in 2000. The result of a successful Olympics (in terms of hosting and Australian athlete success) and the boost to the country's national image was the 'accelerated development of Brand Australia by 10 years' (Australian Tourist Commission, 2001, p. 3).

Such nation branding appears important if soft power is to be leveraged to shape international relations through affecting external perceptions of a country, although, it must be stated, a country's image must rest on something recognisable (e.g., a reputation for producing reliable products) other than simply being a matter of public relations. This becomes more pertinent when emerging states with difficult pasts attempt to project their new, burnished image through such an event that appears to offer the type of 'coming out party' mentioned above, in which countries may have a global audience for their brand (Kuper, 2011).

When a state hosts an SME it effectively takes a gamble with the global media attention this brings. Generally, if a state has something to hide, is involved in malpractice (for example, poor worker relations), and/or is trying to shed a negative image from past events, hosting an SME may shed light on such unsavoury aspects. Take, for example, Qatar, the scheduled host of the FIFA WC in 2022. Unusually, Qatar was awarded the event some 12 years prior to its taking place. This lag has allowed an unprecedented amount of media exposure, which, in turn, has led to unearthing the unpalatable *Kafala* system of monitoring and control of migrant labourers and others, as well as accusations of 'sportswashing', that is, attempting to bury human rights abuses under major sporting spectacles or by investing heavily in sport. The latter has entailed the purchase of European football teams, sports sponsorships, and the development of the *Qatar Aspire* elite sport academy.

In an age of global media audiences and global communications, many more structurally weaker actors can seek to influence world politics using soft power strategies. As Mattern (2005, p. 590) suggests, "soft power is available to any actor that can render itself attractive to another". South Africa, for example, was able to enhance its agency in world politics with a successful soft power strategy of communicating their democratic values in the post-apartheid era, not least through the politics of attraction embodied in Nelson Mandela, the country's first post-apartheid president.

In so doing, it was able to legitimately claim a place at the top table of multilateral summitry, such as the G8 meetings, and join the other emerging powers in extending their agency beyond their regional base. In 2010, for example, South Africa hosted the first African *FIFA WC* that was generally seen as successful and not as negative as pre-event media reports suggested. Other states who came to regret inviting the global media to scrutinise their politics and policies in detail in the build-up to and during an SME and have experienced *unintended consequences* including the *2010 Commonwealth Games* in India and the *European Football Championship* in 2012 in Ukraine. The former event was supposed to be a precursor to an Indian Olympic bid, but instead turned into an unprecedented disaster for India and its global reputation. The intense focus of the world's media was partly to blame for quashing the country's ambitions of hosting an Olympics after the debacle surrounding the preparations for the Commonwealth Games. Similarly, the latter event was similarly faced with an unprecedented level of media scrutiny, and Ukraine attracted the kind of attention that led to a deterioration of its image abroad, rather than the positive boost it was hoping for.

CLASSIFYING THE USE OF SPORTS MEGA-EVENTS

The cross-cultural ethical principles and moral values of sport do not make hosting SMEs the exclusive prerogative of a given government. Moreover, being initially a creation of capitalist democratic societies, SMEs, judging from the latest trend, are far more coveted by non-liberal states. There has been an evident migration of the Olympics and the football (soccer) World Cup from advanced democracies to emerging countries (Hong, 2010), which not only demonstrates their increased financial status but also highlights other major aspects of their agency in the international system. This in turn strongly testifies to the fact that, in spite of claims to the contrary, SMEs historically have been and still are being used to make strong political points (Allison, 1993).

The *1936 Berlin Games*, for example, went down in history as a propaganda triumph and a symbolic legitimisation of Nazi Germany. The 1964 Games in Tokyo are associated with South Africa's expulsion from the Olympic family for its apartheid policies, and the 1968 and 1972 Games are known for the 'Black Power Salute' and the Munich massacre respectively. And the 1980 and 1984 Olympics in Moscow and Los Angeles are infamous for the USA–USSR tit-for-tat boycotts (Goldberg, 2000; Murray, 2012; Rofe, 2016). Sport, therefore, is not just about participation or attendance any more; it is also, and perhaps more so, about the messages being transmitted through it, namely its symbolic and cultural overtones.

One key reason behind the allure of SMEs for authoritarian or developing/transition states is a rigid, though comprehensible, template that they have to follow to win, as they hope, the soft power gamble, which SMEs have been contextualised to reflect (Black and Van der Westhuizen, 2004). The host states have to satisfy a number of obligatory requirements of the IOC or FIFA in the process, ranging from the state-of-the-art infrastructure development to several vital legislative changes, which occasionally run counter to the official line of the ruling elite. In terms of actual self-presentation and identity projection, however, the states are given a lot of room for manoeuvre (Hong, 2010). A growing number of scholars argue in this respect that a host nation's almost decade-long rehearsal for the grand world stage entrance culminates in the opening and closing ceremonies (deLisle, 2009; Arning, 2013). It is during the artistic part of the programmes that the states are given the upper hand to attempt to 'seduce' the global audience by unveiling their new, friendlier face, thus flaunting their most flattering versions.

SMEs and the ceremonies in particular are "the quintessence of the performative politics of attraction". In order to understand why several states achieve more than others in harnessing their soft power by staging SMEs, it is essential to understand what capabilities different states are able to muster, the content of the strategies employed in the process, and the actual set of characteristics the countries in question possess that could fall under the umbrella concept of themselves. In addition, a state's current developmental level and the incumbent type of regime significantly determine the media framing of the event, the feedback of the global community and, accordingly, the broader soft power legacies of the event (Finlay and Xin, 2010; Zhou et al., 2013; Oettler, 2015).

In addition to the host's national circumstances, an analysis of SMEs should be informed by the pertinent temporal and geopolitical contexts, which are different in each particular case (Giulianotti, 2015). Therefore, SMEs of the Cold War era, for example, should be assessed against different benchmarks from the SMEs of the new millennium, which are rooted in evolving challenges and realities. Each host's uniqueness, in turn, becomes particularly evident and manifest during the Olympic ceremonies (Arning, 2013), which showcase a nation at a certain point in time and against the background of 'a constant process of adaption to ever-changing historical and geographical contexts' (Oettler, 2015, p. 247). In short, as noted earlier, the ceremonies dramatically celebrate what the host is and wants to be and, most importantly, they chart its frame of reference, such as, for example, "post-Francoism (Barcelona 1992), multiculturalism (Sydney 2000) and modernisation (Seoul 1988, Beijing 2008)" (Oettler, 2015, p. 247).

Having detailed, in the previous sections, the various objectives and experiences of countries hosting the Olympic Games, we can now turn to proposing a classification of the use of SMEs. The value of such a classification lies not only in the fact that it accounts for the attendant global political circumstances, but also that it makes an important distinction between the Games, the significance of which, as will be seen below, can range from an emphasis on the host city (e.g., Atlanta 1996) to the respective nation (e.g., Beijing 2008).

The classification we put forward in Table 17.1 includes only period-defining Olympic Games primarily based on their geopolitical location (host city and country) and their widely accepted political functions and purposes. As with all types of classification, we have simplified for the sake of clarity. For example, all the Olympics taking place since 1948 (uniformly accepted as the start of the Cold War) could technically

Table 17.1   Comparative analysis of Olympic Games: classification, applicable concept, and host's primary objectives

(a)   1936–1984: Olympic Games in a divided world

Classification	*Applicable Concept* and Host's Primary Objectives
'Propaganda'	
1936 Berlin, Germany	*Propaganda* Official return to world community post-WWI International legitimisation of regime Celebration of Arian ideal Architectural incarnation of Nazi ideology
'Rehabilitation'	
1960 Rome, Italy	*Nation Re-Positioning (political marketing)* Re-admission to club of advanced democracies
1964 Tokyo, Japan	*Nation Re-Positioning (political marketing)* Identity self-reconciliation Nation promotion Acceptance to club of advanced democracies Urbanisation Technological & infrastructural modernisation
1972 Munich, Germany	*Nation Re-Positioning (political marketing)* Re-admission to club of advanced democracies Promotion of peaceful coexistence of nations Coming to terms with the past
'Cold War'	
1980 Moscow, USSR	*Propaganda/Public Diplomacy* Demonstration of superiority of socialist system
1984 Los Angeles, USA	*Propaganda/Public Diplomacy* Demonstration of superiority of liberal-democratic system First profitable Olympics since 1932

(b)   1988–2016: The rise of branding and soft power

Classification	*Applicable Concept* and Host's Primary Objectives
'Branding'	
1988 Seoul, South Korea	*Public Diplomacy/Country Branding:* Graduation to an advanced state Rapprochement with communist block North Korea political isolation Identity construction & projection
1992 Barcelona, Spain	*City Branding:* Entrepreneurial urban development Improvement of CITY (not country) competitiveness International prestige
1996 Atlanta, USA	*City Branding:* Entirely privately funded Games, 'Next best international city' Inclusiveness in planning Positive physical & spiritual legacy
2000 Sydney, Australia	*Country Branding:* 'Brand Australia' as a multicultural & reconciled society 'Green' Games, regeneration of city landscape Reduction of social divide
2004 Athens, Greece	*Country Branding:* Modernisation of tourist infrastructure and transport system Re-branding of Greece as the home of the Olympic Games
'Soft Power'	
2012 London, UK	*Soft Power:* Promotion of London as major world city Regeneration of East London Sustained improvement in UK sport
'Nation-Building'/'Status-Seeking'/'Soft Power'	
2008 Beijing, China	*Soft Power:* 'Coming-Out Party' for China as world power Increase in international prestige Environmental and infrastructural improvements
2014 Sochi, Russia	*Soft Power:* Signalling of Russia's great power ambitions Legitimisation of autocracy domestically Foundation of new Russian identity/national idea Creation of world-class mountain resort Multi-functional city in Russian and global economy
2016 Rio, Brazil	*Soft Power:* 'Brazil – an Emerging Global Power' Physical transformation of city Social inclusion, youth & education promotion Sport promotion

be characterised as 'Cold War Games' (Abel, 2012; Horton and Saunders, 2012), with the 1956, 1960, and 1964 Olympics entrenching the Cold War mentality due to issues related to the East and West German teams that competed as 'one country' at those three events but separately after, until more recent post-1990 times (Balbier, 2009).

There are a number of accounts of ideological collisions and under-the-table diplomacy between the two antagonistic camps in the context of the Olympics (for example, the endorsement of South Korea and North Korea by the democratic West and the communist East, respectively, during negotiations about the prospect of a joint Olympic team; see Radchenko, 2012). However, we classify only the Moscow and Los Angeles Games as being the most characteristic and, at the same time, the apex of Cold War confrontation. Therefore, the 1960, 1964, and 1972 Olympics are included in a separate category of 'Rehabilitation Games', reflecting a more nuanced political milieu (Finlay and Xin, 2010; Horton and Saunders, 2012). 'Rehabilitation' here refers to the attempt of the host to re-enter the international arena after a period as a 'pariah'.

In a manner similar to that of several scholars (Alekseyeva, 2014; Fijałkowski, 2011), this classification shows that the soft power agenda of developing nations or non-liberal regimes is likely to be diametrically opposed to that of advanced democratic-states. Moreover, our approach accords with the argument that states with unassuming brands, which as a general rule are developing or with a poor democratic record and controversial episodes in their past (Gill and Huang, 2006), assign much more transformative power to the act of hosting an SME (Hong, 2010; Jin et al., 2011). That is to say, amongst other dimensions such as economic success or geopolitical aspirations, countries like India, Brazil, South Africa, and, above all, Russia and China strive to "signal diplomatic stature or to project, in the absence of other forms of international influence, soft power" (Cornelissen, 2010, p. 3008). Arning's (2013) precise analysis of the main messages of the nodal Olympic Games ceremonies, in turn, supports the classification suggested above. She argues (p. 537) that:

> The 1980 Moscow ceremony can be read as an attempt to mollify the West and offer up the soft underbelly of the Soviet Union, whimsy, children's anthems and all. South Korea 1988 ceremony attempted to put the country on the map with a discourse of innocence and harmony at its heart. Barcelona 1992 used aesthetic prowess and a shrewd balance of Mediterranean, Spanish and Catalan to roll back stereotypes about backwards, previously autocratic Spain. The USA in LA 1984 had a brief to remind the world of American breeziness and fun and in Atlanta 1996 to promote the South and a more internationally minded country (with chequered results). Sydney 2000 was a coming out party for Australia, to project soft power with an almost blank canvas and with few negative stereotypes to neutralise, except perhaps genocide against aboriginal peoples.

It emerges, accordingly, that due to the relative newness of the term, and hence the lack of conceptual clarity and vague theoretical structure, specific soft power outcomes depend on a rather loose interpretation made by a host state and mean different things in each particular case (Armistead, 2004). Chinese, Russian, and Qatari understandings of soft power, for example, differ substantially from the concept initially introduced by Nye (1990), in particular around the notion of 'attractiveness'. One could argue that human rights issues and non-democratic practices would negate the ability to generate 'soft power' from such states; what is left, if states are not attracting others or persuading them to do what they would not otherwise do, is to put themselves on the map.

SUMMARY AND CONCLUDING THOUGHTS

Our aim in this chapter has been to offer a more nuanced understanding of the motives of a variety of states for wishing to host an SME. We have looked at the key concepts used to discuss and analyse this process: public diplomacy, nation (and place) branding, and soft power. We also sought to distinguish the term 'propaganda' from 'public diplomacy' in the use of sport by states. This ground-clearing exercise is necessary, we believe, because of the ubiquitous use of 'soft power' as a catch-all, broad-brush explanation for the rationale behind wishing to host an SME. The widespread use of the concept is demonstrated most evidently through the increasing number of academics, politicians and governmental authorities, private institutions, and agencies, and journalists and blog writers that have attempted to apply, adapt, and/or measure soft power in their discussions of state-led policies (see Grix and Brannagan, 2016 for a full review).

Part of the problem with distinguishing between the concepts discussed in this chapter is that they all set out to put a city, region, and state in a good light. As discussed, public diplomacy is about impacting (positively) and influencing foreign publics' view of a state; nation branding consists of producing and promoting a particular (positive) image externally; and soft power encompasses the above, but also attempts to draw on a state's culture and institutions as it tries to achieve its goals by persuading others through attraction and not coercion. It becomes clear that many states – especially non-liberal, often emerging and non-democratic – are not applying soft power as Nye set out over 30 years ago. Which states, realistically, will be 'attracted' to the governance of Qatar? Will China really change opinion abroad through hosting both the Summer (2008) and Winter (2022) Olympics? More likely, authoritarian and autocratic states (China, Russia, Qatar etc.) engage in nation branding in an attempt to address their (generally) negative images abroad. For example, the top 24 states in *The Soft-Power-30 Index* (2019) are democracies, with Hungary (25th), China (27th), and Russia (28th) the highest placed non-democratic states.

This chapter has attempted to highlight the fact that often the dominance of a specific concept ('soft power' in this case) can lead to less nuanced accounts of why different states chose to host SMEs. In particular, we need to be wary of the (Western) origins of the concept and question whether it fits the specific case we are attempting to explain or whether another concept, such as 'nation branding' or 'propaganda', is more pertinent.

REFERENCES

Abel, J.R. (2012). Japan's sporting diplomacy: the 1964 Tokyo Olympiad. *The International History Review*, 34(February), 203–220.

Alekseyeva, A. (2014). Sochi 2014 and the rhetoric of a new Russia: image construction through mega-events. *East European Politics*, 30(2), 158–174.

Allison, L. (1993). *The Changing Politics of Sport*. Manchester: Manchester University Press.

Anholt, S. (2008). Place branding: is it marketing or isn't it?, *Journal of Brand Management*, 4(1), 1–6.

Anholt, S. (2010). Definitions of place branding: working towards a resolution, *Journal of Brand Management*, No. 6, pp. 1–10.

Armistead, E.L. (2004). *Information Operations: Warfare and the Hard Reality of Soft Power*. Dulles, VA: Potomac Books.

Arning, C. (2013). Soft power, ideology and symbolic manipulation in Summer Olympic Games opening ceremonies: a semiotic analysis. *Social Semiotics*, 23(4), 523–544.

Australian Tourist Commission (2001). Olympic Games tourism strategy. Canberra, ACT: ATC.

Balbier, U.A. (2009). 'A game, a competition, an instrument?': high performance, cultural diplomacy and German sport from 1950 to 1972. *The International Journal of the History of Sport*, 26(4), 539–555.

Black, D. and Van der Westhuizen, J. (2004), The allure of global games for "semi-peripheral" polities and spaces: a research agenda, *Third World Quarterly*, 25(7), 1195–1214.

Bonde, H. (2009). Danish sport and the Nazi seizure of power: indoctrination, propaganda and confrontation. *The International Journal of the History of Sport*, 26(August).

Bryant, C. (2015). National art and Britain made real: the London 2012 Olympics opening ceremony, *National Identities*, 17(3), 333–346.

Carter, T.F. and Sugden, J. (2012). The USA and sporting diplomacy: comparing and contrasting the cases of table tennis with China and baseball with Cuba in the 1970s. *International Relations*, 26(1), 101–121.

Castells, M. (2008). The new public sphere: global civil society, communication networks, and global governance. *The Annals of the American Academy of Political and Social Science*, 616 (1), 78–93.

Cha, V.D. (2013). The Asian Games and diplomacy in Asia: Korea–China. *The International Journal of the History of Sport*, 30(10), 1176–1187.

Collins, S. (2007). *The 1940 Tokyo Games: The Missing Olympics: Japan, The Asian Olympics and the Olympic Movement*. London: Routledge.

Cornelissen, S. (2010). The geopolitics of global aspiration: sport mega-events and emerging powers. *International Journal of the History of Sport*, 27(16–18), 3008–3025.

Council on Foreign Relations (CFR) (2014). Will South Korea's Olympic diplomacy last? 2 March, accessed 19 October 2018 at https://www.cfr.org/expert-brief/will -south-koreas-olympic-diplomacy-last.

Cowan, G. and Arsenault, A. (2008). Moving from monologue to dialogue to collaboration: the three layers of public diplomacy. *The ANNALS of the American Academy of Political and Social Science*, 616, 10–28.

Cull, N.J. (2010). Public diplomacy: seven lessons for its future from its past. *Place Branding and Public Diplomacy*, 6(1), 11–17.

deLisle, J. (2009). After the Gold Rush: the Beijing Olympics and China's evolving international roles. *Orbis*, 53(2), 179–204.

Endzina, I. and Luneva, L. (2004), Development of a national branding strategy: the case of Latvia, *Place Branding*, 1(1), 94–105.

Evans, A. and Steven, D. (2010). Towards a theory of influence for twenty-first century foreign policy: the new public diplomacy in a globalised world. *Place Branding and Public Diplomacy*, 6(1), 18–26.

Fan, Y. (2010). Branding the nation: towards a better understanding. *Place Branding and Public Diplomacy*, suppl. Special Issue: Places for People in a Turbulent World, 6(2), 97–103.

Fijałkowski, Ł. (2011). China's 'soft power' in Africa? *Journal of Contemporary African Studies*, 29(2), 223–232.

Finlay, C.J. and Xin, X. (2010). Public diplomacy games: a comparative study of American and Japanese responses to the interplay of nationalism, ideology and Chinese soft power strategies around the 2008 Beijing Olympics. *Sport in Society*, 13(5), 876–900.

Gilboa, E. (2008). Searching for a theory of public diplomacy. *The ANNALS of the American Academy of Political and Social Science*, 616, 55–77.

Gill, B. and Huang, Y. (2006). Sources and limits of Chinese 'soft power'. *Survival*, 48(2), 17–36.

Giulianotti, R. (2015). The Beijing 2008 Olympics: examining the interrelations of China, globalization, and soft power. *European Review*, 23, 286–296.

Goldberg, J. (2000). Sporting diplomacy: boosting the size of the diplomatic corps. *Washington Quarterly*, 23(4), 63–70.

Grix, J. (2013). Sport politics and the Olympics. *Political Studies Review*, 11(1), 15–25.

Grix, J. and Kramareva, N. (2016). The Sochi Winter Olympics and Russia's unique soft power strategy. *Sport in Society*, 0437(November), 1–15.

Grix, J. and Brannagan, P.M. (2016). Of mechanisms and myths: conceptualising states' "soft power" strategies through sports mega-events, *Diplomacy & Statecraft*, 27(2), 251–272.

Grix, J., Brannagan, P. and Houlihan, B. (2015). Interrogating states' soft power strategies: a case study of sports mega-events in Brazil and the UK. *Global Society*, 29(3), 463–479.

Guthrie-Shimizu, S. (2013). Transpacific field of dreams: how baseball linked the United States and Japan in peace and war. *Australasian Journal of American Studies*, 32(2), 81–83.

Hepple, P. (2012). Five ways for London to top the Beijing Olympics opening ceremony. *The Huffington Post UK*, 16 February, accessed 5 October 2012 at http://www.huffingtonpost.co.uk.

Hocking, B. (2005). Rethinking the 'new' public diplomacy. In J. Melisson (ed.), *The New Public Diplomacy*, Basingstoke: Palgrave Macmillan, pp. 28–43.

Holzweissig, G. (1981). *Diplomatie im Trainingsanzug. Sport als politisches Instrument der DDR in den innerdeutschen und internationalen Beziehungen*. Munich, Germany and Vienna, Austria: Oldenbourg.

Hong, F. (2010). Epilogue: Branding China: the Beijing Olympics and beyond. *The International Journal of the History of Sport*, 27(14–15), 2642–2650.

Horne, J. and Houlihan, B. (2014). London 2012. In J. Grix (ed.), *Leveraging Legacies from Sports Mega-Events*. Basingstoke: Palgrave Macmillan, pp.107–117.

Horton, P. and Saunders, J. (2012). The 'East Asian' Olympic Games: what of sustainable legacies? *The International Journal of the History of Sport*, 29, 887–911.

Jin, H., Li, H. and Yuan, G. (2011). Status of Beijing Olympic Games brands in establishment of a sports power. *Asian Social Science*, 7(6), 25–28.

Kavaratzis, M. (2004). From city marketing to city branding: towards a theoretical framework for developing city brands, *Journal of Place Branding*, 1(1), 58–73.

Keohane, R. and Nye, J. (1998). Power and interdependence in the information age. *Foreign Affairs*, September/October.

Knott, B., Fyall, A. and Jones, I. (2017). Sport mega-events and nation branding. *International Journal of Contemporary Hospitality Management*, 29(3), 900–923.

Kotler, P. and Gertner, D. (2002). Country as brand, product and beyond: a place marketing and brand management perspective, *Journal of Brand Management*, 9(4–5), 249–261.

Kotler, P., Asplund, C., Rein, I. and Heider, D. (1999). *Marketing Places Europe: Attracting Investments, Industries, Residents and Visitors to European Cities, Communities, Regions and Nations*, London: Pearson Education.

Kuper, S. (2011). Sport: developing nations go on offensive for games. Accessed 14 February 2012 at http://www.ft.com/cms/s/0/aa7cef8c-273f-11e0-80d7-00144feab49a.html#axzz1mMDENFR9.

Li, X. (Leah). (2017). From Beijing to Rio: rebranding China via the modern Olympic Games. *The Journal of International Communication*, 23(2), 252–271.

Manheim, J.B. (1990). Rites of passage: the 1988 Seoul Olympics as public diplomacy. *Western Political Quarterly*, 43, 279–95.

Manzenreiter, W. (2010). The Beijing Games in the Western imagination of China: the weak power of soft power. *Journal of Sport & Social Issues*, 34(1), 29–48.

Mattern, J. (2005). Why soft power isn't so soft: representational force and the sociolinguistic construction of attraction in world politics. *Millennium – Journal of International Studies*, 33(3), 583–612.

Melissen, J. (2005). The new public diplomacy: between theory and practice. In J. Melissen (ed.), *The New Public Diplomacy: Soft Power in International Relations*. New York, NY: Palgrave Macmillan, pp. 3–27.

Moretti, A. (2013). The interference of politics in the Olympic Games, and how the U.S. media contribute to it. *Global Media Journal*, Canadian edn, 6(2), 5–18.

Morgan, N., Pritchard, A. and Pride, R. (eds) (2002). *Destination Branding: Creating the Unique Destination Proposition*, Oxford: Butterworth-Heinemann.

Murray, S. (2012). The two halves of sports-diplomacy. *Diplomacy & Statecraft*, 23(3), 576–592.

Murray, S. and Pigman, G.A. (2014). Mapping the relationship between international sport and diplomacy. *Sport in Society*, 17(9), 1098–1118.

Nickles, D. and Paull (2003). *Under the Wire: How the Telegraph Changed Diplomacy*. Cambridge, MA: Harvard University Press.

Niehaus, A. and Tagsold, C. (eds) (2013). *Sport, Memory and Nationhood in Japan: Remembering the Glory Days*. London: Routledge.

Nye Jr, J S. (1990). Soft power. *Foreign Policy*, 80 (Autumn), 153–171.

Nye, J. (2002). Limits of American power. *Journal of Public and International Affairs*, 117(4), 545–55.

Oettler, A. (2015). The London 2012 Olympics Opening Ceremony and its polyphonous aftermath. *Journal of Sport and Social Issues*, 39(3), 244–261.

Papadopoulos, N. and Heslop, L. (2002), Country equity and country branding: problems and prospects, *Journal of Brand Management*, 9(4/5), 294–315.

Park, M. and Tae, H. (2016). Arts style and national identity reflected in the Olympics opening ceremonies: a comparison of the 2008 Beijing Olympics and the 2012 London Olympics. *Quest*, 68(2), 170–192.

Radchenko, S. (2012). It's not enough to win: the Seoul Olympics and the roots of North Korea's isolation, *The International Journal of the History of Sport*, 29(9), 1243–1262.

Riordan, J. (1974). Soviet sport and Soviet foreign policy. *Soviet Studies*, 26(3), 322–343.

Rofe, S. (2016). Sport and diplomacy: a global diplomacy framework, *Diplomacy & Statecraft*, 27(2), 212–230.

Ståhlberg, P. and Bolin, G. (2016). Having a soul or choosing a face? Nation branding, identity and cosmopolitan imagination. *Social Identities*, 4630(March), 1–17.

Tagsold, C. (2010). Modernity, space and national representation at the Tokyo Olympics 1964. *Urban History*, 37, 289–300.

Wang, G. (2003). "Friendship first": China's sports diplomacy during the cold war. *Journal of American-East Asian Relations*, 12(3), 133–153.

Zhong, X., Zhou, S., Shen, B. and Huang, C. (2013). Shining a spotlight on public diplomacy: Chinese media coverage on the opening ceremony of the 2012 London Olympics, *The International Journal of the History of Sport*, 30(4), 393–406.

Zhou, S., Shen, B., Zhang, C. and Zhong, X. (2013). Creating a competitive identity: public diplomacy in the London Olympics and media portrayal, *Mass Communication and Society*, 16(6), 869–887.

18. Place branding for sustainable development: the role of tourism in sustainable place branding strategies

Anette Therkelsen, Laura James, and Henrik Halkier

INTRODUCTION

The 2010s have been characterized by escalating concerns about sustainability and, in particular, climate change, driven by a broad spectrum of politicians and NGOs, including the Fridays For Future movement, whose goal is to put pressure on policymakers and make them take action to limit global warming (FridaysForFuture, 2020). The UN's *Sustainable Development Goals* (SDGs) have been a common point of reference when nations, regions, and cities have formulated goals in relation to climate change to be attained within the next few decades. Consequently, agendas for sustainable development have found their way into the branding strategies and practices of places.

Though visible climate changes are the main reason for such broad-scale attention, the COVID-19 crisis seems also to have accentuated popular awareness of climate issues and challenges: the lockdown has helped to demonstrate the environmental impact of our daily life activities – in large part because, ironically, it has forced us to curtail them and thus has made them more apparent by their relative absence. However, such challenges demand tangible actions and not just understanding and good intentions, a necessity that was highlighted in a recent analysis of the SDG performance of all UN member states (Sachs et al., 2019). One of the main conclusions of this report is that while rhetorical statements of support are plentiful in relation to sustainable development of cities, regions, and countries, this does not necessarily result in changes to budgetary priorities or concrete developmental actions.

The present study zooms in on the role of the tourism sector in a sustainable place branding strategy. Tourism is particularly interesting to study, not least because the sector has been characterized for decades by a growth imperative and, rightfully or not, this has come to be increasingly associated with 'overtourism', connoting exploitation of natural and socio-cultural resources (Higgins-Desbiolles et al., 2019; Milano et al., 2019). In the face of growing consumer awareness of the importance of climate change, it may be argued that tourism is a sector in need of rebranding itself in order to maintain support among local populations as well as to sustain market attractiveness. For rebranding strategies to be effective, however, the symbolic representation and physical/cultural place-making efforts need to be aligned (Kavaratzis, 2005; Ma et al., 2019; Richards, 2017), and whereas the former may be the domain of tourism actors on their own, the latter necessarily involves the coordinated efforts of multiple place actors.

The literature has shown that reconciling public and private place actor interests is a challenging task (Acharya and Rahman, 2016; Hankinson, 2010; Therkelsen et al., 2010). Public authorities have increasingly learned that the interests of the local population are the starting point of a viable place brand (Colomb and Kalandides, 2010; Hankinson, 2007; Jernsand and Kraff, 2015; Kavaratzis, 2012), whereas tourism actors have their attention directed at tourist target groups and their experience-oriented demands. Variations in target groups and their needs and preferences are also likely to influence the end goal of place actors, in that long-term solutions that will improve the everyday lives of local citizens may lose out to more short-term commercial goals in the pursuit of profit (Andersson, 2016; Andersson and James, 2018; Valencia et al., 2019; Therkelsen et al., 2021).

These differences in terms of target group and goals may be further accentuated in a sustainability context, given that sustainable place-making efforts demand time and resources which may be difficult to reconcile with the existing tourism set-up of the place (e.g., if it is dependent upon high emission activities such as air transport and cruise tourism) and may not generate the tourism revenue needed, at least not on a short-term basis. The prospect of building a place brand around sustainability is, in other words, potentially challenged by the presence among stakeholders of different horizons, in terms of both time and space (Andersson and James, 2018).

The aim of this chapter is therefore to explore ways in which tourism is incorporated into sustainable place branding. More specifically, it considers the extent to which there are differences between the ambitions of public authorities and the tourism sector in relation to sustainable place-telling and place-making. The chapter also examines how local actors attempt to reconcile the tensions between the growth imperatives and non-resident focus of tourism destination branding, on the one hand, and the longer-term resident focus of broader place-based sustainability strategies, on the other.

Empirically, the chapter focuses on the city of Aalborg, Denmark, which has a history of engagement in sustainability as well as a current strategy that signals certain ambitions and dedication. Since the 1990s, Aalborg has held a leading position in the European association *Sustainable Cities Platform* (2020), giving its name to the *Aalborg Charter* – a European version of the 1992 Rio Declaration. In line with its international orientation, the city has a history of local sustainability strategies. The most recent of these (2016–2020) is based on an integrated approach to sustainable development across public and private interests and considers local citizens as important actors in the process (Aalborg Municipality, 2016). Specifically, in relation to tourism, sustainability has been central to the city's conference and convention efforts since the early 2010s, in that the local destination management organization is an active partner in the *Global Destination Sustainability Movement* (2020).

Having outlined the background and aim of this chapter, we subsequently turn to symbolic representation and physical/cultural place-making in the context of sustainability and tourism, before we move on to a discussion of multiple stakeholder cooperation and the different priorities and synergies that this may involve. This forms the basis for the empirical part of this chapter, which uses the case of the city of Aalborg to expand our insight into the challenges and potentials involved in sustainable place branding. The final section concludes the discussion by summarizing the main findings of the empirical case and tying them to the preceding theoretical discussion.

PLACE BRANDING, TOURISM, AND SUSTAINABILITY

Place branding is fraught with inherent tensions, and introducing a sustainability perspective and tourism as the focus point hardly makes things less complicated. As we have argued previously (Therkelsen et al., 2021), the connection between place branding and sustainability is an emerging field of academic endeavor (Maheshwari et al., 2011; Acharya and Rahman, 2016). A recent review (Taecharungroj et al., 2019) uncovered few examples of attempts to brand places on the basis of a holistic approach to sustainability: instead, sustainability is narrowed down to environmental concerns, and the literature highlights the long-standing efforts of 'extra green' eco-cities like Canada's Vancouver (Affolderbach and Schulz, 2017; McCann, 2013) or Sweden's Växjö (Andersson and James, 2018).

In contrast, research on tourism and place branding has produced a sizeable body of literature that covers both the contribution of the visitor economy to wider place brands and vice versa (Almeyda-Ibáñez and George, 2017; Hankinson, 2007; Zenker et al., 2017), as well as the relationship between tourism and other stakeholders in the branding process (Hankinson, 2007; Kavaratzis, 2012; Therkelsen and Halkier, 2011). The literature on tourism and place branding comes across as a specialized version of the general literature on place branding, and therefore it is hardly surprising that sustainability plays a rather limited role within it, with contributions focusing both on environmental (e.g., Andersson and James, 2018) and social sustainability (e.g., Ryan and Mizerski, 2010). Conversely, in the *Journal of Sustainable Tourism*, branding is predominantly discussed in relation to services (e.g., Font et al., 2017) and experiences (e.g., Smith and Font, 2014) rather than places (e.g., Woodland and Acott, 2007).

Symbolic Representation and Physical/Cultural Place-making

Early place branding practices tended to focus on developing more or less elaborate promotional communications platforms, but in recent decades more holistic approaches have become prominent in the research literature, stressing the importance of place-making through the built environment and/or cultural events as an integrated part of building a brand (Eckstein and Throgmorton, 2003; Jensen, 2007; Kavaratzis, 2005; Ma et al., 2019; Richards, 2017; Therkelsen et al. 2010). This change of emphasis recognizes the importance of achieving a reasonable degree of correspondence between the story communicated by the place brand and the experience of being present in the place. Despite its intrinsic appeal and notwithstanding successful examples at such cities as Barcelona, Amsterdam, and Bilbao (Compte-Pujol et al., 2017; Dai et al., 2018; Gomez, 1999), this principle can be difficult to translate into practice. This is simply because the cost of place-making through, for example, urban renewal or a harbor-front opera house greatly exceeds what authorities can spend on marketing and promotion (Maheshwari et al., 2011; Richards, 2017; Ma et al., 2019).

Introducing sustainability as the normative frame for place branding is likely to require very extensive place-making activities. This is because sustainability is such a wide-ranging and contested concept, even when it is narrowed down to environmental concerns – and, given the general appeal of sustainability, the risk of communication-based place branding being seen as 'greenwashing' is a very real one indeed (Andersson, 2016; Andersson and James, 2018; Valencia et al., 2019). A potential gap between communication and practice also presents itself specifically in relation to tourism, in that public initiatives to make places more sustainable are typically aimed at the everyday lives of residents and the operations of local companies/organizations, but not at the activities of tourists. Therefore, it may be difficult to make sustainable measures visible to tourists, let alone turn them into an experience for visitors. Tourism actors may thus be prone to a high degree of 'green speak'.

Place performance indexes may be regarded as one way of overcoming this visibility challenge, and a suitable example for the purpose of this study is the *Global Destination Sustainability Index* (GDSI) (Targeted News Service,

2017; McCartney and Leong, 2018). This constitutes a membership-based, third-party brand certification for tourist destinations that is founded on standardized sustainability indicators and involves publication of annual rankings (Cassinger and Eksell, 2017; Cidell, 2015). It is, however, worth considering whether such an index actually contributes to making the place more sustainable, given its relatively narrow focus.

It could, furthermore, be argued that private investments in sustainable tourism operations may be hampered by doubts about sufficient market demand for such initiatives, and therefore the return on investment and competitive advantage of sustainable practices remain unclear (Bramwell and Lane, 2010; Rowe and Higham, 2007). For example, one study showed that eco certification had no significant impact on general tourist demand but only seemed to influence niche markets in terms of consumers' holiday choices (Karlsson and Dolnicar, 2016). Recent market surveys (e.g., VisitDenmark, 2020), indicate that demand patterns in international holiday tourist markets are changing on a broader scale; however, caution is always needed when considering such data as consumers' intentions may reflect a significant gap compared to their actual behavior (Karlsson and Dolnicar, 2016). These doubts about market demand may be yet another and, indeed, very important reason why sustainable place-telling rather that place-making may be a favored choice of the tourism sector.

Multiple Stakeholder Interests in Sustainable Place Branding Efforts

The discussion above touches upon the difficulties in bringing together stakeholders with different interests around a shared place branding strategy, and this constitutes another central issue in the place branding literature: whereas potential visitors may be in search of culture, leisure, and shopping, local residents are likely to also value quality in public services and a safe living environment (Acharya and Rahman, 2016; Hankinson, 2010). Developing a durable brand requires serious engagement not only with elite stakeholders, such as local politicians and business organizations, but also with NGOs and citizens (Colomb and Kalandides, 2010; Hankinson, 2007; Jernsand and Kraff, 2015; Kavaratzis and Ashworth, 2005). While this sits well with the wide range of issues that can be construed as part of a commitment to good governance and sustainability, inclusive and harder-to-control long-term processes may be less appealing for business actors with short-term bottom lines and a less altruistic mindset.

Given the all-encompassing and fuzzy character of sustainability as a guiding principle, the risk of 'cherry picking' focus areas that promise short-term results that can be achieved by mobilizing relatively limited resources in a targeted manner (Andersson, 2016; Andersson and James, 2018; Valencia et al., 2019) is very real. That is, of course, provided that key stakeholders can actually agree to embrace sustainable place branding, especially in a context where this is no longer a unique position but, rather, one that is quickly becoming fairly mainstream thanks to the rise of climate politics and the newfound reverence for the UN's SDGs (Sachs et al., 2019).

With regard to the branding of tourist destinations, the relevance of sustainability is, as mentioned above, likely to depend on the perceived importance of, for example, green issues or social equity to potential visitors, and the extent to which the destination management organization (DMO) takes its political lead from private or public stakeholders (Acharya and Rahman, 2016; Hankinson, 2010). This point is supported by a UN World Tourism Organization report (UNWTO, 2017), which documents that the perceived importance of the 17 SDGs varies across place actor groups and therefore is likely to hamper cross-sector cooperation on SDG implementation. The report also concludes that competitiveness is the main driver for pursuing a sustainability strategy among tourism businesses, but that this sector does not have sufficient knowledge on how to turn sustainable measures into profitable businesses.

Particularly in the face of climate change, the recent literature on sustainable tourism has, furthermore, challenged a local-scale approach in which a destination could be considered sustainable without consideration of its integration into the wider social and ecological systems (Saarinen, 2014; Espiner et al., 2017). Hence it has become widely accepted among scholars that, as McCool et al. (2013, p. 218) put it, "overly simplistic models and panaceas—such as finding the intersection of ecological sensitivity, economic feasibility and cultural acceptability—are deceptive". Alternative approaches such as resilience (the ability of destinations to bounce back from shocks such as natural disasters and adapt to longer-term processes, such as climate change) have been widely discussed within the academic literature, and more radical ideas, such as degrowing tourism (Higgins-Desbiolles et al., 2019), have been advanced. It is interesting to pursue in the academic discourse whether the deliberations and practices of tourism actors are mainly local and sector-specific, or have a broader orientation both in terms of cross-geographical and cross-sector cooperation.

This brief review of the existing literature suggests that sustainability has so far played a relatively small role in tourism destination branding in general, although there are examples of broader place branding strategies based on environmental policy, such as the eco-cities movement. One reason for this may be that sustainability is an extremely contested concept and its meaning – and therefore the content of any associated brand – is hard to pin down. Whilst this fuzziness may be seen positively because it leaves considerable room for interpretation, it also increases the risk of so-called greenwashing and makes it hard to achieve a clear alignment between brand and reality.

Furthermore, the relationship between communicative place telling and physical/cultural place-making remains challenging. Addressing sustainability challenges requires long-term investments in what might well be 'invisible' infrastructure or changes to everyday routines that are not compatible with the tourism sector's need for visible initiatives that short-term visitors will notice and are willing to pay for. Last, but not least, the preponderance of small tourism firms with limited resources that rely on incoming visitors, most likely brought to the destination in unsustainable ways and potentially representing 'unnecessary' travel, makes the integration of tourism in sustainable place branding efforts inherently difficult.

CASE STUDY AND EMPIRICAL DATA

The Case of Aalborg

Like many other major provincial cities, Aalborg has moved from being an industrial hub dominated by heavy industries (concrete, shipbuilding, tobacco, spirits) towards being a place where digital industries, the experience economy, and major knowledge institutions have reshaped the city (Jensen, 2007; Halkier, 2008). The city has labored hard at establishing itself as an international place, partly through a less successful branding campaign in the early 2000s (Therkelsen et al., 2010), and partly, and more importantly, through investment in modern cultural facilities, accommodating a fast-growing number of students by converting centrally located brownfield sites, attracting an increasing number of international conferences, and hosting high-profile events.

Simultaneously, and what seems to be quite separate from the place branding efforts outlined above, Aalborg municipality has a history of working with sustainability dating back to the 1990s, when the city was one of the initiators of the first *European Conference on Sustainable Cities and Towns* inspired by the 1992 Rio Earth Summit. This resulted in the *Aalborg Charter*, which provided input to the EU's Environmental Action Programme 'Towards Sustainability' and has been signed over the years by more than 3000 local authorities from 40 countries (Sustainable Cities Platform, 2020). Aalborg has remained an active partner of the *Sustainable Cities Platform* association, which supports sustainable transformations through yearly conferences, declarations, and the development and sharing of a database containing good practices of transformative actions.

This international engagement is also reflected in several local sustainability strategies through the 2000s and 2010s and the establishment of the Center for Green Transition (CGT, 2020), which is responsible for implementing sustainability initiatives increasingly directed at citizens. The latter marks a shift in the strategic focus of the municipality, from being centered on the green transition of private firms and public institutions to including the greening of citizens' practices as a major concern. This is clearly reflected in their 2016–2020 sustainability strategy (Aalborg Municipality, 2016).

Although the tourism sector is absent from the 2016–2020 strategy document, in 2018, due to a significant growth in the sector, it was included in the work of the CGT (2020). For the local DMO, VisitAalborg, sustainability is conspicuously absent from their strategic work, including their 2017–2020 strategy, whereas growth through attracting new visitors from international markets is at its center (VisitAalborg, 2017). At the same time, however, VisitAalborg has been one of the driving forces behind the GDSI (2020), and so since the early 2010s sustainability has actually been central to VisitAalborg's conference and convention efforts.

In short, Aalborg has a history of three decades of sustainability efforts which have increased in scope over the years, so that it now includes a broad spectrum of trades and businesses, including tourism, as well as the green transition of individual citizens. The local DMO has not so far included sustainability at the strategic level, but the transition towards sustainability at the operational level, and particularly in relation to the business tourism area, has been a guiding principle for several years.

Empirical Data

Empirically the study draws on data from Aalborg municipality that describes their sustainability visions and concrete initiatives. The 2016–2020 sustainability strategy is of particular interest (Aalborg Municipality, 2016) together with the website of the CGT (2020) that provides insight into the implementation of the strategy. To gain more details on the sustainability visions and practices of the municipality and the importance of tourism, an interview was conducted with the leader of CGT's Green Tourism project in July 2020.

To gain a more detailed understanding of sustainable tourism development, data from the DMO, VisitAalborg, was also collected. As VisitAalborg's 2017–2020 strategy has no specific focus on sustainability (VisitAalborg, 2016), documents describing its efforts in relation to the GDSI are of greater relevance (VisitAalborg, 2019). This is complemented by important insights gained from another interview, also in July 2020, this time with the head of conventions and the sustainability developer at VisitAalborg.

The interviews were conducted online via Microsoft Teams by the first author and lasted for approximately one hour each. They were recorded upon consent from the respondents and subsequently summarized. The respondents agreed that they were to be referred to by their position and organization and that the data would be used for research purposes only. Selected quotations from the interviews were translated into English by the authors and approved by the respondents subsequent to the interviews.

Case Analysis

As outlined in the case description, the city of Aalborg has a relatively long history of working with sustainability. However, it was not until 2018 that these efforts started to include tourism, due to the significant growth experienced within the sector (Interview CGT). The significance of sustainable tourism development is likewise a recent preoccupation for the local DMO. From being absent in its 2017–2020 strategy, sustainability steadily gained importance in relation to one of their main work domains, business tourism, during the strategy period. Since 2018, VisitAalborg has worked closely together with CGT on supporting tourism organizations in implementing more sustainable ways of operating, and they are currently planning a dedicated sustainability strategy for 2021 that is to cover both of their major work domains, business and holiday tourism (Interview VisitAalborg). The recency of the cooperation between the municipality and the DMO, and the addition of tourism to an existing municipal portfolio of strategic actions, provides an important context for understanding stakeholder relations, ambitions, and goals.

Place-making – Synergies and Divisions

Common to the work on sustainable tourism of both the municipal actor and the DMO is that they have directed their focus at changing the operation of local tourism organizations. To this end, CGT offers screening for green potential as well as interns from a *Green Travel Team* to assist with green project development, including identification of partners and applications for funding. Interest in the screening process has been most significant among hotels and conference facilities, whereas only a few visitor attractions have used it and the 'green interns' (Interview CGT). Likewise, VisitAalborg focuses their efforts on hotels and conference facilities, initiating talks about green practices among member organizations and pointing them towards the more hands-on services of CGT. According to the DMO, market demand determines who are the first-movers in terms of sustainability, in that sustainable conference packages are increasingly requested by professional markets, whereas the demand of consumer markets, that is, holiday tourists, is far less pronounced (Interview VisitAalborg). Doubts about sufficient demand in holiday markets hence prevail (Karlsson and Dolnicar, 2016) and hamper the green transition of certain tourism firms.

Some private actors, mainly hotels, choose to use municipal and DMO services as a stepping stone towards environmental designation, typically the

Green Key certification (Interview CGT), combined with consultancy advice on how to turn sustainability potential into profitable businesses, whereas other actors find the certification process too time-consuming and only seek advice on sustainable business development. A third group of actors does not move beyond the screening stage, in many cases because they do not have the human and economic resources to support a green transition (Interview CGT). This underscores the UNWTO (2017) conclusion that the tourism sector does not know how to turn sustainability into profitable business. If they have the financial means, tourism firms may invest in consultancy support; however, in places where the tourism sector consists of many small and micro-sized firms, financial resources are typically scarce and ambitious plans for green transition may therefore be shelved, especially if their market potential is doubtful.

Whereas the municipal unit and the DMO share the purpose of facilitating a green transition of tourism firms' operations, they differ with respect to the general framing of their activities. Central to the work of CGT is to change the habits of private citizens towards more sustainable everyday practices, which is echoed in their sustainability strategy: "The Sustainability Strategy 2016–20 has a new theme: citizens and the good life. Sustainability and green transition is to a high degree about people. Without the involvement and participation of citizens, industry, associations, etc. green transition will not succeed" (Aalborg Municipality, 2016, p. 3).

As a consequence, municipal efforts towards the tourism sector are framed as serving the double purpose of supporting the industry as well as private citizens' green transition, the latter through the sector's extensive customer contact (Interview CGT). The fact that it is mainly hotels and conference facilities that have requested municipal services, however, hampers the fulfilment of this double purpose as local citizens and hotels/conference centers have few contact points compared to local citizens' much more extensive interactions with visitor attractions and restaurants.

The sustainability efforts of the DMO are, unsurprisingly, aimed at safeguarding the interests of a commercial sector, and hence at assisting tourism businesses in attracting visitors. As an illustration, VisitAalborg stresses that "The most significant challenge in relation to sustainable tourism is to convince the trade that it is profitable in the long run" (Interview VisitAalborg). This demonstrates a clear commercial focus as opposed to a general public focus of the municipality. These differences tap into the scholarly debate about altruistic versus profit-oriented goals, which may prove difficult to reconcile (Andersson, 2016; Andersson and James, 2018; Valencia et al., 2019; Therkelsen et al., 2020), but it also underlines the need to 'dig deeper' below grand statements and focus on the specific activities undertaken by different stakeholders. In the case of Aalborg, we have identified a shared goal of facilitating a green transition of tourism firms' operations, and a division of labor between the municipality and the DMO in terms of moving in this direction: while municipal programs provide screening and advice relevant to greener business practices, the DMO focuses on the discursive work of convincing the tourism trade about the long-term profitability of being more sustainable. In this (informal) division of labor, the absence of local visitor attractions and restaurants may need to be remedied in order to promote greater engagement with local citizens, thereby establishing a greater degree of synergy across stakeholder interests and, on this basis, supporting a sustainable place brand that appeals to both citizen and tourist markets.

Making, Ranking, Telling

Looking more closely at the services provided by both the DMO and the municipal unit, these reflect steps that are well-known by practitioners and researchers in sustainable tourism development and are mainly related to hotel and conference operations, as well as being integral to obtaining the special-ized *Green Key* certification. On the one hand, since 3200 hotels and other establishments across 65 countries have been awarded the *Green Key* to date (Green Key, 2020), these steps are obviously widespread and may increasingly be taken for granted by markets, there is good reason for integrating them into operational practices. On the other hand, since they are so widely shared, their usefulness as unique selling propositions is limited, which sits poorly within a sustainable place branding strategy.

One possible way around this apparent paradox is offered by the publicity generated through the more comprehensive place performance indices. To this end, the municipality and the DMO have dedicated substantial efforts to improving Aalborg's position on the GDSI, which covers more than 60 cities worldwide. As a ranking list with sustainability winners (and losers), the potential for differentiation is an integral part of GDSI. Moreover, the index represents a more cross-sector, holistic, SDG-oriented, and destination-wide sustainability recognition effort that sets it apart from the more specialized and piecemeal approach employed by individual tourism actors through, for instance, *Green Key* certification. Covering a wide range of SDGs, the index comprises data on environmental and social conditions of the city, the sustain-ability commitment and performance of the local meeting industry, and the commitment and performance of the local DMO.

After first joining the list in 2016 at the lower tiers of the ranking with a score of 42 percent, by 2019 Aalborg had risen to a (tied) fifth-place position in the global rankings with a score of 76 percent (Seleem et al., 2019). The substantial ranking improvement is undoubtedly due to a concerted effort by the municipality and DMO, in terms of marshalling the data needed to score points across as many of the 69 GDSI categories as possible. However, the

improved score may also indicate a growing sustainable destination partnership with private and public partners involved in delivering business tourism
activities in the city.

The GDSI thus seems to fit well into a broad-scale sustainable place branding strategy, as it taps into other domains of the city's sustainability efforts in
relation to air pollution, green areas, bicycle paths, and public transportation.
A broadening of scope to incorporate holiday tourism is ostensibly on the
agenda of the GDS movement (Interview VisitAalborg), whereby the fit with
a place branding strategy would become even better. Moreover, if cross-sector
contact is facilitated through the efforts to advance the city's ranking on the
GDSI, greater synergy may be achieved between highly innovative industries
(e.g., energy and construction) and the less innovative tourism sector. This,
however, may still be a thing of the future, as indicated by the DMO interview:
"There is a lack of focus on sustainability in hotel construction projects. The
municipality and VisitAalborg should be better at advising hotels towards that
end. When we build something new, we have to think sustainability from the
start" (Interview VisitAalborg).

What the piecemeal and more broad-based place-making efforts described
above have in common is that they are focused at the service level and
behind-the-scene operations, which may be quite difficult to discern by
holiday tourists. Professional business tourism markets – and not least professional conference organizers – may direct their attention towards the ways of
operation of conference facilities and hotels to support their own sustainability
agenda. Holiday tourists, however, are often less inquisitive, and so work on
enhancing sustainability in such areas as waste and water handling or energy
supply may remain quite invisible. This challenges the competitive advantage
of such measures in the context of the private consumer market and calls to
attention the communicative aspects of sustainable place branding.

Green Place Telling – a Double-edged Sword?

The CGT has developed a classical communication toolbox consisting of
a slogan ('Make us all greener'), a logo (a green leaf) and a design manual
for both on-line and off-line marketing, which they use for promoting a broad
range of green municipal initiatives ranging from cycle paths and sustainable
public transportation to green schools and kindergartens. The Center also
encourages private firms to utilize the campaign material, all of which is to
establish a recognizable and strong message across various stakeholders, combined with telling individual company stories about sustainable measures they
have taken (Interview CGT). This profiling strategy should be able to facilitate
both economies of scale through a collective brand as well as individual profiling through close-to-practice storytelling.

So far, however, little success has been achieved in making private firms interested in the communication package. This is attributed both to the broad scope of the campaign, which may impede the profiling of the individual firm, as well as to firms being afraid of flagging sustainability if they are in the middle of a green transition process (Interview CGT). In such cases, firms may be concerned over the limited extent to which they may be able to demonstrate their green intentions through their practices before their transition is complete, thereby taking the risk of being seen as 'green/SDG-washers'. Moreover, the nature of the core product of some firms calls into question the feasibility of implementing a sustainable profiling strategy addressed to consumer markets. Taking the local airport as an example, even though they work hard at reducing the energy usage of daily operations and services to customers, they remain skeptical about adopting a green branding strategy despite its increasing usage by other airports (Interview CGT).

The latter point links up with the DMO's explanation as to why tourism firms are hesitant about green profiling: "Many actors are a bit tired of sustainability as a marketing argument as there has been a lot of greenwashing around" (Interview VisitAalborg). Hence, sustainability in general, rather than specifically the branding effort of the municipality, has become a somewhat empty signifier compromised by actors who have little substance to show for their 'green speak' in terms of their internal operations and product offers. To avoid perceptions of overpromising, some firms opt for a strategy that involves changing their internal operations and products but not promoting these changes, so that the product may in fact offer more than the customer expects (Interview VisitAalborg). This approach holds the potential of generating positive word-of-mouth and customer loyalty, but only if sustainable measures are made visible to visiting tourists. The approach, however, lacks the possibility of creating awareness and attracting new markets on a broader scale, in the same way as economies that could be achieved when tagging onto a common sustainable place brand used by multiple place actors are also lost.

The reservations expressed in relation to green place-telling are more characteristic of tourism firms and less so of the DMO and the municipality. This becomes clear in relation to GDSI ranking, in that the destination's top position is used by the DMO for profiling Aalborg as a green conference and convention city (VisitAalborg, 2020). The marketing value of this international ranking is not questioned, possibly because of the credibility associated with third-party assessments and the benchmarking potential that such ranking lists entail. Ostensibly due to the destination and not an individual actor focus of the GDSI, only one individual tourism firm uses the GDSI ranking as a branding tool so far (Interview VisitAalborg), which indicates that firms have reservations about joining forces in a collective GDSI-based place brand.

CONCLUSION

Based on the Aalborg case study, this chapter has identified three main find-ings, which illustrate both the contribution of tourism to sustainable place branding as well as the challenges involved in such initiatives.

First, the DMO and the municipality work together towards a shared goal of facilitating a green transition of tourism firms (mainly hotels and conference facilities), based on a division of labor: the DMO acts as the initiator of sus-tainability discussions with member organizations, and the municipality pro-vides the more hands-on support for enabling the transition to green business. There is, however, further potential for synergy across stakeholder interests, with tourism contributing to a sustainable place brand, if more members of the tourism sector, such as visitor attractions and restaurants, are also engaged in the transition efforts. This would support a sustainable place brand that would cut across not just holiday and business tourism but also local citizen markets.

Second, the concerted effort of the municipality and DMO towards the GDSI fits well into a broad-scale sustainable place branding strategy, as it taps into a wide variety of the city's sustainability efforts such that what by origin is a tourism sector instrument becomes a general place branding tool. In addition, the GDSI seems to hold more potential as a unique selling proposition than piecemeal certification schemes.

Third, the case study demonstrates a major concern with place-making prac-tices, and more of a hesitant approach toward green place-telling. In particular, international destination rankings may hold marketing value because of their credibility and benchmarking characteristics and may constitute yet another contribution of tourism to sustainable place branding. However, fear of green-washing does exist among tourism firms, and so they seem to neglect the ben-efits of poignant place-telling and the potential synergy between place-making and symbolic representation.

All in all, our case study illustrates public authorities that are pragmatic about greening the tourism industry and its role in the overall sustainability strategy and place brand. They see incremental improvements as a positive outcome rather than fundamentally questioning tourism as an activity in the context of sustainable place development, despite the fact that tourism also involves highly unsustainable practices. However, it is still too early to con-clude whether they, together with the DMO, will manage to balance the twin goals of sustainable development and economic benefits of the tourism sector.

In the wake of the COVID-19 crisis, ambitions of a responsible recovery of the sector have been expressed by international, national, and local organ-izations, including the UNWTO (2020), who, in its *One Planet Vision*, takes a broad SDG-based approach to future tourism development. If such visions and strategic guidance become the blueprint for tourism sector operations, and if the sector is met by pragmatism on the part of other place actors, the way may be paved for further cross-sector synergies towards sustainable place branding strategies in the future. These are important research avenues to pursue in years to come as climate change, biodiversity, inequality, and many other sustainability-related issues become increasingly more urgent to tackle.

REFERENCES

Aalborg Municipality (2016), *Sammen skaber vi et stærkt og grønt Aalborg, hvor mennesker trives*. Sustainability strategy 2016–2020. Accessed 1 September 2020 at https://www.aalborg.dk/media/5759074/aalborg-kommunes-baeredygtighedsstra tegi.pdf.

Acharya, A. and Rahman, Z. (2016), 'Place branding research: a thematic review and future research agenda', *International Review on Public and Nonprofit Marketing*, 13 (3), 289–317.

Affolderbach, J. and Schulz, C. (2017), 'Positioning Vancouver through urban sustainability strategies? The Greenest City 2020 Action Plan', *Journal of Cleaner Production*, 164, 676–685.

Almeyda-Ibáñez, M. and George, B. (2017), 'Place branding in tourism: a review of theoretical approaches and management practices', *Tourism & Management Studies*, 13 (4), 10–19.

Andersson, I. (2016), '"Green cities" going greener? Local environmental policy-making and place branding in the "Greenest City in Europe"', *European Planning Studies*, 24 (6), 1197–1215.

Andersson, I. and James, L. (2018), 'Altruism or entrepreneurialism? The co-evolution of green place branding and policy tourism in Växjö, Sweden', *Urban Studies*, 55 (15), 3437–3453.

Bramwell, B. and Lane, B. (2010). 'Sustainable tourism and the evolving roles of government planning', *Journal of Sustainable Tourism*, 18 (1), 1–5.

Cassinger, C. and Eksell, J. (2017), 'The magic of place branding: regional brand identity in transition', *Journal of Place Management and Development*, 10 (3), 202–212.

CGT, Center for Green Transition (2020), Accessed 1 September 2020 at http://www .xn--centerforgrnomstilling-gjc.dk/.

Cidell, J. (2015), 'Performing leadership: municipal green building policies and the city as role model', *Environment & Planning C: Government and Policy*, 33, 1–14.

Colomb, C. and Kalandides, A. (2010), 'The "Be Berlin" campaign: old wine in new bottles or innovative form of participatory place branding?' In G.J. Ashworth and M. Kavaratzis (eds), *Towards Effective Place Brand Management: Branding European Cities and Regions*, Cheltenham, UK and Northampton, MA, USA: Edward Elgar Publishing, pp. 173–190.

Compte-Pujol, M., de San Eugenio-Vela, J. and Frigola-Reig, J. (2017), 'Key elements in defining Barcelona's place values: the contribution of residents' perceptions from an internal place branding perspective', *Place Branding and Public Diplomacy*, 14, 245–259.

Dai, T., Zhuang, T., Yan, J. and Zhang, T. (2018), 'From landscape to mindscape: spatial narration of touristic Amsterdam', *Sustainability*, 10 (8), 2623.

Eckstein, B. and Throgmorton, J.A. (eds) (2003), *Story and Sustainability: Planning, Practice and Possibility for American Cities*, Cambridge, MA: MIT Press.

Espiner, S., Orchiston, C. and Higham, J. (2017), 'Resilience and sustainability: a complementary relationship? Towards a practical conceptual model for the sustainability–resilience nexus in tourism', *Journal of Sustainable Tourism*, 25 (10), 1385–1400.

Font, X., Elgammal, I. and Lamond, I. (2017), 'Greenhushing: the deliberate under communicating of sustainability practices by tourism businesses', *Journal of Sustainable Tourism*, 25 (7), 1007–1023.

FridaysForFuture (2020), Accessed 20 February 2020 at www.fridaysforfuture.org: #FridaysForFuture.

GDSI, Global Destination Sustainability Movement (2020), Accessed 1 September 2020 at www.gds.earth.

Gomez, M.V. (1999), 'Reflective images: the case of urban regeneration in Glasgow and Bilbao', *International Journal of Urban and Regional Research*, 22 (1), 106–121.

Green Key (2020), Accessed 30 August 2020 at www.greenkey.global.

Halkier, H. (2008), 'Regional udviklingspolitik: Nordjylland som foregangsregion?'. In J.L. Christensen (ed.), *Hvad skal Nordjylland leve af?*, CRU, Aalborg: Aalborg University.

Hankinson, G. (2007), 'The management of destination brands: five guiding principles based on recent developments in corporate branding theory', *Brand Management*, 14 (3), 240–254.

Hankinson, G. (2010), 'Place branding research: a cross-disciplinary agenda and the views of practitioners', *Place Branding and Public Diplomacy*, 6 (4), 300–315.

Higgins-Desbiolles, F., Carnicelli, S., Krolikowski, C., Wijesinghe, G., and Boluk, K. (2019), 'Degrowing tourism: rethinking tourism', *Journal of Sustainable Tourism*, 27 (12), 1926–1944.

Jensen, O.B. (2007), 'Culture stories: understanding cultural urban branding', *Planning Theory*, 6 (3), 211–36.

Jernsand, E.M. and Kraff, H. (2015), 'Participatory place branding through design: the case of Dunga beach in Kinsumu, Kenya', *Place Branding and Public Diplomacy*, 11 (3), 226–242.

Karlsson, L. and Dolnicar, S. (2016), 'Does eco certification sell tourism services? Evidence from a quasi-experimental observation study in Iceland', *Journal of Sustainable Tourism*, 24 (5), 694–714.

Kavaratzis, M. (2005), 'Place branding: a review of trends and conceptual models', *The Marketing Review*, 5 (4), 329–342.

Kavaratzis, M. (2012), 'From "necessary evil" to necessity: stakeholders involvement in place branding', *Journal of Place Management and Development*, 5 (1), 7–19.

Kavaratzis, M. and Ashworth, G.J. (2005), 'City branding: an effective assertion of identity or a transitory marketing trick?', *Tijdschrift Voor Economische En Sociale Geografie*, 96 (5), 506–514.

Ma, W., Schraven, D., de Bruijne, M., de Jong, M. and Lu, H. (2019), 'Tracing the origins of place branding research: a bibliometric study of concepts in use (1980–2018)', *Sustainability*, 11 (11), 1–20.

Maheshwari, V., Vandewalle, I. and Bamber, D. (2011), 'Place branding's role in sustainable development', *Journal of Place Management and Development*, 4 (2), 198–213.

McCann, E. (2013), 'Policy boosterism, policy mobilities, and the extrospective city', *Urban Geography*, 34 (1), 5–29.

McCartney, G. and Leong, V.M.W. (2018), 'An examination of the impact of green impressions by delegates toward a trade show', *Journal of Convention & Event Tourism*, 19 (1), 25–43.

McCool, S., Butler, R., Buckley, R., Weaver, D. and Wheeller, B. (2013), 'Is concept of sustainability utopian: ideally perfect but impracticable', *Tourism Recreation Research*, 38 (2), 213–242.

Milano, C., Novelli, M. and Cheer, J.M. (2019), 'Overtourism and tourismphobia: a journey through four decades of tourism development, planning and local concern', *Tourism Planning & Development*, 16 (4), 353–357.

Richards, G. (2017), 'From place branding to place-making: the role of events', *International Journal of Event and Festival Management*, 8 (1), 8–23.

Rowe, T. and Higham, J. (2007), 'Ecotourism certification in New Zealand: operator and industry perspectives'. In R. Black and A. Crabtree (eds), *Quality Assurance and Certification in Ecotourism*, Wallingford: CABI, pp. 395–414.

Ryan, M.M. and Mizerski, K. (2010), 'Place branding for sustainable futures: a case study', *Place Branding and Public Diplomacy*, 6 (1), 49–57.

Saarinen, J. (2014), 'Critical sustainability: setting the limits to growth and responsibility in tourism', *Sustainability*, 6 (1), 1–17.

Sachs, J., Schmidt-Traub, G., Kroll, C., Lafortune, G. and Fuller, G. (2019), *Sustainable Development Report 2019*, New York, NY: Bertelsmann Stiftung and Sustainable Development Solutions Network.

Seleem, N., Joubert, N. and Bigwood, G. (2019), 'Creating better places to live, meet and thrive in: sustainable destination management trends best practices and insights', *Global Destination Sustainability Index.*

Smith, V.L. and Font, X. (2014), 'Volunteer tourism, greenwashing and understanding responsible marketing using market signalling theory', *Journal of Sustainable Tourism*, 22 (6), 942–963.

Sustainable Cities Platform (2020), Accessed 1 September 2020 at sustainablecities .eu/home.

Taecharungroj, V., Muthuta, M. and Boonchaiyapruek, P. (2019), 'Sustainability as a place brand position: a resident-centric analysis of the ten towns in the vicinity of Bangkok', *Place Branding and Public Diplomacy*, 15 (4), 210–228.

Targeted News Service (2017), 'Global Destination Sustainability Index releases first ever city ranking', *Targeted News Service*, pp. 1–4.

Therkelsen, A. and Halkier, H. (2011), 'Branding provincial cities: the politics of inclusion, strategy and commitment'. In A. Pike (ed.), *Brands and Branding Geographies*, Cheltenham, UK and Northampton, MA, USA: Edward Elgar Publishing, pp. 200–212.

Therkelsen, A., Halkier, H. and James, L. (2021), 'Sustainable Development Goals in place branding: developing a research agenda'. In D. Medway, G. Warnaby and J. Byrom (eds), *A Research Agenda for Place Branding*, Cheltenham, UK and Northampton, MA, USA: Edward Elgar Publishing, pp. 151–161.

Therkelsen, A., Halkier, H. and Jensen, O.B. (2010), 'Branding Aalborg: building community or selling place?' In G. Ashworth and M. Kavaratzis (eds), *Towards Effective Place Brand Management: Branding European Cities and Regions*, Cheltenham, UK and Northampton, MA, USA: Edward Elgar Publishing, pp. 136–155.

UNWTO, UN World Tourism Organization (2017), 'Tourism and the Sustainable Development Goals – journey to 2030. Highlights'. Accessed 1 February 2020 at file://id.aau.dk/Users/at/Documents/SDG%20&%20tourism/UNWTO%20report %20on%20SDG.pdf.

UNWTO, UN World Tourism Organization (2020), 'One planet vision for a responsible recovery of the tourism sector'. Accessed 20 September 2020 at https://www.unwto.org/covid-19-oneplanet-responsible-recovery-initiatives.

Valencia, S.C., Simon, D., Croese, S., Nordqvist, J., Oloko, M., Sharma, T., Buck, N.T. et al. (2019), 'Adapting the Sustainable Development Goals and the New Urban Agenda to the city level: initial reflections from a comparative research project', *International Journal of Urban Sustainable Development*, 11 (1), 4–23.

VisitAalborg (2016), 'Aalborg all in, 2017–2020. Strategi for VisitAalborg og Aalborgs turismeudvikling'. Accessed 1 September 2020 at https://www.visitaalborg.dk/corporate/om-visitaalborg/strategi.

VisitAalborg (2017). 'Aalborg all in. 1000 nye jobs til byen. Ny strategi for byens turisme 2017–2020'. Accessed at https://www.aalborg.dk/media/5065593/praesentation-turismestrategi-2017-2020.pdf.

VisitAalborg (2019), 'Aalborg går all in og får stærk 5. Plads på GDS index 2019'. Accessed 10 July 2020 at www.visitaalborg.dk/corporate/nyheder-og-pressebesog/aalborg-faar-flot-pladsering-paa-gds-index-2019.

VisitAalborg (2020), VisitAalborg Convention Bureau. Accessed 1 September 2020 at https://www.visitaalborgconvention.dk/.

VisitDenmark (2020), Bæredygtig turisme og turisterne fra nærmarkederne. Accessed 20 September 2020 at https://www.visitdenmark.dk/corporate/videncenter/baeredygtighed-og-naermarkeder.

Woodland, M. and Acott, T.G. (2007), 'Sustainability and local tourism branding in England's South Downs', *Journal of Sustainable Tourism*, 15 (6), 715–734.

Zenker, S., Braun, E. and Petersen, S. (2017), 'Branding the destination versus the place: the effects of brand complexity and identification for residents and visitors', *Tourism Management*, 58, 15–27.

19. Place branding practice and scholarship: where we are and whither we may be going[1]

Robert Govers

This book and the contributions in it are being written in the year 2020; and what a year it has been. Some say it will define our time. I hope they are right and that we will learn from the lockdowns, protests, elections, exits, fires, and floods. I hope that after 2020 the worst will be over, but I seriously doubt it.

The good thing is that in 2020 we have been able to separate the wheat from the chaff. In his provocative and controversial 2018 book *Bullshit Jobs: A Theory*, David Graeber, who is professor of anthropology at the London School of Economics and has also been described, among other epithets, as an 'anarchist', wrote about 'shit' jobs and 'bullshit' jobs. While these terms come directly from the cited work, I shall refer to them as Type 1 and Type 2 to avoid potentially offending some readers and/or getting myself in trouble with the publisher (the editors assure me they would have no difficulty with the original terms other than for sharing my concerns about inadvertently making offence). With that out of the way, Graeber's point has clearly been proven in 2020. Type 1 jobs are those vocations many want to avoid as they require hard work, are badly paid, and often scorned. Yet, the people doing these jobs 'make the world go round' and 2020 has made this abundantly clear. They are the people for whom we cheered during lockdown: the nurses, cleaners, and logistical workers. Type 2 jobs are those that we can do without: filled by people like me, now sitting at home reinventing their career while writing to keep busy. Obviously, this is somewhat of a generalization, but it rings true even though many of the authors of this book and I presumably are in honourable labour, teaching, and training.

Yet, despite the nuances, surely, somewhat observant laypersons will be wondering – in light of the 2020 crises – whether we really needed places to design logos, to advertise their bragging rights, or to hire PR agencies to brush over any realistically negative news coverage. They have a point, as did many of the authors of this book when they made the same point before 2020 and make it now in its chapters.

Yet, obviously, considering that we all actually did become engaged in developing this book, we do not yet believe that place branding is all Type 2 work. We still believe there is real value in place branding *strategy*, if not in logos and the like spawned without it. In understanding community identity, in finding purpose, in defining intended positioning. I see strategy as part of the reason why e-state Estonia was quickly able to find tech solutions for the COVID crisis and post-crisis world with their 'Hack the Crisis' initiative (Gessen, 2020); or Bhutan's idea to align GDP growth with gross national happiness gaining momentum (Chassagne, 2020).

One could argue that even the protests against racism in the United States are as fierce as they are because the conflict goes to the heart of what the land of the free is about or not. At least the discussion is being had in the US, unlike in other countries in – for instance – north-western Europe where racism is just as pervasive but not talked about because the dominant narrative, which of course does not refer to it, is that racism does not exist in those liberal progressive societies. Arguably, these examples illustrate how 'place brand values' remain relevant and provide guidance, even – or particularly – in times of adversity.

So, arguably, place branding *is* relevant, but will this insight survive the funding crisis that we already know will occur after the economic impact of COVID-19 fully reveals itself? Surely, in the coming years and years there will be little or no money or attention for serious research, education, or consultancy in something like – seen by many as frivolous – place branding. The funding agencies and governments that appreciate that place branding is of strategic, long-term, and crucial importance are, in my estimation, unfortunately, in a tiny minority.

Sure, place branding will be seen post-COVID as essential as places scramble to recover, notably in tourism but also on other fronts. Under pressure from the private sector or not, there will be resources for tourism, investment, and export promotion. But this will probably come with an urge to do it ASAP and without much strategic thinking as economies need to be rescued. Those few places that have brand strategies in place will benefit from being able to make informed decisions. All the others will not have the time, patience, or resources to take a look at the bigger picture and so they'll keep fighting battles and losing most of them as well as the war itself.

With that in mind, I regret that we have not been able to achieve more advocacy for the discipline so far, but why is that? Why do I feel that in place branding most jobs and their work output have been of the Type 2 variety? Why have we had little success in convincing our institutions, funding agencies, and governments of the value of strategic place branding?

First of all, unfortunately, despite all the writing done by a multitude of scholars including, notably, the authors in this book, place branding still seems to be interpreted by many as a matter of 'just' visual identity. And the thing is, visual design *is* needed. Governments and their agencies need something on their letterhead, for their web-design, and for their posters and exhibition stands. And visual design and campaign initiatives are usually divisive locally. Residents either hate them and get them scrapped quickly, or love them when the initiative resonates with their sense of civic pride. Hence, visual identity projects usually generate lots of (social) media attention locally, which politicians and policy makers obviously love (and if not the policy-making majority, then the opposition).

More often than not there is a launch of the 'new brand' without underlying strategy, without corresponding policies, and, of course, without any impacts on reputation. But who cares if the electorate is happy?

Sometimes, it even goes as far as politicians using 'branding' as an excuse to spend money on getting re-elected. During one of my recent projects a client insisted on advertising the country on a specific regional television channel in a neighbouring state. Naively, I thought that the idea was to win over neighbours, which seemed pointless to me as the neighbours had already been proven to be fans of the country. After a long discussion we eventually figured out that the real reason was that the client's electorate also watches the neighbours' television channel. Hence, the client's electorate could see that their elected official was doing something (or so it should seem) to advance the economic policy of the government. The public budget for nation branding, in which external campaigning was included, was thus really used for political self-promotion. In other words, even though the top-down place branding approach is often criticised in the literature, there are forces at play that one has little control over, particularly if they are sinister, cynical, and resourceful (as in the case of misappropriating taxpayers' money).

In addition, it is often argued that the perceived failure of place branding is the result of a gap between academia and practice. But I wonder if that is an oversimplification. Who are the academics who are – presumably – reluctant to get their hands dirty?

The reality is that there is only really just a handful of true place branding specialist academics, the vast majority of whom are contributing to this book. On the other hand, most publications are written either by junior researchers or academics who publish place branding papers as a side-project. Place branding is an extremely multidisciplinary field, with scholars from fields of study as diverse as geography, economics, marketing, psychology, tourism studies, architecture, international relations, communications, or media studies joining in. Many of them write about place branding at the fringes of their specialisation. As editor of *Place Branding and Public Diplomacy*, more often than not I have to urge authors to clarify their use of our jargon – using place marketing or branding, logos or brands, image or identity, as though they are all interchangeable.

In other words, the bulk of academia disagrees and itself possibly contributes more to the confusion than it clarifies. Recently, I even had practitioner reviewers commenting on confused conceptual definitions in an academic paper. That is the world upside down.

Furthermore, on the other side of the same coin, who are the practitioners who are getting it wrong? The consultants? Which consultants? There is only a handful of true specialist consultants that make a living largely from place branding projects. Much of the work is done by small local agencies that do mostly commercial branding and are therefore no specialists in place branding.

Or is it the policy makers and civil servants who are getting it wrong? But who are they? It could be anyone who is or should be concerned about the reputation management for the city, region, or country, really. Particularly senior government and externally facing agencies such as the tourism management organisations, investment and export promotion agencies, international affairs and public diplomacy units, or talent attraction bureaux are sometimes involved – and the rest of the list of potential practitioners is long and might include, but is not limited to, representatives of chambers of commerce, labour and sector organisations, sports clubs, cultural institutions, major exporters, and local businesses, Olympic committees, real estate developers, hospitality and travel companies, media agencies, tech clusters, and event organisers – and on it goes.

This multitude of policy makers and civil servants is potentially a significant market for us to reach and educate, but nobody knows where to find that market. And if we cannot find that market, can we blame that market for not knowing what they are talking about?

So, yes, we have come some way to build this discipline as is shown through the journal *Place Branding and Public Diplomacy*, the *International Place Branding Association*, this book and others before it and the editors and the authors involved, and a few other contributions including those by thoughtful and dedicated readers who do listen to what we have to say and work to implement it.

But we have a long way to go. The interdisciplinarity, complexity, and potential of place branding make it worthwhile to keep going, but if we do not evolve from place branding Type 2 work to something more substantial ... If we do not do the legwork of collaboration, resident involvement, consensus building – the Type 1 work, not the one in which we just throw money at advertising, PR, and design (and its research) – we are in deep trouble.

The challenge for us specialists is how to get this across to all those involved in place branding full-time, part-time, as dedicated specialist or hobbyist, in academia, the public sector or private enterprise, in senior government and civil service. Because if – after this year 2020 – place branding fails to become a smaller part of the problem (wasting resources) and a bigger part of the solution (providing direction) we are indeed in deep trouble; as a community, but even as a society I reckon. For me, it could go two ways: down the sink or on the list of essential ingredients. It is up to us to make sure we evolve in the latter direction, but the list of challenges to overcome is long and complicated.

NOTE

1. This is an open access work distributed under the Creative Commons Attributio n-NonCommercial-NoDerivatives 4.0 Unported (https://creativecommons.org/ licenses/by-nc-nd/4.0/). Users can redistribute the work for non-commercial purposes, as long as it is passed along unchanged and in whole, as detailed in the Licence. Edward Elgar Publishing Ltd must be clearly credited as the rights holder for publication of the original work. Any translation or adaptation of the original content requires the written authorisation of Edward Elgar Publishing Ltd.

REFERENCES

Chassagne, N. (2020). Here's what the coronavirus pandemic can teach us about tackling climate change. *The Conversation.* 26 March. Accessed 31 August 2020 at https://theconversation.com/heres-what-the-coronavirus-pandemic-can-teach-us -about-tackling-climate-change-134399.
Gessen, M. (2020). Why Estonia was poised to handle how a pandemic would change everything. *The New Yorker.* 24 March. Accessed 31 August 2020 at https:// www.newyorker.com/news/our-columnists/why-estonia-was-poised-to-handle-how -a-pandemic-would-change-everything.
Graeber, D. (2018). *Bullshit Jobs: A Theory.* New York, NY: Simon & Schuster.

Epilogue: 'Between a rock and a hard PLACE'

Mark Cleveland and Nicolas Papadopoulos

The core objective of this book was to bring together the broad range of research on place, specifically associations with, attachments to, and the marketing of places: from place and nation branding to tourism destination image, and from a product–place perspective (e.g., brand/country of origin) to a person–place perspective (e.g., connection, identity, and belongingness). Throwing caution to the wind, we metaphorically charted a course between Scylla and Charybdis: perhaps recklessly, like contemporary versions of Captain Ahab and Captain Bligh, we as editors and our contributors as subject experts navigated within and across different oceans of scholarship and knowledge. The task was to steer the allegorical Ship of State, much like the 'ship on a course' it symbolizes (Merriam-Webster, 2020), through typically hard and often dangerous waters.

Like ships and the affairs of a state – here, the realm of place marketing – we encountered turbulent seas indeed, sailing among whirlpools (*research gaps*), submerged rocks (*unknown pitfalls*), reefs (*known hazards*), tropical isles (*fresh opportunities*), and pirates and opposing ships from other realms (*criticisms* of all kinds, some with merit and some not, such as place/country image and marketing 'is not important' or 'are being researched too much').

Having thrown down the gauntlet, we fielded contributions from 28 researchers based in 13 countries who bring to the place table expertise in a wide-ranging assortment of fields. True to the subject matter in place-based marketing, but also reflecting the breadth of the fields connected to it, the discipline of marketing and its subtopics (e.g., consumer behaviour, advertising, branding, public relations) are well-represented and so are such related fields as tourism, international business, economics, and sports policy/politics, with contributions from authors at universities, other research institutions, and independent associations, by specialists focusing mostly on research and/or with considerable (place) management and consulting experience, and from both newer rising stars as well as seasoned scholars.

Now, 'place', as both authors in this book and readers know, plays a central and critical role in human life, and so it is not surprising that language is filled with numerous idiomatic expressions in English that are inextricably connected to 'place' (rhymezone.com lists 486, as noted in the Introduction) and have equivalents in virtually every other language around the world. As a sort of 'Captain's log' (or Captain's *epilogue*), here we have organized the contributions into a selected eight of these expressions and provide readers with our reflections about future place-associated research expeditions.

1.   'Out of place': That is to say, doing what is *not* ok

Four chapters discuss the pitfalls of erroneous assumptions about place and all its marketing applications and improperly conceived and executed place-associated strategies. Zenker's (Chapter 4) stark assessment of the current state of place marketing/branding research slaughters some sacred cows (with apologies to Hindu readers in India), and rightly so. Govers (Chapter 19) offers a similarly stark appraisal, written as the raging coronavirus (COVID-19) created the most consequential global pandemic crisis since the Spanish flu of 1918–1920, questioning the relevancy of place branding in light of current events, crises, and priorities. Papadopoulos and Cleveland (Chapter 3) skewer both scholars and practitioners on either side of the 'place' versus 'country' Iron Curtain for not talking to one another. And Andéhn and L'Espoir-Decosta (Chapter 9), working from the country of origin (COO) perspective, echo concerns similar to those of these other chapters.

Despite being among the most studied topics in business and marketing, understanding of place and country image-related issues is being held back from realizing their potential due to them being largely atheoretical, self-referential, and beholden to subset silos of research and/or application methodologies and perspectives. Yet it could be said that much of the malaise affecting place-related research domains is likely a by-product of the field's growing pains.

These bear similarity to the debates and identity crises from the late 1970s to the early 1990s (which in many cases continue today, as we note in the Introduction to this book), that rocked place branding's larger cognate disciplines of marketing and consumer behaviour (Jacoby, 1978; Holbrook, 1987; Bagozzi, 1992). We strongly encourage readers to check out these works to see how they inform the challenges accompanying the evolution of place marketing. They, and other similar classic works too many to mention here, emphasize the need for place-marketing researchers of all stripes to look beyond their narrow field in order to implement more rigorous theorizing, more valid construct conceptualizations, and more robust empirical investigations.

2.   'Behind closed doors': Strategizing behind the scenes where no outsiders can watch

The bulk of place branding strategizing occurs behind the scenes, where nobody other than policy makers and managers sees 'how the sausage gets made'. Residents in particular are indispensable stakeholders, as argued by El-Banna and Stoica (Chapter 6) and Insch (Chapter 7), in terms of the key role they play in living, embodying, and perhaps even killing, the place brand. Because these actors are largely independent of, and not coordinated with, place strategizing, they are not easily restrained. Residents thus affect and are affected by place branding strategies and outcomes. They can lend legitimacy and credibility to place branding, but rather like how uncooperative weather will stymie the efforts of even the most experienced sailor, they also stubbornly resist well-intentioned efforts to change place branding course.

3.   'There's no place like home': One is most at ease at home surrounded by kin and kind

Whereas idiom 1, 'out of place', represents mismatches between the various physical, personal, and product components of place marketing, this obverse idiom connects to individual consumers' perspectives of place. Warnaby and Medway (Chapter 1) touch on what 'home' may mean by focusing on a neighbourhood-level versus a cross-national region, while Insch (Chapter 7), leaning on social identity theory, speaks of place belongingness, urban residents' identities, and attachment to the places in which they live, and how they contribute to the authenticity of place image. This is a particular challenge as well as an opportunity for the multicultural gateway cities she cites (e.g., New York, London, Sydney) that serve as the command centres of the global economy. Identity and belongingness in urban living may be anchored in a very 'local' place, such as St Ann's Square in Manchester (Warnaby and Medway), while the overall anonymity of urban environments discourages a sense of community when compared to that achieved by residents of smaller settlements. This issue compounds when people from multiple backgrounds are living in close proximity, as narrated by the 'us and them' notions of social identity theory.

4.   'Every nook and cranny': The devil is in the details

Because consumers possess multiple social identities that are differentially activated according to situational cues in the consumption context, managers are advised to consider the 'nooks and crannies', many if not most of which are hidden from easy view, as they deliberate what place levels and combinations to emphasize when positioning their offerings. Using space analogies and planetary metaphors, and building on the intersectionality of places, spaces, and faces, Cleveland and Papadopoulos (Chapter 8) deliberate multifarious ways that social identity informs consumers' product and brand consumption constellations. Focusing on the image of the US abroad, White (Chapter 16) focuses on an audience perspective and highlights how the popular culture associated with a country's brands and entertainment exports contributes to shaping consumers' perceptions of a country – including a study from the 1980s that discussed how people in some countries learned the ideology of consumption from watching episodes of the TV shows *Dallas* and *Dynasty*.

Likewise, the K-pop phenomenon likely plays a strong positive role in terms of building consumer affinity for South Korea, thus serving as an ambassador for other Korean products and helping to lift the country's overall portfolio. Ironically, it may sometimes be the case that complaints about local customs, traditions, and ways of life being drowned out by American culture ('McDomination') are the loudest where the two cultures are more similar. The cultural differences between the US and the co-editors' country, Canada, are subtle but potent, driving us to obsess endlessly about whether we should bind ourselves closer to, or disengage from, our Southern neighbour. Perhaps Kiwis, Austrians, and Malays experience similar disquiet about, respectively, Australian, German, and Indonesian popular culture? And what of people in bi-cultural countries and their views toward the respective 'parent' cultures (e.g., English-/French-speaking Canadians vs. British/French culture, or Flemings and Walloons in Belgium vs. the Netherlands and France)? While some of these questions have been addressed in some research contexts, they are generally, and sorely, absent from the 'place'-related dialogue.

5.   **'When in Rome, do as the Romans': Following (or not?) local conventions where one is**

This idiom advocates following the conventions of the place where one is residing or visiting. While typical at the consumer level, the advice in this idiom is familiar to sellers in terms of targeting and catering to foreign consumers/visitors. To this end, Wilson (Chapter 14) collates insights from marketing and destination research to detail a strategic process for place-brand advertising, distinguishing functional, symbolic, and experiential place attributes. This recalls the Elaboration Likelihood Model leveraged by Bartsch and Zeugner-Roth (Chapter 12) for advertising purposes, and the attendant central vs. peripheral route to persuasion, and thus, the amount and types of information that should be conveyed. Many destination ads emphasize peripheral, symbolic elements to stimulate an emotional response (e.g., architectural beauty) as opposed to stimulating cognitions (e.g., enumerating the cultural experiences offered) despite the likelihood of high-involvement decision-making.

Conveying a consistent 'place message' is challenged by the disconnect between place branding and strategic spatial planning activities, each run by different constituents having different priorities. Related to this, Oliveira and Hersperger (Chapter 15) reveal the paucity of strategic plans centred on place branding for social cohesion or economic sustainability purposes, and Therkelsen, James, and Halkier (Chapter 18) use the case of Aalborg in Denmark to showcase how tourism can contribute to sustainable place branding. Making sustainability 'pay off' for stakeholders is a challenge not only for place/destination marketing, but increasingly for product branding and corporate image purposes in an expanding number of sectors.

The above said, one cannot help but think of Captain Kirk and his steady hand on the tiller of Starship Enterprise: he and his crew practiced the do-as-the-Romans dictum extensively, always respectful of the many foreign cultures they encountered in galaxies far, far away – but they never once succumbed to the temptation of compromising their own principles to accommodate practices and beliefs they found objectionable. McDonald's does like the Romans do when marketing the Maharajah burger in India, or adjusting its 'I'm Lovin' It' campaign to 'Check our food quality' for parts of the Arab world, or serving beer in Belgium – but it would not compromise on the fundamental ways it conducts its business. Should a city or region present itself as a 'hub of technology' or 'beautiful nature' if it has little of either, and if many residents don't see it this way, to attract investors or tourists? Should a nation present itself as a 'sea of calm' to attract such external targets, if it is racked by civil discord and major constitutional crises?

More generally, the theory of branding teaches us that a brand succeeds only when 'sticking to the knitting' and builds itself based on its core values and competencies, otherwise losing its credibility and suffering as a result. In this context, here is an interesting 'place' question: under what conditions should a city or nation *not* act as the Romans, instead of abandoning reality in the (often vain) hope of appealing to target markets?

6.   'Finding one's way around': Essential navigational skills for connecting with customers

Learning how to tread inside a place or get from one place to another are obviously important navigational skills that lie at the intersection of people, products, and places discussed by Cleveland, Papadopoulos, and Bartikowski (Chapter 11). Successfully charting a course to customers would be greatly enhanced if managers could become skilled in the varying aspects of seamanship by learning from various different captains. Fresh insights can be gained by breaking down the academic silos currently inhibiting the exchange of thoughts from the wide variety of disciplines researching place-related issues. In their review of the evolution of country stereotypes, Magnusson and Westjohn (Chapter 10) note that consensus is still lacking on many concepts, operationalizations, and research approaches.

Despite – or rather, because of – globalization, we believe that the image of a *country* remains an incredibly important construct, while expressly recognizing that there are many levels *above* (e.g., EU, 'Latin America') and *below* the nation-state (cities, regions, neighbourhoods) that also are subject to stereotypes – which may surface as crucial determinants of how any level of place is viewed as nations coalesce or fracture. Appraisals of these alternative levels are often critical for, say, identifying fans of sports teams (cities), for tourism and FDI (nations, regions, cities), and for marketing hedonic products (e.g., Paris, NYC) and foodstuffs (e.g., Gruyere, Parma, Champagne, Kobe). Managers need to appreciate the diagnostic value of these place images, even in those frequent cases when consumers misattribute the origin location, as Magnusson and Westjohn discuss in Chapter 10.

7. 'Location, Location, Location!' There is more than a kernel of truth to this cliché

This common adage about the 'three most critical factors' in determining the desirability of a property in such sectors as retailing and real estate may be quite appropriate in some instances. At the same time, it misses the point that 'location' is just as much a mental place in one's mind as a physical point on a map, and that it is relevant in many more contexts than just within the sectors that have turned it into a cliché. This is showcased by the ways in which COO can be leveraged in place promotion contexts (Bartsch and Zeugner-Roth, Chapter 12), in how COO is a factor in predicting the success or failure of cross-border acquisitions and M&As (Matarazzo, Chapter 13), and in how hosting global sporting events like the Olympics or the FIFA World Cup contributes to the soft power, branding, and public diplomacy of a nation (Kramareva and Grix, Chapter 17). Alongside both hosting and/or performing strongly at sports mega events, one can think of several other opportunities for nation-branding/building. To name but a few, these include achievements in technology, as evidenced by the recent space-faring exploits of China, India, and even the UAE, Nobel laureates in science or the arts, and Britain's reasonably successful efforts (at least in this regard) to strengthen its legacy in culture over time by often evoking iconic 'ambassadors' from Shakespeare to The Beatles, The Rolling Stones, and James Bond to today's Harry Potter.

8.   **'Falling into place': Things should, with the right strategies, but ... easier said than done**

If managers plan their strategies well, everything should then work well – but 'everything' never does, and even 'almost everything' remains a dream in most cases. The complexity of place/brand-building is a direct consequence of the multidisciplinary roots of the field (Florek, Chapter 5), as well as of the myriad possible associations that customers have with brands that can be leveraged to generate place/brand equity. To the rescue, our contributors offer innovative insights and models of place-branding that leverage and blend new and existing theories from psychology, geography, international business, and other cognate fields, and of course from consumer behaviour, advertising, branding, marketing, and international marketing.

As with many things, accomplishing the seemingly straightforward tasks of determining 'what' is to be branded and 'who' should be doing this branding, let alone 'to whom' should the branding be addressed and 'why' should the addressees buy into the brand, requires integrating successfully the intricate and often discrete geographic conceptualizations and scope of place (Warnaby and Medway, Chapter 1). Kavaratzis and Florek (Chapter 2) provide a handy 'primer' on the spheres and vicissitudes of place branding, by delving into the 'five w's' (why, who, what, when, where) and arriving at the sixth and final element, 'how' place brands can be optimally designed and implemented. Perhaps the 'which' might be added as a separate seventh item, in terms of which aspects should be emphasized when designing these place branding initiatives. People (residents, skill sets, other traits)? Culture? Urban/rural fabric? Topography, proximity, and other geographic aspects? Climate/latitude? Industrial/economic sectors? Institutional/regulatory aspects?

The Hydra Challenge

Like the mythical Hydra, who, as legend has it, would regrow two heads for every one chopped off, for every question that gets answered in these chapters many more questions crop up.

The challenges associated with integrating the customer perspective of place branding/marketing with that of the seller do not allow for more than barely *satisficing* strategic objectives, which itself does not happen often, instead of *meeting* them, which virtually never does.

The unfortunate reality is that billions of dollars, euros, yuans, yens, or rupees are spent worldwide on poorly configured dreams of grand branding success that rarely materialize.

But 'we have heart', and we encourage readers to join us by capitalizing on the information, suggestions, and wisdom offered by our constellation of expert contributors so that we can all 'boldly go where no one has gone before'. Let's go to more research by scholars, more careful strategizing and implementing by practitioners, and better understanding by all, so that the 'unfortunate reality' in the previous paragraph can someday become a thing of the past.

REFERENCES

Bagozzi, R.P. (1992). Acrimony in the ivory tower: stagnation or evolution? *Journal of the Academy of Marketing Science*, *20*(4), 355–359.

Holbrook, M.B. (1987). What is consumer research? *Journal of Consumer Research*, *14*(1), 128–132.

Jacoby, J. (1978). Consumer research: how valid and useful are all our consumer behavior research findings? A state-of-the-art review. *Journal of Marketing*, *42*(2), 87–96.

Merriam-Webster Dictionary (2020). Ship of State, accessed 7 December 2020 at https://www.merriam-webster.com/dictionary/ship%20of%20state.

Index